GENESIS

Brazos Theological Commentary on the Bible

GENESIS

R. R. RENO

BrazosPress
a division of Baker Publishing Group
Grand Rapids, Michigan

Published by Brazos Press
a division of Baker Publishing Group
P.O. Box 6287, Grand Rapids, MI 49516-6287
www.brazospress.com

Printed in the United States of America

Library of Congress Cataloging-in-Publication Data

Reno, Russell R., 1959–
    Genesis / R.R. Reno.
      p. cm. — (Brazos theological commentary on the Bible)
    Includes bibliographical references and index.
    ISBN 978-1-58743-091-6 (cloth)
    1. Bible. O.T. Genesis—Commentaries. I. Title.
  BS1235.53.R46 2010
  222′.1107—dc22
                                                   2009025584

10   11   12   13   14   15   16   7   6   5   4   3   2   1

For Peter Ochs and his merry band of scriptural reasoners

CONTENTS

SERIES PREFACE

Near the beginning of his treatise against Gnostic interpretations of the Bible, *Against the Heresies*, Irenaeus observes that Scripture is like a great mosaic depicting a handsome king. It is as if we were owners of a villa in Gaul who had ordered a mosaic from Rome. It arrives, and the beautifully colored tiles need to be taken out of their packaging and put into proper order according to the plan of the artist. The difficulty, of course, is that Scripture provides us with the individual pieces, but the order and sequence of various elements are not obvious. The Bible does not come with instructions that would allow interpreters to simply place verses, episodes, images, and parables in order as a worker might follow a schematic drawing in assembling the pieces to depict the handsome king. The mosaic must be puzzled out. This is precisely the work of scriptural interpretation.

Origen has his own image to express the difficulty of working out the proper approach to reading the Bible. When preparing to offer a commentary on the Psalms he tells of a tradition handed down to him by his Hebrew teacher:

> The Hebrew said that the whole divinely inspired Scripture may be likened, because of its obscurity, to many locked rooms in our house. By each room is placed a key, but not the one that corresponds to it, so that the keys are scattered about beside the rooms, none of them matching the room by which it is placed. It is a difficult task to find the keys and match them to the rooms that they can open. We therefore know the Scriptures that are obscure only by taking the points of departure for understanding them from another place because they have their interpretive principle scattered among them.[1]

1. Fragment from the preface to *Commentary on Psalms 1–25*, preserved in the *Philokalia* (trans. Joseph W. Trigg; London: Routledge, 1998), 70–71.

As is the case for Irenaeus, scriptural interpretation is not purely local. The key in Genesis may best fit the door of Isaiah, which in turn opens up the meaning of Matthew. The mosaic must be put together with an eye toward the overall plan.

Irenaeus, Origen, and the great cloud of premodern biblical interpreters assumed that puzzling out the mosaic of Scripture must be a communal project. The Bible is vast, heterogeneous, full of confusing passages and obscure words, and difficult to understand. Only a fool would imagine that he or she could work out solutions alone. The way forward must rely upon a tradition of reading that Irenaeus reports has been passed on as the rule or canon of truth that functions as a confession of faith. "Anyone," he says, "who keeps unchangeable in himself the rule of truth received through baptism will recognize the names and sayings and parables of the scriptures."[2] Modern scholars debate the content of the rule on which Irenaeus relies and commends, not the least because the terms and formulations Irenaeus himself uses shift and slide. Nonetheless, Irenaeus assumes that there is a body of apostolic doctrine sustained by a tradition of teaching in the church. This doctrine provides the clarifying principles that guide exegetical judgment toward a coherent overall reading of Scripture as a unified witness. Doctrine, then, is the schematic drawing that will allow the reader to organize the vast heterogeneity of the words, images, and stories of the Bible into a readable, coherent whole. It is the rule that guides us toward the proper matching of keys to doors.

If self-consciousness about the role of history in shaping human consciousness makes modern historical-critical study critical, then what makes modern study of the Bible modern is the consensus that classical Christian doctrine distorts interpretive understanding. Benjamin Jowett, the influential nineteenth-century English classical scholar, is representative. In his programmatic essay "On the Interpretation of Scripture," he exhorts the biblical reader to disengage from doctrine and break its hold over the interpretive imagination. "The simple words of that book," writes Jowett of the modern reader, "he tries to preserve absolutely pure from the refinements or distinctions of later times." The modern interpreter wishes to "clear away the remains of dogmas, systems, controversies, which are encrusted upon" the words of Scripture. The disciplines of close philological analysis "would enable us to separate the elements of doctrine and tradition with which the meaning of Scripture is encumbered in our own day."[3] The lens of understanding must be wiped clear of the hazy and distorting film of doctrine.

Postmodernity, in turn, has encouraged us to criticize the critics. Jowett imagined that when he wiped away doctrine he would encounter the biblical text in its purity and uncover what he called "the original spirit and intention of the authors."[4] We are not now so sanguine, and the postmodern mind thinks

---

2. *Against Heresies* 9.4.

3. Benjamin Jowett, "On the Interpretation of Scripture," in *Essays and Reviews* (London: Parker, 1860), 338–39.

4. Ibid., 340.

interpretive frameworks inevitable. Nonetheless, we tend to remain modern in at least one sense. We read Athanasius and think him stage-managing the diversity of Scripture to support his positions against the Arians. We read Bernard of Clairvaux and assume that his monastic ideals structure his reading of the Song of Songs. In the wake of the Reformation, we can see how the doctrinal divisions of the time shaped biblical interpretation. Luther famously described the Epistle of James as a "strawy letter," for, as he said, "it has nothing of the nature of the Gospel about it."[5] In these and many other instances, often written in the heat of ecclesiastical controversy or out of the passion of ascetic commitment, we tend to think Jowett correct: doctrine is a distorting film on the lens of understanding.

However, is what we commonly think actually the case? Are readers naturally perceptive? Do we have an unblemished, reliable aptitude for the divine? Have we no need for disciplines of vision? Do our attention and judgment need to be trained, especially as we seek to read Scripture as the living word of God? According to Augustine, we all struggle to journey toward God, who is our rest and peace. Yet our vision is darkened and the fetters of worldly habit corrupt our judgment. We need training and instruction in order to cleanse our minds so that we might find our way toward God.[6] To this end, "the whole temporal dispensation was made by divine Providence for our salvation."[7] The covenant with Israel, the coming of Christ, the gathering of the nations into the church—all these things are gathered up into the rule of faith, and they guide the vision and form of the soul toward the end of fellowship with God. In Augustine's view, the reading of Scripture both contributes to and benefits from this divine pedagogy. With countless variations in both exegetical conclusions and theological frameworks, the same pedagogy of a doctrinally ruled reading of Scripture characterizes the broad sweep of the Christian tradition from Gregory the Great through Bernard and Bonaventure, continuing across Reformation differences in both John Calvin and Cornelius Lapide, Patrick Henry and Bishop Bossuet, and on to more recent figures such as Karl Barth and Hans Urs von Balthasar.

Is doctrine, then, not a moldering scrim of antique prejudice obscuring the Bible, but instead a clarifying agent, an enduring tradition of theological judgments that amplifies the living voice of Scripture? And what of the scholarly dispassion advocated by Jowett? Is a noncommitted reading, an interpretation unprejudiced, the way toward objectivity, or does it simply invite the languid intellectual apathy that stands aside to make room for the false truisms and easy answers of the age?

This series of biblical commentaries was born out of the conviction that dogma clarifies rather than obscures. The Brazos Theological Commentary on the Bible advances on the assumption that the Nicene tradition, in all its diversity and

5. *Luther's Works*, vol. 35, ed. E. Theodore Bachmann (Philadelphia: Fortress, 1959), 362.
6. *On Christian Doctrine* 1.10.
7. *On Christian Doctrine* 1.35.

controversy, provides the proper basis for the interpretation of the Bible as Christian Scripture. God the Father Almighty, who sends his only begotten Son to die for us and for our salvation and who raises the crucified Son in the power of the Holy Spirit so that the baptized may be joined in one body—faith in *this* God with *this* vocation of love for the world is the lens through which to view the heterogeneity and particularity of the biblical texts. Doctrine, then, is not a moldering scrim of antique prejudice obscuring the meaning of the Bible. It is a crucial aspect of the divine pedagogy, a clarifying agent for our minds fogged by self-deceptions, a challenge to our languid intellectual apathy that will too often rest in false truisms and the easy spiritual nostrums of the present age rather than search more deeply and widely for the dispersed keys to the many doors of Scripture.

For this reason, the commentators in this series have not been chosen because of their historical or philological expertise. In the main, they are not biblical scholars in the conventional, modern sense of the term. Instead, the commentators were chosen because of their knowledge of and expertise in using the Christian doctrinal tradition. They are qualified by virtue of the doctrinal formation of their mental habits, for it is the conceit of this series of biblical commentaries that theological training in the Nicene tradition prepares one for biblical interpretation, and thus it is to theologians and not biblical scholars that we have turned. "War is too important," it has been said, "to leave to the generals."

We do hope, however, that readers do not draw the wrong impression. The Nicene tradition does not provide a set formula for the solution of exegetical problems. The great tradition of Christian doctrine was not transcribed, bound in folio, and issued in an official, critical edition. We have the Niceno-Constantinopolitan Creed, used for centuries in many traditions of Christian worship. We have ancient baptismal affirmations of faith. The Chalcedonian definition and the creeds and canons of other church councils have their places in official church documents. Yet the rule of faith cannot be limited to a specific set of words, sentences, and creeds. It is instead a pervasive habit of thought, the animating culture of the church in its intellectual aspect. As Augustine observed, commenting on Jeremiah 31:33, "The creed is learned by listening; it is written, not on stone tablets nor on any material, but on the heart."[8] This is why Irenaeus is able to appeal to the rule of faith more than a century before the first ecumenical council, and this is why we need not itemize the contents of the Nicene tradition in order to appeal to its potency and role in the work of interpretation.

Because doctrine is intrinsically fluid on the margins and most powerful as a habit of mind rather than a list of propositions, this commentary series cannot settle difficult questions of method and content at the outset. The editors of the series impose no particular method of doctrinal interpretation. We cannot say in advance how doctrine helps the Christian reader assemble the mosaic of Scripture. We have no clear answer to the question of whether exegesis guided by

8. *Sermon* 212.2.

doctrine is antithetical to or compatible with the now-old modern methods of historical-critical inquiry. Truth—historical, mathematical, or doctrinal—knows no contradiction. But method is a discipline of vision and judgment, and we cannot know in advance what aspects of historical-critical inquiry are functions of modernism that shape the soul to be at odds with Christian discipline. Still further, the editors do not hold the commentators to any particular hermeneutical theory that specifies how to define the plain sense of Scripture—or the role this plain sense should play in interpretation. Here the commentary series is tentative and exploratory.

Can we proceed in any other way? European and North American intellectual culture has been de-Christianized. The effect has not been a cessation of Christian activity. Theological work continues. Sermons are preached. Biblical scholars turn out monographs. Church leaders have meetings. But each dimension of a formerly unified Christian practice now tends to function independently. It is as if a weakened army had been fragmented, and various corps had retreated to isolated fortresses in order to survive. Theology has lost its competence in exegesis. Scripture scholars function with minimal theological training. Each decade finds new theories of preaching to cover the nakedness of seminary training that provides theology without exegesis and exegesis without theology.

Not the least of the causes of the fragmentation of Christian intellectual practice has been the divisions of the church. Since the Reformation, the role of the rule of faith in interpretation has been obscured by polemics and counterpolemics about *sola scriptura* and the necessity of a magisterial teaching authority. The Brazos Theological Commentary on the Bible series is deliberately ecumenical in scope, because the editors are convinced that early church fathers were correct: church doctrine does not compete with Scripture in a limited economy of epistemic authority. We wish to encourage unashamedly dogmatic interpretation of Scripture, confident that the concrete consequences of such a reading will cast far more light on the great divisive questions of the Reformation than either reengaging in old theological polemics or chasing the fantasy of a pure exegesis that will somehow adjudicate between competing theological positions. You shall know the truth of doctrine by its interpretive fruits, and therefore in hopes of contributing to the unity of the church, we have deliberately chosen a wide range of theologians whose commitment to doctrine will allow readers to see real interpretive consequences rather than the shadow boxing of theological concepts.

Brazos Theological Commentary on the Bible has no dog in the current translation fights, and we endorse a textual ecumenism that parallels our diversity of ecclesial backgrounds. We do not impose the thankfully modest inclusive-language agenda of the New Revised Standard Version, nor do we insist upon the glories of the Authorized Version, nor do we require our commentators to create a new translation. In our communal worship, in our private devotions, in our theological scholarship, we use a range of scriptural translations. Precisely as Scripture—a living, functioning text in the present life of faith—the Bible is not semantically fixed. Only a modernist, literalist hermeneutic could imagine that this modest fluidity is a liability. Philological precision and stability is a consequence of, not a basis for, exegesis. Judgments about the meaning of a text fix its literal sense, not the other way around. As a result, readers should expect an eclectic use of biblical translations, both across the different volumes of the series and within individual commentaries.

We cannot speak for contemporary biblical scholars, but as theologians we know that we have long been trained to defend our fortresses of theological concepts and formulations. And we have forgotten the skills of interpretation. Like stroke victims, we must rehabilitate our exegetical imaginations, and there are likely to be different strategies of recovery. Readers should expect this reconstructive—not reactionary—series to provide them with experiments in postcritical doctrinal interpretation, not commentaries written according to the settled principles of a well-functioning tradition. Some commentators will follow classical typological and allegorical readings from the premodern tradition; others will draw on contemporary historical study. Some will comment verse by verse; others will highlight passages, even single words that trigger theological analysis of Scripture. No reading strategies are proscribed, no interpretive methods foresworn. The central premise in this commentary series is that doctrine provides structure and cogency to scriptural interpretation. We trust in this premise with the hope that the Nicene tradition can guide us, however imperfectly, diversely, and haltingly, toward a reading of Scripture in which the right keys open the right doors.

R. R. Reno

AUTHOR'S PREFACE

Years ago I suggested to Rodney Clapp that a series of biblical commentaries written by theologians might be interesting. He responded, "Great, let's do it!" I demurred, observing that it was a mad idea. Eventually I guess I got just crazy enough to begin to take the idea seriously—and Rodney never got sane enough to question his initial enthusiasm. To him I owe a great debt, not only for the opportunity to tackle (or better, to be tackled by) Genesis, but also for the Brazos Theological Commentary on the Bible as a whole.

The editorial board of the Brazos Theological Commentary on the Bible has provided indispensable help. Robert Jenson and Robert Wilken gave helpful editorial comments during the final stages of the draft. I am grateful to Ephraim Radner, who offered pastoral support in my moments of despair, reminding me that it is the nature of holy scripture to humiliate the efforts of commentators who imagine themselves capable of the task. Michael Root and George Sumner provided encouragement and good cheer.

I have benefited from the opportunities to present portions of this commentary in public lectures: Gen. 3 at a session of the Bible, Theology, and Theological Interpretation group at the 2007 annual meeting of the Society of Biblical Literature; Gen. 22 at the 2007 Spirit and Letter Conference; and Gen. 1 at Calvin Theological Seminary in 2007 and at Hillsdale College in 2008. Many thanks to Joel Green, Scott Hahn, Arie Leder, and Don Westblade for extending the invitations.

The staff at Brazos Press provided expert support for this volume, as they have for all the volumes in the series. All writers should be as lucky as I have been. Lisa Ann Cockrel provided cheerful and capable assistance, as did Rebecca Cooper before her. David Aiken carefully corrected errors, ironed out confused syntax, and put up with my seemingly invincible inability to get the right chapter and verse for biblical quotations.

I would like to thank Creighton University and the Center of Theological Inquiry at Princeton for institutional support as I worked on this commentary.

Finally, I need to offer a special thanks to Peter Ochs and Stacy Johnson for asking me to participate in the Scriptural Reasoning Project sponsored by the Center of Theological Inquiry (2004–2007). The collective commitment of the group to close and God-saturated reading inspired and energized my own interpretive voice. To Peter and his tribe of postcritical readers I dedicate this attempt to reason scripturally.

ABBREVIATIONS

General

→	indicates a cross-reference to commentary on a Genesis passage
ANF	The Ante-Nicene Fathers. Reprinted Grand Rapids: Eerdmans, 1957.
AV	Authorized Version (King James Version)
FC	Fathers of the Church. Washington DC: Catholic University of America Press, 1947–.
NPNF[1]	A Select Library of the Nicene and Post-Nicene Fathers of the Christian Church. First series. Reprinted Grand Rapids: Eerdmans, 1956.
NPNF[2]	A Select Library of the Nicene and Post-Nicene Fathers of the Christian Church. Second series. Reprinted Grand Rapids: Eerdmans, 1956.
NRSV	New Revised Standard Version
RSV	Revised Standard Version

Biblical

Acts	Acts		Deut.	Deuteronomy
Amos	Amos		Eccl.	Ecclesiastes
1 Chr.	1 Chronicles		Eph.	Ephesians
2 Chr.	2 Chronicles		Esth.	Esther
Col.	Colossians		Exod.	Exodus
1 Cor.	1 Corinthians		Ezek.	Ezekiel
2 Cor.	2 Corinthians		Ezra	Ezra
Dan.	Daniel		Gal.	Galatians

Gen.	Genesis	Matt.	Matthew
Hab.	Habakkuk	Mic.	Micah
Hag.	Haggai	Nah.	Nahum
Heb.	Hebrews	Neh.	Nehemiah
Hos.	Hosea	Num.	Numbers
Isa.	Isaiah	Obad.	Obadiah
Jas.	James	1 Pet.	1 Peter
Jer.	Jeremiah	2 Pet.	2 Peter
Job	Job	Phil.	Philippians
Joel	Joel	Phlm.	Philemon
John	John	Prov.	Proverbs
1 John	1 John	Ps.	Psalms
2 John	2 John	Rev.	Revelation
3 John	3 John	Rom.	Romans
Jonah	Jonah	Ruth	Ruth
Josh.	Joshua	1 Sam.	1 Samuel
Jude	Jude	2 Sam.	2 Samuel
Judg.	Judges	Song	Song of Songs
1 Kgs.	1 Kings	1 Thess.	1 Thessalonians
2 Kgs.	2 Kings	2 Thess.	2 Thessalonians
Lam.	Lamentations	1 Tim.	1 Timothy
Lev.	Leviticus	2 Tim.	2 Timothy
Luke	Luke	Titus	Titus
Mal.	Malachi	Zech.	Zechariah
Mark	Mark	Zeph.	Zephaniah

INTRODUCTION

The book of Genesis presents an inviting prospect. Source of some of the most well-known stories in the Bible, the chapters of Genesis sparkle with memorable characters and dramatic scenes. The six days of creation, the garden of Eden, the subtle serpent who tempts Eve, Cain and Abel, the flood, the tower of Babel, Sodom and Gomorrah, the trial of Abraham on Mount Moriah, Esau selling his inheritance to Jacob for a bowl of porridge, Jacob's ladder and his wrestling match with God—these names and episodes evoke knowing nods, even from folks who otherwise know little of the Bible. Unlike the strange ritual world of Leviticus or the vertiginous logical leaps of Paul's letters, only a person raised without exposure to Western culture will come to Genesis as to a new vista.

The familiarity is not surprising. Esther is a dramatic tale in its own right. Samson's blind fury and David's triumph over Goliath provide memorable images. Renaissance painters devoted many canvases to the chilling moment when Judith slays the sleeping Holofernes. But we know Genesis so well, because of what it promises. The word "Genesis" means *birth* or *origin*, a fitting title for the first book of the Bible, in which the first word—"in the beginning"—expresses the theme of the entire sweep of its fifty chapters. For Genesis tells of the origin of reality, the source of evil, the birth of the many languages and cultures that fill the earth, and then turns to tell the story of Abraham and his troubled descendants, the seed of the people of Israel, who will themselves give birth to the redemption of the whole world. Its episodes and scenes are not just memorable; they are telling.

Therein lies the problem for the interpreter. As a book of origins, Genesis is a seminal text, and its influence extends so far and so deep that discerning and explaining what it says can seem an impossible task. When Gen. 3 depicts the first sin, to explain the full meaning of the verses presses the commentator outward toward a fully developed account of the depths of human depravity. There is nothing about the tasty apple and the fateful first bite that suggests the mud-filled trenches of the Somme or the ash-stained winter skies above Auschwitz or the bodies frozen into cruel Soviet Siberian mud or the shadows of men and women burned into the concrete of Hiroshima—nothing, that is, except the firstness and originalness of the transgression that so quickly bears the fruit of Cain's murder of Abel. Here, then, in just a few short verses, the interpreter finds the whole sad history of humanity, crowding in with its relevance, demanding a place in the exposition. One truly knows the source only when one sees and feels the fullness of its consequences.

Yet the problem is greater still. Genesis is famous for its opening account of creation and then the first sin, both of which give the reader a picture of the origin of the world and human history. But the cosmic and primeval perspectives are not why Genesis has ever been read. This book of origins did not find its way into the sacred scriptures of the people of Israel—and from there into the Christian church and thus into the DNA of Western culture—because it tells us of the origin of things as they are, fascinating and informative as that may be. God's promise to and covenant with Abraham and his descendents are the topic of most of Genesis, and this promise and this covenant are precisely *not* an explanation of the source and origin of what is. The chapters that recount for us the careers of Abraham, Isaac, Jacob, and Joseph reveal the source and origin of what will be. This future is not simply a natural or expected outworking of an original creation. It is something new and unexpected: God creates for a purpose greater than creation itself.

Thus, the truly impossible task for the interpreter of Genesis is to bring into view the fullness of the promised future that pulls on the characters, scenes, and episodes of Genesis like a supernaturally powerful magnet. The small mark of circumcision in Abraham's flesh, the seed of the promise first planted in Sarah's womb, the thin, fragile line of inheritance that finds its way through Isaac to Jacob—these original impregnations of human history reach through the entire history of Israel toward an embrace of Christ. The sweep of the narrative from Gen. 12 onward echoes with the great exhortation of Deuteronomy: Choose life! It is the exhortation repeated and obeyed with all the implacable force of God's own will in the death and resurrection of Christ.

Once the promise is heard, our reading of Genesis inevitably takes on an anticipatory flavor. The seemingly permanent architecture of the universe created "in the beginning" starts to march forward into the promise with joyful anticipation. The painful, familiar reality of human sinfulness becomes an insane, horrifying romance with death, whose rotting image we paint with lipstick and rouge and prop up in the whorehouses of our souls. The primeval past comes alive, both reaching toward the promised future and remaining darkly, mysteriously resistant.

Where, then, can the commentary end? Nothing in the scriptures is manageable, nothing untouched by the consummating gift of life. Yet, in Genesis, the waters of consequence flow from the beginning, and they so quickly divide into the great rivers that irrigate the entire world that the interpreter is quickly drowned in the magnitude of it all. Commenting can feel like standing at the headwaters of the Colorado River and trying to see, as in a vision, its long flow as it reaches to the Gulf of Mexico. How does one bring others to see the Grand Canyon in the reflections of the small ponds of the Rocky Mountains?

I have despaired over the impossible task of providing satisfactory commentary on any one chapter of Genesis, to say nothing of its rich trove of fifty, but I have nevertheless persevered. In order to sandbag against the flood of interpretive possibilities, I have adopted an eccentric but I hope coherent approach.

My main method has been to identify what I hope are some of the telling verses in Genesis and then focus my comments accordingly. Sometimes, the verse is fitting simply because it introduces or summarizes the main thrust of a discrete episode or scene. For example, 5:1 ("this is the book of the generations of Adam") introduces a chapter-long genealogy, and I use this verse as the hook on which to hang comments on the significance of the shift from narrative to genealogy at this point, as well as to discuss the general theological significance of genealogies in the Bible. In other places, I single out a verse because it has long been a point of conflicting interpretations. Genesis 15:6 ("and he believed the LORD; and he reckoned it to him as righteousness") provides the clearest instance. This verse evokes the main issues at stake in centuries of post-Reformation controversy and debate about the relationship between faith and works. Sometimes verses stand out because they suggest important theological questions. Is the serpent in the garden a worldly form of Satan? In what sense is the covenant of circumcision everlasting? In other cases, I dwell on a verse because it provides an image taken up in the New Testament or because it calls to mind a different and seemingly contradictory verse in scripture. If God rests after he completes the six days of creation, then why does Jesus say, "My Father is working still" (John 5:17)? It's a question that gets us very quickly to the crux of the divine plan for the world: God working for us for the sake of our rest in him.

No single rule or principle guides my judgments about what makes for a telling verse, and as a result I do not follow a consistent method or pattern of exegesis. The reasons for commenting on 15:6 are different from those that lead to a focus on 3:1a. This naturally means that what makes for a sensible, useful interpretation will differ as well. For example, by my reckoning, we need to understand the gist of Reformation controversies over the doctrine of justification in order to arrive at a satisfactory reading of 15:6. This is not because the oral and editorial traditions that gave rise to this verse were thinking in terms of sixteenth-century theology, but rather because most contemporary Western Christians continue to think in these terms. We can't bring the authority of God's word to bear on the mind of the church by ignoring the way she thinks. In contrast, the thrust of my comment on 3:1a draws on different material. The church has been of one mind when it comes to reading the serpent as Satan. The interesting question is why.

It should be obvious, therefore, that this diverse and eclectic approach interpolates all sorts of issues and questions into Genesis, and readers who wish for a self-contained commentary that approaches Genesis on its own terms will be disappointed. I can't see any other way to proceed. It is precisely a feature of any view of scripture as the word of God that, when read on its own terms, the seemingly narrow particularity of the texts opens out onto the world. The first chapters of Genesis are obvious examples. They raise fundamental questions about metaphysics, the nature of evil, and the relation of God to the world and humanity. The same holds for the promise that through Abraham all the nations will be blessed. As a result, it is hard to see how anything is irrelevant to reading Genesis on its own terms. The problem is to limit the scope to a manageable size.

Although this commentary ranges widely in topic and method, the individual books of the Bible have unique foci and distinctive themes, and this holds true for Genesis. As a book of origins, Genesis is far less concerned with the source of what *is* than what *will be*. In order to do justice to this overall thrust, I offer an insistent reading of Genesis as a promise-driven, future-oriented text. As the covenant with Abraham makes clear, God blesses his creatures with a new future. The promises break the bonds of sin, because God secures their fulfillment. They perfect our created natures, because God fulfills them in our flesh. I have divided my comments into five main portions in order to draw out this forward movement more clearly.

1. *Creation*: readers quickly notice the odd way in which Genesis gives a double account of creation. I read these two accounts as complimentary portrayals of the same, stage-setting divine act. The architecture of the six days of creation is made plastic and mobile by the possibility of the seventh day, a literary effect that, I argue, reveals the goal of the divine plan "in the beginning." God creates in order to consummate; nature is for the sake of grace; everything leans toward something *more*. The dynamic, forward-reaching structure of creation is even clearer in the second, more human-focused account of creation. It ends with the aching desire of the first man for companionship. This poignant moment of human subjectivity illustrates the way in which all creation groans for fulfillment. It is a yearning taken up and intensified in the nuptial fulfillments that echo throughout scripture.

2. *Fall*: a world yearning for *more* is not a stable place, and Gen. 3 tells of the fateful slide of the human will toward resistance to the divine plan. The choice to seek to rest in the world as it is rather than as God wishes it to become emerges as a mysterious and unexpected possibility. Explaining this choice requires (as I argue at length) the theological hypothesis that human beings do not originate the choice of evil, but instead respond to the devil's prior sinful choice. The consequences of human alliance with Satan's choice for history are soon spelled out in the story of Cain and Abel in Gen. 4, which I group with the famous scene of Adam, Eve, and the serpent as part of the original, continuing fall of humanity.

3. *Dead ends*: creation and fall are standard theological topics, and my training in theology prepared me to think clearly about some of the issues and

questions raised in Gen. 1–4. But reading and rereading Gen. 5–11, I struggled to understand their importance. What are we to say about the genealogy flowing from Adam in Gen. 5, the complicated flood narrative in Gen. 6–9, the tower of Babel and further genealogies in Gen. 10–11? As I worked on the later chapters of Genesis and saw the profoundly future-oriented thrust of the promises to Abraham, I realized that, in spite of the long, seemingly forward moving lists of "begats," these chapters go nowhere. After Cain kills Abel, Adam and Eve start the human family over again with Seth—yet by the time we get to Noah, the human family is stained by sin once again. God seems to regret creating humanity, and the engulfing floodwaters wipe the slate of creation clean. But the stain of sin remains in the sons of Noah, and God utters words that reveal all we need to know about the future role of universal cleansing in the divine plan: "Never again" (9:11). What looks like new initiatives and forward movements turns out to be dead ends.

4. *Scandal of particularity*: the dead ends throw Gen. 12 into sharp relief. When Abraham is called and given the promises of land, prosperity, and progeny, the ensuing sequence of events does not lead to a dead end. On the contrary, Abraham begins a history that works its way toward fulfillment in Christ. The call of Abraham embodies the metaphysical heresy that defines the theological and spiritual essence of Judaism and Christianity. God does not rain down his righteousness from on high. He does not apply the metaphysical balm of eternity to the human condition in a grand, cosmoswide gesture. On the contrary, in the covenant with Abraham, the creator pursues his purposes for the whole world by way of covenant with a single household. The many chapters that recount the career of Abraham and his descendents are preoccupied with impediments to future fulfillment of God's strangely focused plan. Infertility and conflict between brothers draw attention to perilous transmission of the promises from generation to generation. The gate of particularity is frightfully narrow, and the career of Abraham and his descendents inevitably strikes our natural religious instincts as a crazy, fragile, vulnerable way for God to fulfill his plan for all creation.

5. *Need for atonement*: two features of the later chapters of Genesis are striking. First, as readers work their way through the final chapters, they cannot help but feel as though Jacob, the final patriarch, fades into the background. Biblical scholars mark the break at Gen. 37, pointing out that most of the rest of Genesis is concerned with Joseph. By my reading, the break is real, but less distinct, and not entirely focused on Joseph. In the chapters after the wrestling match with God (Gen. 32) and before the clear literary shift to Joseph (Gen. 37), Jacob's clan emerges the main actor in the covenant drama. The shift in narrative agency marks an important change in theological focus. The central chapters of Genesis that concern Abraham and the future of the covenant make no mention of the problem of sin. The driving

question is one of election: who is chosen? For Joseph and his brothers, however, the central narrative problem is different: how will the children of Abraham overcome the deadly, divisive, destructive consequences of sin? My fifth and final division of the text—the need for atonement— brings this question to the fore. By my reading, these concluding chapters of Genesis provide no stable response to the blood of Abel that cries out from the ground. They point forward to the Passover sacrifice, the Levitical principles of atonement, and Jesus's death on Golgotha.

In order to develop this reading of Genesis, I have relied on a wide variety of sources. When I was first orienting myself to the project of commenting on Genesis, a number of friends suggested Claus Westermann's massive, three-volume work as the definitive summation of modern scholarship on Genesis. I dutifully trudged to the library. But I soon discovered that Westermann's great scholarly achievement was impossible for me to use. The elaborate nesting layers of exegetical argument, the parries and thrusts of debate among biblical historians, the slow-motion slides from philological to archeological to anthropological modes of analysis, the long surveys of competing scholarly opinion, the abrupt eruptions of magisterial pronouncement—doubtless others more learned than I have profited from the vast accumulation of scholarly material, but I could only look upon the pages with awe and wonder. I turned to other sources in order to glean from the fields of modern scholarship. Gerhard von Rad's 1972 commentary was consistently accessible and sometimes helpful. James L. Kugel's lucid summaries of modern exegetical reasoning in *How to Read the Bible* were helpful reminders of the main lines of contemporary scholarship.[1]

Kugel's wonderful collections and expositions of ancient interpretive arguments (mostly Jewish but sometimes early Christian) were more important to shaping my exegetical judgments than were his helpful accounts of modern scholarship. I kept his many recently published books close at hand.[2] The voices of ancient Jewish commentators were especially helpful for making my way through the later episodes in Genesis, where early Christian commentary is thin. The relative neglect is not surprising. Why dwell on the shadows and hints of the logic and economy of atonement in Genesis when later portions of the Old Testament provide such rich resources? Yet Jewish readings did more than fill in the gaps. Thinking through some of the recurring priorities of the ancient Jewish interpretation also helped me better understand St. Paul, whose interpretation and use of Genesis in his Letters to the Romans and Galatians has had decisive influence over the development of Western Christian theology. I found that the durable literal sense of Genesis can

---

1. James L. Kugel, *How to Read the Bible: A Guide to Scripture Then and Now* (New York: Free Press, 2007).

2. James L. Kugel, *In Potiphar's House* (New York: HarperCollins, 1990); idem, *The Ladder of Jacob: Ancient Interpretations of the Biblical Story of Jacob and His Children* (Princeton: Princeton University Press, 2006); and especially Kugel 1998.

shed light on the later and often obscure doctrinal controversies over faith and works, controversies for which Paul's letters provide the defining terms.

In addition to Kugel's clear presentations of ancient Jewish commentary, I regularly consulted Rashi, the great medieval Jewish figure whose commentaries on the Bible are among the most influential in the history of Judaism.[3] Readers will see my occasional use of his exegesis, but his influence is greater than the citations indicate. The mere mention of Christ in my interpretations of Genesis surely shows how much I differ from Rashi and the tradition to which he contributed so much. Yet he has been my conscience throughout as I have tried to be faithful to the literal sense of Gen. 17:7: "And I will establish my covenant between me and you and your descendants after you throughout their generations for an everlasting covenant."

If Rashi has been my conscience, then the church fathers have been my inspiration. I have found Origen and St. Augustine to be the most reliable guides to a reading of Genesis that is both metaphysically ambitious and reliably christocentric. When I reread Origen's *On First Principles* with the prospect of this commentary in mind, he helped me understand the possibility of a permanent but plastic role for creation in the divine plan. In concert with reading the remaining fragments of Didymus the Blind's detailed and beautiful commentary, I found that Origen's homilies enabled me to understand the way in which the New Testament's recurring images of the war of the spirit against the flesh need not be read as a static, metaphysical conflict of eternity against time. Instead, these images contribute to a reading of the divine invasion of human history by way of the covenant with Abraham. Thus, it is Origen, filtered through the revisionist Neoscholasticism of Henri de Lubac and Hans Urs von Balthasar,[4] who stands behind my attempt to read Gen. 1–2 in a mobile, forward-leaning fashion.

But I am a man of the West and a child of the Western church, and therefore Augustine looms larger. In his *City of God*, he takes the heavenly Jerusalem and projects it out into the future as the consummating end around which all human history is ordered, either in resistance to her triumph or with a loyalty that desires nothing but her peace. I have found some of Augustine's specific exegetical comments helpful, others not so. But encouraged by Robert W. Jenson's ambitious project of rethinking classical Christian assumptions about time and eternity, I have adopted the future-oriented, historical logic of Augustine's view of the divine plan without hesitation. This theological decision to read our entry into the seventh day as most fundamentally a matter of becoming fully and finally citizens of a city has allowed me to maximize the literal sense of Gen. 12–50. With

---

3. Rashi is an acronym for Rabbi Solomon ben Isaac (1040–1105). I have generally consulted the English translation of his Genesis commentary on the artscroll.com website. There is no critical edition.

4. Henri de Lubac, *The Mystery of the Supernatural*, trans. Rosemary Sheed (New York: Herder & Herder, 1998); and Hans Urs von Balthasar, *The Theology of Karl Barth*, trans. Edward T. Oakes (San Francisco: Ignatius, 1992).

Augustine's historicizing vision as my guide, I have been able to see how the true spiritual sense of 17:11 ("you shall be circumcised in the flesh of your foreskins, and it shall be a sign of the covenant between me and you") intensifies rather than relaxes the literal sense and its emphasis on the permanent role of human flesh in the divine plan. To be marked with the sign of the cross recapitulates a divine stroke that cuts to the marrow of bodily existence.

Two interpreters helped me see the moral and political implications of many of the episodes and themes in Genesis. St. John Chrysostom's homilies are not universally edifying, but often I found myself suddenly seeing once remote biblical scenes with new, penetrating psychological immediacy. Leon Kass's *The Beginning of Wisdom* (2003) also offers a rich array of moral and political insights that are closely tied to textual details. I rarely put down Kass's commentary without feeling myself ready to return to my exegetical labors refreshed. His interpretations are not always convincing. He views the main narrative tension from Gen. 12 onward as the backward-looking problem of preserving a tradition rather than the forward-looking problem of inheriting God's promises. Yet his reading is reliably stimulating.

Before concluding this summary of themes and divisions and sources, I want to identify my polemical interest and argumentative agenda. I have pointed things to say about modern historical-critical study of the Bible. No doubt thin-skinned biblical scholars will image me preoccupied with an antimodern campaign against critical scholarship. In the main, I find modern historical-critical scholarship sometimes helpful, sometimes maddeningly myopic, and sometimes irrelevant to the sorts of questions I find myself asking about Genesis. So, in this commentary I do not reject historical-critical exegesis. I am happy to consult it when helpful. I am only irritated by its unsustainable claims to an exclusive interpretive authority. As a tradition of scholarship, historical-critical cannot provide us with all the resources necessary to interpret the Bible as the living source for Christian faith.

I am especially concerned to set aside distracting and epiphenomenal concerns about modern critical scholarship, pro or con, because this commentary has an enemy that I think much more important: the gnostic temptation. Who hasn't felt its appeal? It is a painful fact that the diversity of nations and cultures has not led to a brilliant pageant of difference, but instead to our bloody world of conflict. Moreover, our own cultural inheritance is fraught with painful moral demands and offensive social mores. The labels of accusation are familiar: racism, ethnocentrism, heterosexism, patriarchy, and most of all the general horror over the way in which we allow the past to claim authority over us. What sensitive observer would not conclude that our historical particularity seems a curse, not a blessing? Our bodies seem no less troublesome. We feel ourselves battered by our fickle desires. We age and decay. Visit a graveyard and ask yourself, Are our bodies anything other than crumbling prisons?

Who, then, wouldn't want to find a way to transcend the cruel restrictions of history and throw off the rusting chains of the body? It was the dream of the Greeks, who contemplated unchangeable forms. It is the hope of modern philosophers, who try to replace hard-won virtue with method and to set aside the vagaries of judgment by appeals to logical and experimental certainties. It is the desire of any spiritual seeker who wants to transcend the differences that separate religions and cultures in order to dwell in their deeper, greater truth. It is the project of the modern educator, who wants critical reason to supervene over and sift through the demands of an inherited culture. It motivates plastic surgery to stave off the wrinkling ravages of time, and it endorses euthanasia in the hope that an act of the human will can somehow control and triumph over death itself.

Beginning with Irenaeus, many have observed that the account of creation in Genesis cuts against the gnostic temptation. The world that God has created is good, and therefore it can't be the problem we need to overcome. The observation is certainly true as far as it goes, but it doesn't go far enough, because the goodness of creation has never been regarded by Jews and Christians as the full and final goodness that God wills for his creatures. God tenses creation with the desire for the seventh day of divine rest, and this greater-than-creation goal seems always to tempt us to turn our spiritual lives into an upward reach that seeks to escape the bonds of finitude. God promises *more*—and we too easily interpret more as *other*, as the sweet nectar of the eternal that will palliate our vulnerability to decay and death, as the balm of indubitable, universal, and necessary truth that will cure our wounded, unpredictable, unreliable wills. My overriding goal in this commentary is to block this slide from *more* to *other*.

For Jews, the *more* is the Torah, and for Christians, the *more* is Christ crucified and risen. The difference is incalculable, all the more so because it contests over the inheritance of promises that both Jews and Christians trace back to Abraham. Jews and Christians are not ships passing in the night. They collide in daylight. The history that has grown out of this collision is painful to contemplate. Nonetheless, Jews and Christians share a common theological judgment, one vividly present in Genesis. God does not give to Abraham anything remotely resembling what we hope for in our perennial and persistent gnostic dreams. True enough, the blessing that God promises is rest in fellowship with him. But God does not remain on a remote heavenly throne while we mutilate our humanity to get to him in vain efforts of spiritual ascent. God comes to us. He gives us a new future in the flesh, not a new metaphysical location. I hope that I do not tax the patience of readers by repeating this truth again and again.

All biblical citations come from the Revised Standard Version unless otherwise noted. Occasionally, I advert to the Authorized Version (also known as the King James Version) in order to accentuate verbal resonances.

1

CREATION

"In the beginning God created" (1:1)

1:1 In the beginning God created the heavens and the earth.

This time-honored translation follows the Septuagint, the ancient Greek translation widely used in early Judaism and Christianity. The verbal formula plays an explicit role in John 1:1 ("in the beginning was the Word"), which itself provides an obvious interpretation of Gen. 1:1, emphasizing a beginning that is absolute and foundational. It is precisely this sense of "beginning," as well as its close association with John 1:1, that is muted by recent translations, which shift the word order: "in the beginning when God created" (NRSV) or "when God began to create" (New Jewish Publication Society Bible).

It is important to realize that we do not possess a quick way to settle the question of which translation is accurate. As Jews began to speak languages further and further removed from ancient Hebrew, a tradition evolved that provided vowel markings to guide pronunciation. This tradition culminated in the Masoretic Text, the oldest manuscript of which dates back to the ninth century after the time of Christ. By and large, modern scholars treat the Masoretic Text as definitive. But consulting the Masoretic Text is not always the obvious way to get to the original sense. The most influential Greek translation, the Septuagint, was made sometime in the third or second century before the time of Christ. In this version, the translators sometimes suggest readings of keywords that differ from those in the Masoretic Text. So, when it comes to the historical question of how to translate in such a way as to be faithful to the original text, the answers are not always easy.

When considering Gen. 1:1, the problem becomes still more difficult, because the concept "beginning" has different shades of meaning. A point of departure can refer to a discrete moment in time. We might say, for example, "The train began its trip at 7:25 p.m.," and following this usage, the preference of contemporary translators for a more temporal and restricted sense of "beginning" is certainly plausible. Yet a point of departure or beginning can also refer to a basis or a rationale, a purpose, or a reason. A scientist can say, "The second law of thermodynamics is the basis—the beginning—of cosmology." Or, "Professor Smith's class was the basis—the beginning—of my love of science." This sense of "beginning" as source and origin is associated with the Greek term *archē*, the word used to translate Gen. 1:1 in the Septuagint and repeated in John 1:1. Of course, the sense of "beginning" as an origin or source rather than first instance in time is not simply a Greek idea. When scripture teaches that "the fear of the LORD is the beginning of wisdom" (Ps. 111:10), the claim is substantive, not temporal. Fear of the LORD is the origin of the wise life, not in the sense of the first step that is superseded by the second and third, but in the lasting sense of providing its basis or root.[1]

With these straightforward observations about the diversity of ancient traditions and the different senses of "beginning," we face an interesting exegetical problem. The old translation brings to mind the traditional theological picture of God as the eternal, self-sufficient deity whose creative act "in the beginning" brings all time and reality into existence. The new translations that are supported by many biblical experts imply a different view. At a certain point in time and in a particular place in a preexisting cosmos, a deity set about to form this particular world. God is a power within the cosmos rather than the power that brings the cosmos into existence. Which, then, shall it be? Are we to cleave to the traditional translation and its implied theology of an absolute beginning, or should we follow contemporary scholarly judgments?

Rashi, the great eleventh-century rabbinic commentator, can help us move toward a satisfactory answer. At the outset of his commentary on Genesis, Rashi reiterates an earlier rabbinic opinion that the Pentateuch should have begun with Exod. 12:2 and not Gen. 1:1. The claim seems fanciful, but it is meant to interpret rather than correct the sacred text. The traditional rabbinic view holds that Exod. 12:2 expresses the first commandment that God gives to Israel. Thus, to say that the Bible *should* have begun with Exod. 12:2 is a way of dramatizing an important theological judgment: God creates for the sake of his commandments, for the sake of the Torah.

---

1. For a full development of the possible senses of "beginning," see Origen's *Commentary on John* 1.16–22 (ANF 9.305–8). I follow Origen in also rejecting a temporal sense of "beginning" for interpreting Gen. 1:1; see his *Homilies on Genesis* 1.1 (FC 71.47–48).

More is at work here than a general theological idea, however. It turns out that Exod. 12:2 is not just the first commandment to Israel. The verse also echoes the key, fraught word "beginning": "This month shall be for you the beginning of months; it shall be the first month of the year for you." Furthermore, the commandment about the beginning of the months is odd, and it draws attention to a richer, more foundational sense of "beginning." Exodus 12 as a whole is concerned with preparations for the Passover, and the implied meaning of 12:2 is that the Passover festival, in a certain sense, provides the beginning of the lunar calendar. But, of course, the verse can't mean that Passover is the temporal beginning of lunar cycles measured by months, since there were countless months before the Israelites were enslaved in Egypt. Thus, the passage must mean that the Passover provides an *ultimate purpose* or *rationale* for the lunar calendar. So our attention is redirected back to Gen. 1:1 and the origin of all things. In a substantive rather than temporal way the Passover serves as the beginning point, the *archē* of human history. The very cycles of the moon exist for the sake of marking the time of the Passover.

We can now see, therefore, that Rashi cites the ancient rabbinic opinion that the Bible should have begun with Exod. 12:2 because he wants to reinforce that larger theological judgment about Gen. 1 as a whole: God's plan for the people of Israel is the most elementary, most fundamental aspect of creation. As another ancient interpretation glosses Gen. 1:1, "God looked into the Torah . . . and created the world" (*Genesis Rabbah* 1.1, quoted from Kugel 1998: 45). The deliverance and sanctification of Israel, the Passover project so to speak, is that in which and for which God creates. Still another ancient interpretation puts the priority of God's plan in paradoxical terms and gives a full-blown account of the divine plan: "Two thousand years before [God] created the world he created the Law; he had prepared the garden of Eden for the just and Gehenna for the wicked. He had prepared the garden of Eden for the just that they might eat and delight themselves from the fruits of the trees, because they had kept [the] precepts of the Law in this world and fulfilled the commandments. For the wicked he prepared Gehenna . . . , [and] within it darts of fire and burning coals for the wicked, to be avenged of them in the world to come because they did not observe the precepts of the Law in this world."[2] God *first* "creates" the future consummation of creation—"the world to come" in which Torah obedience and disobedience define existence—and *then* God creates for the sake of bringing this future to pass in the real time of creation.

This traditional rabbinic affirmation that the revelation of Sinai precedes reality—where "precedes" is given a substantive or foundational sense rather than in a narrow, temporal sense—lines up fairly closely with the prologue to John's Gospel. John 1:1, like Exod. 12:2, echoes the crucial word "beginning." It affirms

---

2. *Targum Neofiti* 3.24 in Martin McNamara, trans., *Targum Neofiti 1: Genesis*, Aramaic Bible 1A (Collegeville, MN: Liturgical Press, 1992), 63–64.

the truth that God creates out of his word or purpose. It is not that Rashi or any other Jewish commentator would agree that Christ, the incarnate Word, is the basis for creation. Rather, the rabbis and the author of John's Gospel explicitly affirm a basic theological principle. The divine plan or project, however spelled out, is the beginning out of which and for which God creates.

At this point contemporary scholars are likely to raise objections. The current formulations such as "when God began" or "in the beginning when God created" stem, at least in part, from an anxiety that traditional theological loyalties have for too long overdetermined our reading of scripture. This anxiety becomes particularly acute when modern biblical scholars see the New Testament (or ancient rabbinic interpretation) functioning as the lens through which we read the Old Testament. Historians worry that later doctrinal commitments exercise an extrinsic and anachronistic control over our interpretive imaginations. The danger is that we end up simply finding what we are looking for: confirmation of our dogmatic prejudices. In the meantime, the real meaning of the biblical text is lost. After all, as biblical scholars point out, the very next verse of Genesis evokes a standard ancient Near Eastern myth of primeval combat between the power for order and the power of chaos.

No doubt it is a good thing to want to recover the integrity of the distinctive voices and historical contexts for the diverse books of the Bible. The methods of historical-critical study allow us to see the biblical text as a multilayered, internally complex document, and this is a gain. There is no reason to think that the word of God should be one-dimensional and immediately accessible.[3] Nonetheless, the modern tradition of biblical interpretation tends to be blind to the wealth of reasons in favor of traditional readings. Exegetical judgments do not emerge out of nowhere, achieve communal authority, and then impose themselves on the interpretive imaginations of traditional readers and translators of the Bible. In the main, traditional readers formulated and gave credence to patterns of interpretation and translation because they discerned any number of intellectual and spiritual advantages that are as relevant today as they were thousands of years ago.

We need to turn, then, to a brief survey of some exegetical reasons in support of the substantive approach to "in the beginning," the approach that the rabbinic tradition cited by Rashi endorses. These reasons very likely guided those who produced the Septuagint and later translations, as well as the implied reading of Gen. 1:1 found in John 1:1. Needless to say, a comprehensive account is out of reach. How we treat the beginning is so fundamental to our overall interpretation of the Bible that reasons for any particular translation are almost coextensive with the articulation of a comprehensive, biblically sensitive theology. Nonetheless,

---

3. On the contrary, the church fathers consistently observe that it is fitting that the sacred scriptures should be difficult and confusing. For an account of the patristic theology of scriptural obscurity, see John J. O'Keefe and R. R. Reno, *Sanctified Vision: An Introduction to Early Christian Interpretation of the Bible* (Baltimore: Johns Hopkins University Press, 2005), 128–39; and R. R. Reno, "Origen and Spiritual Interpretation," *Pro ecclesia* 15.1 (Winter 2006): 108–26.

it is possible to gain some insight into why the traditional translation ("in the beginning") best conveys the meaning of Gen. 1:1.

The larger sweep of Gen. 1 provides the first indication. The days of creation certainly move forward in a temporal sequence. One day follows another, culminating in the seventh day, the Sabbath. But in spite of this apparent focus on *when* things happen, the dominant rhetorical theme of the first chapters of Genesis concerns *how* God creates. Each day is introduced with the refrain "and God said." This forceful rhetorical pattern is echoed elsewhere. Recalling the angels and the heavens, Ps. 148:5 gives all praise to God, "for he commanded and they were created." From this picture of God's voice as the instrument of creation, it is a very short step to something like the interpretation of Gen. 1:1 found in John 1:1: "In the beginning"—that is, in his all-powerful word—"God created the heavens and the earth."

A substantive reading of "beginning" has another, more literal form of textual support. Many ancient commentators saw an obvious difficulty standing in the way of a straightforward, temporal interpretation of the sort found in translations such as "when God began." In Gen. 1 the sun, moon, and stars are created on the fourth day. How, then, can there be a "first day" when the sun, whose movements mark day and night, does not exist? Furthermore, at any moment half of the earth is in darkness, while the other half is illuminated by the sun. So, we never think of the earth as a whole (to say nothing of the larger universe) as existing in the temporally distinct states of day and night. In view of these difficulties, we should not be surprised that St. Augustine worried that a strictly temporal reading of Gen. 1 would entangle interpreters in countless difficulties. "I fear," he wrote, "that I will be laughed at by those who have scientific knowledge of these matters and by those who recognize the facts of the case" (*Literal Commentary on Genesis* 1.10 in FC 41.30; see also *City of God* 11.7 in Bettenson 1972: 436–37). To avoid this problem Augustine subordinated the temporal sense of the day-by-day account to what he took to be the more important, substantive sense of "beginning."

There are still further textual reasons in support of the traditional interpretation and translation of the beginning, reasons that draw on the insights of modern biblical scholarship. In the terminology of modern biblical study, Gen. 1 reflects the interests and worldview of P, the Priestly writer or writers, while Gen. 2 stems from J, the Yahwist source.[4] This is not the place to give an account of scholarly opinions about the historical contexts for P and J or their roles in the overall composition of the canonical form of Genesis. However, it is important to know that isolating distinct traditions and assigning different sections of Genesis to one source or the other has helped modern biblical readers. It allows us to step back from a merely local reading of Genesis in order to consider how the different sections and episodes within Genesis reflect and advance particular theological concerns.

4. "J" comes from the scholars who first developed this theory of the composition of Genesis transliterating their vocalization of the divine name in German as *Jahweh*.

In this case, to know that Gen. 1 stems from the Priestly tradition encourages us to think about how the seven-day account of creation fits with the cultic theology of ritual and sacrifice in Leviticus, as well as the emphasis on the centralized, priest-governed worship in Jerusalem found in the historical books of the Old Testament. As a modern historian, then, the first and most important thing to say about the opening account of creation in Genesis is that it stems from a Priestly tradition that wishes to place temple and sacrifice at the center of our perceptions of the deepest logic and purpose of reality. The Priestly theology of temple and sacrifice is the *archē* or beginning of the P account of creation.[5]

Thus we are pretty much where Rashi and John's Gospel left us. To be sure, there are important differences. The traditional rabbinic opinion that God creates for the sake of the Torah and the traditional Christian view that the eternal Word was with God in the beginning make distinct claims about God and reality. In contrast, modern scholars direct our attention toward sociological rather than theological truths: certain ideologies and political loyalties shape the final form of the biblical text. Nonetheless, the logic of "beginning" is the same in each case. Genesis presents the days of creation in terms of a substantive, underlying source: God's plan for traditional readers, Priestly ideology for modern historical scholars.

Here we encounter a persistent paradox in modern biblical study. The actual implications of its methods and analysis are often at odds with its exegetical judgments (although not always; see von Rad 1972: 46). Rashi, the authors of various New Testament texts, and modern biblical scholars assume that the creation account has a beginning in which or for the sake of which the seven days unfold across Gen. 1. Again, it does not matter that Rashi will say that God creates for the sake of the Torah, over and against the author of John's Gospel, who implies that God creates for the sake of the incarnation of his Word—both of whom are contradicted by the modern biblical scholar who says that the writer or writers of the creation account formulated the seven-day sequence for the sake of reinforcing a Jerusalem-oriented temple ideology. All agree that creation emerges out of a prior plan or purpose—traditional readers putting the plan in the mind of God, and modern readers putting it in the mind of the tradition that stands behind the P source. This striking consensus militates against the contemporary preference for a thin, temporally focused reading of Gen. 1:1 and strongly supports the substantive sense of the traditional translation: "In the beginning."

---

5. One need not depend on the aid of modern biblical scholarship. Canonical writers also emphasized the temple-oriented structure of creation. Thus Jer. 17:12: "A glorious throne set on high from the beginning is the place of our sanctuary." See also Wisdom of Solomon 9:8: "Thou hast given command to build a temple on thy holy mountain, and an altar in the city of thy habitation, a copy of the holy tent which thou didst prepare from the beginning." The same vision of a temple "in the beginning" continues in the New Testament: "We have such a high priest, one who is seated at the right hand of the throne of the Majesty in heaven, a minister in the sanctuary and the true tent which is set up not by man but by the Lord" (Heb. 8:1–2).

The immediate reasons in support of a traditional interpretation and translation are strong, but we should broaden the argument, not only because further reasons are important in their own right, but also because we need to be clearminded about the expansive scope of interpretation. A theological reading needs to approach scripture in such a way as to sustain a coherent, overall view of God's plan and purpose. What is entailed in sustaining such a view is complex and opaque. No one can set criteria ahead of time, and there are no particular methods that will guarantee good results. Sound interpretive arguments are always varied and cumulative. In this case, three broad considerations speak in favor of the traditional translation. A substantive interpretation of "beginning" will allow us to approach the larger question of creation in a way that (1) helps us avoid a false conflict between creation and science, (2) facilitates a fruitful engagement of faith with reason, and (3) gives a proper spiritual focus to our interpretive concerns.

The first advantage of the traditional approach to Gen. 1:1 concerns the relation between Genesis and modern cosmology. Modern physics analyzes the movements of matter and energy, and it operates with the notion of "beginning" as temporal sequence. For this reason, an approach to Gen. 1:1 that emphasizes the temporal sense in which "God began" will run afoul of modern science and its account of the beginning of the cosmos. In contrast, a theological reading of "beginning" as source and basis need not directly and primarily concern itself with modern cosmology. We can interpret Genesis with reference to the beginning out of which and for which God creates, and we need not coordinate the seven-day sequence with the complex physical processes that modern scientists think best explain the evolution of the universe. In other words, to adopt the tradition translation, "in the beginning," helps us focus on the divine purpose for creation rather than on the physical processes that gave rise to the created world.

Of course, a modern scientist may assert, as does Richard Dawkins, that there is no intent or purpose undergirding the world.[6] But a metaphysical pronouncement of this sort reflects the judgment that what modern science can or cannot investigate is coextensive with what is or is not the case. This highly implausible view undergirds the materialist claim that physical processes cause and explain everything, a claim that is an important and influential tenet of modern metaphysical ideologies. But as a clear distinction between "beginning" as first instance in an unfolding process and "beginning" as ultimate source and purpose helps us to see, materialism is neither entailed by nor part of modern scientific cosmology. Thus, a Christian faith that reads Gen. 1 as outlining the substantive rather than temporal source of creation is well prepared to endorse modern science while rejecting the faux metaphysics of modern scientism.[7]

6. Richard Dawkins, *The Blind Watchmaker* (New York: Penguin, 1990).

7. For a clear explanation of the import of modern cosmology and its relationship to classical doctrines of creation, see Stephen M. Barr, *Modern Physics and Ancient Faith* (Notre Dame: University of Notre Dame Press, 2003).

The second broad issue at stake in our approach to the beginning concerns the proper focus of interpretive anxiety. If we adopt a reading of Gen. 1:1 that follows the direction of Rashi's use of Exod. 12:2, as well as John 1:1, then our interpretive question is forthright, and it brings us directly to the spiritual centers of both Judaism and Christianity. What is the purpose or intention from which God, as it were, counts back as the beginning? The New Testament writers were well aware of the crucial importance of this question. The author of John's Gospel was not the only one to frame creation in terms of the divine plan. St. Paul writes: "There is one God, the Father, from whom are all things and for whom we exist, and one Lord, Jesus Christ, through whom are all things and through whom we exist" (1 Cor. 8:6). Paul's formulation is a direct interpretation of Gen. 1:1. In (through) the beginning (Christ), God (the Father) created heaven and earth.

With this account of creation, St. Paul and the subsequent Christian tradition give priority to the specific revelation of the divine plan in Christ, but in a way that harmonizes faith with reason. Knowing the Lord Jesus is crucial to knowing the beginning in which and out of which all things come to be. As Augustine exhorts, "Mark this fabric of the world. View what was made by the Word, and then thou wilt understand what is the nature of the world" (*Tractates on John* 1.9 in NPNF[1] 7.10).[8] Christ is the master plan; he is the "beloved Son" who is "the first-born of all creation." Christ is the beginning, "for in him all things were created" (Col. 1:13–16). His saving death was planned "before the foundation of the world" (1 Pet. 1:20). The Lord Jesus is the "bright morning star" (Rev. 22:16) by which the faithful take their bearings, and "in [him] are hid all the treasures of wisdom and knowledge" (Col. 2:3). In sum: the world has a beginning by and in the divine Word, and we best orient ourselves to reality when we focus on Christ.

This affirmation of the priority of Christ would seem to set up a painful conflict between faith and reason, between knowledge of revealed truth and the sort of knowledge we acquire by scientific study of reality. But a substantive sense of "beginning" prevents just such a conflict. Faith brings us to an ever more intimate union with the *logos* of creation, and as a result, theology is rightfully queen of the sciences. Theology orients our minds toward the truth of all things. Yet, since Christ is the beginning or source of reality, theology does not take our minds to strange places and inculcate antiscientific attitudes. Rather, because Christ is the beginning from which and for which God creates, accurate knowledge of reality (what medieval scholars called philosophy and what we usually refer to as science) can help guide us toward the originating Word. Wisdom of Solomon 9:1 teaches that God has made all things by his word, and Ps. 104:24 proclaims: "O LORD, how manifold are thy works! In wisdom hast thou made them all." Endowed with intellectual powers that can see the outlines of wisdom in creation, our reason can prepare us for faith.

8. The theological judgment is by no means merely antique. See Robert W. Jenson, *Systematic Theology* (New York: Oxford University Press, 1999), 2.27: "The story told in the Gospels states the meaning of creation."

The third warrant for privileging a substantive sense of "beginning" bears directly on a central problem in Christian theology: the relation between nature and grace. A Christ-centered reading of God's creation explains a perplexing, double affirmation that characterizes apostolic Christianity. On the one hand, everything is good—on the other hand, everything must change under the lordship of Christ. Not only are human creatures finite and natural aspects of the created order, they are also chosen and called. As the Genesis story moves forward, Abraham must leave home. He must transcend the natural bonds of filial love and the safety of his clan. This leave-taking is focused and intensified in Christian discipleship. Consider the demands of the Sermon on the Mount. The ordinary, worldly stuff of life—our bodies, our desires, our loyalties, our identities as social creatures—all this has a divinely ordained destiny that stretches well beyond what seems natural and normal.

There is a similar double affirmation in a Torah-centered reading. It leads to the classical rabbinic project of transforming everything into legal problems to be brought under the authority of divine law. In both the Christian and Jewish views, therefore, a problem emerges. There is an apparent contradiction between the goodness of creation and the drive toward sanctification. How can God call creation very good—and then turn around and continue to act upon it for the sake of pushing the human creature forward toward an even higher goal? How can the human body be good—but nonetheless require the commandment of circumcision for the sake of covenant? How can we harmonize the divine directive to "be fruitful and multiply" with the Pauline exhortation to prefer the celibate life?

These sorts of questions capture a deep worry that religious faith encourages an inhumane form of life, an aggressive attack on the natural limitations of our created condition. If God must act upon us by way of commandment rather than simply meet us in our desire for fellowship, then isn't our hoped-for rest in God extrinsic and compelled? Isn't the final end sought in faith an enslaving and alienating state of obedience?

The problem has perplexed Western Christianity ever since Augustine. How can the necessity of the outer pull of divine command be affirmed without supplanting the inner push of desire for God? How can we do justice to both the "attractive" and "imperative" dimensions of the Christian life, the sense in which faith is both exactly what the human creature needs and wants and, at the same time, something new, frightening, and unexpected? How can our free decision of faith be compatible with the sovereign grace of God that is necessary for any true and saving participation in Christ crucified and risen?[9]

These difficulties are resolved if we adopt a substantive sense of "beginning." Christ is the master plan of all creation, and his call is necessarily toward a fulfillment rather than effacement or denial of creation. As Athanasius observes, "There is

---

9. For a clearly developed account of this problem, keyed to the moral life, see Gilbert Meilaender, *The Way Leads There: Augustinian Reflections on the Christian Life* (Grand Rapids: Eerdmans, 2006), 71–76.

no inconsistency between creation and salvation; for the one Father has employed the same Agent for both works, effecting salvation of the world through the same Word who made it in the beginning" (*On the Incarnation* 1). In following Christ toward an end that is supernatural, we will not (to echo Nietzsche) vivisect our fragile, finite, natural lives. That which is created and mortal shall not be defeated or destroyed; it will "be swallowed up by life" (2 Cor. 5:4). In the words of T. S. Eliot: "And the end of all our exploring / Will be to arrive where we started / And know the place for the first time."[10] To put this truth in its popular Thomistic formula: grace perfects rather than destroys nature.

There is more. But we must stop here, because it should now be clear that the traditional translation is part of a fully developed and well-considered theological outlook. A decision in favor of a substantive beginning rather than a temporal sequence sets the interpretive agenda for the Bible as a whole. Creation is for the sake of something prior and more fundamental: the divine project or plan. In the beginning, God subjected all things to his final purpose, just as an archer strings a bow in order to pull it back and load it with a force that strains forward toward its target (Rom. 8:20–21). Thus, the very first verse of the Bible encourages us to read forward, plotting the trajectory of the text in all its extraordinarily rich diversity as it aims toward the fulfillment of the Word that is eternally spoken by the Father "in the beginning," out of which and for the sake of which all things were created.

Unlike the worldly archer, however, we do not possess the divine, consummating target of scripture as an item of knowledge that we can use in syllogisms, which is why wild apocalyptic discourse in the Bible can never be distilled into predictions. The plan and purpose of God is love, and it is revealed in its fullness in the person of Jesus Christ. As we are baptized into his body and follow his way, we participate in his truth rather than examine it as a fact or theory. We live amid the final realization of the divine plan, and we cannot stand still and coolly line up the endpoint of human history in our theological crosshairs. For this reason, our reading of Genesis (or any other book of the Bible) is not a simple retrospective calculation. One does not approach the days of creation with a slide rule, reasoning backward from a fixed point.

Instead, to begin Genesis "in the beginning" gives our interpretation a double quality. At every moment in the unfolding of the divine plan we rightly devote ourselves to the details. But the project of exegesis is not simply to settle purely local questions of meaning. Our goal should be to move forward ever more deeply into the beginning, into the mystery of Christ. For this reason, theological interpretation necessarily combines a global framework with local color. Our overall take on the divine plan interacts with particular moments of scriptural evidence. The best possible reading of any verse of scripture will be one that allows us to

10. T. S. Eliot, "Little Gidding," lines 240–42, in *Four Quartets* (New York: Harcourt, Brace & Jovanovich, 1943), 59.

both make sense of the words in front of us *and* see their role in guiding us toward fulfillment in Christ.

1:2 The earth was without form and void.

Instead of simply speaking all reality into existence, God seems to tame and form a preexisting chaos by acting upon a primal, watery substance. Modern biblical scholars have detailed the connections between this verse and the Babylonian creation myth *Enuma Elish*, a connection that crops up in a number of different places in the Old Testament.[11] But modern scholars are by no means the first to notice the plain sense of Gen. 1:2 and its apparent affirmation of creation out of preexisting, primal substance. As St. Augustine reports in one of his commentaries on Genesis: "The heretics [he is referring to Manicheans] who reject the Old Testament are in the habit of pointing the finger at this passage and saying, 'How can God have made heaven and earth in the beginning, if the earth was already there?'"[12]

Augustine's adversaries had common sense and ancient science on their side. A potter makes pots out of preexisting clay. A carpenter makes chairs out of uncut wood. For this reason, ancient theories of creation consistently pictured the cosmos as formed out of primal matter. Yet, as Augustine recognized, the doctrine of *creatio ex nihilo*, creation out of nothing, speaks against all the ordinary good reasons in favor of accepting the literal sense of this verse. We can't interpret the enigmatic formless void and abyss and watery chaos as preexistent matter, Augustine insists, because "we are bound to believe that God is the author and founder of all things."[13] His solution is to observe that scripture does not tell us everything, and therefore he speculates that God must have created the unformed matter at some point after the beginning announced in 1:1, but before the actions depicted in 1:2. This allows him to harmonize the plain sense of the verse with the doctrine of creation out of nothing.

Many modern readers recoil at the notion that church doctrines should be relevant to a critically responsible approach to the Bible. After all, aside from 2 Maccabees 7:28, the Bible does not specify creation out of nothing. It would seem, then, that the conflict between the doctrine *creatio ex nihilo* and the immediate sense of Gen. 1:2 presents us with a classic case of later theological ideas subverting the literal meaning of the Bible, forcing an implausible, strained reading. Is a rigid system of doctrine being imposed upon scripture and silencing its own voice? "It is one thing to respect the traditional views and interpretations of

11. Jon D. Levenson, *Creation and the Persistence of Evil* (San Francisco: Harper & Row, 1988).

12. *Unfinished Literal Commentary of Genesis* 4 in *The Works of Saint Augustine*, vol. 1/13: *On Genesis*, trans. Edmund Hill (Hyde Park, NY: New City Press, 2002), 119.

13. Ibid., 123.

the Bible," we might find ourselves saying, "but we must be sure not to lose the text in the process."

Who can object to the impulse to defend scripture against simpleminded absorption into a preconceived doctrinal system? Any reading of scripture that ignores or distorts the text makes a mockery of the fundamental Christian commitment to the Bible as the word of God. However, we need to relax for a moment. Doctrines such as *creatio ex nihilo* became authoritative because communities of readers have found them to be helpful guides to a coherent, overall reading of scripture. If we step back from 1:2 and view the issue more broadly, then we can see that the interpretive judgments epitomized in the doctrine of *creatio ex nihilo* find wide and substantial support. An affirmation of creation out of nothing helps readers (1) maximize the plain sense of many other scriptural passages, (2) support a metaphysical framework for coherent affirmations of basic Christian claims, and (3) maintain a soteriological focus for biblical interpretation as a whole.

The Old Testament campaign against idolatry has a recurring structure that implies the doctrine of creation out of nothing. Idols are not weak, ineffective, or inadequate; they are empty and lifeless. Those who set themselves up against the LORD's commands "are nothing; their molten images are empty wind" (Isa. 41:29). "The makers of idols go in confusion" (45:16). Idolatrous practices are, of course, disastrous for Israel, but the images themselves are not evil powers. "Idols are like scarecrows," and "they cannot do evil, neither is it in them to do good" (Jer. 10:5).

The New Testament carries forward the same view. Idols are lifeless and powerless. St. Paul consistently explains the futility of idols by appealing to God's creative uniqueness (Acts 14:15; 17:24). For this reason, Paul is indifferent to any thought that pagan meat sacrifices might be infected by a hidden, shameful potency (1 Cor. 8). Idols are not malignantly potent; they are empty and vacant. The danger is not that idols will bewitch by some internal, semidivine, and primeval power. There can be no such source, because God creates everything out of nothing. Instead, idols transfix solely because we fill their vacancy with the "noisy gong" and "clanging cymbal" of empty prophecy and pseudomystery (13:1).

Given this larger biblical consensus, it's not coincidental that the themes of idolatry and loyalty set the stage for the explicit affirmation of *creatio ex nihilo* in 2 Maccabees 7:28. After all, the doctrine of creation out of nothing gives precise expression to the metaphysical view that underlies the main lines of the biblical analysis of idolatry. There is nothing (*nihil*) other than the one true God and the set of all things he has made. Idolatry is not a simple mistake or miscalculation. In view of the ontological parsimony implicit in the doctrine of creation out of nothing (the parsimony comes from denying that there exists anything other than God and what he has created), the error of idolatry is not loyalty to a primeval, chaotic, and semidivine substance that cannot measure up to the power and glory of the LORD. Idolatry is loyalty to *nihil*, a devotion to the lifeless, empty abyss of death, which is the antithesis of the future promised in the covenant. This is why idolatry is the mother of all sins in the Old Testament and also why St. Paul makes idolatry the fundamental, original sin in Rom. 1.[14]

In addition to expressing the crucial theological principle underlying the biblical rejection of idolatry, the ontological parsimony entailed in the doctrine of creation out of nothing also helps biblical readers manage the apparent conflict between two different kinds of biblical claims about God. On the one hand, we read, "Behold, heaven and the highest heaven cannot contain thee" (1 Kgs. 8:27). God is wholly other and cannot be framed within the finite world. On the other hand, God is a character within the biblical story. He commands and speaks, and, "the LORD appeared to Abram" (Gen. 17:1). So, which shall it be? Is God without or within? Is God wholly other, or is he a participant in the unfolding drama of finite creation?

These questions concern more than intrascriptural tension. They also have to do with contemporary intuitions about the universality of truth and the particularity of cultures. The bumper sticker declaration that "My God is too big for any one religion" reflects the conviction that one must be loyal to 1 Kgs. 8:27 to the exclusion of Gen. 17:1. One must affirm the universal deity over and against the LORD who has a particular name and elects a particular nation. This apparently inevitable and contrastive choice between universality and particularity is all the more dramatic in classical Christology. Divine transcendence would seem utterly inconsistent with incarnation in the person of Jesus of Nazareth.

The doctrine of *creatio ex nihilo* resolves the problem, because it forces us to formulate God's transcendence in terms of uniqueness rather than difference or supremacy. Prior to creation there is no eternal "stuff" present with God as a coexisting reality, and thus God-as-God is in relation to absolutely nothing other than himself. As the traditional translation of Exod. 3:14 states, God is who he is simply because he is who he is, and not because he is not something else.[15] Or, to move to 3:15, which has the same metaphysical implication, God's revealed name (YHWH) is a more fundamental denotation of the one whom we praise and worship than contrastive terms such as the Eternal or Almighty.[16] The "thatness" of God (the God with a particular name) is prior to the "whatness" of God (the Infinite, the Eternal, the Almighty). Or put differently, what the LORD says and does shapes the concept of God in scripture rather than the concept of God identifying whom or what counts as divine.[17]

14. St. Athanasius glosses Rom. 1 in *Against the Pagans* 8.3 (NPNF[2] 4.8): "Evil is the cause which brings idolatry in its train; for men, having learned to contrive evil, which is no reality in itself, in like manner feigned for themselves as gods beings that had no real existence."

15. The logic doesn't change if we read Exod. 3:14 as "I will be who I will be." In neither case is the LORD identified by a quality of godliness or timelessness or universality.

16. For this reason, the use of the divine name by the J material of Genesis involves an implicit doctrine of creation that is every bit as theocentric as the P material in Gen. 1.

17. On this point and with a vigorous polemic against the ways in which a metaphysically prior concept of what counts as divine unnecessarily limits our ability to identify God as the one who delivers Israel and raises Jesus from the dead, see Jenson, *Systematic Theology*, 2.63–114.

Since *creatio ex nihilo* formulates God's transcendence in terms of uniqueness rather than supremacy or difference, what makes God divine is consistent with his immediacy and presence to finite reality. God leaves nothing behind. There is no divine reality other than the singular LORD, and therefore he neither betrays nor contradicts his divinity by drawing near. For this reason, the biblical reader need not choose between the universal God of the philosophers and the LORD who acts in space and time and who is described in scripture with anthropomorphic terms. Nor need the reader of the Gospels parse the divinity and humanity in the unified person of Jesus Christ.[18] In view of these fundamental considerations, the relevance of the doctrine of creation out of nothing to our reading of Gen. 1:2 should be plain. Any interpretation that sets aside *creatio ex nihilo* and its implied ontological parsimony will both undermine the capacity of scriptural readers to interpret the LORD God of Israel as the universal deity and render Nicene doctrine incoherent.[19]

At stake are more than philosophical puzzles about immanence and transcendence, or doctrinal debates about the humanity and divinity of Christ. Our natural religious imaginations tend to formulate an image of God and then assess our finite lives accordingly. If God is eternal, then temporality and history are problems to be overcome. If God is invulnerable and unchanging, then our capacities for suffering and change are the essential sources of the pain and unhappiness of human existence. In short, with the usual idea of God, we give a speculative cast to the human predicament, thinking in terms of metaphysical dichotomies such as eternal/temporal, infinite/finite, unchanging/changeable. These dichotomies back us into a spiritual corner. Either we have to deny our ordinary experience of human reality as temporal, finite, and changeable, positing instead some sort of inner spark of divinity as the true, hidden essence of our humanity. Or we end up resenting our condition as finite creatures through and through. Both ancient and modern philosophies tell the history of these two options.

The ontological parsimony of the doctrine of creation out of nothing challenges the primacy of the metaphysical dichotomies that animate our natural religious imaginations. The identity or *thatness* of God is not like anything at all—and therefore God is not intrinsically unlike anything at all. This makes the so-called analogy of being possible for reflection about God, because it places metaphysical categories (the whatness of God) in a subordinate position in relation to biblical narrative (the thatness of God). While the metaphysical dichotomies can help orient the mind toward the difference between God and creature, they cannot identify or direct the mind to the uniqueness of God.

18. For a helpful discussion of the way in which *creatio ex nihilo* provides crucial background for christological doctrine, see Robert Sokolowski, *The God of Faith and Reason: Foundations of Christian Theology* (Washington: Catholic University Press, 1982), 31–40.

19. For a discussion of the theologically paralyzing consequences of placing God within a well-furnished metaphysical system, see William Placher, *The Domestication of Transcendence: How Modern Thinking about God Went Wrong* (Louisville: Westminster John Knox, 1996).

A subordination of divine whatness to God's thatness effectively removes metaphysical properties from our calculations about what is right or wrong about our lives. Once removed, we can see that our dissatisfactions with human life arise out of history and not nature, out of the way we make choices and live our lives—our disposition toward that which God says and does—and not from our failure to possess divine qualities of eternity, simplicity, and changelessness. In other words, the ontological parsimony of the doctrine of creation out of nothing directs our attention away from a metaphysical assessment of our lives and toward a moral assessment. We are afflicted by the consequences of sin, not by the fact of human embodiment or finitude.

In this way, the doctrine of creation out of nothing and its consequent ontological parsimony give important support to the fundamental humanism of the Bible. We are not to cure our souls by detemporalizing and decreating ourselves. We should not follow the advice that the goddess Justice gave to Parmenides: Cling to that which is and cannot not be. Happiness does not come from palliating our defective metaphysical status with dreams of a godlike, changeless eternity. Instead, faced with the reality of our finitude, the voice of Eccl. 12:13 rings from Gen. 1:1 to Revelation: "Fear God, and keep his commandments." This exhortation to worship and obedience entails many things that our supposedly humanistic modern and postmodern age dislikes and rejects. Nonetheless, it gives powerful voice to something our age finds increasingly difficult to articulate: a transcendent hope for the future that does not encourage an escape from finitude. Keeping God's commandments is a worldly task that we undertake in our finite, embodied lives.

Not only does the doctrine of creation out of nothing help us make sense out of the odd conjunction of universality and particularity in the Bible, as well as the striking combination of theocentric piety with an unashamed loyalty to the human condition, it also motivates the christological maximalism that characterizes classical Christian theology, liturgy, and spiritual discipline.[20] Irenaeus, for example, based his rejection of gnostic accounts of Jesus's role as savior on an extensive refutation of the gnostic doctrine of creation. The gnostic doctrine presumed that the world in which we live is the final fruit of a cosmic evolution characterized by many layers of spiritual or supernatural reality that emanate from the transcendent and eternal deity. With such a nuanced and graduated ontological scheme at their disposal, gnostic teachers were able to avoid the counterintuitive claim that Jesus was God incarnate. They could assign to Jesus an intermediate redemptive role. He is above us in ontological significance, and he offers us a hand up to the next higher link in the great chain of being. Irenaeus's arguments against the gnostics amount to a case on behalf of the doctrine of creation out

20. For the use of the term "christological maximalism" and suggestions about its importance in the early Christian project of forming a coherent overall interpretation of scripture, see George A. Lindbeck, *The Nature of Doctrine: Religion and Theology in a Postliberal Age* (Philadelphia: Westminster, 1984), 92–96.

of nothing. Its ontological parsimony limits the options severely. Jesus is either simply a man or he is God incarnate. There are no metaphysical hybrids available to formulate alternative, mediating accounts.[21]

Irenaeus and his focus on the ontological parsimony of *creatio ex nihilo* is not a matter of merely theoretical Christology, nor is it an instance of using one doctrine to defend another in a circular system of philosophical invention. The analysis that Irenaeus provides grows out of the broad *sola gratia* emphasis of the New Testament's reading of the Old. St. Paul's account of Abraham's justification and the larger project of divine blessing through Israel emphasizes the lack of mediating realities between God and finite reality. Upon what might Abraham rely other than God? After all, it is God alone "who gives life to the dead and calls into existence the things that do not exist" (Rom. 4:17). All other things— and this includes our works—are "as good as dead" (4:19), says St. Paul, because God alone has the power of life, the power to create anew. The terms that Paul uses clearly echo the Old Testament's polemic against idolatry. We cannot rely on worldly powers: neither our own nor the supposed power of idols. Here we can see how the ontological parsimony entailed by *creatio ex nihilo* has direct soteriological significance. It eliminates the half-measures of Pelagianism, which is but the moral form of idolatry, and as a result *creatio ex nihilo* presses us toward Christ alone as the power of salvation.[22]

There are surely further warrants for the classical doctrine of creation out of nothing, but here I must pause to express my exasperation with the antidogmatic sensibilities that seem to dominate modern biblical scholarship. As traditional readers have long realized, the classical doctrine of *creatio ex nihilo* guides us toward a reading of the ambiguous words and phrases in Genesis that downplays the obvious, literal sense. But it does so for the sake of preserving our ability to give very straightforward and intellectually cogent readings of countless other biblical verses. If we set aside *creatio ex nihilo*, then I suppose we can become more intimate with a scholarly construct called "ancient Israelite religion." But this concept is a thin historical construct and can do little to guide our reflection toward the larger biblical vision of God and creation. If we are overly preoccupied with determining the dim outlines of ancient Israelite religion from the various sources of the Old Testament, then we fail to notice that our present approach to the Bible as a whole has become incoherent, and our talk about God vaguely metaphorical and metaphysically sloppy. It was precisely to avoid both this incoherence and intellectual flabbiness that the classical doctrine of *creatio ex nihilo*

---

21. There is no doctrine of the incarnation in Judaism, but one finds a comparable Torah maximalism in rabbinic rhetoric, and the ontological parsimony entailed by the doctrine of creation out of nothing likely plays a similar role in encouraging this maximalism.

22. The same *sola gratia* logic characterizes Jewish thought about the relation between worldly powers and divinely given law. See Joseph Soloveitchik, *Halakhic Man*, trans. Lawrence Kaplan (Philadelphia: Jewish Publication Society, 1983), for the rejection of *homo religiosus*, the religious personality that responds to the perennial urge to climb up the great chain of being.

was developed—and developed with a clear awareness that the literal sense of Gen. 1:2 presents a problem.[23]

Traditional Christian readers rarely felt the need to display explicitly the larger exegetical context for their doctrines, in large part because they trusted the scriptural integrity of the tradition as whole. One of the most important items on the agenda of modern biblical scholarship has been to undermine this trust. However, as modern scriptural readers ignore the resources of the tradition, they too often reinvent the interpretive wheel. Not surprising, it does not turn very well. Or to put the situation in terms familiar to generations of seminary students, modern biblical study does not preach, because it doesn't actually make much sense out of the Bible. The problem is not historical consciousness. Nor is it the critical cast of mind, which, in any event, is well represented in the church fathers, the medieval Scholastics, and the Reformers. The problem is a collective self-impoverishment that stems from the antitraditionalism implicitly endorsed by most modern biblical scholars. Stripped of the interpretations developed over the course of a long tradition of biblical reading, we end up with small pieces of text, which, however carefully surrounded by sophisticated reconstructions of historical context, we cannot bring into synthesis with the other parts of the Bible or with current Christian practice or even with the most basic requirements for a cogent view of God. The end result of the modern historical critical tradition is therefore painfully obvious: a great deal of valuable but localized philological and historical knowledge, combined with crude generalizations and vague theological gestures.[24]

The imperative is clear. We need to stop trying to reinvent interpretation. We need to avoid the vain illusion that our spiritually crippled age can apply historical methods to recover the so-called real Bible. Each and every aspect of our inherited tradition is not always correct, and a great deal of traditional doctrine and theology has become entirely disconnected from a living exegetical practice. For this reason, traditional views need to be constantly tested, and reinvested with scriptural content. This will require renewed exegetical reflection, and contemporary exegesis should certainly include intelligent use of modern historical methods. However, our inherited traditions are themselves strikingly sophisticated and textually sensitive projects. They were developed to answer the single most difficult and central exegetical question of all: how can the Bible be read as a document that can be affirmed as true?

Because we face the very same question today, we ignore our dogmatic, ecclesiastical, liturgical, and spiritual traditions at our peril. The darkness and formless void over which the Spirit of God moved in Gen. 1:2 doubtless admits

23. See, for example, the exegetical work that Basil does in order to turn readers away from the conclusion that the literal sense of this verse requires an affirmation of preexistent matter (*Hexaemeron* 1.9–2.1 in NPNF[2] 8.57–59).

24. See my analysis of the failed exegetical strategies of modernity in R. R. Reno, "Biblical Theology and Theological Exegesis," in *Out of Egypt: Biblical Theology and Biblical Interpretation*, ed. Craig Bartholomew et al. (London: Paternoster, 2004), 385–408.

of many interpretations (→1:4 on darkness and void). It is a mysterious, evocative passage that may be illuminated by comparison to ancient creation myths. But any reading that contradicts the doctrine of creation out of nothing will undermine our capacity to read the Bible as a whole in a theologically coherent fashion.

1:3 And God said, "Let there be light."

Because the sun is not created until the fourth day, we should not think in terms of a literal light, as if there were rays of light before the creation of the sun. Instead, we should direct our thoughts toward the light of divine wisdom, the light of the Word already implied "in the beginning." In this sense, the light of the first day shines with the purpose of the divine plan and its unfolding— Torah, the history of Israel, Christ, the career of the church. The same light is the pillar that guides Israel out of Egypt (Exod. 13:21), preparing for the gift of the law at Mount Sinai. As the great hymn to the law exults, "Thy word is a lamp to my feet and a light to my path" (Ps. 119:105). It is the light of God's purpose reflected in the shining face of Moses (Exod. 34:29). The light of the first day, the world-directed love of God illumines the people of Israel, who will be as "a light to the nations" (Isa. 42:6). As the divine plan shines forth in its final fulfillment, all creation shall dwell in the "everlasting light" of the LORD (60:19).

Similar evocations of the light of the first day are found in the New Testament. The incarnate Word of God comes to us as "the true light" that enlightened the world (John 1:9). He was the light in the beginning, now come near. Dwelling in the shining light of Christ and putting off the works of darkness (Eph. 5:11–14), the church, the new Israel, will be a "light [to] the world" (Matt. 5:14), and she will be the light by which all the nations shall walk (Rev. 21:24). The echo of Genesis rings clearly when St. Paul writes, "For it is the God who said, 'Let light shine out of darkness,' who has shone in our hearts to give the light of the knowledge of the glory of God in the face of Christ" (2 Cor. 4:6).

Thus, when God says, "Let there be light," it is as if he were saying, "Let there be the illumination and divinization of creation that I have planned from the beginning. Let there be the circumcision of Abraham. Let there be the commandments of Sinai. Let there be Solomon's temple. Let there be crucifixion of my beloved people in the captivity of Babylon and their resurrection to life in a renewed Jerusalem. Let the eternal Son be born of the Virgin Mary and made man. Let him be crucified under Pontius Pilate. Let him be raised on the third day. Let him come again in glory." In this way, the light of the first day refers to both the eternal divine purpose and to the scriptures themselves, which tell of the outworking of the divine plan. For it is written: "In thy light do we see light" (Ps. 36:9).

1:4 God separated the light from the darkness.

The light comes into the world, and the darkness is whatever remains outside its fulfillment. This separation is not a necessity forced upon God by human sinfulness. The primal separation is not a response to the malign influence of evil. The supernatural good of heaven needs only natural goodness that it exceeds and transforms: "The sun shall be no more your light by day; nor for brightness shall the moon give light to you by night; but the LORD will be your everlasting light, and your God will be your glory" (Isa. 60:19).

Thus, the first act of separation should be understood as the triumph of love that God intends from the beginning. There was nothing, and nothing cannot participate in the light of the Word that was in the beginning and that shines toward its fulfillment, calling into existence all that is, all for the sake of the divine plan. God bring things into existence. They shine with being, and this creates a boundary between that which is and that which is not.

This boundary between being and nothingness helps us understand the metaphysical reality of evil. God creates everything for the sake of his plan, for the sake of the triumph of light. And because God's purposes are invincible, the only way to opt out of the future for which God creates is to somehow embrace nonexistence, to leap across the edge that separates the original light from the empty darkness it illuminates. This turns out to be the strange, self-defeating, dark desire of evil. There are ultimately only two futures, one real and the other an odd, impossible, invisible shadow of the real. The hungry emptiness of the *nihil* is the only alternative to the triumph of God's light. As St. Paul teaches the faithful in a clear evocation of Gen. 1:4, "You are all sons of light and sons of the day; we are not of the night or of darkness" (1 Thess. 5:5).

It is important, however, to remember that nothingness does not exist. It is not real, as the doctrine of *creatio ex nihilo* teaches. Creation does not give content to the darkness, as if God's word in the beginning somehow requires a negative shadow to resist or negate in order to give outline and purpose to reality. The purpose of creation is precisely not as an alternative to nothingness. "Let there be light" is not motivated by a divine fear or rejection of some sort of cosmically threatening darkness. Creation is not an original combat against chaos. Existence is not first and foremost an answer to a prior nothingness, as if the *nihil* can stand on its own feet as an alternative possibility. On the contrary, creation finds its purpose in its beginning. The anchoring rationale for reality is the consummating goal for which God creates.

Thus, Gen. 1 fittingly gives no weight or content to the darkness announced on the first day. As St. Augustine points out, it is telling that the rest of Genesis and the account of the six days of creation refrain from mentioning night (*City of God* 11.7; see Bettenson 1972: 437). Each day ends with evening—the dusky time between light and darkness. The pure darkness of night is an empty possibility. In the time-filled world of created things, nothingness and the void remain a purely hypothetical future. It is populated only by that which is not, and therefore it exists only as a hopeless, destructive, chaotic desire of a created freedom that wishes it were not created, wishes that it did not exist for the sake of the divine plan. The darkness is a lust for nonexistence, a desire not to be created in the first place—and it is a desire that can have power only as it feeds on the divinely illumined reality it seeks to renounce.

1:5 One day.

"What kind of days these are," writes St. Augustine, "is difficult or even impossible for us to imagine" (*City of God* 11.6, quoted from Bettenson 1972: 436). But we need not worry about this difficulty, because we should not read "in the beginning" temporally. We need not try to mash the seven days of creation into a sequence of twenty-four-hour events. Within the literary atmosphere of Gen. 1, the seven days suggest a structural, architectural order to all things, something made according to a plan rather than the ticking of a clock. The first day is the foundation for the second, and then the third, fourth, fifth, and sixth, culminating in the seventh day, the Sabbath, which does not complete the created order—for nothing is done on the seventh day—but rather crowns it. The first day tilts toward the seventh day, just as the initial separation of light from darkness presses forward through the entire sweep of scripture toward the consummating sunrise of the new creation that "has no need of sun or moon to shine upon it, for the glory of God is its light, and its lamp is the Lamb" (Rev. 21:23).

1:7 And God made the firmament and separated the waters.

Days two through six enact divisions and separations that create the distinct realities that become the location of and instruments for the outworking of the divine plan.

On day two, God separates the waters above from the waters below in order to create the waters of the earth. In the great flood, God returns creation to its primal state of watery disorder: "On that day all the fountains of the great deep burst forth, and the windows of the heavens were opened" (7:11). In baptism, the destructive force of water is released once again as the baptized die in Christ to the power of sin. On the third day, the dry land is separated from the waters, preparing the way for the gift of the land promised to Abraham. In the culminating scene of God's deliverance of the Israelites from the hand of the Egyptians, the second and the third days of creation provide the backdrop: "Moses stretched out his hand over the sea; and the LORD drove the sea back by the strong east wind all night, and made the sea dry land, and the waters were divided" (Exod. 14:21). On the fourth day, the lights of the firmament are created. They mark the days and months, allowing for the distinction between the days of the week and the Sabbath, and the movements of the heavenly bodies signal the celebration of the Passover that frames the passion of Christ. On the fifth day, the separation of life into various plants and animals provides an array of distinct living forms that are subsequently taken up into the laws of sacrifice given on Mount Sinai. These laws and their use of plants and animals become the motor of the ongoing divine purpose in human history: to pry human life out of the grip of darkness and perfect our created nature so that we "may walk before God in the light of life" (Ps. 56:13). Of the creation of man and woman on the sixth day we will have more to say, but it is transparent that the male and the female are partners, not only for each other, but for God as well, who will invite them into his Sabbath rest (→1:26a).

These remarks are simply gestures toward the significance of each day of creation in the outworking of the divine plan. Considering each day and providing a detailed exposition of how water, land, heavenly bodies, plants, animals, and human beings are taken up into the divine plan would entail retelling the entire scriptural story, which is why traditional treatises on the six days of creation are more compendia of theological wisdom than exegetical works narrowly understood. But it is important to recognize that the aspects of creation identified in days two through six do not contain or entail the divine plan that serves as the beginning of all realty. We can contemplate creation and see its fittingness for consummation, but no natural theology can formulate an account of the beginning in which and for which God creates. When we say in the eucharistic liturgy "heaven and earth are full of your glory," we are not giving pious expression to the argument from design. Instead, the Sanctus points to the full role of creation in the future of God's plan. God uses water and dry land, sun and moon, plants and animals, and—most of all—the human capacity for free obedience, and taken into his consummating plan they are filled with his glory.

1:10 And God saw that it was good.

This repeated refrain punctuates Gen. 1 like an exclamation point. The greatness and abundance and generosity of God are evident in his work: "The heavens are telling the glory of God; and the firmament proclaims his handiwork" (Ps. 19:1). Therefore, even though creation provides the stage rather than the plot for the divine plan, creation has its own power of testimony. Guided by revelation, we can read nature as preaching many truths that scripture teaches.

For example, creation stands in active judgment against the disorder of human sin: "Even the stork in the heavens knows her times; and the turtledove, swallow, and crane keep the time of their coming" (Jer. 8:7). The Gospels take up a similar theme when Jesus points to the birds of the air, who do not lay up for themselves earthly treasures, but rely on the Father to feed them (Matt. 6:26). Jesus draws upon the image of birds who devour the seeds that fall by the wayside in order to dramatize the fate of those who lay aside the word of the kingdom (13:4). Our inconstancy and negligent worldliness find worldly symbols of rebuke.

The natural world does not just preach judgment: "The heavens proclaim his righteousness" (Ps. 97:6). The crowing of the cock in the morning reminds us to be ready for the coming of the master of the house (Mark 13:36). The sheep coming to the familiar shepherd to be fed testify that those called by Christ "follow him, for they know his voice" (John 10:4). The abundance of the fields and flocks evokes the overflowing blessings of the marriage feast of God with his people: "The kingdom of heaven may be compared to a king who gave a marriage feast for his son" (Matt. 22:2). Creation does not teach us the good news of God's offer of fellowship with him, but the patterns of nature provide apt reminders and powerful symbols of the purposes of God revealed in the calling of Abraham, the giving of the law on Mount Sinai, and the life, death, and resurrection of Christ. Indeed, the goodness of the created order is so auspicious for the fulfillment of the divine plan that scripture can contemplate the author plagiarizing his own work: "He built his sanctuary like the high heavens, like the earth, which he has founded" (Ps. 78:69).

1:11 And it was so.

The Bible as a whole exalts the power of God: "Our God is in the heavens; he does whatever he pleases" (Ps. 115:3). The image is clear. God suffers no limitation. Any and all things are within his power to accomplish. Yet, we need to be careful in our thinking about what constitutes divine omnipotence. God is not all-powerful simply in the sense of lacking limitations, and we certainly should not picture God as a sybaritic despot free to follow his passing whims. Instead, the fullness of divine power is found in the way in which God's words are reality creating. He is the source of existence. God does not cause or fabricate reality as does an artisan, but rather, as the emphasis on speech as the means of creation indicates, God originates all things out of his power to command reality into existence. The biblical emphasis on the sheer effectiveness of divine speech dramatizes God's omnipotence: "For he spoke, and it came to be; he commanded, and it stood forth" (Ps. 33:9). Thus, in the apocalyptic vision of St. John, the living creatures who surround the heavenly throne glorify God, not because he possesses some sort of omnipotent potential energy, and certainly not because God holds in reserve a power to do otherwise. Rather, they say, "Worthy art thou, our Lord and God, to receive glory and honor and power, for thou didst create all things, and by thy will they existed and were created" (Rev. 4:11).

The creative words of God signal the future-oriented logic of creation. That which God intends invariably comes to pass. The pattern of Gen. 1 is consistent: "God said . . . and it was so." The future-creating power of God's spoken word is also the motor of the history of covenant that begins with Abraham. He utters promises that have the same basic structure as the days of creation: "This was the promise. . . . And so it came to pass" (2 Kgs. 15:12). The pilgrimage of the chosen people, while full of digressions and setbacks, winds its way toward a fulfillment. For this reason and according to the same logic, the New Testament constantly emphasizes that events occur so that the scriptures might be fulfilled. God's words create reality, unrolling the scroll of time.

1:26a Let us make man in our image, after our likeness.

For centuries the first and most obvious puzzle posed by this verse has been its relationship to the second, longer, and more involved account in Gen. 2 of the creation of man from the dust of the earth and of woman from his rib. Why two accounts, and why are they so different?

Ancient readers had their own solutions. Origen is typical. By his reading the two accounts signify what he took to be the obvious, dual structure of human existence. On the one hand, we have an incorporeal, rational nature capable of entertaining the timeless idea of a perfect triangle or the concept of infinity. On the other hand, we are embodied, physical beings who need to struggle forward in life to satisfy our needs and fulfill our desires. Origen reads the two creation accounts accordingly. The direct creation of man and woman in the image and likeness of God points toward our rational nature, which is permanent and unchanging, while the account in 2:7 of Adam created out of the dust of the earth signifies our bodily existence, which is full of time and change (*Homilies on Genesis* 1.13 in FC 71.63).

Origin finds support for his parsing of the two creation stories in the verbal hint provided in this verse. Of the key terms "image" and "likeness," he writes, "Man received the honour of God's image in his first creation, whereas the perfection of God's likeness was reserved for him at the consummation."[25] The "image" denotes the intrinsic spiritual dignity that God has bestowed on humanity, but this dignity awaits perfection as the "likeness." This exegetical move draws on 1 John 3:2 ("beloved, we are God's children now; it does not yet appear what we shall be, but we know that when he appears we shall be like him, for we shall see him as he is"), as well as St. Paul's similar use of "likeness of God" to describe the new nature that the faithful put on in Christ (Eph. 4:22–24). And this way of parsing image and likeness also reminds us that the human creature is not a static entity. We are not two-tiered composites of body and soul doomed to a limited economy of bodily denials designed to transfer loyalty to the spiritual substance of the soul. On the contrary, the church fathers tended to interpret the second

25. *On First Principles* 3.6.1 in *Origen: On First Principles*, trans. G. W. Butterworth (repr., Gloucester, MA: Peter Smith, 1973), 245.

creation ("the LORD God formed man of dust from the ground") in concert with the first. It gives the soul a place in the world, and as befits a Neoplatonic optimism about the plasticity of reality that Origen emphasizes, this is good news. For an embodied soul can be worked upon and changed, which is exactly what happens in the unfolding, divine plan. Through divinely orchestrated events in the bodily realm of time, the man and woman created in the image of God are formed into the likeness of God.

Modern biblical critics do not read salvation history into "image" and "likeness," but they provide their own solution, which turns out to be surprisingly similar to the main lines of Origen's interpretation. The standard approach is to parse the two accounts of the creation of man and woman according to two oral or textual traditions, both of which were combined to form the final form of the book. Genesis 1 is ascribed to P (the Priestly author), and scholars hypothesize that this author is concerned about laws of temple and sacrifice. The second account of the creation of man and woman is ascribed to J (the Yahwist author), whose style and focus turn toward the narrative of Abraham and the history of the people of Israel. Although modern biblical scholars do not use Origen's Neoplatonic vocabulary to describe the theology of P, the differences are not as great as one might imagine. The Priestly account of creation depicts a grand cosmic temple, and this ideal order flows from the Priestly theology organized around temple sacrifices and holiness codes. And in this theology the divine ordinances have a perfect, timeless ideality. Modern biblical historians tell us that the J writer, in contrast, is preoccupied with the dust out of which life emerges, as well as the vagaries of historical time so evident in the account of Abraham and his descendents. In other words, the J tradition reflects Origen's notion of a second, embodied and corporeal creation.

This suggestive similarity between Origen and modern scholarly theories helps us to see how Genesis as a whole depicts created permanence for the sake of the plasticity necessary for the fulfillment of creation. The created image of God, imprinted into our humanity, works in concert with a view of the human condition as an ongoing project of living up to God's original purpose in creation. The first account of human creation signifies what is *done* on the sixth day. Creation in the image of God seals us as those destined for fellowship with God. The image of God is stamped into our human nature, which is precisely why we experience our desires and capacities as fit for more than animal survival.

The traditional emphasis on our rational nature as the seat of the image of God conveys this point. We seem drawn to think about truths that have no place in the mundane affairs of ordinary life. As a permanent feature of our humanity, reason leans beyond our humanity. Then, in a more explicit way the second account of creation out of the dust foreshadows and initiates the events that wind their way through the patriarchs to Moses and Sinai, onward to Jerusalem, exile, and restoration, and then eventually to the gritty details of the passion and death of Jesus. In this sense, the bodily, time-filled realities of history also press forward toward a consummating end, just as reason transcends the limitations of the present by abstraction and contemplation.

We need not follow Origen's strategy of parsing image and likeness, however. In the main, the Christian tradition has treated these two terms as synonyms denoting our distinctive nature as human beings. But Origen rightly recognized a static tendency in our commonsense ways of thinking about human nature that the dual account of creation can help us overcome. The nature of a thing makes the thing what it is, and we tend to think that this analytic truth has a substantial solidity. Hardness makes the rock. Barking makes the dog. Rationality or some other distinctive capacity makes the human. Here, Origen's future-oriented reading of the creation of man and woman can help. We need to join (as does Origen in his own way) the cosmic order outlined by the P material in Genesis with the intimate, narrative emphasis that characterizes the J material. To do so, we need to be clear that the *imago dei* is constituted by the fundamental, permanent characteristics of our humanity that make us capable of receiving the consummating gift of the seventh day, the gift of fellowship with God that he plans for us "in the beginning."[26] Put somewhat differently: the image of God imprinted on human nature provides the basis for our supernatural vocation, the life in Christ that is greater than any possibility resident in our natural powers, but which is nonetheless a genuine exercise of our natural powers. In this sense, the theological concept of the *imago dei* presumes both a nature and a future, both a capacity to do what God intends for us as the consummating vocation of humanity and the actually doing of what God intends.

The following comments diverge somewhat from the main lines of the theological tradition. By and large, classical Christian theology follows the Greek philosophical tradition and designates reason as the distinctive feature of our humanity and the seat of the image of God. In order to place an emphasis on the historical fulfillment of the image of God, however, I will emphasize what I take to be more covenant-oriented human qualities, ones specifically mentioned in the two accounts of the creation of the original man and woman: dominion ($\rightarrow$1:26b) and reproduction ($\rightarrow$1:28). Of course, a close reading of the theological tradition shows that the church fathers dramatically revised the philosophical accounts of what it means to live rationally, and they gave a very different content to the consummating ideal of rational vision or contemplation, a content that comes from the scriptural account of human flourishing. Therefore, although I do not identify reason as the image of God, my approach compliments rather than contradicts the substance of traditional interpretations of the *imago dei*.

26. Thus Panatyiotis Nellas: "The essence of man is not found in the matter from which he was created but in the archetype on the basis of which he was created and towards which he tends"; *Deification in Christ: The Nature of the Human Person*, trans. Norman Russell (Crestwood, NY: St. Vladimir's Seminary Press, 1987), 33. For the fuller development of a future-oriented account of the image of God, see Jenson, *Systematic Theology*, 2.53–72.

1:26b Let them have dominion.

The capacity for dominion is an aspect of the *imago dei* (→1:26a). Our "crown" of "glory and honor" is found in our "dominion over the works" of God's own hand (Ps. 8:5–6). As Gregory of Nyssa writes, that the human is in "the image of that Nature which rules over all means nothing else than this, that our nature was created to be royal from the first" (*On the Making of Man* 4 in NPNF[2] 5.391). Our royal power does not set up the human creature as a petty satrap. Instead, dominion is a natural vocation of headship that guides and governs so that things can flourish according to their proper purposes. Parents guide children in their development. The head of a working group coordinates others toward a productive purpose. Community leaders organize society in an effort to promote the common good. The same holds for our personal lives. A well-ordered soul is one in which reason governs the passions of the flesh, ordering them toward their proper satisfaction as part of a flourishing human life.

Dominion is not just the exercise of the social phenomenon of power, nor is the proper dominion of reason over our passions and instincts simply a matter of sustaining a crushing regime of internal self-discipline. We need to discern what makes for a well-developed child or a productive organization or the common good. We need to know what it means to flourish as a human being. When we distinguish between dominion and tyranny, we are pointing to the difference between successful and failed discernment, which is one reason why the church fathers could give such emphasis to the Greek philosophical tradition of rational inquiry while remaining true to the main thrust of the biblical view. The capacity for dominion always presupposes a power of command that is based on a principle or purpose. The "do this" of the command is the proper exercise of dominion rather than mere display of power when based in a prior judgment that "this should be done." Dominion, in short, commands because it obeys a higher principle.

Human beings can exercise dominion wrongly, sowing discord and seeking a domination that wishes only to command and not obey. We can glorify our own power and we can easily confuse our self-interest with the good proper to that over which we have authority. Everyone knows the leader who makes elaborate protests about the principles of fairness that are invariably interpreted to his or her own advantage. Nonetheless, the basic patterns of human dominion remain, however deeply perverted by sin. For example, everybody feels the need to govern his or her inner life. Even in a hedonistic culture the very idea of living for the sake of pleasure involves taking control of one's life—exercising dominion over transient passions—in order to guide daily affairs toward the goal of the greatest pleasure. The same holds for outer, social dimension of life. The egalitarian family is not leaderless, nor is the consensual community without offices that invest individuals with responsibility. Dominion endures as a fundamental dimension of human life. The circuit of command and obedience must be completed, however imperfectly, however falsely. Even the most tyrannical regimes need to find ways to claim legitimacy. Robespierre claimed to serve the people, Stalin the proletariat, Hitler Germany's destiny. A despot never serves himself. In fact, nobody ever succeeds in serving himself or herself, because we were created for dominion, for the exercise of power in the service of something greater.

Because dominion, however materially corrupted by our misuse, is a part of the *imago dei*, we can set aside two false views of authority. First, we should not aim at a vision of common life that relieves us of responsibility for wise exercise of dominion. We need to resist the fantasies of a world free from authority. Exercising authority is part of the dignity of our created humanity. To govern and be governed is a crucial way in which humans differ from animals, which was why Aristotle designated politics a uniquely noble use of the human power of reason. The political project of arguing about and ordering common life reflects the original gift of dominion.

We have a basic duty to participate in the larger communal project of exercising dominion, contributing to the processes that shape social life to serve the common good. This need not require modern forms of democracy. For example, the Anglo-Saxon common-law tradition bears witness to an earlier conviction that over time every member of the community contributes organically and often unconsciously to social norms. This is why the definition of tyranny should not be understood simplistically as the absence of modern liberal democracy. The term was used long before our era. For a medieval artisan, a tyrant was a monarch or local lord who ignored long-established traditions. The oppression came from the imposition of norms that the population did not develop and infuse with authority by persistent, widespread, customary expectation and behavior.

Today, aggressive monarchs do not threaten the broad participation of most citizens in the exercise of social dominion. Instead, a bureaucratic and administrative state tends to turn political questions into problems of economic efficiency, psychological well-being, and material welfare. The result is governance by expertise; the modern welfare state does not exercise political dominion so much as benevolent social engineering. Tyranny takes for itself the power of command, and it denies a participatory role (however understood) for the ordinary person. The hard tyranny of totalitarianism presses for maximal obedience without any scope for popular participation in the shaping of commands. The soft tyranny of the modern welfare state allows for human rights that limit the zone of obedience, but can also undermine the role of citizens in shaping social norms. Custom and tradition are undermined in order to make room for a supreme individual right to do as one pleases. Soft tyranny is far better than hard tyranny. Nonetheless, human beings were created for participation in the public exercise of authority. Just as a self-governed life is a combination of self-command and self-obedience, a properly ordered politics allows for citizens to participate in a combination of collective command and obedience.

The practices of natural dominion, both in self-government and politics, are ordained by God to train and prepare us for participation in the supernatural dominion of the good shepherd. The circuit of command and obedience is fully completed. When St. Paul sets up a sharp dichotomy between the law revealed on Mount Sinai and the grace of Christ, he is making a claim about the divine plan. According to his reasoning, the external authority of the law does not penetrate deeply enough into our humanity to free us from bondage to sin. As a result, God's will is not the command that the obedient believer gives himself or herself. Christ, however, has invaded to the very core of every person and destroyed the power of sin. He now lives as the source of life. This allows Paul to say that Christ issues commands from within and that our obedience is simultaneously an act of self-command: "For freedom Christ has set us free" (Gal. 5:1).

1:28 Be fruitful and multiply.

Procreation functions along the same lines as dominion. The created order is organized so as to prepare for the ascending logic of fellowship with God. The natural fertility of sexual intercourse plays an important role. The power of "begetting" serves as the engine of history in Genesis and in scripture as a whole. The generations are the streams of forward movement. Procreation gives us a future. It is the human power that realizes the capacity of creation to have time and history.

We need to be very clear that the spiritual significance of sexual union in scripture does not simply encourage romanticized images of intimacy, nor does it draw upon Dionysian images of orgiastic ecstasy. As the command "be fruitful and multiply" emphasizes, we are physically equipped to live in the image of God, because we possess the potential for new life. This is not true for hunger or thirst, both of which can exercise a powerful influence over our souls. Sexual desire is spiritual, then, not because it is more powerful or more sublime, but because of its biological function: its consummation gives birth to a future. For this reason all the longing and desiring and instinctual passions of human sexual identity are ordered toward participation in the larger purposes of God, purposes that require a human future. Just as our capacity for dominion prepares us for the spiritual dominion of the good shepherd, our sexual powers and desires prepare us for participation in the new life of spiritual rebirth.

The productive, future-oriented logic of procreation is widely acknowledged and developed throughout scripture. To have a child is to have a future, and as a consequence, the dead end of barrenness recurs as a threat to the success of the promise that God makes to Abraham. The possibility of having children and the danger of the empty womb are the narrative form of the choice between life and death that is so prominent in the account of covenant loyalty in Deuteronomy. Obedience to God's commandments expresses Israel's trust in the fulfillment of the promised future, and children are the material form of that trust. "These words which I command you this day shall be upon your heart," says the LORD to those whom he loves, "and you shall teach them diligently to your children" (Deut. 6:6–7). The future of the law is given flesh in the obedience of children.

Like all aspects of the human creature that prepare us for fellowship with God, this spiritual potential can be used for ill or for good. The Old Testament's favorite images of idolatry are sexual: prostitution, adultery, and fornication. As sexual sins, they are characterized by a fixation on present pleasure. The adulterer and fornicator want sexual union, but not children. The future-oriented fertility of the sexual act threatens rather than fulfills the adulterer's or fornicator's desires. Fear of the children that naturally come from sexual intercourse—and the future they represent—is why sexual desire misdirected and twisted into service of present pleasures becomes the Old Testament's favored image of idolatry. The idolater is like the man who visits prostitutes. He wants to discharge his need for worship while reserving power to live as he pleases. The silence of idols is no disappointment. On the contrary, like a discrete mistress who neither makes public demands for recognition nor gives birth to children who make claims on the future, idols are charming in their convenient emptiness.

The sexual act and the natural consequence of children do not exhaust the full meaning of the *imago dei*. In its fully realized form, to "be fruitful and multiply" is not simply to have children; more precisely, the forward lean of procreation toward participation in divine life involves more than biological reproduction. Reproduction extends life forward, but only along the horizontal plane as the brute fact of the continued existence of our DNA. Instead, what gives procreation its spiritual potential is the way in which children compel us to serve the future rather than the present. The *imago dei* is found in our giving birth to and nurturing children whom we cannot finally control. Children become independent agents who eventually supersede us. Even the most controlling parent dies. That we should approach this truth about children with hope and joy suggests the fuller form of the *imago dei*, for it reflects an implicit trust that the future will bring blessing and not curse. This trust in the future, a future that we cannot control, is an essential dimension of the act of faith. We give ourselves over to new life in Christ.

Thus, although procreation seems the paradigmatic instance of human creativity, it is, in fact, a moment of profound submission. Parents have more in common with the Virgin Mary than with King David. To have children and exercise dominion over them as they grow up does not give parents an easy feeling of power and control. On the contrary, raising children is fraught with a deep uncertainty and anxiety about the future. This is why parents work so hard to educate their children, save up an inheritance, and do all they can to provide for those whom they love. It is a work that any clearminded person knows can be swept away in a moment by economic, political, and personal tragedies. Therefore, having children is always an act of trust, a moment in which we surrender ourselves and say, however unconsciously, "Let it be to me according to your word" (Luke 1:38).

Of course, we do try to control the future, which is why the worldly schemes from social redemption always focus on education. If only we could raise our children to be cooperative rather than competitive—or so modern liberalism has dreamt. This hope has no stable basis. We can give birth to the future, but in our present bondage to sin, we cannot shape and change it. Nonetheless, modern liberal fantasies are right in this regard: children epitomize the natural promise of life. Birth brings hope. This detail of biological reproduction can help us understand why celibacy can be understood as fulfilling the fundamental imperative to "be fruitful and multiply." Vows of celibacy have nothing to do with the sterility of the present age. They are not a rejection of children and childbearing for the sake of present pleasures or, worse, out of a capitulation to anxieties about a future that we cannot control. On the contrary, the Christian tradition has championed virginity and celibacy as firstfruits of the future promised in Christ. St. Ambrose is typical of the church fathers in his description of Christian virginity as fruitful and procreative. "The virgin's produce is the fruit of the lips," he writes, for her way of life proclaims the dramatic newness of life in Christ. Virgins in their continence bear witness to Christ's victory over the incontinence of sin. They are testimony to the resurrection in which there will be neither giving nor taking in marriage (*Concerning Virgins* 1.8–9 in NPNF[2] 10.369–71). There is no suspension or rejection of the procreative dimension of the *imago dei*. Celibacy and virginity are affirmed because they are spiritually fruitful. They multiply new life in Christ.

1:31 It was very good.

Christians have found it notoriously difficult to think through the way in which the good promised in Christ sustains the goodness of creation. The temptation is to conceive of the divine drama as two acts. The first act, provided in Gen. 1–3, sets the scene and introduces the dramatic problem of sin. The second act depicts the solution to the problem and portrays the final resolution: salvation in Christ and heavenly bliss. In this view, the second act succeeds the first as today replaces yesterday or, to shift the metaphor, we turn from past to future like an eager child who drops the old toy in order to grasp the new. This dramatic vision has a metaphysical counterpart. We can picture creation as our present, physical existence and then imagine redemption as being lifted out of our bodies and delivered to a purely spiritual realm.

A superficial reading of the scriptures can encourage this sequential or two-tiered picture. Consider Isa. 51:6: "Lift up your eyes to the heavens, and look at the earth beneath; for the heavens will vanish like smoke, the earth will wear out like a garment." The first act will give way to the second; the body will wither and the spirit will take its place. St. Paul's persistent juxtaposition of carnal to spiritual can create the same image in our minds. His distinction suggests a movement away from the embodied, created condition toward a spiritual, redeemed one that leaves behind the body.[27] But God's pronouncement that "it was very good" blocks this up-and-out interpretation of Old Testament prophecy and New Testament teaching. The strongly negative descriptions that St. Paul gives of the "body of death" (Rom. 7:24) and "the things of the flesh" (8:5) cannot be interpreted in such a way as to drive a wedge between our created reality and our promised future in Christ. Instead, because creation is very good, we must think more closely about what it means when Paul says that "the flesh cannot please God" (8:8) and when Jesus teaches that "my kingship is not of this world" (John 18:36).

God created the world for the sake of the fullness of the divine plan, thus creation must be the enduring basis for all divine action (→1:1). The created order is not a first act; it is the enduring stage upon which the entire divine drama unfolds: "The world is established, it shall never be moved" (Ps. 96:10). Like a play upon a stage filled with props, the action uses—and in sin abuses—the bodily material of the scenery. In the divine drama, the Pauline terms "flesh" and "carnal" designate our perversion of created reality. The "body of death" refers to the "law of sin" that dominates our desires and shapes our habits into an implicit "no" to the divine plan. The pejorative use of "the world" throughout the New Testament does not denigrate creation; it refers to the worldly regime of sin that is ordered toward the emptiness and futility of life lived solely for the sake of finite, worldly loves. To describe someone as "carnal," as Paul does so often, is not to make the ontological observation that he or she has a body. This cannot be the correct reading, because God pronounces our created condition very good. Instead, the term "carnal" in Paul's letters points to the direction or trajectory of a person's life. To live carnally means to wrongly regard creation as the endpoint or purpose for human life and thus to try to remove one's body and soul from participation in God's plan. This is why "carnal" can mean so much more than desires for pleasure and wealth. Good governance, children, family, intellectual self-development, and human freedom—all the finite goods of this world become carnal when made ultimate.

Therefore, we need to read "fleshly" and "worldly" as moral rather than metaphysical terms. Put more precisely, perhaps, we need to see that what matters most about reality is its role in the future ordained by God, rather than its ontological status. Everything that exists is very good. The body is not a prison. Clay, dust, blood, and flesh—the *realia* of embodied life—are not problems to be overcome. But as good as creation is and always will be, nothing created can provide men and women with the future for which they were created. The gritty facts of life are taken up into a narrative that stretches toward something more, something different, something supernatural. Creation is very good, yet the good things to come in Christ Jesus are still greater and more perfect (Heb. 9:11).

27. For extensive textual analysis to support this spiritualized reading of Paul, see Daniel Boyarin, *A Radical Jew: Paul and the Politics of Identity* (Berkeley: University of California Press, 1994).

The crucial dualism, then, is not between body and spirit, between finite and infinite, between time and eternity. Instead, the great distinction is between creation and consummation, between present and future. As St. Augustine saw with clarity, the fundamental human temptation is to rest in the finite goodness of the created order rather than to participate in the divine project of drawing us into fellowship with God. To live by the law of the flesh means to put our hope in the present order of things rather than in the future promised to Abraham and fulfilled in Christ. The problem, of course, is that the present order of things is not itself a stable, independent place for us to rest. God creates with and for the sake of his Word, and therefore the cosmos groans for completion (Rom. 8:22). Creation is mobilized for the future in the beginning, and there is no enduring present for us to take up residence. As a result, our attempts to opt out of the divinely ordained future must take the form of violent, desperate efforts to uproot and relocate our lives and remake our created condition according to a counterplan, a counterfuture. This explains why sins that begin as seemingly commendable loyalties to the finite goods of creation inevitably pervert and destroy their integrity.

2:2 On the seventh day God finished his work which he had done,
  and he rested.

The day-by-day account of creation culminates in the seventh day, but the end point is not simply the final step in a sequence. The seventh day does not follow the pattern of days two through six. Instead of further furnishing the universe, God finishes and then rests, or more precisely, God finishes *by* resting, and this resting blesses and sanctifies the seventh day. So we should say that the "work" of the seventh day is blessing and sanctification, something that flows from who God is rather than what God does.

That the account of creation in Genesis finishes on the sixth day—and then has more to say—gives the seven-day sequence of the Priestly account of creation a narrative, historical dimension. The prior six days are not crowned with a seventh day that somehow epitomizes or raises the ordering work to a higher pitch. The rest of the seventh day is something new. God has finished one thing and now embarks on something quite different. God has worked to create, but now rests, blesses, and sanctifies. The account of the seventh day does not end with the formula "and there was evening and there was morning." The new "work" of rest takes place on a day that has a beginning, but no ending. The seventh day, it seems, stretches forward and beyond the counting of days. In this sense, the seven-day account of Gen. 1 does not simply provide us with a beginning. It extends to the end of the ages. The seventh day contains within itself the fullness of time. Creation is finished, but the story of God's strategy for blessing and sanctifying still needs to be told. The entire sweep of scripture from this point onward tells us what happens so that the seventh day can be brought to completion.

Because the consummating rest of the seventh day opens out onto the scriptural depiction of the unfolding drama of salvation, there is an impression of paradox. "My Father is working still," says Jesus, "and I am working" (John 5:17). How can this be? Creation is finished and God rests. If the Father is still working, then are we to conclude that he does not rest for very long? Does God need to repair and maintain the world? In a certain sense, of course, God sustains creation. Nonetheless, we should distinguish between the completed work *of* creation and God's work *upon* it or, more accurately, *for* it. The six days anticipate the seventh, and creation yearns for Sabbath. But we need to be careful here. The six days do not automatically lead to the seventh. There is a difference between nature and its cycles and the supernatural end of rest in God. The former is established and finished over the course of the six days, while the later must be achieved in the course of human history. The Father and the Son "work" to bring creation into the rest of their eternal love. This is the work of hallowing, the work of blessing and sanctification.

The creation account supports a distinction between the finished work of creation and the ongoing work of sanctification. The man and woman are created on the sixth day, but we do not read of them joining God in the hallowing of the Sabbath. The human creature does not participate in God "by nature." The Sabbath rest awaits us as a possibility for the future. But this future will not come to the man and the woman along the settled, reliable course of natural events. The seventh day does not follow upon the sixth according to the revolutions of the earth. The Sabbath is not a natural inheritance. As Jesus teaches, man and woman were not made for the Sabbath: the seventh day was made for man and woman (Mark 2:27). It is given as a gift (Exod. 16:29), given by adoption (Gal. 4:5).

When the LORD God commands Israel in the Sinai desert to "remember the sabbath day, to keep it holy" (Exod. 20:8), the seventh day becomes a human possibility within the created order. The LORD instructs Moses to say, "You shall keep my sabbaths, for this is a sign between me and you throughout your generations, that you may know that I, the LORD, sanctify you" (31:13). The gift is not only for humans; the land itself shall enter into a Sabbath rest (Lev. 25:4). The morning stars sing together in concert with the "sons of God," who shout for joy (Job 38:7). In the end, all that was created joins God on the seventh day. This outcome flows from the substantive beginning—the eternal invitation of fellowship that the Father offers in and through the Son—in which and for which God creates. The end is a fulfillment of the beginning.

The New Testament carries forward the fulfillment of the beginning. The mission of Jesus echoes the seventh day, and the peace he brings is the rest of the Sabbath. The disciple whom Jesus loved rested his head on his master's breast (John 13:25), and this foreshadows the fullness of the grace of Christ. After Jesus says "it is finished" (19:30) on the cross—a direct reference back to Genesis—he rests in the tomb and in this rest sanctifies even the dead. The disciplines of the Christian life are preparations for entrance into the kingdom of Christ, a kingdom that is not a place outside or beyond the created order, but is instead a new time, a dawn in which the morning star rises in the hearts of the faithful to mark the beginning of the seventh day (2 Pet. 1:19). And Christ, the root and offspring of David, is that bright morning star (Rev. 22:16), the light of the world by whom and through whom all things were made. Christ rises, but like the seventh day of divine blessing and sanctification, he does not set. There is no end to the day of his triumph.

Obviously, then, we cannot describe the Priestly account of creation as architectural and then, in a simplistic way, contrast it with the Yahwist account and its interest in human history. The structure of the seven-day account of creation reinforces the conclusion that God creates from and for something beyond creation itself. He finishes—but there is still something more. There is a rest into which everything is invited. As Lactantius writes in a pithy summary of the logic of the seven-day sequence: "The world had been created for this purpose, that we may be born; we are born for this end, that we may acknowledge the Maker of the world and of ourselves—God; we acknowledge Him for this end, that we may worship Him" (*Divine Institutes* 7.6 in ANF 7.203). Being (to speak like a philosopher) is for the sake of the specific end, and attaining that end will require a history. The seventh day gives creation its future. "My presence will go with you," the LORD promises Israel, "and I will give you rest" (Exod. 33:14). Thus, those who worship the God of Israel are not engaged in sacrifices and propitiations designed to maintain the equilibrium of the created order. We are animated by an imperative that involves change: "Let us therefore strive to enter [God's] rest" (Heb. 4:11).

The forward lean of the Priestly creation account toward the consummating blessings of the seventh day stands in striking contradiction to the classical view of the ideal life as conformity to unchanging reality. Plato, Aristotle, Seneca, Lucretius, and many other great philosophers of antiquity disagreed about just what was essentially true about the world, and they disagreed about how to shape the human intellect, will, and passions to best accord with this deep, unchanging truth. However, they all agreed that human happiness and fulfillment flows from the deepest possible accordance of the human soul with the timelessly true and changelessly real.

For example, Lucretius viewed the world and the human soul as constituted out of tiny bits of irreducible material reality. His great poem *On the Nature of Things* sets out both to depict a world animated by impersonal laws of nature and to convince us that we must forsake our illusions and live in accord with the "facts." There is no new future, no seventh day different from the order and logic of creation. The fundamental spiritual therapy is straightforward. Instead of imagining impossibilities, we should accept who we are—pain-avoiding and pleasure-seeking animals—and rest in the unchanging laws of the material universe.

Plato was an idealist and not a materialist, so of necessity he had a different view of the permanent reality that we must embrace in order to be delivered from the illusions of time and change. However the upshot is quite similar. We are to shed our loyalties to transient things and attach ourselves to the permanent, essential forms that have in any case always and unchangingly been the source of the reality of our lives. Like Lucretius, the basic cure of the soul is to give up illusions and embrace what is permanent.

It is crucial for us to recognize that the desire of those who worship the God of Israel is different. The Priestly account of creation can seem like the outline of a timeless cosmic structure, written as if to provide a template for our efforts to live in accord with God's creative purposes and designed to encourage us to accept our roles and places in the universe. But the seventh day disrupts this picture. It blocks the spiritual project of so much of the classical pagan world. Needless to say, the created order rightly shapes our lives. It is "very good," and thus we properly seek to live in accord with natural law. The philosophical traditions of pagan antiquity provide powerful intellectual tools for this task. But the "very good" created world is not the end for which all things exist. The world is both permanent and has a future. This future blesses, sanctifies, and transforms the given order of things. Thus, the deepest and most permanent truth about our created humanity is our restlessness. The more thoroughly we follow the advice of classical philosophy and the more we bring ourselves into conformity with reality, the more restless we become and the more powerfully we feel the desire for the seventh day.

We need to emphasize the forward-leaning seventh day, because a great deal of Christian piety interprets our experience of restlessness in a way that backslides into ancient Greek visions of redemption. We too easily imagine that we are restless because this world is not our home, and consequently we are tempted to think of the spiritual life as a journey up and out of finite existence. St. Augustine speaks against this temptation when he interprets the seventh day as the origin of the heavenly city that is our destination. Our end is in the future. But at the same time, although future for us, this heavenly city is already real. Genesis says that God *did* rest, not that God *will* rest. Drawing on numerous verses elsewhere in scripture that speak of angels and heavenly hosts that attend to God, St. Augustine supposes that God already shares his rest with them (*City of God* 9.9; see Bettenson 1972: 354). There is, in short, a heavenly realm in which created reality already participates in God's consummating rest.

With a heavenly realm above and ministering angels who can interpose and communicate with pilgrims here below, Augustine and the early Christian tradition absorbed a great deal of the Platonic project into its own intellectual life. Just as Plato's forms or ideas lure us up and out of our transient perceptions, directing us toward contemplation of what is timeless and unchanging, for the church fathers the heavenly city above offers an already existing spiritual realm that enflames the desires of the faithful for deliverance from our present world of sin and temptation. Unlike the promise/fulfillment tension that animates the history of the covenant and takes up so much of the Old Testament, this *heavenly rest above* versus *struggle with sin below* dichotomy can easily be expressed in formulations that juxtapose spirit and body. It is not coincidental that St. Paul's most dualistic picture of the spiritual and carnal dimensions of life comes along with his explicit affirmation of "Jerusalem above" (Gal. 4:26). There is an already realized spiritual perfection (Jerusalem above, alive with the heavenly hosts and their praise of God; Ps. 148:2), and this cannot help but throw our struggle toward holiness into a dark shade.

To know of perfection and yet also to know that our daily lives are mired in imperfection—this describes the existential insight that animates ancient Platonism. It is not surprising, therefore, that the church fathers mined this tradition very deeply. But the perennial temptation has been to interpret the contrast with easy metaphysical dichotomies (as the Platonists do): perfect, eternal, unchanging, spiritual versus imperfect, temporal, changeable, and bodily. Nonetheless, this temptation does not invalidate the project of Christian Platonism any more than a tendency toward a purely immanent religious imagination in modern theologies of history invalidates an approach that focuses on the promised future. The lure of an already realized perfection plays an indispensable role in Christian piety.

A commentary is not the place to mount a defense of Christian Platonism. However, we should recognize that there is no inherent conflict between a realized ideal and a promised future. St. Paul blends them both. "The Jerusalem above is free," he writes, "and she is our mother" (Gal. 4:26). Only a verse or two later he writes, "We, brethren, like Isaac, are children of promise" (4:28). If I am born and raised in a prison camp, and someone powerful tells me that in the future he will bring me to a city where people walk freely, then this promise will stir up whatever inchoate sense I have that I was not born for slavery. If this person also tells me that this city already exists, it in no way alters my desire for freedom, but only intensifies it all the more. Christian Platonism places emphasis on the second, but not at the expense of the first. Christian Platonism remains loyal to the "very good" of God's creation. We need not escape time and embodiment simply because the prison camp of sin is located in time-bound and embodied creation. Rather, we need only renounce our loyalty to the mores of the prison camp and obey the one who has the power to deliver us. The promise of the gospel is clear: the free city of heaven was made for men and women who are time-bound and embodied.

2:5 The LORD God had not caused it to rain.

The six days of creation crowned by the seventh day of divine rest uses the simple Hebrew word for God (Elohim), while this new account, opening with a formula of "generations" that punctuates Genesis, uses the mysterious divine name (YHWH) revealed to Moses on Mount Horeb. Beginning with the Greek and Latin translations of the Bible, for many centuries Christians followed the Jewish tradition of vocalizing the divine name "YHWH" as "Adonai," which is

Hebrew for "lord." Newer translations try to restore the particularity of the name of God by spelling it out as Yahweh.

There are good reasons to support the older approach. It has the advantage of spiritual and intellectual modesty. In ancient Israel, concern about misuse of the divine name led to the tradition of circumlocution. Better not to pronounce the great and powerful name of God than to risk its abuse. This spiritual modesty meant that the exact pronunciation of YHWH was lost. When Jewish scholars set about to provide vowels for the entire Hebrew Bible more than a thousand years ago, when they came to YHWH, they put in the appropriate vowels to signal the convention of vocalizing the divine name as "Lord." During the Renaissance, some Christian scholars were unsatisfied with the traditional substitution of "Lord" for the actual name of God. They saw the vowels for the Hebrew word "Adonai" written with the consonants for the divine name and took it literally rather than as a device for superimposing the pronunciation of "Lord" over the divine name itself. Thus they came up with "Jehovah" (YaHoVaH). Modern scholars have developed their own, more plausible speculations, and a consensus has emerged that vocalizes the divine name as "Yahweh" (YaHWeH). But at the end of the day, we really don't know, and in any event, the ancient imperative of spiritual modesty remains compelling. In this commentary I follow the older tradition of using capitalized letters in LORD to signal the unique divine name "YHWH."

The newer preference for "Yahweh" is rightly motivated by a desire to recover the particularity of the biblical view of God. The God of the Bible is not generic. He is the LORD who chooses a particular people and makes a unique covenant. After all, if an engaged person is asked, "Who promised to marry you?" then the answer cannot be "a woman" or "a man." The question asks which man or woman, and in order to give a proper answer we need to use a proper name. "Mary Jones promised," the young man might say. The name "YHWH" functions in just this fashion. It draws our attention to the God who "marries" himself to Israel by way of a covenant.

This recovery of the particular name of God as the one who makes a covenant with Israel is well intentioned, but unless we are careful we can lose more than we gain. The New Testament closely associates the divine name with Jesus, who is proclaimed Lord (*kyrios*). This close association creates tremendous difficulties, because Jesus also prays to the God of Israel. How, then, can Jesus be both YHWH and at the same time pray to YHWH? This question is closely linked to a liturgical dilemma. Early Christians prayed in the name of Jesus, as do contemporary Christians. But the jealous monotheism of the Old Testament ("you shall have no other gods before me"; Exod. 20:3) cuts against this basic form of prayer. These problems are at the root of early Christian reflections on the nature and identity of God, reflections we study as the doctrine of the Trinity. Christian thinking and liturgical practice evolved toward a standard identification of God as Father, Son, and Holy Spirit, and this identification allows for an affirmation of Old Testament monotheism along with the divinity of Jesus implicit in the New. As the incarnate Son, Jesus can both be the LORD and at the same time pray to the LORD, the Father.

Unfortunately, the use of Yahweh in Old Testament translations can obscure the logic of this evolution. Readers cannot see the ways in which LORD is used throughout the Old Testament as a proxy for the name of God and then how this proxy name is presupposed in the New Testament. When Paul affirms Jesus as Lord, he is explicitly linking his obedience to Christ with his faith in the God of the Old Testament. In order to see this as clearly as possible, we need to continue in the ancient tradition of pronouncing and translating the divine name so that we can see that the LORD who walks in the garden is intimately connected to the Lord Jesus who walked the streets of Jerusalem. The parts of scripture interact in all sorts of complicated ways. Here as elsewhere we must be aware that changes in traditions of translation, changes supposedly made to achieve greater clarity, can actually generate new forms of obscurity.

Leaving aside the question of how we should represent the divine name on the pages of scripture, one of the most powerful achievements of modern biblical study has been a clear and sustained insight into the way in which the opening chapters of Genesis have a certain theological consistency in their divergent uses of words for God. The Priestly strand uses the generic term for God (Elohim) in its seven-day description of a cosmic creation, while the Yahwist writer uses the particular name of God (YHWH) to tell an intimate story of the origins of humanity. Instead of a cosmic frame of reference, Gen. 2 focuses on a particular place, the garden of Eden. The chapter provides a detailed geography of rivers with names. It is as if the universal perspective of Gen. 1 suddenly telescopes down to a very localized account. God, moreover, does not speak as a disembodied voice. He breathes life into the man formed out of the dust of the ground and then later performs surgery on the man to create the woman. The LORD even walks in the garden and talks to the human beings he has created.

Ancient writers recognized that there were two different accounts of the creation of humanity, and many of them drew conclusions roughly similar to those of modern scholars (→1:26a). The first account, they often observed, concerns timeless matters of the soul, while the second account delivers information about the particularity of our embodied humanity. The scholarly distinction between the Priestly and Yahwist material develops this insight more fully, allowing us to see the doubling of the creation account as a dual focus on what *is* and what *is to become*. In this sense, the Yahwist account of the generations of the heavens and the earth takes up and makes explicit the implicit, future-oriented dynamic of the seventh day in the Priestly account. This is not to deny the difference between the transcendence of the God who rests on the seventh day and the immanence of the LORD who brings the animals to Adam to see what he would call them. But we should not overplay the difference. A bird's-eye view of New York City is quite different from walking its streets, but it remains the same city, and the two perspectives supplement rather than conflict. The map guides the walking, and the walking gives life to the map.

The basic dynamic of Gen. 2 reinforces the complimentary relation between the two creation accounts. "Need" drives the chapter as a whole: the earth needs water; the dust-formed man needs the breath of life; the garden needs cultivation; and most clearly of all, the creation of Eve from Adam's rib stems from the need of the man for a companion, a need directly articulated by the LORD. In this second account, therefore, the ontological fact of creation is presupposed. Attention falls on the restlessness of creation, its needs and desires. God's action moves toward rest in fulfillment—watering the earth, commissioning Adam to give names to the animals, and finally completing the human pair in a dramatic scene of original surgery. If the seven-day account only ends with an implicit suggestion of the divine project of bringing all creation into the Sabbath rest, then the second account clearly focuses on detailing the primordial movement toward the final end. All things yearn for completion, especially the lonely man. The central theme of Gen. 2 is the way in which the LORD acts to satisfy the restless human heart. In this sense, it introduces the leitmotif of the larger witness of scripture, as St. Paul recognizes when he returns to the final verses of Gen. 2 for the image of the consummating love of God (Eph. 5).

2:7 The LORD God formed man of dust from the ground, and breathed into his nostrils the breath of life.

Scripture uses breath as a simple image of physical life. On the sixth day of creation, God gives every green plant as food to all creatures that have "the breath of life." Yet, in the formation of man out of the dust "the breath of life" has a fuller significance. The breath comes directly from God, and this signals that the "man of dust" is to live in a special way, according to the image of "the man of heaven" (1 Cor. 15:49).

The larger import of the original breath and its connection to the *imago dei* is evident in the New Testament's echoes of this verse. The risen Jesus gives his disciples the breath of life when "he breathed on them, and said to them, 'Receive the Holy Spirit'" (John 20:22), and it is with "the breath of his mouth" that the Lord Jesus will destroy the lawlessness that deceives (2 Thess. 2:8). Clearly, then, the divine breath does not simply animate in the sense of giving sentience, or even the higher faculties of reason and will. Divine breath animates toward the end for which God creates. God breathes the potential for a supernatural vocation into the man created out of the dust.

This reading of divine breath is reinforced by the juxtaposition of the two creation accounts. When God creates in his image and likeness, the resulting humans are perfectly formed as potential partners for fellowship with God in his Sabbath rest. The sequence of six days and then a seventh day provides a sense of the creationwide lean forward from "finished" to "rest"; however, the first account gives no suggestion of restless desire *within* human nature. This Gen. 2 provides.

The breath of life creates a lonely figure, a human being who needs something more for completion. It is as if the first account provides a picture of human beings capable of being perfected by grace, but not needing grace in order to live as creatures. The lure of fulfillment remains external, given on the seventh day. In contrast, the second account strikes an Augustinian note, describing our humanity as animated by the intense, inner desire for fellowship with God.

These two pictures of the human creature in relation to the fulfillment of the divine plan are no more incompatible conceptually than the cosmic picture of the first account is at odds with the local detail of the second account. One can and should say that (1) the human is capable of fellowship with God (grace perfects and does not destroy nature), (2) there is nothing about our created capacities and aptitudes that requires fellowship with God for their proper function (God does not owe the creature grace), and (3) all human beings are, in fact, animated by God's supernatural intention to bring all things into his Sabbath rest (our hearts are restless until they find their rest in God).[28]

The breath of life stirs up a desire for fellowship with God, and this impulse in the human heart can often be translated into a desire to escape from the bonds of finitude, to transcend and leave behind the limitations of the body. But the divine plan is not to draw us out of the world. Instead, just as the loneliness of the first man is satisfied in the created order—out of his body is fashioned his helpmate—so also the larger Sabbath project is inner-worldly. As we saw above, the seventh day completes rather than supersedes the first six days. God provides us with a new future, not with a new metaphysical address. In breathing out his Spirit upon us, the Father "remembers that we are dust" (Ps. 103:14) and his Spirit renews "the face of the ground" (104:30). From the beginning the LORD ordered all things so that humans could enter into the divine life and do so precisely as finite creatures. Animated by the breath of life, the dust of the earth is shaped by a desire for fellowship with God. This spiritual vocation is consistent with the enduring role of our creaturely humanity. The consummating light of the Sabbath illuminates rather than eliminates the dusty fact of our embodied condition.

2:15 Till it and keep it.

The particularized focus of the Yahwist account takes the broad outlines of the Priestly account of the *imago dei* and gives it a distinctive shape. The human capacities for disciplined work ("till") and concentrated attention ("keep") are

28. For a classic statement of these principles for describing the relationship between our created nature and divine grace, see Karl Rahner, *Theological Investigations*, trans. Cornelius Ernst (New York: Crossroad, 1982), 1.297–317. For an account of Rahner's formulation in the context of modern Catholic Neoscholasticism as it struggled to makes sense out of both the permanence of creation and the plastic desire for consummation, see R. R. Reno, *The Ordinary Transformed: Karl Rahner and the Christian Vision of Transcendence* (Grand Rapids: Eerdmans, 1995), 85–133.

instances of dominion. They point toward the particular social and cultural practices emphasized throughout scripture. The Bible consistently pictures the cultivation of crops as a natural virtue, and creation achieves a certain immanent, worldly fruitfulness when it is properly tilled and kept: "He who tills his land will have plenty" (Prov. 12:11). The ideal of a good shepherd is even more powerful and widespread. The shepherd who cares for his sheep symbolizes the ideal form of political dominion. The LORD tells David, "You shall be shepherd of my people Israel, and you shall be prince over Israel" (2 Sam. 5:2).

The divinely ordained project of tilling and keeping is not limited to its literal or political senses. One should "till and keep" as a parent, as a teacher, as a carpenter, and as an entrepreneur, in each case seeking to bring out the natural fruitfulness and productivity of our children, students, raw materials, and collective endeavors. All socially productive tasks deserve disciplined work and concentrated attention. However, God does not create us in his own image and likeness in order to make us supremely productive citizens. The fruitfulness of cultivation has a spiritual end. The LORD gives the original man worldly tasks to train his capacities so that he can become fit for a greater purpose. Here we see how, in a specific way, human nature, while not automatically leading to grace, nonetheless provides a fitting basis for fellowship with God. In this instance, the capacities that allow for attentive, concentrated, and disciplined work—capacities properly shaped by natural responsibilities for fields and families, factories and classrooms—find employment and perfection in the supernatural life of faith.

The spiritual senses in which "till and keep" play a role in faith are obvious and manifold. We are to return to the furrows of God's word again and again, and by cultivating his wisdom we will reap his righteousness. Not looking back to the cares of the world (Luke 9:62), the abundance of fellowship with God becomes possible as we "plow in hope" and "sow spiritual good" (1 Cor. 9:10–11). And not only do we "till" in hope, but we must also "keep" in faith: "We must pay the closer attention to what we have heard, lest we drift away from it" (Heb. 2:1). The same tilling and keeping characterizes worship. The entire book of Leviticus should be read as a handbook for ritual agriculture. The community of Israel must be plotted, fenced, and plowed with the laws of purity so that she can bear the fruits of holiness. The contemporary priest and minister are to do the same with the law of Christ. The sacraments bring the purely natural condition of the human under a divinely planned cultivation. It is a priestly work that requires a great deal of determination and discipline. The weeds and thistles of sin can never be fully eradicated, and the yield of righteousness can always be increased.

2:17 You shall not eat, for in the day that you eat of it you shall die.

Given the disaster of transgression, we tend to think of divine commandment and human obedience as a contrastive, competitive pair. God reigns over our natural impulses, and we squeeze ourselves into a tight-fitting, disciplinary suit. God's will supervenes over and imposes itself upon our wills.

Because fallen humanity suffers from disordered desires, we often experience God's commandments as disciplining impositions. However, the contest between our wayward wills and God's greater purposes is not intrinsic to the created order. God issues commands before Adam and Eve fall. Their capacity for obedience—our capacity for obedience—plays a fundamental role in the divine plan of consummating creation. We must obey not simply because we must be disciplined out of our sinful condition. On the contrary, the circuit of commandment and obedience allows God to direct us toward our supernatural end, and our capacity to obey allows us to participate in that end.

Because we can obey, we are teachable. We can be guided, trained, and directed. We can be changed from who we presently are into something more focused, more developed, more perfect. Our natural capacity for language can be trained into an ability to read. Our native mathematical skills can be shaped into advanced knowledge. Our bodies can be strengthened by good coaching, and our moral character given sharp outline by high expectations. In all these instances, commandment and obedience are far from contrastive and competitive. They interlock and work together as the engine of transformation. The teacher gives assignments. The coach barks orders. The parent lays down rules. From the beginning, therefore, the commandment that calls for human obedience is God's grace. Law and our capacity to be law-abiding is the motor of our transformation; it is the engine that moves us from the sixth day toward fellowship with God in the seventh.

The foundational dynamism made possible by the human capacity to receive and obey instruction is plain to see. In his account of human happiness, Aristotle recognized that the human personality is perfected insofar as its native potential is trained toward its proper end, and we are trainable only by virtue of our capacity for obedience. In a metaphorical sense, this is even true of plants. A fruit tree can accept pruning and flourish all the more; a grapevine can be encouraged to climb a trellis and provide shade. In a brute sense, the plants obey. They accept the guidance of human direction, and they flourish in their obedience. Animals are even more receptive to training, and therefore they are capable of even more refined purposes. A retriever can develop a sophisticated capacity to fetch a duck in the water.

Human beings are the most trainable of all animals, and therefore we are the most capable of developing into highly focused, purposeful creatures. This is why the ideal of self-possession and freedom depends upon the capacity for obedience. One must be able to accept instruction in order to begin the process of training that leads to genuine self-command. A person in bondage to passing impulses is hardly free in any desirable sense. Only a person who can first obey the commandments of those who have a rightful claim to authority can later give commandments to himself in the realistic hope that self-command will carry the day. This is why genuine freedom—a natural end that we rightly seek to realize in our lives—requires a capacity for obedience. We are truly free only when we have the ability to obey ourselves.

The larger witness of scripture consistently links obedience with fullness of life—and disobedience with death. In this sense, the divine legislation at Sinai frames a choice that recapitulates the original situation in Eden. "See," says Moses, "I have set before you this day life and good, death and evil. If you obey the commandments of the LORD your God . . . then you shall live and multiply. . . . But if your heart turns away, and you will not hear . . . you shall perish" (Deut. 30:15–18). Disobedience throws us back upon both the inherent immaturity of our untrained wills and, because of the effects of sin, the incoherent disorder of our conflicting desires. In contrast, obedience moves us toward an ever fuller and more disciplined realization of our innate human capacities. In this sense, the scriptures echo Aristotle: the untrained soul is unformed and dissipated, while the trained soul achieves an integrated purpose that realizes our fullest potential. But as Thomas Aquinas recognized in his use of Aristotle, God's commandments do not only train us to realize our natural potential; they also train us for a supernatural end that exceeds our natural end. God commands us to go beyond nature, and because, by nature, we have the capacity to obey, we can become more than natural.

The first commandment in the garden anticipates this supernatural end. The command cannot help but seem arbitrary. Why shouldn't the original man eat of the tree of the knowledge of good and evil? It seems as though he is being commanded only in order to induce obedience and not for a clear, inner-worldly purpose. But this is as it must be. If God is to train the natural man toward the end of participating in the supernatural Sabbath rest of the seventh day, then his commandments must transcend our inner-worldly purposes, must exceed our capacity for understanding. Thus, the original, sinless man finds himself in the same position as the Virgin Mary. The angel Gabriel comes to her with a message. She is to be conscripted into a divine plan that she cannot fathom, and she cannot resolve the angel's prophecy into a plausible, worldly scenario. "How shall this be, since I have no husband?" (Luke 1:34). Instead, she simply obeys: "Let it be to me according to your word" (1:38). In her obedience the Virgin Mary participates in the supernatural end that God wills for human beings. She obeys a call that exceeds what is natural, and in this way the Virgin Mary realizes the fullest possible fruit of the created power of our free will. Because we can obey, grace perfects rather than destroys nature. We cannot discern and choose a supernatural end that exceeds created nature. But we can obey commandments from God that draw us beyond our natural ends.

However we read the Pauline polemics against the works of the law or interpret the larger New Testament judgment that Gentile Christians are not subject to the full scope of Mosaic law, we cannot imagine that new life in Christ transcends the basic pattern of commandment and obedience. Far from relaxing or altering this form of participation in the image of God, the New Testament redoubles it. "He who does not obey the Son shall not see life, but the wrath of God rests upon him" (John 3:36). The good news of Christ is not the announcement of a divine decision to forsake the original commandment-obedience structure of God's plan for the perfection and fulfillment of humanity. If we are to enter life, then we must keep the commandments (Matt. 19:17).

The gospel is an invitation to participate in the incarnate Son's unalterable and omnipotent choice of obedience and life. His obedience and life have swallowed up disobedience and death (1 Cor. 15:54). As we are baptized into Christ's death, we are freed from the body of our own death, which is the fruit of our bondage to disobedience, and in Christ we rise to the newness of his life (Rom. 6:3–4). Christ the good shepherd infuses in us the power of his own dominion, and we are able to master our sinfulness and obey "the law of the Spirit of life" (8:2). Thus, we are not released from the original structure of divine commandment, the "shalt not eat" that is spoken in the very beginning. Instead, we bear "the image of the man of heaven" (1 Cor. 15:49) who was obedient unto death. In him we "become slaves of righteousness" (Rom. 6:18).

2:18 It is not good.

At first glance, this verse seems to contradict 1:31. How can everything that God creates be good and at the same time not good? But the puzzle is resolved if we think back to the dynamic at work in the first account of creation. At the conclusion of the six days of creation, God finishes, but there is something more to be done. From the cosmic perspective of Gen. 1, creation is very good, but its goodness lacks the supernatural, sanctifying rest of the seventh day. Nature is perfect on its own terms, but God adds a supernatural possibility (→2:2). Now, from the anthropocentric perspective of Gen. 2, God breathes into man's nostrils. The breath of life does not set the cosmic stage. Instead, it infuses life into space and time, providing the forward push of human history. The man feels the need for the *more* suggested by the architecture of the cosmos that leans toward the seventh day. Adam lacks "a helper," and alone he cannot "be fruitful and multiply." The situation is "not good," but this is not because creation is flawed. Instead, the "not good" evokes the existential loneliness of the first man, and in this way, the phrase expresses the sense that creation is "not enough." God creates a world that is complete in itself, but because he intends to transform it into something greater, we experience life as unsettled by a restless anticipation of the future.

All of us feel the divine pronouncement "it is not good." We can walk a beautiful beach or hike a stunning wilderness path, but even as we rejoice in the natural beauty, the canker of unmet desires and unfulfilled hopes irritates and intervenes. People make mountains of money and surround themselves with every good thing, and still the human heart will not rest. Our children are charming and successful, but we nonetheless pine for what they are not. We look at our no doubt imperfect society, but instead of sober criticism, we rise up in moral indignation and denounce it as corrupt. At every point, we come up against the limitations of reality, and rather than appreciate the finite goods we truly enjoy, we rebel. The lure of something greater, the attractive possibility of more, the shadows of things not only set right but fulfilled—we gaze upon that which God creates with a dissatisfaction that we cannot understand and cannot justify, but nonetheless feel too strongly to deny or set aside.

The atmosphere of felt incompleteness is not unique to the Gen. 2 creation account. It runs throughout scripture. The sense of incompleteness is a function of the substantial purpose of self-donation that God has in mind "in the beginning." Things exist for the purpose of being brought into the Sabbath rest of fellowship with God. For this reason, the scriptural witness is structured by a movement from *very good* to *better still*. All finite existence is complete and good on its own. But when that existence is brought into relation to the infinite existence of God, it becomes supernaturally incomplete; it becomes palpably "not God." For this reason, creation yearns to be more than itself—to be no longer itself, alone, and without fellowship with God. This is especially true for human beings. The most teachable of animals, and therefore the most plastic and changeable of creatures, we feel the alluring possibility of moving from what is very good to something better still. Because we sense what we can become, we regret what we are not.

2:20 The man gave names.

The giving of names is a primal expression of human initiative. The human vocation of obedience to God's commandments is not free from responsibility and judgment. We must see and grasp reality and render judgment in order to adequately till and watch over creation. God does not call all the plays from the sidelines. The human creature is an actor in the divine drama, a character whom God can train to discern what is to be said and done in the role assigned. King Solomon's glory rests in his capacity to render justice according to the wisdom of God. He was not a prophet receiving an oracle, but a discerning judge (1 Kgs. 3:16–28).

The duty to see reality clearly and render wise judgments is not for royalty alone. The larger scriptural witness emphasizes the royal vocation of all humanity. "Thus says the LORD of hosts, Render true judgments, show kindness and mercy each to his brother" (Zech. 7:9). The same scope for human judgment is often emphasized in Jesus's teaching. Life brings many things before us, and God will see how we name them. Will we name those things that are Caesar's as Caesar's and give them their due consideration (Rom. 13)? Will we name those things that are God's as God's and give them their proper place (Matt. 22:21)? There is no formula that can be routinely applied. Instead, the language of scripture trains our tongues to speak truly and our minds to discern wisely. The future into which we are called from the beginning requires us to till and watch over the present as readers and listeners well versed in the fields of scripture (Acts 15). If we have God's word on our tongues, then we will better be able to give things their rightful names. In this sense, divine revelation helps guide and train our natural reason.

God's revealed word aides us in the project of seeing the world as it truly is—faith perfects reason—and at the same time a disciplined development of our natural capacities prepares us for our supernatural vocation—a well-formed mind can more fully receive the gift of faith. Intellectual integrity urges us to attend to the world as it really is. We must not traffic in verbal manipulations and ideological distortions, as if we can adjust reality and truth to serve our purposes. Here the disciplines of experimental method, peer review, careful argument, and clear exposition train the soul to serve truth rather than passing desires. Seeing through the mists of wistful thinking and self-serving delusion, whether individual or collective, allows us to be arrested by what is real. If we develop this natural capacity, then we are better prepared to receive the truth of Christ. If we train ourselves to name the things of the world truly and judge worldly affairs wisely and honestly, then we can more fully and unequivocally confess that Jesus Christ is Lord, giving him his true name, the name above all names (Phil. 2:9).

2:22 The rib which the Lord God had taken from the man he made into a woman.

The primal loneliness of the first man and his desire for a fuller fellowship foreshadow the great biblical theme of consummation. "The open side of the new Adam," writes Joseph Ratzinger, "repeats the mystery of the 'open side' of man at creation."[29] Just as the answer to the first man's yearning for fuller life comes from his side, so also does the answer to our desire for salvation—the blood and water of the church's sacraments—come from the pierced side of Jesus (John 19:34). Just as the Eucharist does not merely symbolize or point to Christ's saving death, but rather is his saving body and blood, the history of the covenant does not represent or point to God's plan of redemption: it is God's plan incarnate. The *more* that God plans for humanity is made out of human flesh.

2:24 They shall be one flesh. (AV)

Our reading of creation has emphasized the way in which creation in Genesis is ordered toward consummation. The cosmos and the contours of human existence are established, and they are good in themselves. They endure by virtue of the

29. Joseph Ratzinger, *Introduction to Christianity*, trans. J. R. Foster (San Francisco: Ignatius, 1990), 241.

ongoing gift of existence bestowed by God. Yet the created order, however good and enduring on its own, is tensed with a purpose that is supernatural. We saw this in the seven-day sequence of creation (→2:2). God finishes on the sixth day—but then a further, seventh day follows. Now, just as the seventh day points beyond creation to the divine drama that will draw all things to their fulfillment, so also does the second creation account end with an anticipated consummation.

In accord with the highly anthropocentric focus of the J material, the lean toward fulfillment is not cosmic but personal. A background of loneliness and desire colors the depiction of the creation of the woman from the rib of the man. The LORD God announces, "It is not good that the man should be alone" (2:18). God immediately populates the earth with beasts of the field and birds of the air (2:19). Yet the great menagerie of animal life is not enough. Something more is required, and God uses Adam's rib to create the woman. "At last" sighs the man when he sees his mate. The first man has found the one whom he has desired. Then, in a manner strikingly similar to the conclusion of the seven-day account of creation, this second creation account ends with open-ended expectation. After Adam's sigh of recognition, readers find themselves expecting consummation. The scene of desire is vivid, but the narrative shifts focus before Adam and Eve embrace.

There is more at work in the narrative than a demure discretion. In other places, the Bible is certainly forthright about the sexual union of men and women. Therefore, we do well to see the loneliness of the first man as transcending his desire for a mate. The desire for companionship felt by the first man—a desire that is the naturally experienced compound of physical desire and emotional need—is one of the original elements of human existence. This impulse toward sexual union is like the capacity to exercise dominion in obedience to the proper purpose of things. The thirst of the body and our longing for companionship is always already enrolled in the divine drama of breathing life. They are tensed with a future-oriented desire that anticipates the life of faith.

The church fathers disagreed about the role of sexual desire and intercourse in the garden, and they gave a variety of answers to the question of how Adam and Eve would exercise their creative power of procreation if they had not sinned. However we wish to approach this hypothetical question, we cannot treat marriage and sexual desire as simply natural aspects of life, any more than we can treat acts of the will or efforts of the intellect as merely biological. Without doubt, human sexuality is instinctual, just as our cognitive faculties are part of the natural equipment of our bodily existence. But instincts and natural abilities must be educated and shaped so that they take a specific form in an actual human life. From the beginning, the divine plan was and remains the same: to order our natural capacities toward our supernatural vocation, which is our entrance into the seventh day, the future of living in fellowship with God.

The complex array of emotion and desire that characterizes the relationship between male and female has long inspired a sense of transcendent purpose. Of all the instinctual features of human life, the intensely felt desires of the heart are the most transparently open-ended. As countless poets have recognized, "love is strong as death" (Song 8:6). Love presses toward the infinite. The full force of the exclamation "I love you" outstrips the natural order, breaking bonds of familial and clan loyalty to form a new household: "A man leaves his father and his mother and cleaves to his wife" (Gen. 2:24). The emotional and physical bond between male and female reaches toward new life in children. This drive toward new life reflects the divine intention in creation. Just as the original man feels a lonely longing that reaches forward, we all exist for the sake of something more, something fuller, something that evokes the "at last" of our spiritual desire.

Finally, it is not coincidental that the account of longing concludes the twofold account of creation and serves as a hinge in the narrative as it turns to the original transgression. The forward push of desire, the restlessness of human loneliness, the future-oriented reality of procreation in the act of sexual union—these features of created human reality are capable of being formed in fellowship with God. But this future will not happen automatically or naturally. Love can break the bonds of a man to his father and mother, sending us into the arms of our beloved. For precisely this reason, our restless longing can also destroy the ties of human solidarity and wreck the goodness of God's creation. The same love that is as strong as death can become an agent of jealous possession and suicidal despair. The restless heart and its desire for fulfillment can rage against the limitations of the present, and driven by a longing for something more, we can seek perverted, false forms of rest, clinging to false loves with an almost supernatural determination, even when faced with their failures. No feature of the human dynamism toward fellowship with God will automatically realize the potential of his image imprinted on our natures. Grace perfects nature; it is not an outgrowth or result of created powers and capacities. This is especially true of the power of love, which seeks to rest in the arms of the beloved.

2

FALL

"Sin is crouching at the door" (4:7)

3:1a The serpent was more subtle.

On the sixth day God creates "the beasts . . . and the cattle . . . and everything that creeps upon the ground" (1:25). Yet, now appears something "more subtle" and seemingly of a different order. Just who or what is the subtle serpent? The voice of the tradition is unequivocal: it is a worldly form of Satan, the fallen angel. The modern historical-critical tradition rejects this reading; von Rad is typical: "The serpent which now enters the narrative is marked as one of God's created animals. . . . In the narrator's mind, therefore, it is not a symbol of a 'demonic' power and certainly not Satan. What distinguishes it a little from the rest of the animals is exclusively its greater cleverness" (1972: 87). So which shall it be: demonic power personified or the animal trickster of folklore?

At the very minimum, Jewish and Christian readers expect this verse to cohere with other parts of the Bible. For example, Job 1 portrays an interaction between God and Satan that sets up another scene of temptation. God allows Satan to afflict Job in order to tempt him to curse God (1:6–12). Wisdom of Solomon 2:23–24 interprets the original temptation along similar lines: "God created man for incorruption, and made him in the image of his own eternity, but through the devil's envy death entered the world." The New Testament only reinforces the presumption that temptation and transgression come from the devil. In Luke's Gospel, Satan and the demons are closely associated with serpents and scorpions

(10:17–20), and in John of Patmos's vision of end times, the power of Christ is depicted as dethroning "that ancient serpent, who is called the Devil and Satan, the deceiver of the whole world" (Rev. 12:9). Even when the image of the serpent is absent, the link between Satan and temptation is clear. In the New Testament scene that recapitulates the circumstances in Gen. 3, Satan tempts Jesus in the desert (Matt. 4:1–11; Luke 4:1–13).

Scripture interprets scripture, and the weight in favor of reading the serpent as Satan is overwhelming. But we can do more than adduce intracanonical warrants. It is useful to think through *why* there is such a strong consensus that a demonic power lay behind the original transgression. The benefits of pursuing this question are significant. We not only understand Gen. 3:1 more fully, but we also develop a deeper, more intelligent grasp of why angels and demons become so important in the later books of the Bible and why so many later theologians developed systematic accounts of nonbodily, spiritual creatures.

The way forward is not obvious. As Origen notes, "In regard to the devil and his angels and the opposing spiritual powers, the Church teaching lays it down that these beings exist, but what they are and how they exist it has not explained very clearly."[1] But Origen, however tentative in his speculations about Satan, gives him a central role in the cosmological drama of fall and redemption. The role is emphasized in the many later scriptural passages that implicitly comment on Gen. 3:1. As the larger tradition affirms again and again, evil and the possibility of transgression begins with the angels.

It is very important to see that this view of the origin of evil is not the product of an ancient view of the world as bounded by a heaven above and a spiritual realm below, the so-called three-tiered universe often adduced by modern scholars as a sufficient explanation for early Christian (and Jewish) interest in angels and demons. The devil is not a mythological figure invented by a prescientific, credulous spiritual imagination. On the contrary, the idea of a fallen angel helps biblical readers of Gen. 3 in two ways. First, a reference to Satan immediately conjures a cosmoswide power, and this helps dramatize the cosmoswide scope of the divine plan and the sinful resistance to it. Second, the concept of the devil serves as a placeholder for the most extreme possible negation of the divine plan that is consistent with the belief that God is the all-powerful and all-good creator of everything out of nothing.

Let us begin, then, with salvation history. In the broadest possible sense, if we assume that the serpent is not just a particular animal in the garden of paradise, but is instead a grand spiritual being who has already embarked on the deepest and widest possible rebellion against God, then at the very least we have succeeded in reframing a quite intimate and concrete story of temptation in Gen. 3 within a cosmic context. What the serpent says is not just a localized event. Recourse

---

1. *On First Principles* preface.6 in *Origen: On First Principles*, trans. G. W. Butterworth (repr., Gloucester, MA: Peter Smith, 1973), 245.

to the devil inflates the significance of the events. The story is not merely about a serpent and a woman and a man. On the contrary, the garden scene depicts the ultimate adversary at work. The transgression, therefore, is infected with the depth and breadth of Satan's prior rebellion. It is universally consequential, or as the terminology of traditional doctrine would have it, the sin is original.

One might object that this enlargement of the events in Gen. 3 does violence to the plain sense. But the objection ignores the context, which positively begs from a cosmic frame of reference. The seven-day account of creation that opens Genesis is part of the Priestly tradition; in contrast, the second account of creation of man and woman in Gen. 2 reflects the Yahwist tradition. The standard modern approach to reading these two accounts emphasizes their differences. The P writer provides an account of the architecture of the cosmos, while the J writer is more interested in the human-focused flow of history. However, the two perspectives overlap. The Priestly material suggests a historical dynamism toward the seventh day (→2:2). Now we can see how an interpretation of the serpent as the devil opens up a cosmic frame of reference for reading the Yahwist. Instead of trying to give a conceptual answer to the question of how a particular event in the past can have universal consequences, the tradition gives an exegetical answer. The episode is cosmic in significance because the serpent is Satan, the primordial agent of rebellion.

Job, the biblical text most closely related to Gen. 3 in theme and situation, evokes a similar conclusion about the human condition. The main body of the book is highly particularized. Job's flocks are stolen, his house destroyed, and his children killed. These personal tragedies trigger a long series of debates with Job's friends about the justice of Job's sufferings, debates that turn on whether Job is a righteous man. The central premise is that God rewards the righteous and punishes the wicked. The assumption is that our actions determine our destinies. Have I obeyed? Have I transgressed? As readers familiar with the book know, Job's friends argue that Job must have transgressed. Job counterargues that he has not. But for our purposes, the important point of the debate is more general. Throughout the back and forth of argument, all the focus falls on the human condition. In a sense, Job and his friends live in the Yahwist strand of Genesis. The discrete details of our lives provide exactly the right frame of reference for thinking about the human condition. And yet, Job neither begins nor ends with this focus. Instead, the story opens with Satan approaching the LORD God in his heavenly court. He challenges God, suggesting that God lacks the ability to attract spiritual loyalty without buying off the faithful with worldly rewards. The story ends with the famous divine appearance out of a whirlwind, an appearance in which God recounts to Job, not the details of his life and actions, but instead the divine acts of creation. In short, the cosmic perspective frames and contextualizes the human-focused concerns of Job and his friends.

The devil functions in the same way in the New Testament. Again and again St. Paul reminds his readers of the true scale of their struggle against sin. Worldly trials and temptations are not just local; they are afflictions of the devil. The faithful are to resist with confidence, for in due time the God of peace will crush Satan under their feet (Rom. 16:20). This image of triumph draws on Gen. 3:15—the divine prophecy that the children of Eve shall crush the head of the serpent. In the same way, Hebrews uses the greater spiritual powers of angels and demons in order to frame the significance of the passion and death of Jesus. The one who was greater than angels was made lower in order to destroy what the writer calls "the power of death, that is, the devil" (Heb. 2:14). Luke's Gospel makes a similar move when it evokes the intruding agency of evil: "Then Satan entered into Judas called Iscariot" (22:3). The reader is put on notice. The events in Jerusalem, like the events in the primordial garden, have the gravest and greatest of consequences.

Our goal is not to try to reconstruct a New Testament angelology or demonology and transpose it back onto Genesis. The point is much simpler. When 1 Pet. 5:8 warns that "the devil prowls around like a roaring lion, seeking some one to devour," the effect is not to conjure up pictures of a trident-carrying, horned creature with cloven hoofs. Instead, this and other appeals to Satan function in the same way as the apocalyptic visions of Daniel, Zechariah, and Revelation, all of which portray our destiny in the context of more powerful forces. Here a reading of the serpent as Satan begins to pay theological dividends. As we allow the image of Satan to guide our reading of Gen. 3, we learn something about the large biblical vision of human freedom. Although our actions are free and we genuinely shape the directions of our lives, we do not define the moral and spiritual atmosphere in which we live. As any mention of the devil reminds us, we are cast into a world already shaped by a creationwide history of resistance to the divine plan. Our freedom is not pristine, unaffected, and uninfluenced by prior events. We must decide and act in circumstances beyond our control.

Of course, not every portion of scripture can be brought into harmony with every other part. The Bible is fundamentally heterogeneous and cannot be reduced to general theological principles. We should avoid the impulse to interpret scripture simply in order to draw out a theological point, even the very important point that human freedom is constrained by a larger contest between good and evil. Theological concepts are never fully adequate, and no single theological conclusion does justice to the plentitude of the scriptural text. For this reason, it is worthwhile to digress into some further, more technical reasons for calling the tempting serpent "Satan." These reasons emerge out of the problem of theodicy, the conceptually difficult need to acknowledge the reality of evil while affirming the power and goodness of God.

We can best begin by considering the contrary interpretation. The text says the serpent was an animal—admittedly a strangely clever and talkative animal—and that is the end of it.[2] With this approach we gain in literalism, but an immediate

---

2. A talking animal is not sufficient reason to hypothesize about demonic (or angelic) agents. Balaam's ass talks, but the role of the ass is that of a sensible animal and not a spiritual being (Num. 22:21–30).

problem emerges. As human beings, our acts are voluntary or free insofar as they are motivated. An unmotivated act is accidental, not free. But as embodied rational beings, we are motivated by what we perceive and by conclusions we draw from our engagement with the world. As St. Augustine writes, "Nothing draws the will into action except some object that has been perceived."[3] If this is so, then the first transgression must have been motivated by something perceived in the garden. Perhaps it was the novelty of a talking snake. Perhaps it was the loveliness of the fruit. Perhaps the slipperiness of human language, a faulty memory, or the all-too-natural tendency of the human mind to be distracted led the woman to eat. Perhaps the natural affections and loyalty of the man to the woman led him to follow suit.

The point is not to specify the motive or cause. Instead, we need to see what is entailed in allowing the serpent to be just a clever snake. Because our freedom is embodied and responsive rather than purely spiritual and originative, if the serpent is just another bodily creature in the world, then the temptation toward primal sin follows as a consequence of the way God creates. He makes us free in a certain way, but the created order contains realities and impulses that are intrinsically tempting and out of balance: a talking animal such as the serpent, a lovely fruit, the bond of companionship, or some other feature of created, embodied existence. In short, if the serpent is just an animal, then sin emerges out of the human encounter with the natural order.

This conclusion immediately runs up against the problem of evil. The notion that the original transgression occurs as a result of our embodied freedom seems to contradict the biblical assertion that God creates everything and calls it good. Not surprisingly, then, the tradition reads Satan into this verse. There are (so the traditional train of thought presumes) free spiritual beings whose created free wills are not moved by their perception of other created realities. In their independence, these spiritual beings are capable of a pure choice, a choice unmotivated and uncolored by instinct and natural desire. For this reason, spiritual beings can make choices that are originative and not responsive. A spiritual being can choose evil without being motivated by anything God has created. Angels are, as it were, self-moved.

If we suppose the existence of an angel who has fallen, then we have a way out of the problem of evil in our reading of Gen. 3, or at least a way of giving a more subtle form to the problem of evil.[4] By interpreting the serpent as Satan, we have created exegetical space for a prior, purely spiritual choice of disobedience, one not motivated by the desire for something in the created world that is perceived

---

3. Augustine, *De libero arbitrio* 3.25.74. I draw this formulation from the translation provided in Scott MacDonald's nuanced analysis of St. Augustine's approach to Adam and Eve's sin in "Primal Sin," in *The Augustinian Tradition*, ed. Gareth B. Matthews (Berkeley: University of California Press, 1999), 110–39 at 118.

4. Here I follow Augustine's line of reasoning in his long digression at the beginning of his treatment of the fall in *The Literal Meaning of Genesis* 11.

as good. The fallen angel is motivated solely by his choice of evil, the darkness of a world without the supreme goodness of God (→1:4). Of course, the pure freedom of the devil is a finite freedom. The devil is not a primordial being who exists before creation, and in this sense the devil's freedom is part of the divine project from the outset. However, although the finitude of a purely spiritual freedom constrains its scope and consequences, finitude does not mitigate the capacity of a disembodied freedom to do and become something out of its own pure choice. In a certain sense, God is still on the hook. But for God's creation of the angels, none would have fallen. Yet the important point is secure: no aspect of creation other than freedom itself is implicated as the *reason* for an angelic fall. The devil falls strictly because of his choice and not because of any other feature or quality of the created order. This allows us to say that the first transgression, the fall of the devil, occurs *in* creation, but not *because of* creation. "It was," writes St. Augustine, "an evil arising not from nature but from choice" (*City of God* 11.19, quoted from Bettenson 1972: 450).

These suppositions about the finite spiritual freedom of fallen angels open up conceptual space for an interpretation of Gen. 3, and this allows us to pursue a reading that avoids the problem of implying that the ordinary conditions of our embodied freedom lead to sin. Interpreted as Satan in bodily form, the serpent in the garden can be understood as the vehicle for the intrusion of a more original evil choice into our world of embodied freedom. Aspects of creation (e.g., the attractive tastiness of the apple) are obviously implicated in and serve as the medium for transgression, but we need no longer presume that created goods trigger the first human sin. Instead, Satan's prior, purely spiritual, and self-directing choice influences Eve's subsequent, embodied, and responsive choice. She is not thrown off balance by anything God has created. Her transgression turns on her response to a prior form of evil that is, in itself, an act of finite but pure freedom. Of course, Adam's sin has precisely the same form. She hands him the fruit, and he responds to Eve's prior choice. Once the infection is introduced it spreads.

The conceptual advantages of reading the serpent as Satan shows why it is terribly naïve to imagine that the classical interpretation is motivated by a love of mythological figures.[5] To read the serpent as Satan is not to think of the snake as

5. The modern historical-critical tradition is hopelessly confused on this point. See, for example, Claus Westermann, *Genesis 1–11: A Commentary*, trans. John J. Scullion (Minneapolis: Augsburg, 1984), 237–39. Unable to countenance "the mythological explanation of the serpent," Westermann concludes that the origin of evil must be a purely human phenomenon. Westermann is apparently unable to imagine that biblical readers (including readers whose writings would subsequently be incorporated into the canon) would develop interpretive hypotheses in order to avoid contradicting basic theological convictions about the nature of God and creation. Von Rad also falsely assumes that classical demonology is mythical and summarily rejects the traditional reading of the serpent as Satan by insisting that the narrative treats temptation as "a completely unmythical process" (1972: 87). The dichotomy works only if one supposes that hypothetical or inferred beings are by definition mythical, but this is absurd, since it would make a great deal of scientific and mathematical reasoning mythological.

a wicked elf or a rebellious satyr. On the contrary, the traditional exegesis of the serpent as Satan resolves the dilemma posed by a literal reading of the story. To suppose the serpent to be Satan's worldly guise allows us to coordinate the strong affirmation of the intrinsic goodness of creation in Gen. 1 with the narrative of disobedience, resistance, and rebellion of Gen. 3.

At this point we should step back and consider an obvious objection. The reading of the serpent as Satan may help us with the difficulty of affirming the intrinsic goodness of God's creation. The hypothesis of an angelic fall allows us to assert that freedom alone can pervert itself; it cannot go awry simply as human freedom engaged in response to created goods. Yet this approach, we might worry, undermines human responsibility. If the fall is triggered by Satan's earlier choice, then how can we be held responsible? It would seem that the original sin is the devil's fault, not ours. And if this is the case, doesn't the entire Pauline economy of guilt in Adam and forgiveness in Christ collapse?

The objection is helpful, because it forces us to be clear about the nature of our embodied freedom, as well as more attentive to what scripture actually says about our roles in both the empire of evil and the reign of Christ. It is certainly true that we are free participants in the divine plan—for good or for ill. However, transgression is like Caesar's army crossing the Rubicon. Our freedom does not determine us all at once. It sets us down a particular path. More important, in crossing any number of moral and spiritual Rubicons, we are like soldiers deciding to follow, not generals leading their legions. Our freedom is real; we must decide to move our feet in one direction or the other. But that freedom is reactive and responsive, not executive or commanding. We need a leader to trigger our movement. This is why human freedom never provides a sufficient explanation for the march toward sin—or the countermarch toward righteousness. Humans seem capable of a depravity—and righteousness—that far exceeds our ordinary capacities, which is why ordinary language stretches toward adjectives such as "demonic" and "saintly" when describing human extremes. We can follow much further than we can lead.

There are scriptural and commonsensical reasons for thinking of human freedom more on the model of an enlistee than an officer. Joshua ends with a restatement of the choice that determines us. We cannot create endlessly new and different paths into the future. On the contrary, we must decide whom to follow: "Choose this day whom you will serve" (Josh. 24:14–15). We are free to switch loyalties, but we cannot invent new armies and new objectives. With exactly the same underlying assumptions about the human condition, St. Paul insists that our choice, which recapitulates the original choice of Adam and Eve, is about whom to serve and not an invitation to brainstorm about the good life. "You are slaves of the one whom you obey," writes Paul, and in Adam we are conscripted into the army of sin (Rom. 6:16).

The gospel stories evoke the same view of freedom when they portray the good news as a challenge to "the powers" that hold us in their thrall. We seem always beholden to a prior evil that gives us orders that we willingly obey, and Christ frees us by giving countercommands. Mammon leads us one direction; God leads us in another. When Paul says that "for freedom Christ has set us free" (Gal. 5:1), he does not mean that we can opt out and wait for a third option. We are freed from sin precisely because we are taken captive in Christ. In him we serve the life-giving master.

Thus, an appeal to Satan in our interpretation of Gen. 3 reinforces a general biblical claim about our created condition. Our freedom is always a matter of whom we obey, and in sin we seek a perverse fulfillment of our natural desire for obedient service. Promethean self-direction is a fantasy, for we are not created with the capacity to serve ourselves. We can only serve that which is greater, which is why the supposition that the serpent is Satan fits nicely with the larger biblical tendency to see the fundamental form of sin as idolatry. The perverted human will follows false gods, false leaders, and false promises, all the while imagining them to be the source of life.

This view of human freedom as a decision about whom to obey finds ample confirmation in everyday life. We cannot follow our instincts, but we can follow the *idea* of following our instincts. We cannot live as natural men and women, but we can follow a *philosophy* of natural existence. We cannot live only for ourselves, but we can adopt the *principle* of egoism. By St. Paul's analysis, in sin we pervert rather than undo or destroy the purposes for which human nature was created. We live a distorted facsimile of covenant. We are "slaves to the elemental spirits of the universe" (Gal. 4:3). We were created to know and worship the living God, but in our blindness we serve dead idols (Rom. 1:21–23). Thus, when we introduce the greater power of Satan into our interpretation of Genesis, we are not undermining human responsibility for sin, nor are we compromising the Pauline vision of salvation history. Instead, we are bringing our reading of the fall into conformity with the New Testament account of our slavery to sin. Sin is a perverted obedience, a false following, a deceived discipleship. To suppose the serpent to be a form of Satan helps us see the true form of our slavery to sin—and by contrast to see the obedient form of our participation in Christ.

Although there are strong reasons in support of a traditional reading of the serpent as Satan, neither scripture nor the classical theological tradition gives Satan an ongoing, central role in the unfolding of the divine plan. St. Paul observes that "sin came into the world through one man" (Rom. 5:12) and that the divine campaign against the entire empire of evil is conducted through "that one man Jesus Christ" (5:15). While we may not be commanders in the cosmic conflict, salvation history turns on our loyalty. Although the possibility of evil should be traced back to the purely spiritual freedom of fallen angels, we need to be careful. The origin of evil should not be confused with the location of its ultimate conflict with goodness. The centers of government may have been in Richmond and Washington, but the tide of the Civil War turned at the small Pennsylvania town of Gettysburg.

For Gregory of Nyssa, the human focus of the scriptural story is clear from the outset, and he explains why God fittingly chooses our embodied freedom as the place to work out his redemptive plan. Our amphibious existence as both embodied and free places us at the center of the cosmic drama. "God, taking dust of the ground, formed the man," Gregory writes, "and, by an inspiration from Himself, He planted life in the work of His hand, that thus the earthy might be raised up to the Divine, and so one certain grace of equal value might pervade the whole creation, the lower nature being mingled with the supramundane" (*Catechetical Orations* 6 in NPNF[2] 5.480). The human creature has a unique role. We are what angels and demons can never be: a hybrid of body and spirit that participates in all aspects of the created order. Through us, therefore, God can reach into all the corners of his creation. Neither pure spirit nor mere body, we are at the crossroads of reality. The future of the cosmos is in the hands of whichever army controls this strategic point.

Thus, for all the biblical concern about demons and for all the theological principles that warrant the hypothesis of the devil, focus falls on the human. We live out our loyalties in the quotidian realities of everyday life. It is here and now that we do the work of Satan, and it is here and now that we encounter Christ, who has the power to free us from the thrall of our own past choices, from the primordial choice of Adam and Eve, and from the original wickedness of Satan. We do the most to defeat the devil and sanctify the world when we focus on our core competence: obedience to the call of Christ in the midst of human affairs.

3:1b Did God say . . . ?

The subtle serpent creates a disorienting atmosphere of uncertain questions. Is it "this tree" or "any tree" that God has fenced with a commandment not to eat of its fruit? What did God actually command? And why? What are the real consequences of transgression? The ambiguity is crucial. As the self-defeating perversion of goodness, sin is ugly and repulsive. Transgression can only allure in a world of distortion and dreamlike fantasy, where what is real becomes malleable, capable of seeming to be what it is not. The robbery won't require any killing, the thief imagines. The one-night stand won't lead to any bad feelings. The lie is for the best. Our lives are full of gauzy pictures that our imaginations conjure in order to make the ugliness of sin look more appealing. This is why deception and the lie loom so large in Christian thought about Satan. We can consistently desire what is bad when we imagine that it will add up to something good, a mental operation only possible if we are deceived about reality. As Gregory of Nyssa writes, "Good is in its nature simple and uniform, alien from all duplicity or conjunction with its opposite, while evil is many-coloured and fairly adorned, being esteemed to be one thing and revealed by experience as another" (*On the Making of Man* 20.3 in NPNF[2] 5.410). Or as St. Paul writes, "Even Satan disguises himself as an angel of light" (2 Cor. 11:14).

In the garden, the serpent's distortion has the effect of throwing doubt on the divine plan. "Is this not," he seems to be saying, "the garden of joy? You are surrounded by food for life, and yet you are commanded not to fully enjoy it? Is this the sort of God you obey, one who promises life and yet requires renunciations, one who claims to give blessings but always ends up placing limits and making demands?" These questions have been repeated many times. A Jew is not to eat pork or shrimp, and what are we to think? Does God wish to cut us off from the good things in life? St. Paul inveighs against fornication, and what are we to think? Is God so opposed to sex and the human capacity for pleasure? Is not the whole scheme of divine commandment a diminishment of life that cuts us off from the bounty of creation, condemning us to endless sackcloth and ashes?

The woman's response is corrective, but the serpent's opening gambit produces an echoing exaggeration. She recounts that God forbade eating from the tree in the middle of the garden, and she then adds, "Neither shall you touch it." Unsettled by the distortions of the serpent, the woman wants to return to the reality of God's commandment, but her grasp is unsteady. It is as if Satan's insinuation has taken hold on her imagination. She begins to assume the role of lawgiver herself, puffing up as one giving orders and establishing rules. It is an untenable position of pride: "Everything that I command you you shall be careful to do; you shall not add to it or take from it" (Deut. 12:32).

Midrash is a traditional Jewish style of reading. It involves a supplemented retelling that interprets by way of added emphasis, color, and dramatization, as I have done above. The skeleton of the biblical story is retained, but flesh is added. Midrash, however, is not unique to Judaism. These few verses depicting the original transgression provide the basis for an extensive tradition of Christian midrash. Milton's *Paradise Lost* provides one of the most famous examples. But there is nothing uniquely poetic or premodern about the tendency to fill out the story of the fall. Modern biblical critic Gerhard von Rad produces exegesis in this genre, and he does so with a panache for inventing motives and emotional responses that shed light on the psychology of sin (1972: 88–90). These examples of creative retelling are not surprising. This short portion of biblical text combines narrative realism with economy of expression, a combination that positively invites the reader to fill out the story with more detail. Here, then, the literary form matches the ambition of Genesis. The suggestive brevity of the verses invites us to interweave our many and diverse thoughts about the nature of sin into our reading. In the silences of the text we find a place for our own knowledge of the concrete form of human wickedness, and in so doing we vindicate the traditional view that this story tells us about the original sin.

3:2 And the woman said.

Perhaps the serpent arrives on the scene more ignorant than wise, and he opens with a clever question designed to provoke the woman to betray crucial information. "I've heard that all these trees are off limits. Is it true?" he asks. "No," says the woman, "with God as my witness, I was told to refrain from eating the fruit of the one tree in the middle of the garden." "Oh, I see," he responds. Now, with this missing piece of information, the lawyer can proceed, knowing just where to focus his attention. "You foolish woman," he says to himself, "you have given me what I wanted to know, because you could not restrict yourself to a simple 'yes' or 'no'" (Matt. 5:37). Eve is too eager, too chatty, too forthcoming. She allows herself to be lured into a discussion with the evil one about the substance of God's commandment. "Do not throw your pearls before swine," warns Jesus (7:6), and that seems to be exactly what Eve does. "Such is the evil of idly and casually exposing to all and sundry the divine mysteries," John Chrysostom observes in his extraordinarily rich reading of Eve's transgression (*Homilies on Genesis* 16.6 in FC 74.211).

This might seem a fanciful reading, but the larger scriptural witness suggests otherwise. A negligent, careless tongue looms large in the biblical concern about sin, much larger than most Christian readers realize. Restraint of the tongue is the object of two of the Ten Commandments: do not take the LORD's name in vain, and do not bear false witness. James identifies the control of the mouth as the key to vice and virtue (Jas. 3:2–5) and warns that "the tongue is a fire" (3:6). Sin has made our tongues "a restless evil, full of deadly poison" (3:8). The Pastoral Epistles place great emphasis on the properly trained tongue, one that knows when to be silent and when to command and teach according to the sound doctrine.

This larger biblical concern about the tongue and its dangers forms the background for Chrysostom's portrayal of Eve as the original gossipy housewife, whose wandering, undisciplined tongue leads to the original human sin. It is not prideful self-assertion that is the source. For Chrysostom, the root sin is negligence, expressed most clearly in the easy familiarity of neighborhood gossip. For in gossip we treat other people's lives as occasions for entertainment and titillation, as opportunities to express complacent superiority or to express a burning envy. With Chrysostom's interpretation, therefore, we see an important aspect of our sinful selves. We are not hyperalert seekers after advantage, men and women who puff ourselves up with arrogant self-importance. More often than not we are somnolent, lazy, and complacent folks who drift along with the crowd. We don't rush off to join the devil's party. Instead, we wake up one day and find that, after an unthinking, offhanded career as a fellow traveler, we have signed a loyalty oath as full members.

There is no one right way to read the story of the first sin. The early monastic tradition developed a list of seven deadly sins: pride, envy, anger, sloth, avarice, gluttony, and lust. Under the influence of Augustine, Western Christianity has tended to presume that pride is the cardinal, original sin. But the early monks who lived in the Egyptian desert often thought otherwise. For some greed loomed large. They observed a deep human fear of dependence upon God that manifested itself in a perennial desire to accumulate some small margin of protective, sustaining property. For others, a languid, despairing, spiritual pessimism (sloth) was the deepest problem we face.

We should not be surprised that the Christian tradition has not settled on a single account of material form of the primal sin. The scriptures themselves equivocate. Proverbs 16:18 gives St. Augustine his favorite text: "Pride goes before destruction, and a haughty spirit before a fall." But Wisdom of Solomon 2:24 teaches, "Through the devil's envy death entered the world." (St. Augustine harmonizes these verses by supposing that the devil's pride causes him to envy God's supremacy.) In 1 Tim. 6:10 we read that "the love of money is the root of all evils." And 1 John 2:16 gives a threefold formulation (drawing on Ezek. 24:21) that has been used to probe the deep sources of sin: "the lust of the flesh and the lust of the eyes and the pride of life."

This diversity should not trouble, because it reflects a deeper, formal truth about sin. Transgression is, at root, a spectral romance with nothingness. It is epitomized by idolatry, devotion to an image powerless to deliver on its promises. Lacking an underlying truth or reality, our actual sins take countless forms without ever coming into focus as instances of some deeper, more stable, more fundamental form of life. As a strange, impossible love of nothingness, sin always twists itself toward some semblance of reality. Sin is the perverted love of a finite good, and therefore has no stable, fundamental form. For this reason, there is no one way to characterize the original sin in Gen. 3.

3:4 You will not die.

The serpent's deceiving promise is a primordial lie. It is to the ears what an idol is to the eyes: a fantasy about the power of life. As a promise, the lie is a claim about the future, a faux covenant. In the subtle, indirect, and deceiving form of a negative claim, the serpent seems to promise life: "You will not die." "Have no fear," he implies. "Do as you please. You can have what you want right now—and at the same time you can have the fullness of life in the future. You can have the lovely fruit, and it will provide you with all the happiness you seek." At root, this lie, and the covenant it implies, is like the golden calf at the base of Mount Sinai. It is like Mammon, whom we so often serve. It is like the ideological totems of modern men and women. Satan's lie always takes the same form. It creates the illusion that there is some path to fullness of life other than obedience to God's commandments.

Evil is negation, and pure evil is complete privation or negation. Therefore, pure evil cannot exist, not even as a possibility. As a result, the lie can endure only in the mind of the woman and tempt her if it somehow participates in truth, as do all believable lies. And indeed Satan's lie does. When they eat the fruit, neither the man nor the woman drops dead. The LORD, who has said, "In the day that you eat of it you shall die" (2:17), seems to be shown the purveyor of falsehood, while the serpent speaks the truth.

The seeming truth of Satan's lie rests on the equivocal meaning of life and death. God creates the man and the woman for a purpose: to enter into his Sabbath rest. Spiritual life and death turns on our acceptance or rejection of that divine purpose established in the beginning. Moses's exhortation to the Israelites restates the choice that Eve faces in the garden: "I call heaven and earth to witness against you this day, that I have set before you life and death, blessing and curse; therefore choose life, that you and your descendents may live, loving the LORD your God, obeying his voice, and cleaving to him" (Deut. 30:19–20). Christ presents the same choice to all the nations: "In him was life" (John 1:4), he is "the bread of life" (6:35), and his words "are spirit and life" (6:63). Christ gives his flesh over to death for the sake of "the life of the world" (6:51), and in his resurrection death is "swallowed up by life" (2 Cor. 5:4). In this way, from Eve onward the original choice of life or death is recapitulated again and again: "He who has the Son has life; he who has not the Son of God has not life" (1 John 5:12).

The serpent's lie was brilliant and effective, because it shifts the focus of human concern. He directs attention to what the woman already possesses: the gift of physical life that she shares with all living things. "What you have now you shall not lose," he promises, and in a strict sense he speaks truthfully. But the strict sense of Satan's promise is not the implied sense. "You shall not die" conjures the promise that we will have life abundant. The deception thus breaks the bond between "life and godliness," and the lie turns our attention away from "him who called us to his own glory and excellence" (2 Pet. 1:3). The serpent's lie tempts the woman to believe that what matters most is sentient, bodily existence: "Take the fruit. It's not going to kill you!"

The lie remains effective to this day. St. Augustine makes a distinction between two dispositions toward things: use and enjoyment. To use something means to see its finite goodness and its role in God's larger plan or purpose and then to love it contingently, that is, not for its own sake but for the sake of God's plan. To enjoy, by contrast, means to embrace something as our final rest and ultimate purpose, to love it for its own sake. God alone is our proper rest, and thus we are created to enjoy him alone, and others in him, while we are to use created reality to attain that end. But we are tempted to rest in countless finite goods, and the temptation is strong, because, as Satan promises, we really can love them and live in them for their own sake—at least for a while. My professional success is genuinely rewarding. The five-star chef cooks wonderful food. Patriotism is a noble sentiment. All of these finite goods make life better in the short and medium term. "The tree was good for food" (Gen. 3:6), and its apple does not kill Adam and Eve—or us. In fact, an apple might satisfy our hunger and keep the doctor away. Thus, it's very easy to think that apples and other finite goods are what make life worth living. The lie works because it has a ring of truth.

3:6a The woman saw that the tree was good for food, and that it was a delight to the eyes, and that the tree was desired to make one wise.

First John 2:16 suggests a view of sin as "the lust of the flesh and the lust of the eyes and the pride of life." This threefold formula is not so much a specific theory of original sin as a deliberate echo of the story of original transgression. The woman sees that the fruit is good for food (lust of the flesh), a delight to the eyes (lust of the eyes), and the source of wisdom (pride of life). The same tripartite scheme is at work in Jesus's temptation by Satan in the wilderness (Luke 4:1–13; Matt. 4:1–11). The temptation to turn stones to bread echoes the tasty fruit (lust of the flesh). The vision of the kingdoms of the world from the mountaintop echoes the delightful appearance of the fruit (lust of the eyes). The temptation to compel God to rescue his beloved son echoes the allure of wisdom (pride of life). Sin enters the human condition by many doors, and if we are to follow the genealogy of sin outlined in Rom. 1, the diversity of entrances lead into the culminating form of idolatry, the sine qua non of covenant faithlessness in the Old Testament. Idolatry is the final, spiritualized strategy of life based on the hope that the lie might be true, for idolatry epitomizes the spiritualized hope that something other than God has deathless power.

3:6b He ate.

Who is finally responsible? Upon whom may we pin the original fault? The man or the woman? The testimony of scripture equivocates. Compare 1 Tim. 2:14 ("Adam was not deceived, but the woman was deceived and became a transgressor") with Rom. 5:12 ("sin came into the world through one man"). It is tempting to throw up one's hands in exasperation—or to suppress the contradiction by discounting 1 Timothy as pseudo-Pauline.[6]

Here we can reap some further dividends from the traditional decision to interpret the serpent as Satan (→3:1a). Human sin is not original in the sense of emerging out of human freedom as a new possibility. As embodied agents, our freedom is enacted in our relation to the world and others. Eating the fruit is a possibility that must be presented to the woman, both by the physical form of the fruit and by the provocative suggestion of the serpent. Her fatefully disobedient choice emerges from the encounter with the voice of the devil's prior disobedient choice. Eve's sin is reactive, responsive, and reiterative. The same holds for the man. He eats in disobedience after encountering the fruit held up to him by the woman's prior disobedient choice. In this way the human original sin circulates

6. Modern biblical scholarship insists on a particularized focus that has helped bring out the unique voices of scripture. To think through the Pauline view of x or the Matthean theology of y has been fruitful. However, this strategy of reading has also tempted biblical scholars to discount and ignore the problem of canonical consistency. Faithful readers want to understand the overall biblical view.

like a rumor. And like the evil of a rumor, what matters is not so much the origin as the impulse to pass it along. Only Satan's spiritual fall is originative. Both Eve and Adam repeat it, and the fault rests in the repeating. One cannot plead innocence and say that "she gave me fruit of the tree" (3:12) or that "the serpent beguiled me" (3:13). Once the lie is available, the order of the sin has no moral significance. One's place in the chain of deadly gossip makes the guilt neither lighter nor heavier.

3:7 The eyes of both were opened.

Are we to think that the man and woman were blind before they transgressed and that somehow sin is necessary for wisdom and knowledge? In Romans, Paul distinguishes between two kinds of seeing. "I would have you wise as to what is good," he writes, suggesting a power of sight with respect to the things of God, "and guileless as to what is evil," he continues, suggesting blindness with respect to the subtle, false promises of the devil (16:19). The distinction is reinforced by Jesus's statement of a dual purpose with respect to sight: "For judgment I came into the world, that those who do not see may see, and that those who see may become blind" (John 9:39). This dualism suggests a spiritual interpretation of the blindness and sight in the garden. It is a reading common among the church fathers.

For the church fathers, vision is not just a physical capacity. The soul has eyes in the sense that our lives have focus and our intentions are directed toward larger objectives. If I choose to go to law school, then it is because I "see" how the degree will serve to advance my goals. Didymus the Blind applies this sense of vision to the original man and woman. Before they sin, they do not simply look upon material reality; instead, they see reality in the light of the reason or *logos* of creation that was established in the beginning. They see that what has been created is good and that it serves to prepare them for fellowship with God. After the fall, however, their vision changes. The eye of the soul is blinded, and the eye of carnal desire opens. The original pair now think of material reality itself as the endpoint or purpose of creation. Seeking to rest in finite things, they no longer think of material reality in the light of the original *logos* or reason for which and with which God creates.[7]

We need not follow Didymus's dualistic view of human nature that divides the rational from the sensual, but we should acknowledge the underlying insight. To live in the image of God is to see everything with the "eyes" of faithful obedience. The plants are to be tilled; the animals are to be kept. They are real and they are seen, but their meaning and purpose is illuminated by God's plan for all things: entrance into Sabbath rest and participation in divine life. However, when the man and woman believe the serpent's lie, they give priority to physical life, and

7. *Didyme l'aveugle: sur la genèse*, ed. Pierre Nautin, Sources chrétiennes 233 (Paris: Cerf, 1976), 1.193–97.

their vision shifts focus. Everything is now seen in terms of the project of bodily existence, one that involves satisfying transient desires and ensuring survival. Thus, the nakedness that they see is really the truth of the lie they believe. After their transgression, they see themselves as they have chosen to live: for the sake of physical life unadorned by God's purpose.

The man and woman feel shame—and not surprisingly. When we fail to see what reality is for, we cannot help but disfigure the intrinsic goodness of creation. The sight of life stripped of divine purpose is not pleasant: "Woe to those who call evil good and good evil. . . . Woe to those who are wise in their own eyes" (Isa. 5:20–21). The perversion of sin is evident, even to eyes no longer focused on the divine purpose for creation. The *logos* or law of God is written on the hearts of the human creatures (Rom. 2:15). When the eye of the soul becomes carnal, taking the physical and finite as the measure of all things, the testimony of creation awakens a sense of shame. We know ourselves pursuing a futile life-project—even as we commit ourselves to its futility.

Adam and Eve seek cover to hide their shame with clothes sewn from fig leaves. So it shall be for subsequent generations. Vice rarely parades itself in public. More often than not it takes on disguises.[8] Pride becomes what we imagine to be a healthy self-confidence. Shameless sin disguises itself as an authentic existential stance that will not stoop to hypocrisy. We're not so much greedy as responsible parents, laying up prudent reserves for the education of our children. It's not gluttony or lust, but instead a world-affirming ethic that takes life seriously. The alchemy of rationalization sews together the fig leaves in many different ways. We do so in order to reclothe ourselves in a greater moral purpose, hiding the deep truth that we are living carnally, living as if the material world was the final truth that constrains and governs human life.

The gaze of holiness sees through these rationalizations and assays the heart, just as Jesus sees the fig tree by the road as it truly is. The mass of leaves disguises a lack of fruit (Matt. 21:19). We are subject to this gaze, which is why divine goodness and generosity cannot but be felt as judgment and accusation. God responds to sin by coming close to the sinner and forcing the issue. As he walks in the garden, the sinner flees and hides. To overcome the power of the lie, however, the opposite must occur: "Draw near to God and he will draw near to you" (Jas. 4:8).

3:14 Cursed are you.

God creates for a purpose, and when the original choices of the man and woman go against his purpose, God does not wash his hands of creation. "They

---

8. Gregory of Nyssa says of Satan's lie: "This deception would never have succeeded, had not the glamour of beauty been spread over the hook of vice like a bait" (*Catechetical Orations* 21 in NPNF² 5.492).

heard the sound of the LORD God walking in the garden" (3:8). He speaks to the man and woman: "I will question you, and you shall declare to me" (Job 38:3). Both respond, "I ate" (Gen. 3:12–13). Now the initiative returns to God, and he fulfills their choices. The man and woman chose sentient life, the realm of physical pleasures and the project of natural survival. Their punishment is to have what they have chosen. As Chrysostom says, imagining God speaking directly to the man and woman, "Lo, you have become what you expected—or rather, not what you expected but what you deserved to become" (*Homilies on Genesis* 18.6 in FC 82.7). Divine justice is not only incorruptible and beneficent ("the LORD reproves him whom he loves"; Prov. 3:12); it is also fitting. According to Augustine, "The retribution for disobedience is simply disobedience itself. For man's wretchedness is nothing but his own disobedience to himself" (*City of God* 14.15, quoted from Bettenson 1972: 575). We try to live according to Satan's lie, as if the material world were sufficient for life. But just as the restless loneliness that Adam experienced extends beyond the bodily union of man and woman, so also do we twist and turn in order to extract more than survival from our inner-worldly projects. We tie ourselves into knots of self-contradiction in our efforts to use finite goods to satisfy our infinite longing.

Before God gives specific form to human punishment, the LORD curses the serpent. The half-truth of the lie—that we really can find happiness as physical beings—is an unequivocal lie for Satan. The devil needs neither bread nor breath, and there is no physical flourishing that can give even the semblance of reality to the dream that what matters most is our enjoyment of created reality. So the devil reaps the fruit of his lie. He shall eat the dust of physical life that gives him nothing at all. Thus, the devil is condemned to the perpetual frustration of trying to spiritualize our hunger, our fear of death, our sexual desire, our desire for the admiration of others. It is a fool's errand, for the bodily realities of human nature (which includes the psychological as well as the more narrowly physical) cannot become the consistent, transparent objects of our loyalty. Dust cannot be turned into that than which nothing greater can be conceived. It can only be formed into golden calves that are capable of transfixing our vision, but cannot become the living center of our lives.

The punishment of the man and the woman focuses on the conditions for mortal life: childbirth for the woman and the toil of tilling the ground for the man. Both are tinged with death, because both are central to the project of physical survival. Childbirth perpetuates the species, and agricultural work staves off the disaster of famine ("if any one will not work, let him not eat"; 2 Thess. 3:10). Both echo the original tasks of the garden, tasks that are ordered to eternal fellowship with God. Both retain the dignity of their original purpose. "Be fruitful and multiply"—we can attain a tantalizing taste of eternal life in our children. They extend us into the future, and in them we can place our hopes. "Till and keep"—tilling the ground is a proper form of dominion over the natural fruitfulness of the earth. It allows us to builds up stores of grain that provide abundance for festivals of celebration. Our capacity for work produces the material and cultural inheritance we pass on to our children. However, the project of species survival and contributing to the common good can never succeed for any particular person. All finite flesh shall "return to the ground" (Gen. 3:19). Thus, the punishments of the man and the woman are reformatory. They raise hopes even as they remind us that natural processes of reproduction and labor cannot lead us to the Sabbath rest.

Because of the way in which the punishments echo the blessings of the garden, we should not read childbirth, labor, and even death as extrinsic to the human condition, as if God is angry and imposes particularly bitter punishments that reverse the logic of creation. Childbirth, labor, and death are not new possibilities. "Be fruitful and multiply" and "till and keep" precede the fall, and the man and woman were not created as immortal beings. However, the man and the woman have rejected their future in the image of God, and they have chosen instead the project of physical survival. "The wages of a hired servant shall not remain with you all night until the morning" (Lev. 19:13). The LORD is true to his own word, and he does not withhold the wages due to Adam and Eve: "The wages of sin is death" (Rom. 6:23). With his judgment, God does not introduce an evil into the world—such a thought is inconsistent with his holiness. Rather, he acknowledges the full fruit of the harvest of transgression, and he pays the man and woman in the currency they favor. If they wish to live on bread alone, then bread alone and the finitude of the body shall be their future. Their punishment will be to live out the half-truth of the deception "you will not die." Now the human creature must survive under the dominion of biology and by the rules of mere physical survival. If we wish to live for the sake of the world, then we must live strictly according to what the world can give us: the painful labor of birth, which is an emblem of the dire and difficult psychological mating dance that characterizes every culture, and the toilsome labor of the harvest, which encompassed the entire project of building and sustaining civilization. Both are darkened by the forces of decay and dissolution that end in death.

Where the punishment of the man and the woman involves God giving us what we want, the history of salvation is a series of gifts shaped by what God wants for us—and that we consistently regard as alien and frightening. This difference does not, however, entail any conflict between the all-too-natural conditions of physical life and the gift of salvation. In Isa. 65:23, the consequences of sin are redeemed rather than removed: "They shall not labor in vain, or bear children for calamity." For St. Paul, death has lost its sting; it has not been erased as a fact of natural life. This is because salvation is a change in personal loyalty, not a change in metaphysical location. The purpose of creation is to create the conditions for human beings to "become partakers in the divine nature" (2 Pet. 1:4). To enter into the seventh day of Sabbath rest is a way of being human; it is not a suprahuman or extrahuman possibility. Thus, to reverse the punishment of men and women requires breaking the bonds of our perverse loyalty to Satan's lie, the belief that the natural conditions of life can fulfill and satisfy. Salvation does not eliminate or destroy those natural conditions.

3:21 Garments of skin.

In this enigmatic verse the theme of clothing and nakedness in the story of the original transgression reemerges. God seems to express care by providing the fallen man and woman with clothing to replace the woven garments of fig leaves. These clothes prepare the man and woman to live under the burden of their transgression. But what, exactly, are these garments?

The leather clothes suggest a thickening or toughening of the human condition. Human life takes on greater density and weight. The Catholic tradition calls this weight concupiscence, the condition of disorder within the human soul caused when the lower appetites, what Paul calls "passions of our flesh" (Eph. 2:3), push us in directions contrary to our rational desires. For example, I want to study for a test or practice a musical instrument, but hunger distracts or sleepiness overwhelms or an attractive woman has me off and running. This added weight or sluggishness blunts and reduces the power of the human will by dissipating it into desires of the moment. What we plan for the future is corrupted by what we want in the moment.

The Council of Trent teaches that concupiscence is not itself sin, but rather "comes from sin and induces to sin" (session 5.5).[9] If so, then we are faced with an important question. Assuming that the garments of skin represent the thickening of the human condition, in what sense could this sluggishness and capacity for distraction be an act of divine care? To provide a satisfactory answer we need to think clearly about the consequences of concupiscence, the consequences of base desires overriding our well-considered intentions.

Human beings are poised halfway between animals and angels. We are embodied, rational animals, capable of long-term projects and sustained loyalties. As a result, the original transgression has momentum. As Rowan Williams observes, "The corruption of the human will is a more far-reaching disaster than the corruption of the animal will." We can follow through with our decision to be loyal to finite reality. For this reason, "a wicked human is an immeasurably greater problem than a wicked hamster."[10] In order to restrain the effects of sin, God makes the garments of skin. Concupiscence places a governor on the intensity of the human will. It makes us more like hamsters, seeking the pleasures of the moment, and

---

9. Although often characterized as a dualist opposed to bodily desires, Augustine is also quite clear that bodily desires are not themselves the problem. "It is not the corruptible flesh that made the soul sinful," he writes, "it was the sinful soul that made the flesh corruptible" (*City of God* 14.3, quoted from Bettenson 1972: 551).

10. Rowan Williams, "Insubstantial Evil," in *Augustine and His Critics*, ed. Robert Dodaro and George Lawless (London: Routledge, 2000), 111.

less like the devil, who has no body to limit the intensity of his perversely formed will. Clothed with the garments of skin, we remain incapable of fully focusing our minds in order to completely follow through with our ill-fated plans. We often experience this as a curse. Who hasn't rued the weakness of the flesh? Yet, as the young poet John Keats saw, our slavery to bodily limitations has benefits as well. He bemoaned his tendency toward a depressive dormancy and "an indolent enjoyment of the intellect," but he also saw a blessing in the heaviness of his concupiscence. "There are no Men thoroughly wicked," he writes. We are limited by lower desires "so as never to be self-spiritualized into a kind of sublime Misery."[11]

St. Paul describes the effects of concupiscence in a similar way. The fallen human condition is more a somnolence or paralysis brought on by desires working at cross-purposes than an ever refined project of demonic transgression. "I do not understand my own actions," Paul writes of his efforts to live according to the law, "for I do not do what I want, but I do the very thing I hate" (Rom. 7:15). The "law" of his "members" wars against the "law of [his] mind" (7:23). "The passions of our flesh" (Eph. 2:3) are the garments of skin that shackle his will. This limitation of the will stands in the way of living in obedience to the will of God, but it also protects Paul (and us) from living out the full perversity of a self-destructive loyalty to sin. Heroes and saints are said to have clay feet. Perhaps, and the blessing of the garments of skin is that the wicked have them as well.

Redemption also involves garments. As we are restored to our roles in the divine plan of bringing all things into the Sabbath rest, Paul exhorts us to change our clothes: "Let us put on the armour of light" (Rom. 13:12 AV). He continues: "Put ye on the Lord Jesus Christ, and make not provision for the flesh, to fulfil the lusts thereof" (13:14 AV). Even more pointedly, and echoing this passage in Genesis, Paul says that we are called to enter into the covenant with "the whole fullness of deity," and we do so "by putting off the body of flesh in the circumcision of Christ" (Col. 2:9, 11). A similar dynamic of exchange is at work when Paul describes our desire to "put on our heavenly dwelling" (2 Cor. 5:1–2), which is, perhaps, the costume of the "beautiful garments" of Zion (Isa. 52:1). The echoes of Genesis ring clear yet again, this time reinforced by Job 19:26 and following a pattern also found in Wisdom of Solomon 9. Paul leans forward in expectation: "For while we are still in this tent, we sigh with anxiety; not that we would be unclothed, but that we would be further clothed, so that what is mortal may be swallowed up by life" (2 Cor. 5:4).

3:24 He drove out the man.

The fall is not a singular event. It is a trajectory of human destiny that arcs away from the divine plan. The expulsion from the garden is part of the motion away

11. Lionel Trilling, ed., *Selected Letters of John Keats* (New York: Doubleday, 1956), 93.

from fellowship with God and toward the counterfeit *imago dei* that will manifest itself in murder, mismarriage, and perverse dominion—all given false spiritual unity in the practice of idolatry. In this sense, the story of the fall stretches all the way to Gen. 12 and the calling of Abraham.

Within the cascade of events that make up the fall, the expulsion of Adam and Eve expresses the substance of the doctrine of original sin more clearly than the primal transgression of the man and the woman. Adam and Eve choose loyalty to the lie—life according to its physical reality—and this sends them marching away from the Sabbath fulfillment for which they were created. All subsequent human beings are born into this futile countercovenant, and for this reason we are invariably fellow travelers away from God. Original sin, then, is our inheritance, our place in the trajectory of self-willed expulsion, the back-turned-toward-God orientation that characterizes the default direction of human life.

However burdensome the movement away from God will be for the human race, the expulsion is not without divine blessing. Disobedience cannot bear the consuming reality of holiness. As the Israelites say to Moses at the base of Mount Sinai, "Speak thou with us, and we will hear: but let not God speak with us, lest we die" (Exod. 20:19 AV). As a result, although we experience the distance created by expulsion, like the garments of skin, as curse, because the distance provides the human creature with space and time to live in sin, it is also a gift. The existence of a human space and time at a distance from the immediacy of the divine presence provides an opportunity—not for us, but for God. As the human race departs, God can begin to formulate a strategy that redeems rather than annihilates the transgressor. As humanity moves away from the presence of God, the conditions emerge in which God can come to humanity. "Where sin abounded, grace did much more abound," Paul writes (Rom. 5:21 AV).

4:3 To the LORD** an offering.**

The text offers no explanation for Cain's and Abel's sacrifices. No divine commandments evoke or specify the ritual act. Instead, within the narrative atmosphere of the primal history, the impulse to sacrifice seems to follow from the sheer humanity of Cain and Abel. They are animated by what the later theological tradition calls a natural desire for God. As St. Augustine writes in a famous affirmation of this desire: "You stir man to take pleasure in praising you, because you have made us for yourself, and our heart is restless until it rests in you."[12] The powers and capacities of humans are for the sake of fellowship with God, and those powers and capacities, however distorted by the false covenant with the lie, continue to

12. Augustine, *Confessions* 1.1, quoted from *Saint Augustine: Confessions*, trans. Henry Chadwick (Oxford: Oxford University Press, 1991), 3.

seek God. In this seeking, the economy of sacrifice—offering the fruits of human labor—bridges the distance between God and the now-remote creature.

A doctrinal commitment to the enduring desire for God in fallen humanity, like all doctrinal commitments, does not rest on any single verse of scripture. Petitions in the psalms testify to the perennial longing of the human heart. Of course, this longing is not always reliable. The longing heart often finds false loves. However, as the larger witness of the scriptures depicts again and again, even in their perversity false loves testify to an enduring desire for God. We consistently spiritualize sin, and in so doing try to satisfy our need for worship. We take love of luxury or love of wealth and turn it into "covetousness, which is idolatry" (Col. 3:5). We justify our domination of others by appealing to higher purposes. In these and many other ways, the darkening of the human heart in sin does not signal the cessation of religious desire or an eclipse of the need for worship. The darkened heart is a perverted heart. Idols become a necessity so that we can worship something, even if it is intrinsically impotent—or rather precisely because it is intrinsically impotent. A dead idol allows us the illusion of worship without renouncing our covenant with the lie.

Cain and Abel represent the two diverging trajectories of love. "A glad heart makes a cheerful countenance" (Prov. 15:13) we read, but the countenance of Cain is anything but cheerful. His heart is hardened against God's favor to Abel, and "Cain was very angry, and his countenance fell" (Gen. 4:5). Cain falls more deeply in the thrall of the evil one, whose lie has gained dominion over the human future, and "his own deeds were evil" (1 John 3:12). By contrast, the younger brother moves in the opposite direction: "Abel offered to God a more acceptable sacrifice than Cain, through which he received approval as righteous, God bearing witness by accepting his gifts" (Heb. 11:4). The altar of sacrifice marks a place of division. As the human reaches toward God, the difference between sin and righteousness becomes clearer. Worship is the great precipitant.

How and why Abel can escape bondage to the devil and offer an acceptable sacrifice finds no answer in Genesis. We read about Cain's anger, his plot to lure Abel to a remote field, his effort to evade divine judgment, and his plea for mercy, but we learn nothing of Abel's sentiments. This silence is fitting, for the larger scriptural witness traces the distinction between the wicked and the righteous back to the mercy of God and not to a difference between two types of human beings. We persevere in wickedness by our own continued recapitulation of the primal choice of Adam and Eve, but we become capable of righteousness by the grace of God. "The wind blows where it wills" (John 3:8). The particularity of election—the one rather than the other—comes to the fore in Genesis from the calling of Abraham forward, and it reaches a crescendo in the election of Jacob over Esau in Rebekah's womb (→25:23), but the mechanism of election is foreshadowed in Abel's sad fate. Cain is the active author of his wickedness; Abel is simply the recipient of God's favor.

If we explain the LORD's regard for Abel's offering in terms of election rather than the intrinsic merit of his character and sacrifice, then it is tempting for us to rebel and deride the difference between Cain and Abel as arbitrary. But on what basis do we protest? "Has the potter no right over the clay, to make out of the same lump one vessel for beauty and another for menial use?" (Rom. 9:21). By preferring Abel, God seems to be saying, "I will be gracious to whom I will be gracious, and will show mercy on whom I will show mercy" (Exod. 33:19; Rom. 9:15). This declaration of divine prerogative is a rhetorical extension of the divine name *ehyeh asher ehyeh* in Exod. 3:14: "I am who I am" or "I will be what I will be." Does Cain's (and our) bitterness over salvation being in God's hands (and not in his or our own) amount to a cursing of the divine name? Of such an outcome we are warned: "You shall not take the name of the LORD your God in vain; for the LORD will not hold him guiltless who takes his name in vain" (20:7).

4:7 Sin is crouching at the door.

Cain inherits a life of exile from Eden. He is born into sin and concupiscence. But his distance from God is not the same as actual sin. It waits upon his decision. The same holds for all who inherit the legacy of exile. Because we are born as children of Adam, the momentum of our lives is away from God. Left to ourselves we choose always to believe the lie that we can live on bread alone, and with this choice, we enter into our inheritance with actual sin. "There is no man who does not sin" (1 Kgs. 8:46). It is a judgment taken up by Paul: "All have sinned" (Rom. 3:23). The sin that crouches by the door of our free choices inevitably enters, because we invite it in.

The doctrine of original sin seeks to convey the logic of this scriptural judgment. On the one hand, the legacy of Adam and Eve always leads to sin. And on the other hand, the "always" is a function of free choice, not human nature. Maintaining the "always" in conjunction with free choice can be difficult, because we are easily tempted to substitute some species of "necessity" to explain the "always." St. Augustine's speculations about the transmission of original sin through the sexual act and conception clearly lean in this direction. Just as the cause-and-effect sequence of physical life marches forward according to the laws of nature, by a similar mechanism sin infects the future, or so this way of thinking often seems to suggest.

The problem with an approach that locates the transmission of original sin in a natural process is obvious. If we explain the impulse toward sin by recourse to the physical reality of our humanity, then we end up contradicting the essential goodness of creation, which St. Augustine clearly did not wish to do (→3:1a). To avoid this danger, we need to recognize that, speculations aside, the doctrine of original sin has limited scope. It asserts rather than explains a fact about the human condition. The doctrine affirms *that* the children of Adam and Eve invariably sin; it does not specify *how* this gloomy fact works its way into every human life.

A doctrinal commitment to the infecting power of original sin does not entirely depend upon the story of the fall or the fate of Cain or our general observations of the human condition. Original sin is also an inference from the universal necessity of reconciliation in Christ. If some do not sin, then all are not redeemed in the death of Christ. But this contradicts a basic tenet of faith; therefore, all sin.[13] The difficulty of explaining how the first sin casts such a long and expansive shadow—and the complexity of showing how the ubiquity of sin is consistent with free choice and personal responsibility for all actual sins ("but you can master it")—is less of an obstacle to a coherent faith than denying the universality of sin and, by implication, denying the universal scope of Christ's saving death.

Genesis seems reluctant to explain how the sin crouching at the door enters. But one feature foreshadows Paul's seemingly paradoxical teaching that the law, though the divine instrument of righteousness, actually provokes and heightens sin (Rom. 3:20; 5:13, 20; 7:8–9). With Cain, God intervenes and gives counsel: in effect, "Do not let the sun go down on your anger, and give no opportunity to the devil" (Eph. 4:26–27). But the admonition to turn away from sin adds to rather than detracts from Cain's anger. As Augustine observes, God's instruction stiffens Cain's resolve, "for the fault of jealousy grew stronger, and he planned and carried out his brother's murder" (*City of God* 15.7, quoted from Bettenson 1972: 606).

Why was Cain angry in the first place? Again, the text is reticent, leaving ample room for speculation, which inevitably reflects the interpreter's more basic judgments about the original transgression of Adam and Eve, the first sin that infects the human race. Thus, *Targum Pseudo-Jonathan* depicts Cain as fathered by Adam, but in concert with a wicked angel, the same angel whose presence precipitated Eve's original transgression (Maher 1992: 31). Just as the devil gives birth to sin by way of his primal fall, he now gives birth to the primal sinner, Cain. Indeed, in our slavery to sin the devil gives birth to us all.

There is canonical support for this seemingly fanciful explanation. First John 3:10–12 distinguishes those born of God and those who are children of the devil. But as 1 John makes clear, we should not naturalize the source of our sinfulness, as if sin is inherited in the same way as blue eyes or brown hair. Our "birth" in Satan is the same as the counterbirth in Christ. Both are spiritual rather than natural. They give us our identities—we are shaped and formed by our loyalties—but neither birth gives us our natures. Our natural capacities are created, and human nature endures, no matter what form it takes as we exercise our innate powers. Because the image of birth can so quickly slide in a literal direction, we can easily fall into

---

13. The apparent exception is the Virgin Mary, but in a fully developed account of her sinlessness we see that she participates in Christ's redemptive death in an anticipatory but full way. Thus her sinlessness stems from her being prospectively saved from sin by Christ.

the gnostic reading: Cain sins because he receives the weighty burden of finite flesh or because he inherits demonic genes. It is a reading to be resisted.

Augustine's reading of Cain's murderous desire gives priority to God's election rather than to Cain's original moral character, and this allows Augustine to give a subtle interpretation that avoids these dangers of a naturalized account of human wickedness. The crux of the story, Augustine astutely notices, comes *after* the divine decision to prefer Abel's sacrifice rather than Cain's. Augustine digresses to explain why Cain's sacrifice was rejected by God, but it is clear in the larger context of his exegesis that what really matters is how Cain responds to God's initiative. By Augustine's account, Cain's anger is rooted in a self-regard that is jealous of his brother's successful sacrifice. "This is a sin which God particularly rebukes," Augustine writes, "namely, sulkiness about another's goodness, and a brother's goodness at that" (*City of God* 15.7, quoted from Bettenson 1972: 604). Instead of imitating his brother, Cain envies him. In this way, Augustine ends up following the larger Pauline insight: God's election—in this case the divine favor shown to Abel—precipitates sin. Although Augustine does not pursue the connection of Cain's sin to later brotherly enmity in Genesis, the notion that sin is stirred up by God's initiative anticipates a major theme of the later chapters of Genesis. Cain is angry about the LORD's preference for Abel, and he rebels against the divine plan that "the elder shall serve the younger" (Gen. 25:23). Like Joseph's brothers, who will nurse a murderous jealousy of Joseph's preeminence, Cain hates Abel "and could not speak peaceably to him" (37:4).

Augustine's reading is persuasive, not only because it gives cogent form to the cryptic Pauline claims about the actual effect of God's commandments and anticipates the later theme of brotherly jealousy in Genesis, but also because the exegesis has remarkable systematic integrity. The doctrine of creation out of nothing eliminates all the metaphysical resources necessary for a substantial account of evil. God creates all reality, and he calls it good. Therefore, as Augustine sees very clearly, nothing real can be evil. What we experience as evil, therefore, must be defined only over and against created goodness. It is a diminishment or privation of goodness. And this is precisely the narrative logic of Cain's murder of Abel. The good of worship sets the scene; the blessing of divine favor brings forth bitter jealousy; the righteous counsel of God heightens the enmity: in each instance Cain's sin takes on a reactive quality. It negates rather than affirms; it rejects rather than embraces. Murder is the fitting endpoint: Cain destroys the one whom God loves.

Augustine's explanation of evil as privation of goodness can seem abstract and unreal in its own right. How can we say that evil is *unreal* when we experience it as such a powerful and painful force in our lives. Part of Augustine's genius was undoubtedly his ability to suggest how metaphysical truths have historical or existential reality, which we see so clearly in Cain. Reality is the created order, and the created order is tensed with the possibility of fellowship with God. At its deepest level, then, evil is not an abstract privation of goodness. It is a demurral from the future that God intends for creation in the beginning. God wants to bring things to fulfillment in the seventh day. He calls us to enter into his Sabbath rest. In contrast, evil wants _____. We cannot, in fact, fill in the blank. Like Cain's anger, evil wants nothing stable. Abel's death serves no purpose other than to negate God's favor and mercy.

Evil rarely aims directly at the empty void of death. At times, evil acts are motivated by desires for pleasure. At other times evil is motivated by a desire for status or novelty or any number of other real but finite goods. But these motives never last, and they cannot serve as a permanent basis and purpose for human life. True enough, Adam and Eve eat the apple, but they immediately discard it. Thus, taken generally, evil wants all sorts of particular things but nothing overall. Evil is coherent only when defined negatively. As Cain's murder of Abel epitomizes, evil is the desire for anything other than the fulfillment of God's purpose from the beginning. In the perverse blindness of this desire, even murder and death are better than the triumph of divine love.

Pure evil cannot exist in any positive or enduring sense. As God says to Cain, "You shall be a fugitive and a wanderer on the earth" (4:12). But our evil desires invariably seek to rest in substantive affirmations rather than mere negations. As Cain laments, "My punishment is greater than I can bear" (4:13). The human heart wants to rest in a lasting loyalty rather than wander in an endless cycle of negation. The desire of wickedness for rest explains the fundamental importance of idols in human life. We give ourselves to the finite goods that we imagine will endure as our ultimate good. These idols, some graven in metal and stone, others in theories and philosophies of life, give the empty rejection of God's love the illusion of an alternative path for history and for life.

Modern humanism claims to deliver us from our restless condition. We are not to struggle over the final meaning of history or the ultimate purpose for life. We are not to throw ourselves into any grand affirmations. Instead, we are to simply live. We should embrace reality as it is, and not compulsively seek to bend it one way or another. This, it seems to me, is the thrust of a great deal of postmodern philosophy: set aside grand narratives, renounce the desire for deep and lasting knowledge, give up fantasies about truth. The goal is not to cultivate a nihilistic despair. After all, a cosmic rejection of a divinely ordained purpose for creation is as vainglorious as a universal affirmation. Instead, the postmodern approach—which has its roots in the modest but urgent humanism that runs from Montaigne through Hume to twentieth-century figures such as Albert Camus—wishes to encourage a humane clarity about the fragile, finite, and irreducible particularity of our lives. Let us no longer imagine ourselves children of the devil or children of God, it urges. Let us see ourselves as merely human.

Cain, a play by Lord Byron, explores the personality of Cain in a way that sheds some light on the possibility of a third way, the humanistic stance between a "yes" to God's call to fellowship and the nihilistic "no" that embraces the devil's clearsighted rejection of the divine plan.[14] The result is an extended retelling of the original murder that is fanciful with respect to the account in Genesis, but deadly serious about the way in which modern humanism collides with the life of piety.

The play opens with a scene of religious devotion. The entire family of Adam and Eve gathers to offer prayers of thanksgiving to God. But Cain cannot join. The curse of mortality oppresses him. He cannot give thanks for the good gifts of life, because he knows himself doomed to die. Cain's rightful sense that death is wrong stiffens his resolve. Yes, original sin merits punishment, but Cain asks, "What had *I* done in this? I was unborn."[15] Yes, God has the right to command and prohibit, but why did God perversely plant a tree that would tempt, and why at the very center of the garden where it would attract attention? Still again, they say God is all-powerful and perfectly good, but Cain observes, "I judge but by the fruits—and they are bitter—which I must feed on for a fault not mine."[16]

Doubting God's justice and goodness, Byron's Cain would seem a sure candidate for alliance with Lucifer, the original rebel. But it is not so. In the longest scenes of the play, Byron portrays Lucifer engaging Cain in conversation, first on earth and then in the shadowy realms of hell itself. At every turn Lucifer encourages Cain's unbelief and tempts him with the promise of bittersweet happiness: he can achieve immortality by embracing and affirming death as the proper and true end for human beings. "It may be death leads to the highest knowledge," counsels Lucifer, "and being of all things the sole thing certain."[17] In other words, accept human mortality and dissolution into dust as a law of life, and you will be at peace with your circumstances. It is an ancient counsel familiar to Lucretius and other materialist philosophers, and it is very much in the air these days.

But Cain will no more fall down and worship Lucifer down below than he will offer prayers to the glory of God on high. He loves existence too much to embrace and affirm death. In this sense, Cain is a modern humanist after the fashion of Albert Camus—or perhaps it is more accurate to say that Camus was a humanist in the way that Byron was. Cain resists the lure of death. "I thirst for good," Cain protests.[18] But he cannot believe in God and the promise of eternal life. Cain will serve neither God nor the devil. He wants to remain neutral, loyal to life alone.

Can it be so? The Bible as a whole consistently speaks against any lasting middle position between a saving faith and a damning unbelief. Theologians can theorize about the fullness of time that God gives for us to work out our salvation in fear and trembling, but as St. Augustine observes in *City of God*, there are only two cities, one earthly and doomed to perdition, and the other heavenly and redeemed

---

14. Truman Guy Steffan, *Lord Byron's Cain* (Austin: University of Texas Press, 1968).
15. Ibid., 163 (emphasis original).
16. Ibid., 164.
17. Ibid., 212.
18. Ibid., 216.

by God. There is no third, neutral option. Byron seems to agree. Much like the gospel accounts of Satan's temptation of Jesus, he has Lucifer give voice to an orthodox theological judgment. He observes in his cold, matter of fact way, "He who bows not to him has bowed to me!"[19]

Lucifer's pronouncement is the turning point of the play. A long scene in hell follows, but the drama is largely at an emotional standstill (which is very likely why it was a failure on the stage). Cain swings between a despairing hatred of his own mortality and a love of the beauty of existence, but he does not move to a decision. He remains uncommitted. He will neither damn God nor worship him.

In the climactic scene, Abel approaches Cain. The younger brother has prepared a sacrifice to the Almighty, and he wishes his older brother to join him. He sees his brother agitated by dark thoughts, and he wants to share with him the peace that comes from an affirmation of God's providential love. Abel defers to his elder brother, the model of solicitude. He has built two altars, and he wants Cain to take precedence before God as the firstborn. Cain resists this idea, but soon enough Abel's sweet piety coaxes him to cooperate in the joint offering to God.

It is in the smoke that surrounds the altars of sacrifice that Cain becomes inflamed with anger. Cain offers a diffident prayer to God—something like a contemporary Unitarian-Universalist appeal to God, whomever he or she may be. When the sign from God indicates that Cain's sacrifice has been rejected, Abel does not gloat or distance himself from Cain. Instead, he pleads with Cain to offer another, more fitting sacrifice. However the ambivalent Cain has now become steely and determined. "I will build no altars," he announces, "nor suffer any."[20]

Byron is, I think, quite perceptive as he depicts Cain hurtling toward murder. The piety he tolerated in his brother now enrages him. The sacrificial ritual he had so halfheartedly performed now disgusts him. Cain's ambivalent neutrality is now being forced toward decision by the reality of his brother's faith. He will not thank God for what he hates: the reality of life lived under the curse of death. The very idea of holiness seems to throw the small pleasures and finite goods of life into a dark shadow of insignificance. When faced with his brother's determination to give another offering to God, Cain asks: "I have toiled and tilled and sweaten in the sun according to the curse; must I do more?"[21] Shall we add still more burdens, the burdens of piety and obedience to God, when we are already heavily laden with the challenges of simply living authentic human lives? Thus, before the altar of sacrifice, Cain's decision comes clear. "Give way!" he screams as he pushes toward Abel's altar to destroy it: "This bloody record shall not stand in the sun to shame creation."[22] Faced with piety, unbelief will not—and, as Byron suggests, cannot—stand at ease.

19. Ibid., 176.
20. Ibid., 243.
21. Ibid., 234.
22. Ibid., 244.

Nor will or can faith. In Byron's account, Abel does not allow Cain to desecrate the altar. He stands to bar the way. "If thou lov'st thyself," warns Cain, "stand back."[23] Of course, Abel loves God, and thus he precisely does not love himself. "I love God far more," he confesses, "than life."[24] These words of faith, at once simple and fundamental, bring Cain to the white heat of homicidal fury. How can his brother betray the one, fragile, finite but beautiful thing we have—human life? The die is cast. "Then take thy life unto God," Cain replies, "since he loves lives."[25] Taking up a flaming brand, Cain strikes his brother down. Thus, for Byron, Cain's primal murder is not a premeditated act motivated by an envy of God's favor for Abel; it is instead a blind, enraged act of loyalty to worldly life in all its imperfections and limitations. It is an act of protest that seeks to defend our fragile, temporary hold on life against the impulse to transfer our loyalty to something higher, something greater, something transcendent and suprahuman—something, therefore, that the humanist cannot help but regard as antihuman.

Christians should seek to enlist as many as possible in the cause of humanity. It is one of the central principles of the Genesis account of creation that that grace of the seventh day perfects rather than destroys the nature created on the prior six days. For this reason, most Christian traditions have not formulated sharp antagonisms between Christ and culture, between church and world, between revealed truths and the truths accessible by natural reason, or between men and women of good will and believers in Christ. As the Second Vatican Council made clear for Catholic theology and practice, we don't all need to believe in the God who raises Jesus from the dead in order to share and support a humane social order.

Yet what is possible in theory often remains painfully remote in life. As Byron recognized, modern humanism can easily become cruelly jealous of the modest claims it makes on behalf of the noble but fragile human condition. To believe in something *more*, to hope for something that transcends rather than simply continues our present mode of life, to love something as more precious that life itself—the central yearning desire that animates the life of faith can easily seem a betrayal of the finite goods that the humanist thinks we should cherish. Of this Byron was acutely aware: the ambitions of faith intrude upon the present and force the issue of our deepest loyalty and love. As St. Augustine observed, we are disposed toward that which is higher; we stretch toward God. This thirst for God, this God-smitten fact about our humanity helps explain the rhetorical violence of modern crusaders against belief. They accurately fear the contagion of piety. To defend the finite goods of this world against the perceived assaults of holiness, they turn the earthly city into a fortress and drive out anyone they see as disloyal to its this-worldly principles. When faced with faith in God's plan on our behalf, what seems like a modest and humane affirmation of the finite goods of this world all too quickly gathers itself into a violent posture of negation.

23. Ibid.
24. Ibid.
25. Ibid.

4:8 Cain rose up against his brother Abel, and killed him.

"Alas!" says Eve in Byron's *Cain*, "the fruit of our forbidden tree begins to fall."[26] What began as wrongful eating is now murder. In the wake of the murder, Cain behaves like Adam and Eve in the garden. When asked by the LORD, "Where is Abel your brother?" he imagines that he can hide his actions from God. Cain answers, "I do not know; am I my brother's keeper?" (4:9). Punishment is forthcoming, and the direction of humanity's expulsion from the garden is reiterated: "Cain went away from the presence of the LORD" (4:16).

The order of transgression and expulsion in Gen. 3 is not simply recapitulated. Because the fall is a trajectory and not a singular event, it is intensified. Obedience to the lie has a dark future, a future of death. "You shall not die," promises Satan. On the contrary, we may indeed live as we wish and according to our natural desires. We can have lovely, tasty fruit—and as Cain shows we can follow our enraged desire to eliminate all those who stand in the way of our hopes and dreams. "From the misuse of free will," writes St. Augustine of the long shadow cast by the original transgression, "there started a chain of disasters" (*City of God* 13.14, quoted from Bettenson 1972: 523). The gift of physical life can provide an at least temporary basis for wickedness.

In Abel's murder, the logic of the fall is now clear. "The fruit of righteousness is a tree of life, but lawlessness takes away lives" (Prov. 11:30). "He who does not love abides in death" (1 John 3:14). In Adam sin comes into the world, and through Cain death (cf. Rom. 5:12). Compare this logic with the countermovement of redemption. Through one man we receive the free gift of grace (cf. 5:14), and he teaches the opposite of Cain, who will not be his brother's keeper: "Greater love hath no man than this, that a man lay down his life for his friends" (John 15:13 AV). The two futures—one in loyalty to the lie and the other in obedience to the covenant—are antithetical. We will be either children of the devil or children of God. "This is the message which you have heard from the beginning," writes the author of 1 John about Christian fellowship, "that we should love one another, and not be like Cain who was of the evil one and murdered his brother" (3:11–12). Cain farmed the land, and his murder of Abel was as a beating of his plowshare into a sword; the alternative future does not ignore or forget or sidestep Cain's deed. The way of the covenant goes down exactly the same paths of sacrifice, blood, and death, but it goes in the opposite direction, beating swords into plowshares.

Augustine depicts these two futures as two fellowships, two cities knit together by two very different goals. "The two cities," he writes, "were created by two kinds of love: the earthly city was created by self-love reaching the point of contempt for God, the Heavenly City by the love of God carried as far as contempt of self" (*City of God* 14.28, quoted from Bettenson 1972: 593). The antithesis is not physical or metaphysical. The earthly city is not to be equated with embodiment, and the

26. Ibid., 161.

heavenly city with ethereal, spiritual existence. Nor is the earthly city simply the secular political realm set in contrast to the sacramental life of the church. Cain and Abel are both men with bodies, both participate in the economy of sacrifice, both are animated by a natural desire for God. Yet, according to St. Augustine's reading of Gen. 4, "Cain . . . belonged to the city of man; the later son, Abel, belonged to the City of God." They are citizens of the two cities by virtue of their loyalties. Cain remains in bondage to the future chosen by Adam and Eve. He lives only in the sense of surviving. His plaintive cry to God for mercy gives a clear indication: "My punishment is greater than I can bear," because "I shall be a fugitive and a wanderer on the earth, and whoever finds me will slay me" (Gen. 4:13–14). In contrast, by Augustine's reckoning, Abel is "predestined by grace, and chosen by grace" (*City of God* 15.1, quoted from Bettenson 1972: 596). But Abel is dead. Whatever life he lives in grace must wait for the calling of Abraham in order to emerge as an embodied, human reality.

4:10 Your brother's blood is crying.

The image has a complex, twofold meaning. On the one hand, the blood of life mixes with the earth out of which Adam was formed, and it cries out. Abel's death is contrary to the purpose woven into the fabric of creation from the beginning. The blood cries out because murder violates the moral law, which is a law of nature. What is wrong is not only contrary to what is right; it contradicts and offends against what is real. This is one reason why evil can reign but never triumph. Generations of indoctrination in the Soviet Union could not succeed in extinguishing an awareness of the essential brutality of the regime. The many justifications for Jim Crow racism in the American South could not entirely obscure the natural equality of human beings.

Nonetheless, the crying out of Abel's blood also signifies the painful fact that wickedness, however contrary to reality, seems able to endure and even flourish. "The nations conspire" (Ps. 2:1), "the wicked hotly pursue the poor" (10:2), and the "prophets and wise men and scribes" sent to restore the covenant of the LORD are killed and crucified (Matt. 23:34). Abel's blood cries out, not only as a protest, but also as an appeal to God: "Why dost thou stand afar off, O LORD?" (Ps. 10:1). "Arise, O LORD! Let not man prevail; let the nations be judged before thee!" (9:19–20). Render judgment, the blood petitions, so that upon the wicked "may come all the righteous blood shed on the earth, from the blood of innocent Abel to the blood of Zechariah" (Matt. 23:35).

God respects the blood of the innocent: "I will execute judgment: I am the LORD" (Exod. 12:12). But in his punishment of Cain, the LORD does not wash away the blood of one man with the blood of another. Cain is not killed in order to balance out the killing of Abel. Instead, in judgment the LORD can "see the blood" of the Passover and the blood of the paschal lamb, Jesus Christ, which "speaks more graciously than the blood of Abel" (Heb. 12:24). In the eyes of God, blood does not demand blood in an unending cycle of death. Instead, the blood of Christ purifies ("the blood of Jesus his Son cleanses"; 1 John 1:7) and changes the future ("freed us from our sins by his blood"; Rev. 1:5). We are not burdened with the unquenchable cry for retribution.

4:12 A fugitive and a wanderer.

How do we square Cain's wandering with the subsequent report that he settles "east of Eden" (4:16) and builds a city named after his son, Enoch (4:17)? The paradox is apparent rather than real, as our experience demonstrates. A great deal of modern humanism encourages us to overcome our religious fantasies and affirm the finite world of flesh and blood as our true inheritance. Instead of pining for the transcendent, we should be loyal to the present. Instead of trying to be citizens of heaven, we should be happy with our citizenship in this world.

The problem, however, is that we cannot settle down into the city of Enoch or any earthly city. Because the human creature is created for the future of fellowship with God, we are amphibious and we cannot rest in the world. We cannot find lasting rest in human projects, whether amassing wealth or assuming power or satisfying passions and desires or any other worldly endeavor. Libertines will groan in their overindulgence—or take to the streets to protest against the repressions of society that they imagine still limit them and deny them the rest they seek. Our age is full of fugitives and wanderers, resolute in their loyalty to the earthly city as they pant and strain for more. Even being normal and well adjusted becomes an anxious project surrounded by an industry of counselors and self-help books.

Citizenship in Cain's city, the earthly city, requires loyalty to the covenant of Satan's lie, the promise that this world will be sufficient for the fullness of life that we desire. This citizenship cannot help but give rise to dissatisfied agitation. We become fugitives and wanderers trying to find ways to do the impossible: to be fully and honestly loyal to our worldly hopes. This is why the larger vision of the Bible so consistently divides our human future into two religious destinies: we either turn to seek God, or we perform a spiritual alchemy that transforms our finite commitments into idols rich with imagined mystery and power.

4:15 Mark on Cain.

What is the mark that protects Cain as he wanders in the city of his founding? The text gives no clue as to the nature of the mysterious mark. An Aramaic version of Genesis, however, suggests that God lends Cain the power of his holiness as a protection against retribution: "Then the Lord traced on Cain's face a letter of the great and glorious Name, so that anyone who would find him, upon seeing it on him, would not kill him" (Maher 1992: 34).

This reading may seem fanciful, but the larger canonical context encourages an interpretation of the mark along these lines. Aaron's priestly garments include a plate of gold engraved with the words "Holy to the LORD," and we read that "it shall always be upon his forehead" as he takes the offerings of the people of Israel before the LORD (Exod. 28:36–38). This marking is extended to all the people in the commandment for the daily use of tefillin, the ritual act of strapping to one's forearms and forehead small boxes containing a portion of scripture: "You shall therefore lay up these words of mine in your heart and in your soul; and you shall bind them as a sign upon your hand, and they shall be as frontlets between your eyes" (Deut. 11:18). The idea of a mark of holiness on the forehead recurs in the Old Testament. During the apostasy of the house of Israel, the LORD commissions "the man clothed in linen" to put a Passover mark on the few who remain righteous. "Put a mark," God commands, "upon the foreheads of the men who sigh and groan over all the abominations that are committed in [Jerusalem]." As is the case with Cain, the mark protects from destruction. For six men of vengeance are to "pass through the city after him, and smite . . . , but touch no one upon whom is the mark" (Ezek. 9:3–6).

Revelation takes up the same role for marking. The forehead becomes the place where the servants are sealed in the service of the master (Rev. 7:3). Some are marked for service to Satan. Of the martyrs, however, John's vision testifies that they "had not worshiped the beast or its image and had not received its mark on their foreheads or on their hands" (20:4). The servants of the Lamb "shall see his face, and his name shall be on their foreheads" (22:4). They make up the company of the elect: "I looked, and lo, on Mount Zion stood the Lamb, and with him a hundred and forty-four thousand who had his name and his Father's name written on their foreheads" (14:1).

The ancient church followed the biblical witness. Marking the forehead with the sign of the cross was part of the ritual of initiation for those seeking baptism, a practice that continues to this day. Thus, Augustine can appeal to the baptismal mark as a lasting emblem of loyalty. "Belonging to Christ," he writes, "upon the forehead we bear His sign" (*Tractates on John* 3.2 in NPNF[1] 7.19).

4:23 Lamech said to his wives.

Time does not stand still in Genesis. Instead, what is latent comes to the fore; the seed of the future develops to maturity. Where Adam and Eve eat, Cain murders. Where Cain murders and then pleads with God for mercy, Lamech murders and then boasts of his deadly anger: "I have slain a man for wounding me, a young man for striking me" (4:23). Lamech's voice brags about rather than laments his fate: "If Cain is avenged sevenfold, truly Lamech is avenged seventy-sevenfold"

(4:24). "Hah," Lamech says, "Cain killed his brother in a fit of anger, but I've killed a young man simply because he inconvenienced me, simply because he offended my honor, and unlike Cain I'm man enough to face my future." Like the frenzied crowd in Jerusalem who cry "Crucify him! Crucify him!" Lamech embraces the covenant of Satan's lie. The crazy, impossible dream of countermanding the divine plan that began with a tasty fruit and the promise of life now spirals toward a forthright lust for death.

3

DEAD ENDS

"Never again" (8:21)

5:1 The book of the generations.

Genealogies evoke the forward thrust of time. They are emblems of the future. The return to Adam as the source of the generations, including an explicit repetition of the first creation of the original man and woman, signals a restarting of primal history. This new genesis, coming after the descent of Cain's line into the pit of death, evokes the possibility of new future, one not implicated in the first transgression. It is as if the incoming tide of sin has so flooded the human condition that a new beginning must be made. And in this genealogy, tellingly, Cain and his progeny are excluded. The future evoked seems to bend away from the trajectory of sin.

In a sense, therefore, we can say that Gen. 4–5 expresses the full cycle of decay and cleansing so prominent in the larger sweep of Genesis from the fall to Noah and the flood story. Lamech signals the bitter end of a genealogy of sin, the equivalent of the great wickedness in Noah's time that grieved the LORD (6:6). Now, beginning again with Adam, a countergenealogy erases Cain (and Abel) from memory, just as the flood destroys the inhabitants of the earth.

The cleansing of memory in a fashion that parallels the purifying floodwaters gives us a clue. Just as the flood fails to deliver the world from sin, the countergenealogy from Adam based on forgetfulness fails. Seth is not born in the image and likeness of God, but instead in the image of Adam, his father: "When Adam had lived a hundred and thirty years, he became the father of a son in his own likeness, after his image, and named him Seth" (5:3). Seth is enrolled with Adam in the project of physical survival that brings death as its future. He cannot help but live in the shadow of the first sin. The patriarchs of old live long lives, but they die in the end. Thus the genealogy flowing from Adam gives us a picture of a fresh but failed effort to escape the gravitational force of the first sin. Even as the genealogy begins anew with Seth, he and his descendents slowly but inevitably trace a declining arc toward the target of death.

The pessimism latent in this genealogy and its foreshadowing of the flood narrative tell us something important about the opening chapters of Genesis. They are preoccupied with beginnings: the beginning of all things, of course, but also the genesis of our fantasies about finding a way out of the legacy of sin by starting over again. The warning of this chapter is clear: we cannot forgive and forget. Even if Cain is erased from history, the children of Adam fall under the sway of sin. This holds for the radical erasure caused by the flood as well. The divinely ordained cleansing of the entire created order does not succeed in altering the future of sin. We cannot simply stop the forward flow of history and wipe the slate clean.

Genesis 5–11 is often opaque. Readers feel the text moving in fits and starts. But as a whole the diverse material speaks clearly. The various dead ends suggest that the solution to the distorting power of sin will not come by way of the new beginnings so often favored by utopian dreamers. God's plan does not involve a radical reengineering of human life after the fashion of one of Stalin's five-year plans, nor does it depend upon a method of therapeutic reconciliation that puts bad experiences behind us. The remote and timeless hand of God does not press an automatic reset button. Instead, with the calling of Abraham in Gen. 12, God does not start the human race over again. Abraham is not a new genesis. Instead the promises to Abraham create the possibility of a new future that divides rather than restarts history.

5:24 Enoch walked with God.

In the previous section we saw that for all its hopeful beginnings in Seth the genealogy has the same hopeless logic as the genealogy of Cain—and as the flood story (though the theological meaning of the flood account is much more complicated). But what of Enoch? To "walk with God" signals righteousness, and he did not die, but instead was "taken" by God.

In the Jewish and Christian traditions, Enoch is read as someone who merits exemption from the general trend of humanity toward destruction. *Targum Pseudo-Jonathan* portrays him as "worship[ing] in truth before the Lord" and ascending into heaven to take up the role of "the great scribe" (Maher 1992: 36–37). Sirach 44:16 pictures him as the model of repentance: "Enoch pleased the Lord, and was taken up; he was an example of repentance to all generations."

Jude 14–15 assigns him the role of prophet. Across these differences a common pattern emerges. The strange and unique fate of Enoch serves as a screen on which to project an account of how righteousness is possible even amid a humanity whose history is defined by sin.

Hebrews illustrates. Enoch's deliverance from the punishment of death was not arbitrary: "Now before he was taken he was attested as having pleased God" (11:5). And how did Enoch please God? Genesis is silent, of course. So, as did the editors of the targum, the writers of Sirach, and the author of Jude, the author of Hebrews reasons backward from a theological account of salvation developed in an overall reading of scripture to arrive at an exegetical judgment about Enoch. "Without faith it is impossible to please [God]" (11:6), and therefore we can infer that "by faith Enoch was taken up so that he should not see death" (11:5). Like rightful worship and knowledge of the law (*Targum Pseudo-Jonathan*), repentance (Sirach), and the gift of prophesy (Jude), the saving power of faith is a this-worldly possibility for all of us. Even Enoch, born into a genealogy that goes from Adam to the wicked generation of the flood, can participate in God's redemptive plan.

The larger point bears on Reformation controversies. The Reformers placed such a great emphasis on the debilitating effects of original sin, and they attacked so vigorously the concept of merit, that Catholic opponents often supposed that Reformation doctrine effectively denied the possibility of any form of life pleasing to God in this world. Volleys of polemic went back and forth. Catholics accused Protestants of denying the efficacy of grace, and Protestants accused Catholics of denying the necessity of grace. Yet beneath this furious antagonism there seems to have been a more fundamental but hidden consensus. Both Protestants and Catholics largely followed the general lines of the intracanonical interpretation of Enoch. But for the victory of Christ, a victory still working its way toward final triumph, the current of sin races toward the disaster of death. The good news is that now—and even from the very beginning of human history—God has made it possible to taste the fruits of that triumph.

The Reformation debate about faith and works focused on disagreements about how to describe the possibility of participating in the righteousness of Christ rather than whether to affirm it. The fathers at the Council of Trent endorsed the human capacity to perform meritorious works (always, of course, made possible only by the prevenient grace of God), while the Reformers pointed to faith (also always made possible only by the prevenient grace of God) as the sine qua non of a life pleasing to God. I cannot pretend to resolve this debate, which in spite of important ecumenical statements that underline essential compatibilities remains very much alive in the culture of contemporary Christianity. But it is important to see the underlying consensus that was always present. Here and now, and even in the most inauspicious circumstances, a life pleasing to God is possible. The affirmation is especially important today, because a desire to blend into modern post-Christian culture has tempted modern Protestant theology to adopt the

Catholic assessment of Reformation teaching, treating any distinctively Christian form of life as an instance of "works-righteousness."[1]

6:2 The sons of God saw that the daughters of men were fair.

It is not easy to identify just what the text wishes to convey by the miscegenation of "sons of God" with "daughters of men." Perhaps the verse signals an ongoing and ill-fated commerce between fallen angels and fallen humanity. The Septuagint tradition suggests as much with its formulation "angels of God." By this reading, "the mighty men that were of old, the men of renown" (6:4)—and again the Septuagint encourages this train of interpretation by calling them "giants"—are the progeny of spiritual beings and fallen humanity: enlarged with demonic powers and able to dominate in the earthly realm.[2] But perhaps recourse to fallen angels stretches the text too far, and we should read the verse as signaling the broad decline of humanity into the covenant of the lie. The trajectory from "sons of God" to "daughters of men" symbolizes the decline of history into a singular focus on physical life as the end or purpose of human striving. With this approach we can gloss God's judgment that he will not "abide in man for ever, for he is flesh" (6:3) in the following way: "I will not abide in man, for he has become entirely a slave of the flesh." For as Paul observes, "The mind that is set on the flesh is hostile to God; it does not submit to God's law, indeed it cannot" (Rom. 8:7).

The specific form of decline remains open for speculation, but the larger significance is clear. The flood story begins with emphasis on the disaster of sin: "Do not be mismatched," warns Paul, "for what partnership have righteousness and iniquity?" (2 Cor. 6:14). The mismatching began with Adam and Eve. They did not marry their wills to God's purpose for creation; instead, they turned and wed themselves to the lie that worldly goods are the highest good. Just as wrongful eating becomes wrongful killing in Cain, once again Genesis emphasizes a trajectory of intensified consequences as the genealogy of Seth heads toward disaster. "The LORD saw that the wickedness of man was great in the earth," and there was "only evil continually" (Gen. 6:5). It is Lamech all over again (→4:23). The descendants of Adam and Eve live in "a covenant with death" (Isa. 28:15). "The

---

1. David Yeago, "Gnosticism, Antinomianism, and Reformation Theology: Reflections on the Costs of a Construal," *Pro ecclesia* 2.1 (Winter 1993): 37–49.

2. The Septuagint reading has, apparently, returned to favor. Von Rad 1972: 114 writes: "The question, which has been asked from the time of the early church down to our own day, whether, namely, the 'sons of God' are to be understood as angelic beings or as men ... can be considered finally settled." They are "beings of the upper heavenly world." One doubts that the answer remains settled, however. For an early Christian reading along these lines, see Lactantius, *Divine Institutes* 2.15 (ANF 7.64). For a patristic argument against reading "sons of God" as angelic beings, see Chrysostom, *Homilies on Genesis* 22.6 (FC 82.71–72). The long history of exegetical debate, as well as the relatively fixed range of arguments for and against, testify that much modern biblical study often reframes rather than resolves interpretive debates.

earth was filled with violence" and "all flesh had corrupted their way upon the earth" (Gen. 6:11–12), and so "the earth lies polluted under its inhabitants" (Isa. 24:5); "the earth was corrupt in God's sight" (Gen. 6:11).

6:6 The Lord was sorry.

It seems strange for the Bible to say that God was sorry. Did he regret creating the world because his plan was defeated by the power of evil? Is he like the father of a rebellious teenager, sadly looking back and wishing he had done a better job? Here and in so many other places in the Bible we need to be careful. God is not one thing among others in the world. God is not just another person, another mind, another soul. Therefore, scriptural descriptions of God need to be read carefully.

In general, words mediate by signifying or triggering appropriate thoughts in our minds. We hear somebody say, "It's raining outside," and we come to the appropriate mental state of thinking about rain outside. The words point to a fact about the weather. Another person might say, "I'm angry," and in so doing suggest a mental state or emotion. Signs obviously cannot refer to God in this way. God is certainly not a state of affairs or a fact about the world, nor is God a mental state or emotion that we can experience. God transcends creation and cannot be observed or experienced. This is why verses such as "they heard the sound of the Lord God walking in the garden" (3:8) and "the Lord was sorry that he had made man on the earth" (6:6) cannot be read literally. To do so would entail allowing ourselves to become bewitched by the directness of the language into supposing that signs could convey facts about God or indicate mental states that God has.

Too often modern biblical readers presume a false dichotomy. Either signs convey something discrete and digestible, something we can point to or identify as the clear referent, or they convey nothing at all. Either we say something that can be understood on its own terms, or we are speaking nonsense. But this is palpably false. A great deal of what is important in human communication is dependent upon complex, interlocking systems of sentences. Consider the final lines of "The Second Coming," W. B. Yeats's poem of dark foreboding: "And what rough beast, / its hour come round at last, / Slouches toward Bethlehem to be born?" The signs are poetic and not factual. The literal sense might stimulate thoughts of a mangy grizzly bear lumbering toward a Palestinian village, but the mental image is patently misguided, or at least inadequate to the interplay of signs. Instead, our minds are encouraged to move in any number of directions: toward grimy industrialization, toward militaristic nationalism, toward beer-sodden brawlers on road trips to distant soccer matches. A good reader knows how to refer back to earlier lines in the poem to build a case for one reading or another—or to other poems by Yeats, or images from other poets, or historical context, or general knowledge, or, by Yeats's own suggestion, verses from the biblical text itself.

There is nothing uniquely poetical about this process. When we learn modern physics, words such as "mass" and "energy" and "time" take on very specific meanings that are expressed in mathematical formulas that convey their relationships rather than defining the terms by reference to facts or experiences. As a student of physics quickly discovers, obvious facts about mass and time turn out to be false, not true. Scriptural statements about God work in the same way. Therefore, sentences that describe divine action or emotions must be read as part of the overall system of scriptural language, designed to convey our minds toward divine reality rather than conveying divine reality to our minds.

God is no more sorrowful or angry in a human way than the weight of an object is its mass. Our sin does not evoke an emotion of grief or regret in God, at least not of the sort we can identify in our own lives. Since God is the source of creation itself, we must think of God sorrowing only in a way consistent with the complete absence of the vulnerability, despair, and impotence that are so closely associated with human experiences of sorrow, grief, and regret—that is, God sorrows in a way unfamiliar to our experience. But this denial of an inner-worldly sense for divine sorrow does not make the verse meaningless. Reference to divine sorrow suggests that humanity is deeply relevant to God's identity. What happens to us matters fundamentally to God, so much so that God cannot be God if our sin has the final say over the future of creation. In this sense, our sin grieves the LORD. It strikes to the quick of his inner life. Our sin enters into the love of the Holy Spirit that binds the Father to the Son, giving that love a specific, cruciform shape.

6:8 Noah found favor in the eyes of the LORD.

The contrast between Noah and "the mighty men that were of old" (6:4) is striking. What brings renown in the world and satisfies human standards of wisdom and excellence is not what pleases God. What counts as "wise according to worldly standards," what counts as "powerful" and "of noble birth," stands in contrast to "the foolishness of God [that] is wiser than men" (1 Cor. 1:25–26). The covenant of the devil's lie creates its own culture, its own economy of praise and blame, and that culture presses toward death, an end antithetical to the Sabbath for which the human creature is created. As Paul writes, "If I were still pleasing to men, I should not be servant of Christ" (Gal. 1:10). Noah is not pleasing to his generation, but he finds favor with God.

In a surprising way, Noah foreshadows the role of Mary. Like Noah, she finds favor in the eyes of the LORD. "Hail, O favored one," says the angle of annunciation, "the Lord is with you" (Luke 1:28). And like Noah, Mary cannot count her favor as a reward, for the grace of God "depends not upon man's will or exertion, but upon God's mercy" (Rom. 9:16). Furthermore, one of the most striking features of Noah's relation to God is his passivity. He does not formulate a plan or make independent preparations for the flood. He never speaks. He waits upon the LORD in his silence, suggesting very much the passivity of one chosen to bear the savior: "Let it be to me according to your word" (Luke 1:38).

Noah builds the ark. It is certainly a moment of busy human agency, but the action in no way alters the priority of God's agency. We should not confuse human activity with human independence: "Unless the LORD builds the house, those who build it labor in vain" (Ps. 127:1). At no point does the narrative suggest any controlling factor in Noah's life other than God's initiative. God conveys the design of the ark just as he lays out the architecture of the tabernacle and announces the role assigned to Mary. Of his role, Noah can only say, "He reached from on high, he took me, he drew me out of many waters" (18:16).

6:13 I will destroy them with the earth.

Sin pushes toward its self-chosen future: death, the dissolution of our flesh that simulates the nonbeing of pure evil. But God will not remain passive, and his response involves using the primal power of water to give evil what it wants: "The LORD will lay waste the earth and make it desolate" (Isa. 24:1). God will not preserve "the old way which wicked men have trod" (Job 22:15). "They [will be] snatched away before their time; their foundation [shall be] washed away" (22:16) "when the overwhelming scourge passes through" (Isa. 28:15). "With an overwhelming flood he will make a full end of his adversaries" (Nah. 1:8). As was the case in the garden, God punishes fittingly. He gives evil the dissolving, disintegrating future it seeks (→3:14). Contrast this with the conquering "water of life [that is] flowing from the throne of God and of the Lamb" (Rev. 22:1). The waters of the deep that flood the earth signify the primal vitality of biological life, which has no future in itself, but only the endless cycles of birth and death. They are the primal, undifferentiated waters first separated and ordered on the second day of creation (Gen. 1:6–8). In contrast, the water of life that comes from the throne of God and the Lamb signify the refreshment of the Sabbath rest of the seventh day. It is the life-giving water of the river that flows out of Eden that divides and irrigates the whole earth in the second account of creation (2:10–14).

A spiritual sense also follows the pattern of fitting punishment. To inundate sinners with the natural elements is to fulfill the desire of Adam and Eve to rest in finite things. God does not pour out an alien wrath or muster an invading force. He opens the floodgates of our desire for things of the earth. The flood is what happens when the decision of Adam and Eve is given free reign. We drown in the consummation of our finite loves. The soul that desires pleasures of food and drink becomes bloated and bursts. Envy finds perverse pleasure in implacable grudges. Anger burns and overflows. Greed piles up coins and hungers for more. We want to live by bread alone, and in the flood, God allows water, the primal power of finite, organic life, to reign supreme.

6:14 Make yourself an ark.

An extended ode in 4 Maccabees 15 to the mother of seven martyred brothers takes up the Noah story as a rhetorical device: "Just as Noah's ark, carrying the world in the universal flood, stoutly endured the waves, so you, O guardian of the law, overwhelmed from every side by the flood of your emotions and the violent winds, the torture of your sons, endured nobly and withstood the wintry storms that assail religion" (15:31–32). A life disciplined by religious duty is like Noah's ark; it carries the individual to safety through the storms of emotion and passion that arise in the midst of worldly trials and afflictions.[3]

Wisdom of Solomon also refers to the Noah story, treating it as pregnant with significance for our efforts to find safe passage through the trials of temptation: "For even in the beginning, when arrogant giants were perishing, the hope of the world took refuge on a raft, and guided by thy hand left to the world the seed of a new generation," and thus, "blessed is the wood by which righteousness comes" (14:6–7). In the larger context of Wisdom of Solomon, the wood is wisdom, the teachings of righteousness that alone are trustworthy in this life.

A Christian reader needs no great literary imagination to link the saving wood of the ark with the saving wood of the cross and the body of Christ on the cross to the body of Christ that is the church. Augustine unpacks these connections in his multifaceted allegorical reading:

> Noah, with his family is saved by water and wood, as the family of Christ is saved by baptism, as representing the suffering of the cross. That this ark is made of beams formed in a square, as the Church is constructed of saints prepared unto every good work: for a square stands firm on any side. That the length is six times the breadth, and ten times the height, like a human body, to show that Christ appeared in a human body. That the breadth reaches to fifty cubits; as the apostle says, "Our heart is enlarged" [2 Cor. 6:11], that is with spiritual love, of which he says again, "The love of God is shed abroad in our heart by the Holy Ghost, which is given unto us" [Rom. 5:5]. For in the fiftieth day after His resurrection, Christ sent His Holy Spirit to enlarge the hearts of His disciples. . . . That it is thirty cubits high, a tenth part of the length; because Christ is our height, who in His thirtieth year gave His sanction to the doctrine of the gospel, by declaring that He came not to destroy the law, but to fulfil it. Now the ten commandments are to be the heart of the law; and so the length of the ark is ten times thirty. Noah himself, too, was the tenth from Adam. That the beams are fastened within and without with pitch, to signify by compact union the forbearance of love, which keeps the brotherly connection

3. Chrysostom echoes this reading of the ark as the vessel of virtue: "[Noah] was like a skillful pilot, controlling the rudder of his mind with great vigilance, not allowing the craft to be submerged under the violence of the billows of wickedness, but getting the better of the storm and riding it out at sea as though safely berthed in port; in this fashion by steering the tiller of virtue he kept himself clear of the deluge that was about to engulf everyone in the world" (*Homilies on Genesis* 23.1 in FC 82.87).

from being impaired, and the bond of peace from being broken by the offences which try the Church either from without or from within. (*Reply to Faustus the Manichean* 12.14 in NPNF[1] 4.188)

Although this exegesis is traditional, modern readers often find it fanciful. For example, the notion that the dimensions of the ark might be divided and added and multiplied in such a way as to generate hidden references to the Ten Commandments or to the thirty years before Christ began his earthly ministry seems to many an absurd abuse of the text. "The Genesis narrative is about the ark," the objection runs, "it is not about Christ or the church or anything else."

I do not want to gainsay the skepticism. It is wise to ask for warrants for interpretations that wander far from the plain sense of the text, but we need to understand what motivates traditional allegorical readings. Augustine admits that readers may agree or disagree with spiritual readings that take mere mention of wood and water as cause to expound upon the saving power of baptism and the redemption of all by Christ on the cross. However, he is also concerned to lay down an important principle of interpretation. "No one ought to imagine," he observes, "that this account [of the flood] was written for no purpose, or that we are to look here solely for a reliable historical record without any allegorical meaning" (*City of God* 15.27, quoted from Bettenson 1972: 645). According to Augustine, a basic assumption of a Christian reading of scripture is that God is the creator of all things and author of history. So, if we assume that God's providence shapes history (which includes the writing, editing, and transmission of the scriptural text), then we need always to be open to the following question: what is God telling us by doing things *that* way (and by causing it to be remembered/written/edited *that* way)? Why thirty cubits instead of forty? Why forty days and forty nights instead of fifty? Why a dove instead of a pigeon?

There is nothing remotely strange or occult about these kinds of questions. If we read the daily paper or watch the news on television, we encounter many political commentators who make their livings by decoding governmental decisions and political platforms. "Today's appointment of so-and-so," a commentator might say, "confirms a strong neoconservative trend in the current administration." Spiritual reading operates in the same way. God runs the administration of worldly affairs to remedy the fall and return humanity to the possibility of entering into his Sabbath rest. The divinely ordained administration is rationally run; that is, it functions according to a *logos* or plan. Should we be surprised, then, that competent biblical readers who trust that the Bible reports the details of the divine plan set about to discern patterns and connections between different stages of the divine plan for the redemption of the world?

Here we need to be clear about the impulse to deny the legitimacy of allegorical interpretation. An outright denial of traditional efforts to discern patterns and connections entails a prima facie denial of God's power over history—or a denial that God is sufficiently competent to pursue a coherent plan that has a *logos* or structuring rationale. If we say that the story of safe passage through the floodwaters *cannot* point to subsequent Christian teachings about safe passage in Christ through divine judgment, then we are denying that God has either the power or the desire to organize events (and memories and texts and editing and traditions) according to a coherent plan.

Needless to say, the New Testament writers were confident that God is sufficiently powerful and solicitous of our humanity to work according to a comprehensive and effective plan. They treated Noah, the ark, and the flood as revealing the economy of salvation. Both Luke and Matthew contain a prophecy of coming judgment that draws upon the flood story. "As in the days of Noah," says Jesus of his own coming passion, "so will it be in the days of the Son of man. They ate, they drank, they married, they were given in marriage, until the day when Noah entered the ark, and the flood came and destroyed them all" (Luke 17:26–27; Matt. 24:37–39). As the gospel story unfolds, the pattern of the flood is recapitulated in Christ. On the cross, the flood of divine judgment destroys the power of sin, and in the tomb the Son endures solely by the will of the Father.

Second Peter also evokes Noah in a complex train of thought that focuses on the recurring scriptural evidence that God has a consistent plan for saving the righteous few amid the judgment of the wicked many. The "eyewitnesses" to the "majesty" of the "Lord Jesus Christ" bear testimony as "men moved by the Holy Spirit" (2 Pet. 1:16–21). "But false prophets also arose among the people," and in their "licentiousness" and "greed" and "false words," they assail the true way of the gospel (2:1–3). The faithful need not worry, however. God will deal with the wickedness of the present day as he has done in days of old. "For if God did not spare the angels when they sinned, but cast them into hell and committed them to pits of nether gloom to be kept until the judgment" (2:4), then surely he will condemn the false prophets who flourish in the present age. But God does not just condemn the wicked; he preserves the righteous remnant. "If he did not spare the ancient world, but preserved Noah, a herald of righteousness, with seven other persons, when he brought a flood upon the world of the ungodly," and, continuing with the pattern, "if by turning the cities of Sodom and Gomorrah to ashes he condemned them to extinction and made them an example to those who were to be ungodly; and if he rescued righteous Lot . . . , then the Lord knows how to rescue the godly from trial" (2:5–9). In other words, the author of 2 Peter presumes a pattern: "When the tempest passes, the wicked is no more, but the righteous is established for ever" (Prov. 10:25).

How then does God rescue the godly from trial? Where do the righteous find refuge in the deluge of divine judgment? In Matthew's Gospel, yet another echo of the flood story suggests an answer. Matching the theme of 2 Peter, Jesus warns against the danger of false prophets: "Every one who then hears these words of mine and does them will be like a wise man who built his house upon the rock; and the rain fell, and the floods came, and the winds blew and beat upon the house, but it did not fall, because it had been founded on the rock" (7:24–25). The gospel message is the ark of salvation.

Since the Reformation, Western Christianity has been locked in a struggle over how to understand the rock that provides the ark of protection for the faithful as they try to navigate through the flood of worldly teaching, infidelity, and wickedness. Is the rock the word of God in scripture, or should we follow the images of "rock" and "building" to Matt. 16:18: "On this rock I will build my church, and the powers of death shall not prevail against it"? Thus the great question: is scripture or the church the refuge of salvation? I incline toward the latter, because it is animated by the former. But the larger point is much more important. The Genesis narrative foreshadows the larger economy of salvation depicted in scripture. The flood story provides clues for discerning the pattern of the divine plan. We need not flounder and sink in the face of divine judgment. God provides an ark for those whom he rescues.

7:5 Noah did all that the LORD had commanded him.

The LORD says, "You are righteous before me in this generation" (7:1). Obedience marks the path to righteousness. But how can Noah succeed in pleasing the LORD? "How then can man be righteous before God," for "even the moon is not bright and the stars are not clean in his sight" (Job 25:4–5)? Is it not a consequence of original sin that "no man living is righteous before thee" (Ps. 143:2)? Is it realistic to expect fallen humanity to "keep the commandments" to the point that we "would be perfect" (Matt. 19:17, 21)? The answer rests neither in exempting a small group of humans from original sin nor in ascribing heroic powers to a few great saints. No human quality or capacity can make us righteous before God. "With men this is impossible, but with God all things are possible" (19:26).

7:9 Two and two.

The entry into the ark provides an important piece of evidence about the divine plan for salvation. God presses creation toward the promised Sabbath rest, and he does so by way of an intensified focus rather than with a generalized, universal act of benevolence. The calling of Abraham gives explicit expression to the narrow way of the "two and two," as does the scriptural emphasis on the few who survive the destruction of Jerusalem. The later authors of scripture saw the link: "Noah was found perfect and righteous; in the time of wrath he was taken in exchange; therefore a remnant was left to the earth when the flood came" (Sirach 44:17). The pattern recurs in the devastating flood of invasion (Jer. 4) and in the prophesied restoration of the people in the ark of divine care:

"Come, my people, enter your chambers, and shut your doors behind you; hide yourselves for a little while until the wrath is past" (Isa. 26:20). In the rescued few rests the future hope for all.

In Christ, the remnant moves from a chosen few to a single individual, and here we see the metaphysical heresy of the divine plan in its most naked form (→12:1a). God's goal of returning creation to the trajectory toward Sabbath rest is universal in scope. All things are to be brought to fulfillment. But the plan is intensely focused and particular in execution. The fulfillment comes through a narrow gate. With this future in mind, we can see how the flood story both retells and alters the original creation story. The primal waters return in the flood, and the world reverts back to its original, undifferentiated state. Then, the waters recede, and the world seems to reemerge as creation reborn and cleansed of sin. Although the water symbolism certainly points toward a replay of the six days of creation (the inundation from below and rain from above clearly evoke the waters below and above on the second day of creation), the narrative detail points toward the new creation in Christ. The flood does not destroy or wipe creation clean so that God can undertake a broad refurbishment of the cosmos as a contractor might gut and then restore a dilapidated house. Instead, the flood holds up the ark. The tiny vessel carries forward the human future: creation is renewed two by two, anticipating the time when "one man's act of righteousness leads to acquittal and life for all men" (Rom. 5:18).

7:12 Forty days and forty nights.

The genealogy in Gen. 5 gives a prospective interpretation of Noah's role that hearkens back to the punishment of Adam: "Out of the ground which the LORD has cursed this one shall bring us relief from our work and from the toil of our hands" (5:29). But how does this relief from the burden of original sin come about? In the New Testament we read, "By faith Noah, being warned by God concerning events as yet unseen, took heed and constructed an ark for the saving of his household; by this he condemned the world and became an heir of the righteousness which comes by faith" (Heb. 11:7). The puzzle is that Noah brings "relief" by "condemnation." How, we might wonder, does God bring salvation through destruction? "I will blot out man," says the LORD (Gen. 6:7). But if this is so, then how can the earlier prophecy of Noah's role as bringer of relief be true? Where is the relief in being blotted out? Where is the hope of salvation in the word of condemnation?

The first feature of the flood is that divine intervention prevents sin from spiraling to its conclusion. The destructive power of the water turns back the corruptive power of evil, and in this way the flood prevents sin from descending all the way into nothingness. In an important sense, therefore, just as the garments of skin and expulsion from the garden are punishments that protect human beings from the full force of their sinful decisions, so also does the flood block the realization of the future promised in the covenant of Satan's lie.[4]

Furthermore, as the use of forty days (or years) throughout scripture suggests, the rains sent by God last for the standard period for purgation and purification: "Wash me, and I shall be whiter than snow" (Ps. 51:7). This link between purgative destruction and salvation culminates in the saving death of Jesus Christ. Written in a context of persecution, the author of 1 Peter describes the trials of the faithful as tests of fire that purify the soul (1 Pet. 1:7, 22). In these trials, the suffering of Christ serves as an example (2:21). He is the one who, "when he was reviled, . . . did not revile in return" (2:23). The application is clear: the faithful are to resist the temptation to return evil for evil. Like Noah in the ark and Jesus in the wilderness, they should patiently endure affliction for the sake of righteousness.

Yet, there is a decisive twist that distinguishes Jesus from Noah and his ark. Jesus Christ does not endure death simply as a trial; his death brings life. For "by his wounds," writes the author of 1 Peter, echoing Isa. 53, "you have been healed." His death took place so "that we might die to sin and live to righteousness" (1 Pet. 2:24). Christ even "went and preached to the spirits in prison, who formerly did not obey, when God's patience waited in the days of Noah, during the building of the ark, in which a few, that is, eight persons, were saved through water" (3:19–20). It is as if, when the waters begin to rise, Christ leaps from the ark and dives into the destroying flood of death so that he can reach all the way to the bottom and rescue those drowning in the covenant of the lie. Perhaps the imagery breaks down at this point, because Christ and the church are the ark into which the faithful are incorporated. The author if 1 Peter presumes this shift: "Baptism, which corresponds to this, now saves you" (3:21)—although this assertion of allegorical correspondence is itself complex and plays across different aspects of Noah's story. Baptism is both immersion in Christ's death (a recapitulation of his dive into the waters of destruction) and incorporation into his risen life (a first draught of the water of life).

8:16 Go forth from the ark, you and your wife, and your sons and your sons' wives with you.

Note the difference between the entry into the ark and the exit. In 6:18, God says to Noah, "You shall come into the ark, you, your sons, your wife, and your sons' wives with you." The men are separate from the women as part of the two-by-two entry of all the animals into the ark. But now, after the waters have subsided, God sends forth each man with his wife. Ancient readers saw this textual detail as telling. On the ark, men and women are separated (so this reading supposes

4. On the benevolence of punishment that blocks the downward spiral of sin, see Chrysostom, *Homilies on Genesis* 26.3 (FC 82.146).

on the basis of the sequence of entry). Didymus the Blind, for example, reads this separation as indicating that Noah and his sons did not have sexual intercourse on the ark. It was not fitting, Didymus thought, to enjoy the pleasures of marriage while the rest of humanity was being destroyed in judgment.[5]

At issue here is not prudery about our sexual identities. Instead, these older interpreters wanted to both follow the literal sense in its detail and also deepen the reader's grasp of the spiritual sense in which the flood ends human history. The ark exists as a limbo. Without the possibility of reproduction, it floats through a time outside history. Only after exiting does sexual union—the production of a new generation that is the fundamental biblical structure of human history— become possible again.

9:1 Be fruitful and multiply.

This echo of 1:28 is repeated in 9:7. Together they frame the blessing that God gives to Noah and his sons. The effect is to emphasize the future-oriented content of the blessing. The generations lean forward in time, and the divine blessing takes the sterile limbo of the ark and reignites the reproductive engine of history. But this history cannot go back to the conditions of life in the garden. Sin has entered human history, and therefore God now addresses the problem by changing the conditions of dominion and expanding the work of human life. The earth may have been cleansed by water, but the inhabitants of the ark are untouched. They still need to be purified by divine righteousness, which takes the form of new commandments given and old ones reiterated. A very different flood is necessary: "May my teaching drop as the rain, my speech distil as the dew, as the gentle rain upon the tender grass, and as the showers upon the herb" (Deut. 32:2).

The scope and conditions of human dominion over the animals changes. In the first creation, God gives animals into the care of human beings, and plants as food. Now, God gives the animals as well for food: "Every moving thing that lives shall be food for you" (9:3). There is both a price and a condition for this new bequest. The animals will fear humans, and thus they will now be very difficult to find, domesticate, and put into the service of humanity. The work of sustaining the human community has become more complicated and strenuous even as it acquires more potential resources. Moreover the new animal food cannot be taken in any fashion. God lays down a clear restriction that must be obeyed: "You shall not eat flesh with its life, that is, its blood" (9:4).

5. *Didyme l'aveugle: sur la genèse*, ed. Pierre Nautin, Sources chrétiennes 244 (Paris: Cerf, 1978), 2.79, 107. And not only Christian readers; commenting on 6:18, Rashi conveys an older exegetical opinion from the Babylonian Talmud (tractate *Sanhedrin* 108b): "The men separate and the women separate. [We derive] from this that marital relations were prohibited to them."

The new form of dominion over the animals is important, but even more decisive for the future is the emergence of an explicitly social and moral realm of dominion. The commandment to refrain from consuming the blood of animals serves as a bridge to the commandment to punish murder with the death of the murderer: "Whoever sheds the blood of man, by man shall his blood be shed; for God made man in his own image" (9:6). The simple sense of this extraordinary verse suggests that murder is wrong and is fittingly punished, because to kill a human is to kill someone made in the image of God. This reading is certainly correct, but the verse also directs our attention to a fundamentally new aspect of human history. By causing the flood, God has taken justice into his own hands. The wickedness of humanity has been punished. Now, however, God takes the most heinous of crimes and puts justice into human hands. We are to exercise dominion over each other, punishing those who wrongfully take life. And why can we police our collective behavior? What makes us fit to be our brother's keeper? We can do so, this verse suggests, because we are made in the image and likeness of God: we have the capacity for dominion, the capacity to exercise authority for the sake of a higher principle (→1:26b).

Thus, the commandment to punish murder signals the beginning of divinely mandated political authority, a dramatic extension of the work of dominion assigned to human beings in the garden. Here, the nascent world of Noah and his sons foreshadows the false dominion manifest in the building of the tower on the plains of Shinar (→11:4). The tower is the product of social dominion that serves humanly defined goals. The people of the plains want to make a name for themselves, and they work furiously to build their tower and secure their reputation in the world. In contrast, the social agency necessary to punish murder serves a divinely given principle of justice. In order to rightly lord over humans, one must obey God's commandments.

In a modern secular society, the idea of a sacred order seems unworkable. We can't ask our leaders to agree on any particular account of divine law, and we don't ask our presidents, legislators, or judges to sign confessions of faith. However, the basic notion that political authority is justified by a higher principle remains central to the concept of the rule of law. Whether mandated by popular vote or secured by backroom influence, the projects and goals of the moment can govern justly only insofar as they serve a legal or constitutional order that transcends them. It is telling, moreover, that this transcendent order so easily acquires a sacred dimension. The American Constitution has quasicanonical status. It is not just a prudentially justified agreement that can be modified according to shifting judgments of political gain and loss. The Constitution embodies eternal principles of justice—or so we must believe if we are to accept its claim upon our obedience based on more than fear of punishment. Social life ennobles us, because its basic principles are justified by something greater than collective utility.

Some intermixture of secular authority and transcendent mandate, while volatile, seems inevitable, even in modern political cultures that are skeptical of the direct, unmediated influence of church doctrine and ecclesiastical authority. To fully secularize authority invariably undermines its claim to be a just authority, since it reduces human life to survival and the satisfaction of desires. To be sure, modern liberal democracies do not draw their transcendent mandates from the Bible or any other religious tradition. Instead, affirmations of democracy, freedom, and human rights fill the role. But these affirmations are consistently loaded with far greater moral content than any rigorous analysis of the concepts can produce. Democracy and freedom are shibboleths that express the eschatological dreams of modernity, and human rights gathers up and gives legal form to intuitions about the true end and purpose of human life, intuitions often deeply indebted to the religious traditions that modern liberal democracies keep at arm's length.

Finally, the new commandment to shed the blood of those who shed blood sets the stage for the final chapters of Genesis. This commandment threatens to lead Abraham's descendents toward communal disaster. Joseph and his brothers must find a way to prevent the blood of one brother (Joseph) from coming down on the head of those who conspired against him. Avoiding the cry of a brother's blood for the blood of his brothers requires a strategy of atonement that fulfills the requirement of retribution without extracting its penalty from the human transgressor.

9:9 Behold, I establish my covenant.

Aside from the ark, the flood story has all the features of decreation and a return to the beginning of creation. Yet the ark would seem to be the main point, and it introduces the dominant pattern in the rest of scripture: "For a brief moment I forsook you, but with great compassion I will gather you" (Isa. 54:7). Floods of trial, slavery, exile, persecution, and even the flood of death on the cross—all these winnowing and purging episodes of suffering are for the sake of finding our way into the future of fellowship with God. In this sense, the flood sets out patterns of divine loyalty to his creatures: "Many waters cannot quench love, neither can floods drown it" (Song 8:7).

The covenant with Noah, however, is the ambiguous first stage in the divine project of realizing this loyalty in the flesh and blood of human life. It does not so much move history forward as stay the destructive effects of sin. For this reason, the flood is best understood as the covenant of God's patience.[6] The protecting mark of Cain stays the hand of those who seek to kill him. The covenant with Noah has similar effect. The blessing that changes human relations to animals and establishes the basic duty to punish transgression lays the foundations for human survival. The family tribe, held together by rough justice, enters the flow of history. This human-centered change is mirrored in the divine-centered promise never

6. Von Rad 1972: 133 writes: "The Noachic aeon . . . is an aeon of divine forbearance."

again to unleash the primal forces of nature against humanity. Water will return as a remedy for sin in the history of the covenant, but it will be the irrigating, life-giving water of Gen. 2 rather than the primal waters of Gen. 1 that overwhelm the world in Gen. 7: "I will sprinkle clean water upon you, and you shall be clean from all your uncleannesses" (Ezek. 36:25). Looking back on the flood episode, therefore, we can see that the massive project of worldwide cleansing does not create a new future for humanity. It hits the pause button on the doleful, destructive thrust of sin and brings a modicum of stability to human history.

In Ps. 104, the stabilizing purpose of the covenant with Noah is given a broad, cosmic expression. In the flood the LORD covered "the deep as with a garment; the waters stood above the mountains" (104:6). Then, after the waters receded, "the mountains rose, the valleys sank down to the place which thou didst appoint for them. Thou didst set a bound which they should not pass, so that they might not again cover the earth" (104:8–9). The work of dominion is expanded to deputize us to police our own transgressions (→9:1). In this sense, the covenant with Noah is the foundation for rather than a prefiguration of the subsequent, sanctifying covenant begun with Abraham, given full form on Sinai, and completed on Golgotha. "Be still before the LORD," the covenant with Noah would seem to signal, "and wait patiently for him" (Ps. 37:7). "The LORD will fight for you, and you have only to be still" (Exod. 14:14).

Faced with disorder and dissension caused by conflict over the role of the law of Moses in the lives of Gentile followers of Christ, the apostles and elders in Jerusalem reiterated a version of the covenant with Noah as the basis for Paul's mission to the Gentiles: "Abstain from the pollutions of idols and from unchastity and from what is strangled and from blood" (Acts 15:20). These laws had the same stabilizing role in the apostolic age that they had in the primordial time of Noah. They do not supplement the gospel Paul wishes to preach, nor do they provide the prophetic and figural anticipations of Christ found in the later covenants with Abraham and the people of Israel. Instead, the ordinances still the chaotic hearts of those in bondage to sin. The absence of chaos or violence is merely a negative peace; it is not the fulfillment of creation promised in the seventh day. But this negative peace is necessary. The human heart, once awoken to the need for basic, simple principles of communal discipline, gains a margin of freedom from the chaotic din raised by the powers of disordered desire. There is a natural good in this negative peace: "Better a dry morsel with quiet than a house full of feasting with strife" (Prov. 17:1). And this natural good serves the gospel. Only in a relative quiet can we hear the promise of salvation in Christ: "Be still, and know that I am God" (Ps. 46:10).

Many passages in the so-called Pastoral Letters of Paul that are not substantively related to the covenant with Noah or Acts 15 nonetheless point to the need for the negative peace of basic communal discipline. Conduct in worship ("men should pray, lifting holy hands without anger or quarreling" and "women should adorn themselves modestly"; 1 Tim. 2:8–9), instructions regarding church leadership ("a bishop must be above reproach"; 3:2), rules for communal order ("bid the older men be temperate, serious, sensible" and "bid slaves to be submissive to their masters"; Titus 2:2, 9)—all these and other ordinances function in a fashion similar to the covenant with Noah. The din of sin—"a noisy gong or a clanging cymbal" (1 Cor. 13:1)—drowns out the soundest, most clearly articulated truths.

9:20 Noah was the first tiller of the soil. He planted a vineyard.

The possibility of bread and wine comes with Noah. Here again, like the creation story it partially recapitulates, the flood does not usher in a new future, but instead provides the basis or foundation on which the divine plan can develop. Noah's work with the soil and in the vineyard produces the elements that can become for us the bread of life and cup of salvation. "'Behold, the days are coming,' says the LORD, 'when the plowman shall overtake the reaper and the treader of grapes him who sows the seed'" (Amos 9:13).

9:22 The nakedness of his father.

After the creation and fall of humanity, the story of Cain and Abel tells a tale of woe. After the cleansing of the earth and the apparent opportunity to start humanity afresh with the small family of Noah, the original fault finds its way into human life once again, this time corrupting the relations of father and son. The cleansing flood does not go deeply enough into the human heart. Just as the new beginning in Seth fails to evade the consequences of sin ($\rightarrow$5:1), so also the new beginning after the great cosmic erasure of the flood fails to fundamentally alter the trajectory of human history. The covenant with Noah may bring restraint, but not a new future.

Ham sees Noah in his drunken nakedness and tells his brothers. Shem and Japheth then follow a careful, eyes-averted procedure to cover their father's nakedness. When Noah awakens and "knew what his youngest son had done to him," he curses Canaan, Ham's son (9:24–27). But what, exactly, did Ham do to draw down this curse upon his son? This is not an easy question to answer. One tradition reasons backward from the severity of the curse to deduce an equally severe transgression. Ham did not just see his naked father: he castrated him.[7] More modest is the suggestion that Ham is indiscrete, and this is the source of his harm to his father. Ham sees something embarrassing and then runs to tell his brothers, sinning in the way that James envisions the tongue sparking a fire

---

7. *Targum Pseudo-Jonathan* (Maher 1992: 46): Ham "was the cause of his [Noah's] not begetting a fourth son."

of gossip (Jas. 3:6–8).[8] There is a time for silence and a time for speaking (Eccl. 3:7), and apparently Ham spoke when he should have remained silent.

The brevity of the text gives little support to any attempt to identify the transgression that motivates Noah's curse of Ham's progeny. But the larger witness of the Bible gives strong support to an interpretation of Ham's sin as a public broadcast of embarrassing facts about his father. Not only do the Ten Commandments exhort us to honor our father and mother, the commandments also place a disproportionate emphasis on sins of the tongue, prohibiting both abuse of the divine name and abuse of the truth in bearing false witness. Jesus reinforces this emphasis on the tongue when he warns against things that come out of the mouth and defile (Matt. 15:18). What we say—and how and when and to whom—matters a great deal. "With his mouth the godless man would destroy his neighbor" (Prov. 11:9). This is a truth our age wishes to ignore, not only in the perpetual spin of political discourse that evades, dissembles, and traffics in innuendo, but also in the tell-all culture of self-exposure, the insatiable public appetite for celebrity gossip, and the pervasive recourse to the crude and violent expletives that soil everyday conversation.

The story of Ham's transgression, however, has another element that cannot be assimilated to the sins of the tongue. Ham sees his naked father, and the seeing itself seems to be something that harms Noah. The importance of sight is reinforced by the solution that Shem and Japheth provide. With faces turned away, they clothe their father, walking by something other than sight. What Shem and Japheth do is admirable ("I was naked and you clothed me"; Matt. 25:36), as was their method of approach ("we walk by faith, not by sight"; 2 Cor. 5:7). The eyes of Ham betray him, just as the eyes of Eve betray her. The sin is one of sight and not just speech. Ham looks when he should have averted his eyes.

Unlike the restraints on the tongue, the disciplines of the eyes are not as obvious to the modern reader. But they are equally important in the Bible as a whole and in the subsequent Christian tradition. The eyes are the windows of the soul, and the transfixing allure of idols captures our vision. In this sense, then, the entire sweep of the biblical polemic against idolatry functions as a constraint upon the eyes. In contrast to idols, the divine presence is discretely clothed in the inner courts of the temple. We should no more wish to suddenly look upon God without long preparations of the heart than Ham upon Noah. This sentiment lies behind the early Christian doctrine of reserve, the policy of sending catechumens from the church before the celebration of the holy mysteries of the altar. Only those prepared by baptism can look upon the nakedness of the crucified Lord.

In our age we believe that truths are clothed only to hide their falsehood and the shame of their ideological origins, and thus we want to see everything immediately

8. This reading is suggested in the expansion provided by *Targum Pseudo-Jonathan*: "Ham, the father of Canaan, saw his father's nakedness and told his brothers in the street" (Maher 1992: 45–46). *Targum Neofiti* has Ham telling his brothers "in the market place" (Martin McNamara, trans., *Targum Neofiti 1: Genesis*, Aramaic Bible 1A [Collegeville, MN: Liturgical Press, 1992], 80).

and in its nakedness. Bewitched by the images of enlightenment, we think that anything worth believing should be brought out into the public square for scrutiny and examination by all. This is an extraordinarily naïve view, for two reasons.

First, truth is powerful, which is why the biblical tradition is so anxiously fearful of the immediacy of any vision of the searching truth of God's holiness. To see the purity of God's righteousness is to know the deep sources of our motives and action. This self-knowledge is a painful, disorienting, debilitating blow to those spiritually unprepared. Truth judges us, and seeing truth directly threatens to consume us. We see this debilitation in contemporary intellectual culture. Modern critical education can easily conduce to despair—or a cynical nihilism that loves its own knowingness.

Second, human beings are crude, cruel animals. We are attracted to the power that we imagine truth will give us, but we are often insensitive to the obedience that truth demands. The know-it-all expert can pass judgment with serene indifference to the need for wisdom. The ambitious journalist can write the exposé without considering the larger social implications. The cocksure professor can congratulate himself for enlightening his students and delivering them from what he confidently knows to be their ideological bondage—and do so with disregard for their moral and spiritual well-being.

Like parents who give us life and give themselves to our education and training for the future, truth genuinely empowers us. But we also need to train ourselves to honor the deeper claims of truth rather than presuming upon its bounty. Anything worth believing must be approached with pious humility. We will never see the truth in its full depth, and therefore all genuine reflection is deeply intertwined with continuous preparation of the soul. As A. G. Sertillanges observed in his reflections on the intellectual life: "Truth visits those who love her, who surrender to her, and this love cannot be without virtue." Or more pungently and memorably: "Truth serves only its slaves."[9]

10:1 These are the generations of the sons of Noah.

"Be fruitful and multiply"—the imperative of reproduction constitutes the divine blessing of time. History does not stretch endlessly or aimlessly; it is measured out in the forward movement of the generations. At this point, therefore, a new genealogy echoes the new thread of life that began with the birth of Seth (→5:1). Time is restarted, and fittingly so. Human beings are uniquely shaped by the passage of time; the very notion of character and personality requires the formation we receive in education, experience, and the accumulated acts of will that form our habits. We are by nature "time-full" creatures, and only as such are

9. A. G. Sertillanges, *The Intellectual Life: Its Spirit, Conditions, Methods,* trans. Mary Ryan (Washington: Catholic University Press, 1987), 19, 4.

we able to manifest "the first fruits of the Spirit" (Rom. 8:23), which will be given in the covenant with Abraham.

The same plasticity characterizes the natural world as a whole. It is not inert. Creation also has a future, as the prophecies of Isaiah remind us when they look forward to a restoration of the peaceable kingdom of Eden (Isa. 11:6; 65:25). But to have a future, creation itself must participate in the reality of time. Because neither lions nor lambs nor trees nor rocks have histories, creation can have a new future only through humanity. As the head of creation, we are uniquely suited for the role. As amphibians poised between the dust of the earth and the glory of the image of God, human beings can be made anew without being ripped out of the natural context (→1:26a). We can be sanctified without severing our relation to the physical world, divinized without being disembodied.

Thus, the vision of fulfillment in the Old and New Testaments consistently sees history as the engine driving the consummation of the entire created order. Daniel tames wild animals (Dan. 6:16–24), showing how the cosmos finds its future in the generations of Noah. The restoration of Israel triggers the restoration of the whole world in Isaiah's prophecies. St. Paul follows the same train of thought, putting the logic into the clearest possible terms: "The creation waits with eager longing for the revealing of the sons of God" (Rom. 8:19). Nature as a whole has no power to make history; it cannot shape the future. But as uniquely changeable creatures we can—or more accurately though us God can.

11:4 Let us make a name for ourselves.

The men of Shinar set about to build a great city and a high tower "with its top in the heavens" (11:4). The drive toward greatness grows out of a perverse truth. Self-exaltation is a kind of spiritual ascent, an inflating attempt to rise above the limitations of earthly life on the strength of one's spiritual achievements. The desire for rest from the futile strivings of human life seeks satisfaction in a pale imitation of fellowship with the divine: the seeming immortality of fame among humans. We imagine ourselves finding a solution to the threat of death by surviving in human memory. Like the deeds of Achilles before the gates of Troy, we hope to live forever in the songs of great achievements.

But this strategy inevitably fails, as the author of the *Iliad* half-knew and suggested, not only in his observation that, given enough time, the relentless coming and going of the tides will obliterate all signs that the Greeks once camped upon the beaches of Pergamum, but also in the elegiac atmosphere of the entire poem, which ends with the burial of the vanquished man whose city will soon fall: "So that is how they buried Hector, tamer of horses" (*Iliad* 24.804). The *Iliad* savors the memory of great deeds because memory itself is so fragile and so quickly goes to destruction. Thus, as Ecclesiastes makes plain, we cannot attain the rest of eternal life by way of worldly achievement, whether the glorious verses of Homer or the pyramids of Egypt or the monuments of Washington, D.C. We cannot say, "I will ascend to heaven; above the stars of God I will set my throne on high," for the LORD will bring the arrogant "down to Sheol, to the depths of the Pit" (Isa. 14:13, 15), and destroy the great cities that are "fortified up to heaven" (Deut. 1:28). "Man cannot abide in his pomp, he is like the beasts that perish" (Ps. 49:12).

Faced with an accelerating project of prideful ambition on the plains of Shinar, God acts on the same rationale he gave for the expulsion of Adam and Eve from the garden of Eden. The LORD says, "This is only the beginning of what they will do; and nothing that they propose to do will now be impossible for them" (Gen. 11:6). We need to be sure readers here. It cannot be the case that human beings can make themselves divine by dint of their efforts, any more than the fruit of the tree of life and sheer deathlessness would give Adam and Eve divine life—"like one of us" (3:22). Nor can God be threatened by human striving, as if he were a vulnerable despot anxious to protect his prerogatives. No, the temptation of the covenant of the lie is precisely the false promise that worldly abundance is enough to bring rest to human beings.

Can we really fulfill this false future for ourselves? True enough, we can construct a shadowy existence that runs on a seemingly endless sequence of worldly desires manufactured and satisfied. We can seek the worldly renown that we hope will make our names remembered across the centuries. We can try to control our future, either by giving our entire being over to the burning of bricks, with complete loyalty to the affairs of the worldly city, or by stretching ourselves to secure fame as a leader. These are very real possibilities. In fact, as Augustine recounts, they make up the history of the earthly city. Therefore, the danger that God identifies in both the tree of life and the tower of Babel is simple. It is the limitlessness human capacity to live according to the covenant of the lie. However impossible the pure negation of radical evil, we really can say an enduring "no" to the covenant of life. As "slaves of corruption" (2 Pet. 2:19), we have a striking ability, day after day, to give ourselves over to sin. God intervenes not to protect his power, but in order to protect us from the tenacious power of our own corruption.

The story of the tower, however, does more than just recapitulate the logic of sin. Sin works its way into relation of brother to brother, and Cain slays Abel (→4:8). Sin finds its way into the relations of male and female, and God looks upon the wickedness of the mysterious sons of God who wed themselves to the daughters of men (→6:2). Sin corrupts father and son as Ham looks upon Noah's nakedness (→9:22). Each is an instance of familial disorder. The reproductive dimension of the *imago dei* is corrupted, distorted, and stained by Adam's fault. Now we see the social and political dimension of human life fall under the sway of sin. The people who build the city and its tower "migrated from the east" and "settled there" (11:2). In the covenant with Noah, God gives human beings dominion over each other so that they can do the work of maintaining social order (→9:9). As a result, humanity forms itself into political units and organizes itself for coordinated, collective efforts. What were individual or narrowly familial projects and histories in Genesis now become social. Making bricks and burning them thoroughly enough to use for a building project is a technical fruit of the human orientation toward social existence. The grandiose image of the tower points to a fundamental truth about social cooperation. Collective effort magnifies the power of the human will. In this sense, then, the tower of Babel shows us the consequences of human sinfulness magnified and intensified by the human power of social dominion. It is one thing for a person to seek renown. It is quite another for the collective will of a city to do the same.

Devotion to the collective projects of society is very tempting, because it has the form of self-sacrifice that can seem similar to the life of devotion to God. But we cannot escape our slavery to the covenant of the lie through patriotism or some otherworldly form of selfless service. If we "settle there," if we make any aspect of the political project of the earthly city into the object or goal of our lives, then we will turn the finite goods of social life into perverting idols. Indeed, a life devoted to firing bricks to alleviate poverty and building a global cooperation, or any other social ideal, may be the most dangerous and tempting form of the covenant of the lie, because it requires such selfless service to humanity. The depth of this temptation animates the famous tale of the Grand Inquisitor in Dostoyevsky's *The Brothers Karamazov*. The Grand Inquisitor's commitment to serve the unreformable worldliness of humanity is inseparable from his betrayal of Christ. In a lesser known but fuller and richer diagnosis of the spiritual dangers of modern philanthropic idealism, Vladimir Solovyov depicts an earnest pacifist disciple of Tolstoy as the paradigmatic modern instrument of Satan.[10]

Dostoyevsky and Solovyov were prophets of the deadly tyranny of philanthropy. The history of the twentieth century is littered with the bodies of those sacrificed to a particularly powerful form of the covenant of the lie: that the finite human project of politics can be brought to fulfillment in the universal dictatorship of the proletariat. The failure is plain to see. But even in the rubble we continue to build strange new towers. The only alternative to the worship of a finite good made into an idol is the worship of the one true God, the lord and creator of all. Without a predominating love of God, love of neighbor will become a limitless project, and the good things we seek for each other "is only the beginning of what [we] will do" (11:6). What begins as a fitting philanthropy ends with us rallying all the forces at our disposal to serve whatever god of worldly flourishing we have made for ourselves. If people will not be free, then they must be forced to be free. If our global economic system cannot eliminate poverty, then we'll wipe it all away and force people to produce wealth in a new way—even to the point of using fear in place of

10. Vladimir Solovyov, *War, Progress, and the End of History: Three Conversations, Including a Short Story of the Anti-Christ*, trans. Alexander Bakshy and Thomas R. Beyer Jr. (Hudson, NY: Lindisfarne, 1990).

the old motive of greed. We cannot live by bread alone, and if we insist on making bread the entire focus of service to our neighbor, we will end up tying others down to force the food down their throats—and all the while we will reassure ourselves that the cutting ropes of bondage are there for their own good.

11:5 And the LORD came down.

The confusion of languages is like the expulsion from the garden and the flood. Just as the punishment of death puts a limit on the downward spiral of corruption and prevents us from having the time to purify our devotion to the serpent's lie into the spiritual project of pure negation, so also does the confusion of the languages bring an end to the building of the tower. Unable to communicate, human beings are no longer capable of combining their wills into worldwide action. Differences in language signal the emergence of differences in cultures, which even the most fluid translations cannot overcome. We are loyal to our own culture, so much so that the evils of ethnocentrism and nationalism easily arise. But we need to be sure that we understand the alternative. There is no guarantee that global cooperation and a hoped for world-unifying culture will seek what is good. It may well use the leverage of unity to magnify the human capacity for evil. It is not difficult to imagine the horrible perversions that could easily emerge from a sustained global effort of eugenics and genetic engineering. The dispersion of the peoples is a punishment that limits. Less good can be done—but also less evil.

The confusion of the languages and scattering of the peoples also signals the end of the universal perspective of Genesis. Humanity is no longer a coherent entity that can be treated as a narrative actor. Humanity becomes a crazy quilt of tribes and nations with their own genealogies—and thus their own histories. Overinfluenced, perhaps, by modern dreams of universal reason, we tend to think this a loss. How can God restore a consummated creation if there is no unified collective humanity? But the biblical witness points in an utterly different direction. The fragmentation of humanity is a positive step forward, because the divine plan of redemption requires a particularized instrument, a nation rather than what contemporary pundits refer to as the "global community." The people of Israel are the key to the future, and the coming of Jesus Christ does not reunite humanity into a great, global culture unified by a single language. The Holy Spirit at Pentecost does not teach everyone Esperanto. Instead, the nations are brought into the covenant through their own languages (Acts 2:1–13). However we understand Christ's fulfillment of the law and the prophets, it does not involve a deviation in the divine plan of redemption in and through human particularity. Scattered peoples are gathered in a spiritual unity, not a cultural-political unity that mimics the structures and methods of the earthly cities.

11:10 These are the descendents of Shem.

The narrative presses forward toward the narrow gate. The stream of humanity that exits the ark two by two is further winnowed down to the one man, Abraham, through whom the nations shall be blessed. Babel concerns "all the earth," but the future of "all the earth" does not depend upon the collective fate of the many. It turns on the faithfulness of the one. The narrowing is conjoined with a literary device that foreshadows the future. In the genealogy leading up to the flood, the generations are marked by birth, but also by the refrain "and he died." The account of the descendents of Shem omits this refrain. The accent falls upon the future represented by birth: the covenant of life.

11:31 They settled there.

Terah recapitulates the way of the people who migrated from the east and settled on the plain in the land of Shinar to build their great tower (11:2). He stops moving, and in settling in one worldly location he is absorbed into the world that is defined by the past choices of Adam and Eve.

4

SCANDAL OF PARTICULARITY

"So shall my covenant be in your flesh" (17:13)

12:1a Now the Lord said to Abram.

The fall of Adam and Eve is primordial, and this raises an expectation in the readers of Genesis that God's remedy will also be worked out against the same background of universality. If all of humanity has been implicated in the covenant of the lie that we can live by bread alone, then wouldn't it stand to reason that the divine plan should deal with humanity at the same level of inclusive generality? Adam and Eve, Cain and Abel, the sons of God and daughters of men, the global flood, the tower of Babel—these figures and events have the timeless, archetypical feel of myth or legend. The literary forms are diverse, but one feels an expansive frame of reference and a general relevance: the first family, the first sin, the first murder, the first city. Shouldn't Genesis continue in this manner? Shouldn't this book of origins provide a broad outline of God's remedy to match the universality of the problem of sin?

But Genesis disappoints our expectations. As von Rad observes, "The transition from primeval history to sacred history occurs very abruptly and surprisingly. . . . All at once and precipitously the universal field of vision narrows. . . . Previously the narrative concerned humanity as a whole, man's creation and essential character, woman, sin, suffering, humanity, nations, all of them universal themes. In [Abraham's call], as though after a break, the particularism of election begins" (1972: 154). From Gen. 12 onward, Genesis is concerned with one household, a tiny portion of humanity that would be otherwise invisible—indeed, uninteresting—to anyone whose religious categories and concepts had been formed solely by the grand account of creation in Gen. 1.

This change in atmosphere from Gen. 1–11 is one of the single most important moments in the Bible. Because Christian theology has inherited its conceptual vocabulary from Greek thought, there has been a perennial temptation to treat universality as opposed to particularity, and eternity as antithetical to time. But these contrasting terms, which are so central to the commonsense metaphysical intuitions that we all tend to have, will not help us read Genesis—and they certainly will not help us think clearly about the God who comes to us in the person of Jesus of Nazareth.

The first chapters forewarn. The cosmic perspective of the Priestly writer is closely followed by the historical perspective of the Yahwist writer, and the final version of the text seems to relish rather than regret the effect. In a more explicit way, the early chapters of Genesis highlight dead ends that throw into doubt our assumptions about a creationwide salvation. The new beginning in the genealogy of Adam through Seth turns out to be a failure (→5:1). The cleansing of the world by way of the flood only stabilizes the effects of sin rather than washes away its stain. Only now, with a shift of focus from the global and universal to the narrowly tribal and particular, does the Bible reveal the true nature of redemption. God's plan is universal *in scope*—it sets about to redeem the entire cosmos—but the plan is not universal in method or means. Abraham, a particular head of a particular household, is called to live in a particular way, in a particular place. The divine plan injects a new possibility *into* the flow of history rather than acting *over* or *upon* humanity from the outside. Therefore, if we seek deliverance, we are not to appeal to God's timeless universality, nor should we imagine that God saves by way of some sort of direct application of his metaphysical properties, as if we were sipping the nectar of eternity from the cup of salvation. Instead, "you who pursue deliverance, you who seek the LORD; look to the rock from which you were hewn, and the quarry from which you were digged. Look to Abraham your father and to Sarah who bore you" (Isa. 51:1–2).

We are to look to Abraham, moreover, not because he represents something larger or more long-lasting. Abraham is not the father of faith because he is god writ small enough to be visible but large enough to be impressive, or time-bound enough to be part of history but somehow edging out toward a timeless invulnerability to change. Quite the contrary, Abraham is important because God's covenant with him quite simply *is* the divine plan. The full force of the *is*, which we cannot evade with terms such as *represents* or *symbolizes* or *mediates*, runs against the grain of our mental habits. To say that the calling of Abraham *is* God's plan means this. What God has promised in his covenant with Abraham and done to secure its fulfillment leads us to fuller knowledge of who God is, rather than the other way around. "Thus says the LORD" identifies God more surely and more profoundly than philosophical reflection on the being and nature of God.

This simple principle has been widely ignored by modern theologians, who often set about to discern what God must be like (inclusive, relational, universal, etc.) and then reinterpret covenant history accordingly. But this way of proceeding theologically goes against one of the most obvious features of Genesis. The architecture of Gen. 1 leans toward the seventh day, and from this we can see that God creates toward the end of consummation (→2:2). But nothing in Gen. 1–11 gives us a clue about how God plans to achieve this consummation of creation in the aftermath of human disobedience. We learn only of blind alleys: forgetfulness and grand schemes to scrub the world clean. Only in Abraham do we discover the extraordinarily unlikely nature of the divine plan: to call one man and his household and to invest this narrow slice of humanity with the promise of a new future.

The modern drift of theology into the analysis of concepts at a remove from their scriptural content, exemplified in the slide into notions such "incarnational ethics" or "trinitarian relationality" or "sacramentality," gives a special urgency to our reading of the disjunction between Gen. 1–11 and the highly particularized characters and events that follow Gen. 12. The extraordinary and unexpected shift in focus from universal to particular is the clearest way in which the Old Testament prefigures the fulfillment of the divine plan in Jesus Christ. In Abraham, God does something he does not do with Abel or with Seth or with Enoch or with Noah. The particularity of Abraham—he matters for the sake of the whole world—prepares us for the claim that the salvation of all rests on the death and resurrection of Jesus. Therefore, it is not possible to overemphasize 12:1. It is the beginning of the gospel. And this gospel commits us to what our inherited traditions of philosophy train us to regard as a metaphysical heresy: ascribing permanent universal significance to the particularity of Abraham and his household.[1]

12:1b Go from your country and your kindred and your father's house.

Sin defines the future for Adam and Eve's children. A tear in history is necessary, and it must be deep. Abraham's call is like the flaming sword that issues from the mouth of the Word of God (Rev. 19:21). As Jesus teaches, "If any one comes to me and does not hate his own father and mother and wife and children and brothers and sisters, yes, and even his own life, he cannot be my disciple" (Luke 14:26). Because the children of Adam and Eve are beholden to the lie that

1. Of course, a particular with universal significance is not in fact a metaphysical heresy, but only "foolishness to the Greeks." Metaphysics is a descriptive enterprise. The world is the way the world is, not the way that the conventional use of concepts would lead us to believe, and the Bible is a more reliable source of information about the way the world is than our habitual use of concepts. Scientific inquiry is also a more reliable source of data for our metaphysical reflection than our habitual use of concepts, and as the history of science shows, new scientific theories often make sense only if we set aside our metaphysical prejudices.

worldly life can satisfy our desire for rest, God must interrupt the cascading flow of time, tear out a family from the drumbeat of the generations, in order to cut to the joints and marrow of human history, dividing soul and spirit in order to sever the nerve of sin (Heb. 4:12).

This disruption is always a theological challenge, because we need to do justice to its depth and force without suggesting any alteration of the divine purpose established "in the beginning." Abraham is not called out of the human condition. He is called out of a history made through a false loyalty. Before the call, Abraham was enrolled in the movement of the generations, and he received a cultural inheritance from his mother and father. Joshua describes the situation: "Long ago your ancestors—Terah and his sons Abraham and Nahor—lived beyond the Euphrates and served other gods" (Josh. 24:2 NRSV). How could they do otherwise? Left to the future chosen by Adam and Eve, idolatry is our destiny. As Paul observes, all humanity has exchanged the living God for dead idols (Rom. 1:23). Our eyes are transfixed by what we imagine to be life-giving in this world, which we overleaf with gold and worship as if it were divine. We settle down into an identity that is defined by our past. We are satisfied to eat the fruit of our own way and be sated by our own desires (Prov. 1:31).

How can God break the hold of this past over our future? At root, the power of sin rests in Satan's promise in the garden: If you eat, you will not die—you can have what you want and enjoy it as the eternal end or purpose of your life. It is a covenant based on a lie: you can find your heart's desire by satisfying your desires for the things of this world. We all know the extraordinary power of this false promise, which like all convenient, self-serving beliefs has an ability to charm us into thinking that it must be true. Because it is a claim about the future rather than a present thing or reality, it cannot be isolated, examined, and destroyed by its contradiction to reality. Hope springs eternal, and even aging baby boomers sustain the vain hope that they can stay forever young. Thus, the power of the false promise cannot be defused by cool reason. It must be overcome by a counter-promise, a different claim about the future, a different covenant. Thus the divine promise: "Go from your country and your kindred and your father's house to the land I will show you. And I will make of you a great nation, and I will bless you, and make your name great, so that you will be a blessing" (12:1–2).

The promise makes the difference. We often think that metaphysical disjunctions such as material/immaterial, time/eternity, and particular/universal mark the sharpest, most dramatic differences. But the history of human religiosity suggests otherwise. We are attracted to the idea of a metaphysical transformation, because the remote world of concepts is safely distant from what we care about most. Our embodiment and temporality and particularity are abstractions that we easily manipulate in pious talk. We are more than happy to change metaphysical locations, because the transformation is notional rather than real. In fact, it can be very reassuring to believe that the embodied particularity of my life is unreal in comparison to my disembodied, eternal soul, because such a belief leaves me free to live here and now as I please. But the greatest appeal of easy metaphysical dichotomies is that they deflect attention away from a painful fact: we deeply fear giving up the specific loyalties that guide our wills and define our lives. Unlike embodiment and temporality, these loyalties must be killed by renunciation rather than be transcended by supposedly higher realities. A history created by the deformed human will cannot be cleansed or reformed or rehabilitated by some sort of application of a metaphysical balm, a dose of the spiritual or the eternal. Our belief in the false promise must be "cut off" and "plucked out" (Matt. 5:27–30). The life, community, and history of sin cannot be readjusted, repaired, or reeducated. Our self-wrought and futile future in the lie must be left behind: "The wicked will be cut off from the land, and the treacherous will be rooted out of it" (Prov. 2:22).

12:1–2 The land that I will show you . . . a great nation . . . make your name great.

Abraham's leave-taking is not simply a personal or interior departure. The divine plan is not secret, nor does it work in the privacy of the human heart. The tear in history is communal and public. In the generations between Noah and Abraham, an undifferentiated mass of humanity settled on a plain in the land of Shinar, and they tried to form a great city to make a name for themselves (→11:4). Now God promises to give Abraham-in-particular what humanity-in-general sought to achieve by its own hands when it gathered to build a tower to heaven: a place, a nation, and a name remembered by future generations.

In this way, God promises a future that redefines rather than rejects the false hopes of Babel. We are to "take delight in the LORD, [for] he will give you the desires of your heart" (Ps. 37:4). But our desires are not satisfied as we foolishly imagine them to be fulfilled. Instead, the LORD, who sees our true desires in their original integrity, now promises to satisfy them according to his own plan. In the promise to Abraham, we can see the divine fulfillment of our presently deformed desires for place, nation, and immortality. The original garden provided a place, and human beings rightly desire a homeland. The same holds for a nation. Patriotic impulses, nationalisms, tribal loyalties, family pride—all these drives toward collective greatness emerge from the original condition of our humanity. It is our nature to "desire a better country" (Heb. 11:16), and we rightly work toward a greater and more glorious common life. Finally, immortality is approximated by the forward reach of reproduction toward future generations. There is nothing unnatural about the human rebellion against death.

God does not deny these impulses toward homeland, nationhood, and immortality in order to overcome their distortions, excesses, and perversions. The disruption of Abraham's call is not a change in our humanity. Instead, in the promise to Abraham, these desires are guided toward their proper fulfillment.

The disruption is a change in our loyalty. St. Augustine's reading of salvation history in terms of the two cities, one earthly and the other heavenly, captures perfectly the purpose of the divine project. Our future depends on our citizenship, on the direction of our will and the object of our loves, not on our metaphysical status as embodied and finite. We are called out of our loyalty to the earthly city and its account of where we belong and what gives us hope of eternal life, so that we can transfer our loyalty to the heavenly city "whose builder and maker is God" (Heb. 11:10).

This shift in direction is the real nature of the change that God effects in Abraham, and it stands against a perennial gnosticism that tempts us. It is easy to see how our natural impulse to be loyal to place and tribe can lead to a destructive ethnocentrism that rages against the outsider. The blind patriotic fervor of the modern era led to destructive wars. Hitler's rise to power was aided by appeals to German national pride, as well as to anti-Semitism. In the aftermath of these destructive forms of ethnic pride and nationalism, it is not surprising that postmodern Western culture has used multicultural exhortations to try to soften our impulse toward local loyalties. But this effort too easily turns into gnostic erasure of particularity. If our human nature feeds a desire for loyalty that we satisfy in a sinful way, this covert gnosticism reasons, then we are to promote various moral and social therapies that neuter the underlying desire. The divine plan, in contrast, seeks to cure our false loves by providing us with the opportunity to satisfy our native human impulses with true loves. We are not to be other than human; instead, we are to be human in the right way.

12:3 By you all the families of the earth shall bless themselves.

As we have seen again and again, in Genesis reproduction and the promise of children is the primary way of signaling the forward thrust of time (→5:1). It is telling, therefore, that now, for the first time in Genesis, the LORD takes up the human capacity for reproduction. The generations that flow from Abraham will not simply move forward. Abraham's progeny will incarnate God's plan to provide blessing for all the families of the earth. The New Testament adopts this view without deviation. The genealogy of Jesus in Matthew's Gospel begins with Abraham; the genealogy in Luke's Gospel passes through Abraham.

The theological point is clear: God does not conquer the power of Satan's lie with a strategy of saturation bombardment from a distance (e.g., the flood). God establishes a small, unnoticeable beachhead in history through the forward thrust of the generations flowing from Abraham. Abraham's children become the immanent, this-worldly instrument of divine purpose. A small company presses its way into enemy territory, unnoticed as it penetrates deeply and gains the strategic crossroad. Again, the New Testament does not deviate. For St. Paul, the crucial question is covenant membership. Who, exactly, are Abraham's children? He argues for a spiritual patrimony, one that makes uncircumcised but baptized Gentiles children of Abraham. The underlying principle remains the same. God will bless all the nations in and through the children of Abraham.

Thus, the drama of redemption is neither a story of changing personalities, moving from Abraham to Moses to Jesus as a varied gallery of religious figures, nor one that shifts from law to gospel. The drama of redemption is the story of scripture as a whole, and the main plot is about how God adds more and more weight to the single history begun in Abraham. To use a term from patristic theology, scripture and the history it tells recapitulate rather than supersede or advance by way of changed focus or changed theme. Abraham's departure from the household of his father is recapitulated and intensified in his departure from his own household to sacrifice his son on Mount Moriah in obedience to the divine command ($\rightarrow$22:1). The covenant of circumcision is recapitulated and intensified in the holiness codes of Leviticus. In the same way, the shadows of the Old Testament are not ciphers solved and then discarded by the New Testament. They are illumined and saturated with the light of the Son's departure from his Father's house to journey into the world of human flesh. Throughout the Bible, the focus remains the same: the same obedience and the same blessing intensified and deepened and fulfilled. For when one thin thread of generations, one provincial history, and one obscure clan is saturated with divine purpose, even to the point of incarnation in the person of Jesus Christ, the balance of history changes. The covenant with Abraham is a single finger of divine intention pressing with unimaginable force on one spot in the endlessly complex inner-worldly factors that shape the future.

12:4 So Abram went, as the LORD had told him.

The call of Abraham signals the divine plan, which is to restore humanity to the Sabbath future and to do so by way of history, by the actions and affairs of men and women. Therefore we must say that human agency plays a real role. It's not enough for the LORD to call; Abraham must answer. But a real role is not the same as initiative. Abraham's independent human agency is responsive, not originative, just as Adam and Eve's choice of evil was responsive and not originative ($\rightarrow$3:1a). What we do matters for the future of the covenant, but its mattering depends on a prior divine initiative. Abraham does not debate or deliberate; he does as the LORD tells him. He "obeyed, and he went out, not knowing whither he went" (Heb. 11:8 AV). Abraham's feet do the walking. The grace of God's call does not replace human effort. Yet the "whither" is given by God rather than planned out by human efforts. We have no power to formulate an alternative to the path of sin. We can only follow the divine promise that points us away from the false future promised by Satan in the garden.

12:7 To your descendants I will give this land.

The promised land is the place of Sabbath rest, the destination for which God created all things in the beginning and for which he formed the man and the woman. The call of Abraham is for the sake of this promised rest. Should we think, therefore, that the call to "go forth" is temporary and preparatory? Are Abraham's descendents to settle down and build their own city? Is there a place in this world for those who receive the blessing of Abraham? Does God's call sanctify a place and a time in this world? Or is the pilgrimage of faith ongoing, even extending to an eternal journey into the mystery of God?

These are fundamental questions, and at root they concern the relationship of the finite order of space and time to the Sabbath future for which all things were created. This Sabbath future allows us to "receive the crown of life" (Jas. 1:12), "abide in the Son and in the Father" (1 John 2:24), "be known by God" (Gal. 4:9), and "become partakers of the divine nature" (2 Pet. 1:4). It is a puzzle to understand how all the stuff of life—specific times and things and places—can figure in such a future. I have argued *that* the reality of the created order must figure in the Sabbath future of the seventh day (→2:2). The creed confesses "the resurrection of the flesh." Nonetheless, *how* this comes to pass is a matter of theological speculation. No confessional affirmations stipulate how our embodied, time-bound nature comes to rest in fellowship with God's transcendent, infinite difference from creation.

The church fathers exploited the participatory emphasis of Platonic metaphysics in order to explain how the particularity of historical time and place can abide in God. Medieval theologians adopted Aristotle's analysis of reality in terms of a robust, fourfold scheme of causes, and this approach allowed them to explain how things can have both an immediate rationale (an efficient and material cause) and an ultimate purpose (a final cause). St. Thomas gave an account of the final vision of God that carefully preserves the mechanisms of finite perception and thus both affirms and transcends created nature. Each approach has strengths. However, there are no entirely satisfactory metaphysical explanations of how historical events or geographically specific places or particular persons both fully participate in the eternity of the divine life and still retain their local, time-bound reality. The difficulty of giving an adequate account is one reason why we so often fall back on simplistic views that downplay real fellowship with God. For example, popular views of heavenly reward keep us far removed from the divine: we enjoy this or that blessing, but not intimacy with God, whose magnitude seems to threaten to absorb the particular *me* who enjoys the heavenly reward. If we keep our distance, then we can retain the time and place that we need in order to be particular persons.

"At that time the Canaanites were in the land" (Gen. 12:6). The metaphysical problem of conceptualizing how historical particularity participates in the eternity of God's Sabbath rest is not a problem that Genesis worries about. Instead, the problem of participation takes a personal, experiential form. The promise is not immediately realized; in fact, throughout Genesis, the fulfillment of the promise remains remote and improbable. The promise concerns the future, and insofar as he obeys, Abraham serves that which will be rather than that which is the case at present: "He sojourned in the land of promise, as in a foreign land" (Heb. 11:9). Thus the existential puzzle. The future is "not yet" and therefore, even if we could get a clear picture of the metaphysical union of our time-bound and place-specific identities with God's rest, the concrete fact remains: the promised future does not exist now, but instead remains ahead of us. The question naturally arises: how can a future be real for us, how can it make a difference here and now? The question is not simply one for Abraham; it arises as a result of the countless ways in which the New Testament warns us against "the world." As many modern critics of Christianity have worried, if we live amid what presently exists "as in a foreign land," then aren't we courting disconnection from the real world, aren't we disloyal to the present?

It is certainly true that the future, as future, has no present reality. It can't. But the future can have reality as part of a promise, and it makes sense for Abraham (and us) to live and act on the basis of promises about the future.[2] The weather report promises rain, so we take our umbrellas. The company promises a decent salary, so we take the job. The state promises to prosecute those who cheat on their taxes, so we keep good records. The reasonableness of allowing statements about the future to govern our lives depends on the present trustworthiness of the promise rather than on our ability to directly inspect the future. Of course, if God makes a promise, then it is absolutely trustworthy, more trustworthy in fact than any judgment we might make on the basis of past or present realities. Thus, if we believe in the promises of God, then we necessarily live in the present as if it were a foreign time and in the world as if it were a foreign land. What is promised by God is more reliable—and in that sense more existentially urgent and real—than present circumstances and conditions, which, as we know, are never entirely clear and often change without notice.

2. The church fathers typically express the reality evoked by a promise with language of a "heavenly country" as opposed to the earthly land we walk upon; see, e.g., Didymus the Blind on this verse in *Didyme l'aveugle: sur la genèse*, ed. Pierre Nautin, Sources chrétiennes 233 (Paris: Cerf, 1976), 1.160–61. The effect is to transpose the future ahead into a place above. It is easy to criticize the transposition as an example of Platonic otherworldliness, but it is not entirely clear that Platonism governs these formulations. On the one hand, the church fathers tend to formulate their account of the heavenly country on the basis of God's promises rather than on metaphysical principles. In this way of thinking, what is ahead takes precedence over what is above. On the other hand, as Didymus's commentary indicates, the church fathers often read the calling of Abraham as important only insofar as it illustrates a general spiritual pattern of renouncing worldly loyalties, and this approach gives precedence to what is above. Augustine's genius was to place St. Paul's "Jerusalem above" (Gal. 4:26) into a scheme of world history in which what is above is precisely what is ahead, a combination suggested by St. Paul himself, who combines the temporal with the spatial when he juxtaposes "the present Jerusalem" with "Jerusalem above."

We need to be careful, however, about understanding the way in which God's promises make Abraham a wandering foreigner. God does not promise something other than historical, temporal existence. Abraham is not a metaphysical foreigner, as if his time and place were too small, too limited for the one who is called by God. He is not a man out of place; instead, he is a man before his time.[3] The land is "not yet" the place of rest—but it will be. Thus the importance of the altar he builds. The logic is clear: God promises, therefore Abraham builds. His trust in the promise creates an "already" of what is promised. The altar is a beachhead of the future into the present, a foretaste or firstfruit of the promise.

Abraham moves onward and builds altars elsewhere in the land (12:8–9). His progeny do the same. The world is the real place for our future: "Blessed are the meek, for they shall inherit the earth" (Matt. 5:5). God promises a place, and Abraham trusts in the promise of a place, not in the place of the promise. Abraham's trust in the promise makes the future present. He builds the altar, and his building of it on the basis of the promise makes the spot sacred. Abraham does not discover a sacred spot and then build the altar.

We see a similar dynamic at work in Leviticus. The LORD commands the Israelites to restore each plot of land to its original owner during the year of Jubilee. At first glance, the policy of restoration seems to serve the purpose of preventing families from permanently losing ownership. Yet, a close look suggests something different. "The land is not to be sold in perpetuity," says the LORD. The rationale does not concern the dangers of landlessness, but instead the temptation to hold the land too closely: "For the land is mine," the LORD continues, "for you are strangers and sojourners with me" (Lev. 25:23). The Jubilee redemption of land is meant as much to loosen the grip of places on those who possess them, as to restore land to those whom poverty and bad fortune has dispossessed. The message is clear: "Wait for the LORD, and keep to his way, and he will exalt you to possess the land" (Ps. 37:34). It is not this or that land that is promised: it is the promised land. The promise makes the place.

12:10 Now there was a famine in the land.

The divine plan moves forward through a series of narrow openings. In this instance, Abram is called to the land, only to be driven out by famine and into perilous circumstances in Egypt. The trial is just one of many. The promise to

3. This is largely what the church fathers mean by "spiritual." To interpret the spiritual sense of the Old Testament means to read it as a "sign before its time." The same holds for living "spiritually." This does not mean to live at a distance from physical reality. It means to live in accord with the fulfillment of God's plan, which, though completed in Christ, still awaits final fulfillment in our lives.

Abraham does not provide him with a straight and easy road. Traditional readers find ten trials (Kugel 1998: 297–99):

1. He must leave his homeland.
2. He suffers the affliction of famine.
3. He endures the burdens and temptations of wealth.
4 Two times his wife is taken by powerful men.
5. He faces dire consequences of childlessness.
6. He must undergo circumcision.
7. Hagar threatens to bring turmoil to his household.
8. He must cast out Ishmael.
9. He must ready himself to sacrifice Isaac.
10. Sarah's death tempts him with despair.

In these trials, the way of the promise comes clear. It will not be without tribulation: "If any man would come after me, let him deny himself and take up his cross and follow me" (Matt. 16:24). If the burden is light, then it is only because of our trust in the power of God to make good his promises, not because the way is pleasant.

12:13 Say you are my sister.

"Lying lips are an abomination to the LORD" (Prov. 12:22). In this episode and in a similar one later (Gen. 20), ancient commentators exercised themselves to exculpate Abraham, for they thought it unseemly that the father of faith should continue to appear as a servant of the father of lies. But perhaps this anxiety mistakes the nature of these episodes. The doubling of the stories (indeed, tripling, since a similar story is told about Isaac and Rebekah in 26:6–11) suggests an importance not immediately obvious. The atmosphere of deception echoes the primeval deception of the serpent, and Sarah's cooperation recalls the original complicity of the man and the woman in the garden. The primordial problem of sin rather than a patriarch's flawed character seems to be the primary issue.

The episodes also end with an important twist. In the garden, the serpent lies, and then events tumble forward toward their destructive end. In contrast, in both stories, Sarah's captivity to worldly powers is reversed. The LORD will not allow Abraham's lie and Sarah's captivity to define the future. God intervenes and sends plagues to afflict Pharaoh and his household (12:17). This leads to a good outcome. Abraham is enriched and escorted back to the land of the promise. The pattern is repeated with King Abimelech of Gerar in Gen. 20, with differences: instead of plagues, Abimelech receives a dream from God that saves Sarah from defilement. But the outcome is the same: he ends up paying homage to Abraham and Sarah, offering them silver and a welcome in his land.

Therefore, instead of reading the stories of Abraham's lie back into the original lie and then worrying about how to reconcile the sin of prevarication with his role as recipient of God's promise, perhaps these episodes are meant to be read forward, providing a narrative synopsis of the entire divine plan. The episodes begin with captivity to sin (both Abraham's spiritual captivity in his recourse to the lie and Sarah's literal captivity). Then a plague or dream afflicts the agent of captivity, and this leads to release and enrichment. We see the pattern in Joseph. He is held captive in prison until dreams afflict Pharaoh, and then he is not only restored to freedom but, like Abraham, raised to a higher level. And, of course, the pattern defines the beginning of the story of Israel's exodus. The Israelites fall into slavery under Pharaoh, but the LORD intervenes to reverse the direction of the story. Plagues afflict Pharaoh, and the Israelites leave Egypt enriched. Not surprisingly, therefore, Ps. 126:5–6 uses the pattern to express the basic promise of the covenant: "They that sow in tears shall reap in joy. He that goeth forth and weepeth, bearing precious seed, shall doubtless come again with rejoicing, bringing his sheaves with him" (AV).

More than captivity and liberation are at work. The stories of Abraham's lie and Sarah's captivity point toward a feature of the divine plan that does not become evident until later. Those called remain under the influence of sin. It is transparently the case that Abraham tells a lie. Sarah falls into the hands of powerful men who wish to have their way with her. We see, therefore, that the promise alone—and Abraham's trust in the promise—is not powerful enough to alter the trajectory of events. God needs to intervene. The way of the promise is difficult (→12:10), and our ability to successfully walk in this way depends upon God's work in history (→15:8 and →15:18). God does not just call, promise, and make a covenant. "The LORD is a man of war" (Exod. 15:3) who performs mighty deeds for those whom he has chosen: "Thou overthrowest thy adversaries" (15:7).

13:7 There was strife.

Lot participates in Abraham's wealth and abundance, but with wealth comes conflict. As we read in 1 Tim. 6:10, "the love of money is the root of all evils." Yet we need to be careful here. The story of Abraham, indeed, the Old Testament as a whole, depicts wealth as a blessing. This bars us from imagining that wealth is a power for evil, any more than the fruit of the tree of the knowledge of good and evil was the source of transgression. The fruit attracts a rightful desire to enjoy its goodness according to the divine purpose for creation. The same holds for all human economic activities that create wealth. The problem is that our disordered souls desire good things wrongly. It is not money that brings strife; the deep problem is a love of money that comes to supplant the love of God.

A tacit distinction between wealth in itself and wealth as the occasion for strife and disordered desire allows the scriptures to praise the great golden vessels of the temple while denouncing the city of Jerusalem sick with oppression. Again and again the prophets give voice to the LORD's judgment against those who crush the people and "devour the poor" (Hab. 3:14), those who do "not aid the poor and needy" (Ezek. 16:49) but instead are "grinding the face of the poor" (Isa. 3:15) with a restless greed (Job 20:20). Wealth and power give leverage to the human will, and when we are ill with sin, our bank accounts and social position serve to magnify the scope and consequence of our distorted aspirations. Yet fine china is not to be smashed, just as apple trees are not to be put to the axe. We are not to dismantle modern industrial society, nor should we imagine that a vibrant, growing economy is a sign of social disease. The idolatry of wealth cannot be cured by iconoclasm, "for we are not contending against flesh and blood" (Eph. 6:12). What must be smashed and cut down is our loyalty to the covenant of the lie, in this case, the lie that wealth can be the source of life. The axe must fall within the human heart.

Spiritual abundance can have a similar magnifying effect on human sinfulness. The history of religions is a history of conflict as rich in bitterness, jealousy, and rivalry as the marketplace or the senate chamber. One need be no despiser of faith to notice that a preacher's ability to give his speech the ring of holiness, as well as the sacred robes of priest and pastor, increases perversion and intensifies a power for evil. The noble human desire for God can be just as deftly and wickedly manipulated as the more commonplace human desire for comfort, luxury, respect, and dominion. Indeed, because spiritual desires are finer and less hindered by concupiscence (→3:21), their manipulation can lead to more extreme and disastrous evils. The cults of Baal are more dangerous than economic oppression and the violence of power politics. Modern ideologies have exploited high ideals of social equality, national loyalty, and collective sacrifice in order to defile the twentieth century with mass graves.

Just as strife caused by wealth cannot be overcome by smashing the machines that create wealth, so also the death wrought by ideologies cannot be prevented by removing occasions for social idealism or patriotic commitment. One dimension of the moral project of postmodernism has been to deconstruct and deflate by recourse to irony. We hope that by believing less we will become less vulnerable to spiritual manipulation. We cannot be duped, we imagine, if critical doubt weakens the force of our commitments. If there is no truth, then we will not quarrel over our visions of the truth. If nothing is worth fighting for, then nobody will fight. However, an iconoclasm of truth will not succeed. Hell can be as easily built of apathy and diffidence as of megalomania and fevered ideological zeal—perhaps more easily, for it is difficult to wake from the narcosis of a velvet barbarism that desires no truth.

13:10 Lot lifted up his eyes.

Abraham is the older and the greater, yet he cedes the choice of portions to Lot, and in so doing Abraham shows himself greater still. For as Jesus teaches the disciples who fall into strife in a dispute over status, "Let the greatest among you become as the youngest, and the leader as one who serves" (Luke 22:26). But should Lot accept the choice in the first place? To separate from Abraham is a mistake, for Abraham is the source of blessing.

Lot chooses the Jordan valley, a well-watered place like the garden of the LORD. The choice reflects a common impulse. Lot sees what seems to be an Edenic place of repose, and he desires to return to the state of original happiness. He imagines himself retracing the steps of past generations, going back to the innocent abundance of the garden of Eden in a dream of forgetfulness. In this way, Lot's choice is similar to the genealogy of Adam in Gen. 5 (→5:1). Just as the genealogy of Adam that excludes Cain and Abel fails to avoid the stain of sin, so also do the consequences of Lot's choice serve to warn readers in a similar way about false solutions to the problem of sin. Lot's nostalgia and desire to get back to primitive purity will not succeed. Forgetfulness will not reverse the forward flow of the history of sin.

Lot's choice is very much with us today. Jean-Jacques Rousseau dreamt of returning humanity to its original purity, to a way of thinking and living undefiled by the perverting influences of social expectation. He thought adults too deeply infected by social customs, but Rousseau held out hope that a radical revolution in education would allow children to preserve their innocence and retain their instincts of natural dignity. Our time shows his dream for the fantasy it was. We cannot reverse the history of the covenant of the lie by sending our children to progressive summer camps, where the wickedness of adult life is magically excluded and where they can play in sinless nakedness, relating to each other according to an innate, childlike purity. (Although it is amazing how tenaciously we hold to Rousseau's dream, even against all the evidence.) There is no future in the worldly mirages of the garden of Eden, for Adam's sin now reigns. At a distance, what seethes with conflict and violence can easily seem to be a well-watered and inviting place. Soon enough, Lot's imagined garden of happiness is overrun by warring armies, and Lot is taken captive, a prize of war.

13:14 Lift up your eyes.

The LORD commands Abraham to look and see, but according to St. Paul, those chosen by God are to walk by faith, not by sight (2 Cor. 5:7). Hebrews reinforces the contrast between faith and sight: "Faith is the assurance of things hoped for, the conviction of things not seen" (11:1). Abraham is the father of faith, for "by faith he sojourned in the land of promise" (11:9), and therefore we should assume that he does not navigate by sight. Yet in this passage, Abraham is commanded by God to see.

The contradiction is apparent and not real. Faith is contrasted to sight not as blindness to vision, but instead as obedience to self-direction. Lot lifts up his eyes and sees the well-watered Jordan valley. Then, by what he appraises to be his best bet for a happy future, he chooses his way forward. In that sense, he walks by sight. Yet his eyes deceive him, for they are the eyes of worldly desire. As Calvin writes, "Let us then learn by this example, that our eyes are not to be trusted; but that we must rather be on our guard lest we be ensnared by them, and be encircled, unawares, with many evils; just as Lot, when he fancied that he was dwelling in paradise, was nearly plunged into the depths of hell."[4] In contrast, Abraham waits upon the LORD to be shown the way. In this sense, he is walking by faith. Only after the LORD commands does he lift up his eyes to see the future that has been chosen for him by God. The land of the promise was invisible to Lot. He did not have the eyes to see. To Abraham, however, God has given the power of sight. He can see the land that awaits him in the future, visible only to the eyes of faith. "To you it has been given to know the secrets of the kingdom of God," Jesus tells his disciples, "but for others they are in parables, so that seeing they may not see, and hearing they may not understand" (Luke 8:10). Abraham sees the secret—the land to be limned and populated by the promise—while Lot sees a parable of Eden restored, the Jordan valley that outwardly seems to be the perfect place of rest.

13:16 I will make your descendants as the dust of the earth.

The promises of place and posterity are repeated throughout the cycle of stories about Abraham, but here with an interesting twist. How many shall be the descendents of Abraham? In a telling echo of the creation of the primordial couple, the children of Abraham shall be as many as the dust of the earth itself. From the dust and stones of the land can God raise up children of Abraham (Matt. 3:9). The promised land will not be just Eden restored, but enlarged and teaming with life. It will be Eden fulfilled.

13:17 Arise, walk.

In the larger context of the divine plan, the promised land is closely linked to the law given at Sinai. Just as Abraham is commanded to walk the length and breadth of the land, the people of Israel are commanded to walk in the law of God (Exod. 16:4). The way of the law has priority, because it brings abundance to the land. It is the way of the promise, and the promise makes the place. The LORD promises, "Walk in my statutes and observe my commandments and do them, then I will give you your rains in their season, and the land shall yield its

---

4. John Calvin, *Commentaries on the First Book of Moses, Called Genesis*, trans. John King (repr., Grand Rapids: Eerdmans, 1948), 1.373.

increase" (Lev. 26:3–4). As Israel walks in the paths of righteousness according to the commandments, she is torn from the blinding falsehoods of Satan's lie. By walking in the ways of the LORD, she sees, however darkly, the place of rest that is her inheritance. The seeing, then, comes from the way of the walking, not the way of walking from a prior seeing. The petition comes first: "Teach me thy way, O LORD, that I may walk in thy truth" (Ps. 86:11). Then, as we walk, what is promised can be "seen with our own eyes . . . [and] looked upon and touched with our hands" (1 John 1:1).

However we wish to interpret the complex teaching of the New Testament about the covenant with Abraham, the laws of Sinai, and the conflicts that Jesus (and Paul) had with Jewish authorities in first-century Palestine, we must recognize that to walk in the way of Christ is to continue along the pathways first walked by Abraham and his descendents (→17:7). Jesus says to the lame man what God says to Abraham: "Rise and walk" (Matt. 9:5 and parallels). Peter sets the lame man on his way: "In the name of Jesus Christ of Nazareth, walk" (Acts 3:6). Paul urges us to "walk in the steps of . . . faith" (Rom. 4:12 AV), "walk as children of light" (Eph. 5:8), and "walk by the Spirit" (Gal. 5:16). The path is not a dark passageway fraught with uncertainty, nor is it spiritual and remote in an occult or otherworldly sense. To walk in the Spirit requires the follower of Christ to "walk in love, as Christ loved us and gave himself up for us, a fragrant offering and sacrifice to God" (Eph. 5:2). To the eyes of the world, the way in which the follower of Christ walks the length and breadth of love seems to lead into a hopelessly hostile land of persecution, crucifixion, and death. But with the eyes of faith, the way of Christ walks in the land of the promise, where the faithful "walk in newness of life" (Rom. 6:4).

14:2 Kings made war.

Human beings have a natural sense of justice and a desire to live in peace. Original sin does not extinguish our native intuition that social life ought to be ordered toward the common good. Moreover, we have the capacity to organize social life according to humane principles. Economic relations can be regulated by principles of fair dealing. Diligent police can protect communities from crime. Wise leaders can balance interests and forestall eruptions of revolution and civil war. Diplomats can grease the gears of international cooperation. However, the relative justice and peace made possible by good kings are like quiet conversations easily drowned out by the clatter of a rapidly moving train. The children of Adam, willingly or unwillingly, knowingly or unknowingly, are being swept into the future chosen by Adam and Eve. Because fallen men and women mistakenly vest their hopes in the finite goods of this world, our collective life is always unbalanced, always ready to fall into violence and disorder. The threats of a few can bring terror; the wealth of a few can whip up greed and envy; lassitude, indifference, and preoccupation with private well-being can leave the public realm unguarded. In ricocheting political action, reaction, and counterreaction, events easily cascade toward conflict and war.

14:14a Abram heard.

Jesus warns that those who live by the sword shall die by the sword, and from the earliest Christian communities through St. Francis to Dorothy Day, the way of faith has been juxtaposed to warfare. This strong dichotomy would seem to apply to Abraham. The way of obedience to God's call separates Abraham from the history of the covenant of the lie. He trusts in the promise of a different future. He need not enter into endless human striving to build up kingdoms by force of arms. But this difference does not remove Abraham from the world. Faith *contra mundum* ("against the world") is not life *supra mundum* ("above the world").

Abraham may not place his hope in the covenant of the lie, but he retains responsibility for those ground up in the machinery of death. He hears of the plight of his brother, and he knows himself to be his brother's keeper. Abraham's response to Lot's captivity epitomizes the basic logic of Christian analysis of just war. The Good Samaritan helps the neighbor who has been struck down by bandits and, by extension, is prepared to free the neighbor held prisoner by brigands. Thus, Abraham rallies his small band of men in order to come to Lot's aid.

14:14b He led forth his trained men.

The text is silent about the kind of training that qualified Abraham's men for battle. The context, however, is suggestive. An improbably small force of 318 men defeats the allied armies of the Eastern kings and rescues Lot. The narrative reinforces one of the great themes of scripture: salvation by a remnant. Yet the remnant is not a tattered band of survivors. They are trained and disciplined by the oaks of Mamre, where Abraham has built an altar to the LORD (13:18). There, the remnant girds its loins with truth, employs the shield of faith, puts on the helmet of salvation, and wields the sword of the word of God (Eph. 6:14–17). As the psalmist proclaims, "Blessed be the LORD, my rock, who trains my hands for war, and my fingers for battle" (Ps. 144:1).

14:18 Melchizedek king of Salem brought out bread and wine.

Who is the mysterious king-priest Melchizedek? He is not mentioned in the genealogies of Genesis. Announced as a priest of God most high, he appears out of nowhere to officiate over Abraham's victory celebrations, and he disappears just as suddenly. As Calvin observes, "This Melchizedek, whoever he was, is presented before us, without any origin, as if he had dropped from the clouds, and . . . his name is buried without any mention of death."[5]

The strangeness of Melchizedek appeals to the author of Hebrews. The silence of Genesis about the birth and death of this first priest in the Bible becomes positive testimony concerning the finality and eternity of Christ's priesthood. Melchizedek "is without father or mother or genealogy, and has neither beginning of days nor end of life, but resembling the Son of God he continues a priest forever" (Heb. 7:3).

In the context of the Old Testament, that Genesis refers to him as a priest raises a key question: How can there be a priest before the institution of the sacrifices by God? How can there be a priest without a tabernacle or temple? For the author of Hebrews, these troubling questions are resolved. He contrasts the inherited priesthood of Israel with the apparently unique status of Melchizedek. The argument draws upon Ps. 110, which is read as appointing someone to the priesthood simply by declaration: "You are a priest for ever after the order of Melchizedek" (Ps. 110:4, quoted in Heb. 7:17). This mode of priestly consecration by declaration stands in contrast to the temple priesthood, which comes "according to bodily descent" (7:16) and "without an oath" (7:20). With this contrast in mind, the author of Hebrews concludes: "This makes Jesus the surety of a better covenant" (7:22). Direct divine appointment has priority over the mediation of office by way of inheritance. Not surprisingly, therefore, the dome of St. Peter's in Rome is inscribed with God's declaration from Ps. 110. The message is clear. Christ's eternal sacerdotal role is established "in the beginning," and it continues in the sacramental life of the church until the end of the age.

For the author of Hebrews, therefore, the account of Melchizedek in Gen. 14 prefigures Christ. It is important to see, however, that this prefiguration does not move beyond the Old Testament to rest in the New. We are not to file away a few points about Melchizedek as proofs of the high priestly office of Christ. The figure is to the fulfillment as an analogy is to the subject matter at hand. The one illuminates the other. This relationship invites readers to return again and again to the original figure in order to see more fully the fulfillment. We need to go back in order to search for the treasure "hidden in the field" (Matt. 13:44).

For example, one of the striking features of Hebrews is the conjunction of intense focus on a God-directed economy of ritual sacrifice with exhortation to "let brotherly love continue" (Heb. 13:1). The same double focus is found in this episode in Genesis. Melchizedek brings bread and wine to the scene of victory. Like the eucharistic feast it prefigures, these elements serve as an offering and sacrifice to God—and, without any compromise in purpose, they are refreshment for the tired warriors. In this way, the strange figure of Melchizedek conforms to the double love of God and neighbor. The story illuminates the way in which ritual

5. Ibid., 388.

devotion does not detract from but rather works in concert with the corporeal works of mercy.

14:24 I will take nothing.

If the great alliance of kings manifests the violent consequences of sin, then the king of Sodom points back to the sweet, ingratiating voice of the serpent. "Please," he says, "let me be generous. You can have all the spoils of war." Abraham resists the temptation. He accepts nothing but what has been necessary for subsistence: "what the young men have eaten" (14:24). Abraham has been made rich by the power of the promise. He does not take and eat the fruit of war. By refusing, Abraham remains outside the economy of gift and tribute that links lord to vassal. He remains indifferent to the social practices that define power and position. He is in the world but not of it, the prototype of all the faithful who are "strangers and exiles on the earth" (Heb. 11:13).

Abraham's situation is not unique. The spoils of war function as an important temptation in Old Testament accounts of battle. Saul is depicted as disobeying God, who has commanded the complete destruction of the Amalekites, sparing nothing. But Saul allows plunder, and he takes the ultimate symbol of worldly superiority: the vanquished king as a captive. In so doing, he forfeits his future: "The LORD has torn the kingdom of Israel from you this day" (1 Sam. 15:28). David is Saul's successor, but he too is implicated by love of spoils. Leaving on a rescue mission not unlike Abraham's expedition to save Lot, David is able to defeat his adversaries, the Amalekites, who are themselves debauched by long enjoyment of the great spoils they have taken. David may not be given to the excesses of the Amalekites, and he is portrayed as scrupulously fair in the distribution of the bounty of victory, but unlike Abraham, he participates in the military conventions of taking and distributing the spoils of war. It is a harbinger of the inexorable decline of the royal houses of Israel into petty principalities distinguished from other kingdoms only in their weakness.

15:1 The LORD came to Abram.

The voice of God to Abraham recalls the victory of Abraham just narrated: "Fear not, Abram, I am your shield; your reward shall be very great." Abraham's military campaign was conducted with a proper confidence, and his refusal of the spoils of war was fitting. He enjoys the favor of God, and he has no need for the king of Sodom to make him rich. God's reward will be great. But Abraham is thinking about the future, not the past. He can see only his childlessness. Abraham has seen and walked the land of the promise, but because he "see[s] through a glass, darkly" (1 Cor. 13:12 AV), he cannot see how he will enter the promise:

"O Lord GOD, what wilt thou give me, for I continue childless?" (Gen. 15:2). Can his inheritance be great if he has no inheritors? What is the value of possessions and a great name if he has no children? How can a childless man pass along an inheritance? The question turns to lament: "Behold, thou hast given me no offspring; and a slave born in my house will be my heir" (15:3).

The lament is quite realistic and reflects a common trial of faith. Abraham notices that the divine promise has not borne fruit. He remains childless. He has heard the promise, but he can see no future, because he sees only himself as a barren vessel of divine blessing, incapable of participating in the great forward current of the generations that mark biblical time. The lament is perennial. The Israelites enslaved in Egypt "groaned under their bondage, and cried out for help" (Exod. 2:23). How could God forsake them? "How long, O LORD? Wilt thou forget me for ever? How long wilt thou hide thy face from me?" (Ps. 13:1). It is a lament that runs through the psalms and recurs again and again in the prophets as they contemplate the iniquities of Israel: "O Jerusalem! How long will it be before you are made clean?" (Jer. 13:27). These laments have the same logic as Abraham's complaint: "O LORD, you have promised righteousness and blessing, but wickedness and suffering prevail. You have promised, but how long can I endure the delay of fulfillment? I am at the end of despair. Like childless Abraham, I cannot see any future other than sin and death."

The Christian tradition has its own forms of lamentation. The plea "Come, Lord Jesus!" ends Revelation (22:20). It expresses a yearning desire for the final triumph of Christ, in a present reality that seems unpromising. However, the main focus of a great deal of Christian lamentation concerns our personal participation in Christ's fulfillment of the promise of righteousness. We have faith in Christ's saving death, but we wonder why we can't seem to enter into his way of righteousness with any confidence or regularity. Where, we ask, are the good works? Where are the children that faith produces? As we fight against our sinful habits, we can easily picture ourselves in Abraham's position. We look at our lives and the barrenness of our faith, and we lament, "What good is the promise in Christ? Truly, Abraham speaks for me: 'Behold, thou hast given me no offspring, for I continue childless.'"

James addresses Abraham's situation, transposed into the question of faith and works. The new life in Christ is given to the baptized and is a "good ... and ... perfect gift ... from above" (Jas. 1:17), so there can be no question of the source of righteousness, which is God alone. The faithful are like Abraham: he is blessed because called, not called because blessed. So, in a primary sense, the good things of God come from above. He elects. Yet the promised future is real, and we rightly expect "that we should be a kind of first fruit of his creatures" (1:18). In other words, just as God promises Abraham descendents—a future in his flesh—so also God promises righteousness in the flesh to the servants of Christ. And thus, just as Abraham expects a child, the faithful should expect their faith to give birth to good works. The faithful are impregnated by "the implanted [divine] word" (1:21). They should be "doers of the word, and not hearers only" (1:22).

Not surprisingly, then, James's main thrust echoes Abraham's lament: where are the promised children? After explicitly evoking Abraham's encounter with God narrated in Gen. 15, James goes on to paraphrase the reasoning that lies behind Abraham's lament: "As the body apart from the spirit is dead, so faith apart from works is dead" (Jas. 2:26). The blessings promised to Abraham are spectral and notional as long as he remains childless. Without an heir, his faith is as good as dead, since there will be no one to inherit the promises. In the same way, the promise of new life in Christ is remote and distant as long as we fail to give birth to good works: "Faith apart from works is barren" (2:20). Without works, faith gives voice to Abraham's plight. How can we persevere in the promises of Christ if we can see no way forward in our flesh?

The whole question of faith and works has been hopelessly muddied by centuries of Protestant and Catholic polemic.[6] Two points are worth keeping in mind, however. First, in the main, the Reformers endorsed Abraham's lament as spiritually legitimate. All the Reformation talk of forensic and imputed righteousness was meant to clarify the source of the possibility of good works, which comes from the grace of God alone. We do not give birth to the promise that creates an alternative to sin. The promise comes from God; it is imputed. But the Reformers also agreed that we rightly expect God to make good on his promise of new life in Christ. On this point they were on common ground with their Catholic adversaries, who tended to think that the emphasis on grace alone had the effect of denying any actual human capacity for righteous deeds. In spite of polemical distortions that can lead us to think otherwise, according to both, if the promises of God are true, then faith must make a difference. The second point is to remember that Genesis gives a great deal of space to the extraordinary delays and complications that emerge in God's response to Abraham's lament. Isaac is a long time coming, and the child disrupts Abraham's household, bringing as much pain as joy. Thus, to return to the terms of James and the Reformation debates, we should not expect faith to produce good works immediately, and when faith does, we should not expect the righteous deeds of the true servants of Christ to be aglow with a pleasant, easy sanctity.

The Catholic doctrine of purgatory is best understood as a theological hypothesis developed to do justice to the fact that the children of faith (works) often come late in the game. Few of those baptized into the promises of Christ end up visibly manifesting very much of their participation in his righteousness. We look at ourselves and say, "How long, O LORD, must I remain under the sway of my sinful habits?" The answer given at the Council of Trent was simple: there is a time and place where we are given more time to bear the children of the promise. Just as Abraham had to wait a long time for Isaac, so also do many (most) Christians

---

6. In this and subsequent discussions of Reformation controversies, I am indebted to the substantial body of literature produced during the Lutheran–Roman Catholic dialogues begun after Vatican II.

need a long time—more time than the normal duration of life here on earth—to be purified of the effects of sin and fully inhabit the righteousness of Christ.

15:4 This man shall not be your heir.

If Abraham's lament evokes the great question of faith and works, then God's answer takes us back to the very source of the new future he promises. Unable to see his way forward, Abraham proposes his own solution. He intends to take the initiative in order to bridge his way from a barren present to a fruitful future. Abraham allows that his inheritance will default to a certain Eliezer of Damascus. Whether we read these verses as an expression of Abraham's acquiescence and reliance upon worldly principles of inheritance or as a more active attempt to take the future into his own hands by designating an heir, the logic remains the same. Unable to see his way forward into the fulfillment of the promise, Abraham relies on human laws, principles, and actions. It is a strategy for securing the future that is more fully developed in Sarah's plan to use Hagar to secure what God seems unwilling or unable to provide (→16:2a).

Reliance on worldly principles and powers to secure the future of the promise is precisely what the Reformers meant by works-righteousness. They were not opposed to prayers or acts of charity or church attendance, any more than the law given at Sinai stands opposed to principles of inheritance for those who are childless. But God rejects Eliezer of Damascus: "This man shall not be your heir." In a similar manner, the Reformers rejected the use of prayers or good works or spiritual devotions as bridges from our present sinfulness to the promised future of righteousness. The way forward cannot depend on our actions, even pious actions, just as Abraham's future cannot depend on his reliance on worldly principles or his own decisions. It is for the LORD alone to bring the promise to fruition. Abraham rightfully expects to participate: faith gives birth to good works. But God alone brings him into the future: salvation is by grace alone.

15:6 He believed the LORD; and he reckoned it to him as righteousness.

This verse has been a point of controversy since the Reformation. James cites it as part of the argument that faith must give birth to works (→15:1). St. Paul restates this verse in Gal. 3:6 as a key part of his argument against the requirement of circumcision for Gentiles. And Paul cites the verse again in Rom. 4:3, again as part of an argument against the necessity of circumcision for covenant membership. By my reading, Paul's view of covenant fulfillment never disagrees with James's view that God's promise will be fulfilled in our flesh: "Present your bodies as a living sacrifice, holy and acceptable to God" (Rom. 12:1). But Paul does not draw attention to Abraham in order to address questions about the fruitfulness of God's promises. Instead, his concern is with membership in the covenant. How are we to receive or enter into God's promises?

In both Galatians and Romans, Paul appeals to Abraham, because in the sequence of events narrated in Genesis it is clear that God chooses Abraham and makes the crucial promises before issuing commandments, in particular, before commanding the mark of circumcision. This reasoning is most clearly developed in Romans. First, Paul makes a narrow argument based on the verbal sequence of Gen. 15:6: Abraham believed—God reckoned it as righteousness.[7] By Paul's way of thinking, the plan is to deliver us from the power of sin by way of the blessing of forgiveness, and Abraham is blessed with the liberating promise of forgiveness insofar as he believes. Faith, in other words, is the key to Abraham's participation in the divine plan. Works may follow, but they do not bring Abraham into God's plan. To use the language of this commentary: the promise creates a new future for Abraham, one free from the future of sin, and insofar as he believes, he lives toward this new future.[8]

St. Paul's verbal argument in Romans quickly gives way to a broader observation about the sequencing of events in Genesis. Paul asks, "Is the blessing [of the forgiveness of sins] pronounced only upon the circumcised, or also upon the uncircumcised?" (Rom. 4:9). Well, Paul says in effect, let's take the case of Abraham. Did he or did he not receive the promise of a new future? Genesis is, of course, quite clear that the answer is yes. The whole point of the repeated reiterations of the promise at various points is to drive home that Abraham receives them. But was he circumcised when he first received the promise? Since the covenant of circumcision does not come until Gen. 17, the answer is once again clear: no. For Paul, then, the witness of Genesis is conclusive: "The promise to Abraham and his descendants, that they should inherit the world, did not come through the law, but through the righteousness of faith" (Rom. 4:13).[9]

We certainly cannot resolve Reformation controversies in a commentary, to say nothing of the implications of Paul's argument for a Christian theology of Judaism. However, it is instructive to remember that since the Council of Trent

---

7. The Hebrew lends itself to different formulations, not all of which support Paul's reading, as many commentators point out.

8. One striking feature of Genesis is that the entire cycle of stories from the calling of Abraham in Gen. 12 through Jacob's wrestling match with God in Gen. 32 seems entirely disinterested in the problem of sin. Paul's supposition that the promises of land, prosperity, and descendents will eventually amount to the promise of forgiveness is based on a larger reading of the sweep of covenant history. Yet his intensive focus on Abraham is germane. Forgiveness breaks the hold of sin over the future, and in this sense, Paul's sin-and-forgiveness framework fits the basic logic of Abraham's situation. I have found it helpful to consider Jewish commentators on Genesis who are not influenced by Paul's gloss of the promises. This helps the Christian reader to see that, however necessary, a solution to the problem of sin is not all that God promises—as Paul himself observes elsewhere in his letters.

9. Ancient rabbinic readers saw precisely the same logic at work in Genesis, which is why they read the foreshadowing of Mosaic commandments into the earlier chapters of Genesis.

Catholicism has accented the concerns found in James, where Gen. 15:6 is deployed in a different but not contradictory way. In James, the emphasis falls on Abraham's faith insofar as it is reckoned as righteousness—that is, insofar as God gives Abraham's faith the visible, real form of righteousness. This reading points readers forward to Gen. 17 and the covenant of circumcision. There, the promised righteousness is inscribed in Abraham's flesh, just as good works are implanted in the hearts of those who believe in Christ. Paul, in contrast, reads the relationship between faith and righteousness according to a different theological concern. In Rom. 4, he focuses on covenant membership, not covenant fruitfulness. How, he wants to know, do we come into the future promised in Christ? We do so, he argues, just as Abraham did: by trusting in God's promise. According to Paul's reading of Gen. 15:6, then, the key verse points back to Gen. 12: the initial call, promise, and Abraham's trusting response. Here we find important exegetical support for recent ecumenical statements. The capacity of 15:6 to point in both directions underlines the now-official judgment of both Lutheran and Catholic ecclesiastical authorities that Protestant and Catholic views of the doctrine of justification (the technical name for post-Reformation analysis of these questions) need not be seen as mutually exclusive.[10]

15:8 How am I to know?

Abraham's question does not contradict his belief. To trust in God is entirely consistent with a petition for understanding and assurance. Abraham cannot see how he will be able to enter into the promised future, for he has no son after his own flesh. In this sense, he is quite anxious. He has no knowledge of the precise unfolding of the divine plan, and what he can see of his present situation seems to contradict fulfillment. But this condition of uncertainty does not speak against Abraham's faith, just as Mary's question, "How shall this be?" (Luke 1:34), does not cast doubt on her acceptance of the divine word. Faith seeks to understand, and hope yearns to see the way toward its fulfillment.

Across Genesis, Abraham and Sarah struggle to see their future in the promise. They are turned back in their attempt to force a way forward through Sarah's plan of using Hagar to secure a son. When the LORD reveals his plan to give Abraham a son by way of aged and barren Sarah, both respond with an incredulous laugh. They hear the details of the divine plan, but they cannot see how it will come to pass. In these narrative moments, Gen. 15–20 emphasizes Abraham's blindness to the unfolding of the divine plan, a blindness that puts a spotlight on his patient faithfulness to the promise. We may need to walk a long way in "hope for what we do not see" while "we wait for" the inheritance of those born again in Christ "with patience" (Rom. 8:25).

10. *The Joint Declaration on the Doctrine of Justification* (2000).

Even as Abraham walks by faith, God does not deny him a spiritual form of insight and assurance about the future. God commands a mysterious ritual involving a three-year-old heifer, she-goat, ram, turtledove, and pigeon. Abraham kills (sacrifices?) the animals, cutting the mammals in half, but not the birds. Abraham must then fend off the birds of prey that seek to feed on the carcasses.

At this point, the reader is rightly puzzled. How does this strange ritual answer Abraham's question: "How am I to know?" Luther is typical of the tradition. He reads the ritual as foreshadowing the great act of divine deliverance that becomes a touchstone of assurance for Israel, and the paradigmatic figure for salvation in Christ:

> This is the explanation of the sign. The slaughtered animals are the people of Israel, who were abused and afflicted in various ways in Egypt. The birds about to consume the pieces of flesh are Pharaoh and the Egyptians. Abraham, who is the father of this nation, drives the birds away; for the promise made to Abraham does not permit this nation to be completely crushed, even though it is severely oppressed.
>
> Furthermore, the slaughtering of the four kinds of animals depicts the four-hundred-year affliction in Egypt of the descendents of Abraham. The birds denote the final period, during which Israel flew away from slavery to freedom and the Promised Land.[11]

We do not need to accept Luther's interpretation in order to accept the underlying insight. By way of signs, Abraham receives a prophecy of a future act of God, one that demonstrates God's power to fulfills his promises.

Immediately after the cutting of the animals, a dream or vision comes to Abraham as he falls into a deep sleep, and it reinforces the symbolic economy of the sacrifice. God teaches Abraham his future, giving him a synopsis of Exod. 1–14: "Know of a surety that your descendants will be sojourners in a land that is not theirs, and will be slaves there, and they will be oppressed for four hundred years; but I will bring judgment on the nation which they serve, and afterward they shall come out with great possessions" (Gen. 15:13–14). Finally, Abraham has a night vision that seems to dramatize symbolically the future foretold in the dream. He sees "a smoking fire pot and a flaming torch passed between these pieces" (15:17). These images can be read as the pillar of cloud by day (smoking fire pot) and fire by night (flaming torch) that will lead the Israelites out of captivity and through the walls of water in the divided Red Sea (between these pieces).

15:18 On that day the LORD made a covenant with Abram.

Genesis 15 can seem very disjointed. What began as a narrow preoccupation with childlessness and the problem of inheritance ends with a broad vision of

11. Martin Luther, *Lectures on Genesis*, ed. Jaroslav Pelikan, Luther's Works 3 (St. Louis: Concordia, 1961), 32.

the deliverance of an entire nation. But what unifies the entire chapter is the constant concern about the future: How can the promise be fulfilled? How can it be fulfilled if Abraham remains childless? And how can it be fulfilled if his descendants are threatened by genocide hundreds or thousands of years later? Insofar as Christianity reads God's promise to Abraham as fully revealed and fulfilled in Christ, the questions are different, but nonetheless still concern the future. How can a man hanging on a cross be the way to the triumph of life? How can a church besmirched with sin and lead by mediocrities be an instrument for the redemption of all? How, in short, can the poverty of the present give birth to the blessings promised in the future?

The signs and visions of Gen. 15 give Abraham knowledge of the future, and they point not only to God's power to act on behalf of those whom he has chosen, but also to the future fact of his actually doing so. In the signs and visions, it is as if God were answering Abraham's original lament in the following way: "My friend, if you worry about my commitment to fulfilling my promises to you, then just take a look at what I have already decided to do in the future for your descendants." In a prophetic way, Abraham sees the promise fulfilled. God will stand behind his promises, and he will do so when the stakes are much higher. The symbolic ritual, the divine pronouncement, and the dreaming vision are thus the first moments when promise is transformed into covenant. Genesis is no longer a story of what God promises to do. Now Abraham (and the reader) knows what God will do—and from the perspective of his eternity already has done.

Early rabbinic readers interpreted Abraham's vision in an expansive way. Since the deliverance of the Israelites is the epitome of the divine gift of life to the people of Israel, it made sense to them that Abraham saw God's plan in its full, completed form. This first mention of covenant in Genesis, then, is not a preliminary pact, but the entire covenant in latent form. The rabbis offered the following interpretation: "Simeon b[en] Abba said in the name of R[abbi] Yohanan: [God] showed him [Abraham] four things: Hell, the foreign kingdoms [that would dominate Israel], the giving of the Torah, and the future temple. He said to him: so long as your descendants busy themselves with the latter two, they will be saved from the former two" (*Genesis Rabbah* 44.21, quoted from Kugel 1998: 300). *Targum Pseudo-Jonathan* has a different scheme, but it also supposes that God reveals the entire sweep of the divine plan at the outset of the covenant. The "four hundred years" of captivity foretold in 15:12 become four eras of captivity, the last of which is Rome, and "from there the people of the house of Israel will come up" (Maher 1992: 60–61).

Christianity shares in this expansive vision of the divine plan, one that comes to fullness and completion in Jesus Christ. Needless to say, this makes for a dramatically different view of the way in which God fulfills his promises to Abraham. Yet, formally speaking, the response that Jesus gives to the Jews who wondered at the magnificent claims on his own behalf has the same expansive logic as the ancient rabbinic interpretations: "Your father Abraham rejoiced that he was to see my day; he saw it and was glad" (John 8:56). What Jesus says about Abraham is an interpretation of Gen. 15. The signs and visions revealed Christ to Abraham, for in Christ the promises are fulfilled.

16:1 Now Sarai, Abram's wife, bore him no children.

The dominant narrative tension throughout the story of Abraham is one of delay: promises made but still to be fulfilled. The promised son is the first step, and he is a long time coming, because Sarah is barren. Not until 21:2 ("Sarah conceived") does the promised son appear. The overall effect accentuates patience as the signal virtue of Abraham's faith, and it foreshadows the role of patient endurance amid spiritual afflictions throughout scripture. The promised future can seem terribly remote, and Sarah's continued infertility draws attention to the need to "be patient in tribulation" (Rom. 12:12). Even after the death and resurrection of Christ, the womb of human history remains barren, waiting for the final fulfillment of the promise of life. Thus, the saints who enter the kingdom of heaven are called to endurance (Rev. 14:12).

16:2a I shall obtain children by her.

In her old age, Sarah sees her own body. Her womb seems a dead end, empty of any future, dark as a grave (Prov. 30:16) and in "bondage to decay" (Rom. 8:21). Under the shadow of sin, Sarah's barrenness epitomizes the emptiness and desolation that is the true fruit of disobedience. As the LORD warns, "If you walk contrary to me, and will not hearken to me, . . . I will let loose the wild beasts among you, which shall rob you of your children, and destroy your cattle, and make you few in number, so that your ways shall become desolate" (Lev. 26:21–22). Jeremiah sees this warning fulfilled. He returns again and again to images of slaughter, famine, destruction, and desolation. The evil seek loyalty to nothing, and the upshot is a descending spiral of fruitlessness and infertility. Altars are laid waste, prayers are empty, women are barren, the greedy consume the poor, the powerful eat up the weak, and the kingdom of the people of God becomes a place of death. Sarah, like all the children of Adam and Eve, is "captive to the law of sin which dwells" (Rom. 7:23) in her womb. Her human flesh, created for fertility in the service of God, is perverted and brought to naught by the human disobedience that infects us all.

Sarah does not affirm her barren condition; she wants to struggle against it. The impulse is correct, even if the means she chooses are misguided. On this point, the passage can be read on two levels, for the human is a unified being with natural and spiritual desires. Understood naturally (or as the tradition often says, literally or carnally), Sarah's desire for a child and family is entirely in accord with God's original purpose: "be fruitful and multiply." She is barren, and she cannot fulfill the desire for children by intercourse with her husband. So she seeks another, alternative path. In effect, she contracts with a surrogate mother.

The spiritual meaning is closely intertwined with the natural. Sarah wishes to enter into the promises of God, and again this is entirely in accord with God's plan for the restoration and completion of the original purpose of creation. The covenant of the LORD is the way of life, and Sarah wishes to enter into it. To do so she and Abraham must have a son, just as faith must give birth to good works in order for the promise of righteousness to be fulfilled (→15:1). The author of 2 Peter urges his readers forward into the fulfillment of the "very great promises" of new life in Christ: "Add to your faith virtue; and to virtue knowledge; and to knowledge temperance; and to temperance patience; and to patience godliness; and to godliness brotherly kindness; and to brotherly kindness charity." Sarah's desire to find a way toward an heir is based on an important truth: the life of faith in the promises of God "shall neither be barren nor unfruitful" (1:3–8 AV).

Though her desire is pointed in the right direction, Sarah's mistake concerns the way forward. She devises her own plan to deliver herself and her husband from bondage to her barren condition. To use the theological vocabulary that has been so influential in arguments over the economy of salvation in Western theology, the way of the slave child is the way of works-righteousness. The core issue is not one of works strictly speaking. In the entire account of the promises to Abraham and their many reiterations in Genesis, there is no question of whether Abraham will have a son. God's promises require the real flesh and blood of human life for their fulfillment. The promises cannot be inhabited by an idea or a sentiment or a feeling of absolute dependence. Abraham must have descendents; otherwise, the promises are for naught. In the same way, the promise of new life in Christ is fulfilled in the flesh of believers. As Jesus tells us, "Unless your righteousness exceeds that of the scribes and the Pharisees, you will never enter the kingdom of heaven" (Matt. 5:20).

Yet the promised future cannot be made real by our own schemes and plans. Here, Sarah's initiative parallels the collective efforts of the Israelites to compensate for the apparent delay of Moses, who remains on Mount Sinai while they wait for word below. "Make us gods, who shall go before us," they say to Aaron, "as for this Moses, the man who brought us up out of the land of Egypt, we do not know what has become of him" (Exod. 32:1). Faced with the delay and uncertainty that follows the departure of Moses, the people have every good intention. Like Sarah, they see that something needs to happen, and they decide to take the future into their own hands. But the people of Israel can no more make for themselves a way forward in true worship than Sarah can make for herself and her husband an heir of her own devising. The golden calf shall not be an object of worship; the slave child shall not be heir. God will provide the path in which Israel shall walk; God will provide a son to Sarah and Abraham.

The same holds for our own self-wrought projects. We cannot move forward by way of human schemes that seek to compensate for what God seems to delay in providing. It is not our will that shapes the future; instead, it is, as Jesus teaches, "the will of my Father who is in heaven" (Matt. 7:21). We cannot stretch forward to find our future in the economy of salvation. Instead, the LORD defines the way forward in his commandments: "If you would enter life, keep the commandments" (19:17). And the LORD comes to us in Christ as the one who goes before us in the commandments, showing the way: "Come, follow me" (19:21). Faith cannot force the future: "Be still before the LORD, and wait patiently for him" (Ps. 37:7). Sarah has the commandment: "be fruitful and multiply." But she will not wait upon God's initiative to secure its fulfillment. She relies on the resources of her household to overcome the limitations of her body.

16:2b Abram hearkened to the voice of Sarai.

Abraham has lamented his lack of an heir (→15:1), and God made an explicit promise: "Your own son shall be your heir" (15:4). Sarah's plan does not seem to be at odds with this promise. After all, should Hagar conceive and give birth to a male, he would indeed by Abraham's own son. Yet the verbal formulation signaling Abraham's assent to Sarah's plan is inauspicious. The image of the husband hearkening to the voice of his wife returns the reader to the garden of Eden and the fateful choices of first Eve and then Adam.

This scene also recalls an earlier episode that puts Sarah's plan into a dark light. Sarah has formulated a course of action that seems quite sensible. She is barren, so the only way forward seems obvious: conception through the slave girl. Abraham listens to the plan and sees its cogency. "Yes," his subsequent actions seem to say, "I married well. In her selflessness, Sarah will put forward the slave girl as a substitute." His wife is willing to sacrifice her status in the household by allowing Hagar to become the mother of Abraham's heir. The logic of the scene reminds us of the good wife who will say she is Abraham's sister in order to protect him from the murderous lust of powerful men, the wife who will lie and put herself at risk to protect Abraham's future (→12:13).

These negative echoes, however, are less decisive than the dramatic contrast between this first episode in the long and tangled story of Abraham's heir and the last episode, the dramatic scene of Abraham's faithfulness as he ascends Mount Moriah to sacrifice his son. Tellingly, Gen. 22 is very explicit: Abraham hearkens to God's voice, not Sarah's, and he waits for God to provide the lamb for the burnt offering rather than relying on his wife's clearminded reasoning, humility, and devotion to his cause. Even more poignantly, unlike Sarah's barrenness, which she schemes to avoid by conscripting Hagar, on Mount Moriah there seems no clear way forward. How can God's promises be fulfilled if Abraham sacrifices his son? But God does provide. In this way, the episode of the binding of Isaac serves as a concluding commentary on the long and eventually failed effort of Sarah and Abraham to provide for themselves by way of Hagar.

In view of these considerations, it is important to see that the effort does not fail because Hagar is a maidservant rather than a wife. Historical scholars like to remind us that the legal customs of the era considered children by concubines to be legitimate children of the household, as the narrative of Jacob and the births of his many sons testify. In fact, the New Testament has an even more expansive view of the means that God can use to fulfill the promise to Abraham. Tamar is Judah's daughter-in-law, and Solomon is the product of David's adulterous (and murderous) pursuit of Bathsheba. Yet both extraordinary moments are made explicit in Matthew's genealogy of Jesus (Matt. 1:1–16). More dramatically, as Jesus teaches, God can even turn stones into children of Abraham (3:9). Clearly, God can use many different means to ensure the succession of the generations, a succession that is necessary to fulfill his promise. Thus, Hagar is not a false path forward because of her status. Instead, the promise cannot go in her direction because Abraham hearkens to the voice of a human scheme—works-righteousness—when he should wait for God to provide.

16:4 She looked with contempt on her mistress.

The problem with works-righteousness is not that it offends against divine pride, as if the LORD is a greedy sovereign who wishes to have everything under his control. Instead, works-righteousness is a spiritual disaster for us. When we try to devise our own ways forward into God's promise, we end up slaves to our self-wrought schemes, just as the Israelites fell under the thrall of the golden calf of their own devising. Paradoxically, we become the servants of that which we create in order to satisfy our heart's desire.

Hagar's contempt, therefore, is an instrument of divine purpose. She represents the judgment that works-righteousness brings down upon the heads of those who try to plot their own ways forward into the promises of God. No condemnation is more severe than the lofty path one has set for oneself as the means of salvation. We say, "I will fulfill the promise of righteousness in Christ through a life of unqualified prayer and devotion." Then, as is always the case with works-righteousness, the ideal judges us unworthy and holds us in contempt.

16:6 Sarai dealt harshly with her.

Unlike Eve in the garden, Sarah regrets her plan. She turns against the way of the slave child. But regret is not the same as repentance, which draws fault close by accepting responsibility and asking for forgiveness rather than trying to drive the fault away. Sarah cannot put Hagar away, just as we cannot put away the consequences of our transgressions by driving them out of our memories and into the wilderness of forgetfulness. The voice of the LORD does not endorse this expulsion of Hagar, and she returns.

16:11 The LORD has given heed to your affliction.

Genesis begins with an account of the beginning or source of everything, and then it turns to explain the source of sin. The main narrative from Gen. 12 onward tells of the beginning of the covenant with the people of Israel. But Genesis is also full of many other beginnings as well: Cain is the founder of cities (4:17), the tower of Babel is the source of the diversity of human languages and cultures (11:1–9). Within this diversity of peoples, Genesis is keen to identify the original ancestors of the many nations and tribes that figure in the later history of Israel. For example, Noah's curse of Ham's son, Canaan (9:25), serves to both explain the origins of the inhabitants of the land of Canaan and justify Israelite dominance over them. Lot's daughters engage in incestuous relations with their father and give birth to Moab and Ben-ammi, fathers of Israel's enemies, the Moabites and Ammonites (19:36–38). Jacob's brother Esau becomes the father of the Edomites (36:9).

Modern biblical scholars call these episodes etiologies, or accounts that explain the cause or source of things. In this case, readers are told that Hagar's son, Ishmael, will father the nomadic Ishmaelite tribe. What is striking, however, is that this episode also includes an echo of the promise to Abraham. Hagar has been cast out of Abraham's household. Without a clan to protect her, she seems doomed. But an angel of the LORD tells her to return, reassures her, and blesses her womb: "I will so greatly multiply your descendants that they cannot be numbered for multitude" (16:10). The scene is repeated later, in a different form, with Hagar and Ishmael as a young lad (21:14–21). God lifts Hagar up to heaven itself in a vision and makes her a promise: "I will make [Ishmael] a great nation" (21:18). The effect in both cases is dramatic. No less than Sarah, Hagar's womb is conscripted into the service of the divine plan.

What kind of plan can this be? Why would God bless Hagar's womb if the nation that comes forth afflicts his chosen people? Why would God allow Lot's daughters to bear progeny that become Israel's enemies? For the historical scholar, the answer seems easy. These nations already exist, and the narratives of Genesis are handy ways to convey folk legends about their origins. However, this answer neglects the theological implications of placing these legends into the larger Genesis narrative in the first place. To put Israel's enemies into stories of barrenness and fertility that are so clearly under the hand of divine providence has the effect of making God responsible for Israel's trials and tribulations. To put them so close to the births that are integral to the fulfillment of the promises—in Hagar's case echoing the same promise of a flourishing nation—makes it difficult to carefully cordon off these tribes as accidental adversaries. They seem to have a role and purpose within the divine plan.

This is, of course, the position taken by the prophets. Just as God blesses Hagar's womb, the LORD endorses and supports those who defeat Israel and destroy Jerusalem. In this way, the prophets outline a theology of divine providence that is suggested in the story of Hagar. Within the economy of the covenant, the LORD afflicts those whom he loves: "I will come against the wayward people to chastise them" (Hos. 10:10). Sarah has devised a plan to fulfill the covenant, but the result is bitterness, not joy. Hagar lords over Sarah, just as the Babylonians eventually lord over the Israelites. God prospers the womb of Hagar, and this humiliates Sarah, and in her humiliation she sees the foolishness of her plan to take the fulfillment of God's promises into her own hands. But God does not afflict simply in order to chastise, "for he has not despised or abhorred the affliction of the afflicted" (Ps. 22:24). The dark night of the humiliated soul prepares us to glorify and praise the coming fulfillment. It is as if Hagar's role is to lord over Sarah with her natural fertility, just as Pharaoh's or Nebuchadnezzar's role is to lord over the Israelites by virtue of their earthly military and economic power. They predominate so that God can set their natural advantages aside and in this way manifest his power to make the future and give greater blessings—blessings that are supernatural rather than natural. Therefore, we should read the etiologies in Genesis as more than localized explanations of the origins of this or that tribe. They are part of the larger biblical claim about divine control over history.

17:2 Walk before me, and be thou perfect. (AV)

God's appearances to Abraham are not simply reiterative. They have an ascending logic. First, Abraham is called by the promises (12:1–3). The promises create the possibility of a new future and break the hold of the covenant of the lie. Then, in the second divine appearance, Abraham is told to walk within the land of the promise (13:14–18). The new future is not just hypothetical. With the eyes of faith, it can be seen as a real possibility. Next, the covenant is announced (15:1–21), and a vision of God's mighty deeds in the future serves as a down payment on the fulfillment of the promise. In the fourth appearance, the focus shifts. Abraham has walked the land, and now he is directed to walk in the covenant. The promises give a new future. In order to inhabit those promises, Abraham must change. He must become a different kind of man, one fit not only to walk in the land, but also to walk before the LORD. He must be altered in his flesh beginning with the act of circumcision.

For this reason, Gen. 17 is the second great hinge on which Genesis turns. Genesis 12 reveals the metaphysical heresy of the divine investment in a particular clan. God will use a particular people, time, and place to achieve his universal plan of drawing all creation into his Sabbath rest. Now we find out how God will use particularity. As echoes throughout the Old Testament make clear, God will shape the plasticity of the human creature. He commands, and we have the power to obey and, in obeying, to become different (→2:17). The way forward is thus set: "You shall walk in all the ways which the LORD your God has commanded you" (Deut. 5:33). This will not only provide a remedy for sin, but will also serve as a means for the sanctification of human life. To walk in the ways of the LORD is to partake in his will, and by doing so our humanity is formed according to God's purposes. In obedience, our flesh is marked in a way that takes nature beyond creation. The male member that is essential to the primal commandment ("be fruitful and multiply") and the part of the body that is integral to Abraham's complaint in Gen. 15 and the dramatic tension of Gen. 16 (acquiring an heir of his own) becomes the object of ritualized, sanctifying focus.

In the course of its development, Western Christianity has never denied the importance of the sanctification of the flesh, as the history of monasticism and religious life amply demonstrates. Nonetheless, in the aftermath of the Reformation, Western theology has tended to emphasize the dynamics of forgiveness and remission of sins. As a result, certain questions predominate. How can we take the first step necessary to free ourselves from bondage to sin? What provides the strength of will? Does the gospel create a future free from the past life of sin, or do we need to cooperate by making efforts to change? Thus the many debates about the relationship between divine grace and human free will, divine power and human initiative, faith and works. They revolve around the early chapters of Abraham's career, because until Gen. 17, the *fact* of God's call and promises to Abraham is the driving force in the narrative. Abraham matters solely because of the promises, and this is the deep, narrative form of theological conviction that salvation comes by grace alone as a free gift. To follow St. Paul's reasoning, righteousness understood as faith in the promise of forgiveness comes before circumcision. What makes us properly hope in our future with God—the gospel and our faith in the gospel—comes before any actions that shape and transform us into sanctified creatures fit for our future with God.

Because of an overriding concern to sustain the priority of God's promises (faith) over our fulfillment of the commandments (works), the leaders of the Reformation tended to insist that justification (that we are included with Abraham as recipients of the promises) was entirely distinct from sanctification (that we genuinely inhabit the promises in our flesh). The impulse is not entirely misguided. There is a crucial distinction between inheriting the promises and inhabiting the promises, as the narrative development in Gen. 12–17, as well as the larger sweep of the history of Israel, demonstrates again and again. Moreover, the issue that concerns St. Paul when he insists that Abraham's faith was reckoned to him as righteousness is quite different from the worries that animate James (→15:6). We need to make a distinction between justification and sanctification to properly see the difference.

However, the ambiguity of the term "righteousness" can create (and has in fact created) all sorts of misconceptions. The Greek and Latin words for righteousness are *dikaiosynē* and *justitia*, both of which carry legal as well as moral connotations. The legal connotation suggests a sense of justification as forensic pronouncement, as when a judge determines that a claimant is right or justified in a case. The moral connotation, however, points toward the virtue of justice or righteousness. Because the judge is righteous, the judge correctly justifies those who bring forth just claims. In other words, the virtuous judge *inhabits* righteousness (*justitia*) and therefore can reliably determine who shall receive, that is to say *inherit*, the favorable verdict.

Interpreters properly look to context in order to determine and clarify the interaction of the legal and moral senses. For example, in his commentary on this passage, Luther is very concerned to deny that the act of circumcision makes Abraham righteous in the eyes of God. Like St. Paul, Luther wants to draw attention to the narrative sequence in which promise precedes commandment as the power that gives Abraham a new future. As Luther explains, "Abraham was righteous before circumcision; and because he is accounted righteous through faith, righteousness comes about, not because of the Law or works, but simply from faith, or trust in the promise."[12] What he means to say is that Abraham is not freed from the bondage of sin and justified in the eyes of God as a suitable partner for his covenant by any action or achievement of his own. However, because the term "righteousness" can also mean the perfection that God now commands Abraham to seek by way of the sign of circumcision, Luther can easily seem to be turning Gen. 17 into an empty text. If Abraham is already righteous, then what more does he need? Indeed, since his faith is reckoned to him as righteousness, then why bother at all with any further teachings from the Old Testament? So, a careless reader of Luther and other Reformers can conclude that the whole idea of sanctification (becoming righteous) is a misguided (Catholic!) temptation into works-righteousness.

But this reading of Luther and the Reformation tradition cannot be right. The scriptural seriousness of the Reformers could not possibly allow them to write off the vast preoccupation of the Old Testament with holiness—and the clear link between holiness and obeying God's commandments. In keeping with the Augustinian tradition of Western Christianity, Luther wishes to emphasize the central theological conviction that the crucial turn from a future defined by disobedience and death to a future of obedience and life is entirely God's doing. We are saved by grace alone. Yet this clear affirmation of the priority of grace does not rule out the obvious importance of "walking before" the LORD according to his commandments. In fact, Luther observes, "The Law binds not only the Jews but also the heathen, for it is the eternal and immutable decree of God concerning the worship of God and the love of one's neighbor."[13] God does not make the promises to Abraham simply as items to be held in a purely mental or

12. Ibid., 84–85.
13. Ibid., 84.

internal faith. The promises are fulfilled in the flesh of our humanity. Justification is necessarily linked to sanctification.[14]

To be sure, the promised future cannot be ours unless we renounce the illusory future of the covenant of the lie: "If a man does not repent, God will whet his sword" (Ps. 7:12). As is the case with the call and promises to Abraham, so also with all those called to righteousness in Christ. Only the prior call and promise of God can make repentance possible. Yet, the promised future does not remain ever before us as a goal. The future has a present reality as well, given form and shape by God's commandments. "Hope does not disappoint us," writes St. Paul, "because God's love has been poured into our hearts through the Holy Spirit which has been given to us" (Rom. 5:5). Even now we are empowered by the Spirit of God to "walk in the law of the LORD" (Ps. 119:1). The law of the LORD shapes bodily life, and this is its singular blessing. As the divine commandments are obeyed, we are brought—in our flesh!—to participate in God's holiness. Faith formed by love, which is a grace empowered obedience, perfects our human nature: "My flesh . . . shall see God" (Job 19:26).

17:4 Behold, my covenant is with thee. (AV)

The formulation of the covenant in this chapter has a clearly defined, three-part structure. First the LORD outlines his promises. In the second element the LORD renames Abraham and gives the commandment of circumcision. The third and final part addresses Sarah, renaming her and confirming her role as "mother of nations."

The second and third parts shift from the structure of Gen. 15 and the first mention of the covenant. There, Abraham has a lament. God responds by reiterating the promises (explicitly descendents, but also implicitly land and national greatness), and then God provides signs and a vision that foretell what he will do in order to fulfill the promises. Now the situation seems reversed. God has an implicit lament: "You, Abram, are to be my covenant partner, but look at you, you're terribly inadequate. You need to live up to your vocation as the one I have chosen to walk before me." Then, instead of revealing what he will do for his human partners in order to secure the future of the covenant, the LORD turns the table. What are Abraham and Sarah going to do?

Of course, readers know that Abraham and Sarah are not competent to decide. They have already embarked on an ill-fated plan to fulfill the promises by way of Hagar's fertile womb. How could it be otherwise? God's plan is to draw all things into fellowship with himself in his Sabbath rest. This goal is supernatural, that is, it involves an end that exceeds or surpasses what we can see or predict or hope for

14. On the fundamental link between justification and sanctification, see John Calvin, *Institutes of Christian Religion* 3.16.1.

on the basis of the created order. So Abraham and Sarah do not—cannot—see how to walk before God and be perfect. Thus, God does not expect Abraham to know the way forward. The LORD needs to outline the completion of the human side of the covenant. He must tell us what to do. This brings out the asymmetry of the two forms of covenant pronouncement in Gen. 15 and Gen. 17. God will do what God will do (Exod. 3:14), as the signs and visions in Gen. 15 reveal. In contrast, God's commandments do not produce obedience with the same divine necessity, as the long history of Israel (and the church) testifies. God can command circumcision, but he cannot perform it. The doing of the deed will depend upon Abraham and his descendents.

In the interplay of Gen. 15 with Gen. 17 we see the theological drama of the New Testament and the penultimate mighty act of God in Christ. God does by himself what he commands in a way that includes and perfects human obedience. Viewed exegetically, the incarnation involves the union of the mighty deeds that seal the covenant formulation in Gen. 15 with the way of obedience in Gen. 17. In Christ, God's invincible power to make the promised future real enters into and galvanizes our very feeble human power of obedience. Thus St. Paul's formulation: we die in Christ's death and rise with him in his resurrection. The works of righteousness are properly human. They take place in our flesh. But as Paul insists, the agency is divine: "I have been crucified with Christ; it is no longer I who live, but Christ who lives in me" (Gal. 2:20). It is difficult to express this union of divine power with human agency without collapsing the human into the divine—or the divine into the human. This conceptual difficulty should give us a great deal of sympathy for the tangled web of misunderstanding and mutual condemnation in the aftermath of the Reformation. If God really does fulfill the human side of the covenant in the perfect obedience of Christ, then the roles of our present decisions and actions can easily seem pale and empty (the Catholic worry about Protestant doctrines of justification)—or they can seem hopelessly vainglorious and full of presumptive sanctity (the Protestant worry about Catholic doctrines of sanctification).

17:5 Your name shall be Abraham.

The new name seals Abraham and binds him to the future ordained by God. Reflecting a rabbinic tradition that sees a divinizing power in Abraham's new name, Martin Buber writes, "God names him anew, by casting a letter from His own name into the midst of the original name of the man."[15] The LORD (itself a convention for the unspeakable divine name "YHWH") gives a natural man a supernatural destiny by divinizing his worldly name with the addition of a divine

15. Martin Buber, *On the Bible: Eighteen Studies*, ed. Nahum N. Glatzer (New York: Schocken, 1968), 39.

letter (the H from Yhwh). It is a verbal anticipation of the act of circumcision that adds a supernatural mark to Abraham's flesh.

Personal names and individual identities are closely related, and name changes seal commitments of loyalty. The new name confirms the direction and destiny of the individual. Postulants who enter monasteries traditionally adopt new names to signal the depth of their commitment to a future defined solely by the monastic life. The same holds for baptism. The name pronounced at baptism is the Christian name, not the family name, and like the name the Lord gives Abraham, it is given as part of the covenant of new life in Christ.

Genesis, the scriptures as a whole, and the Jewish and Christian traditions take God at his word. The Lord says, "No longer shall your name be Abram," and never again is he called anything but Abraham. The covenant makes an irreversible difference. I have followed this convention, referring to Abraham from the outset even though Genesis calls him Abram. God says the same to Jacob when he renames him Israel, and yet neither the subsequent chapters of Genesis nor the tradition makes the same unequivocal, irreversible change to his name. The difference is telling, suggesting in its ambivalence the open-ended career of Israel (→32:28).

17:7 An everlasting covenant.

The Acts of the Apostles records the first great controversy of the church. St. Paul preached the good news of Jesus Christ among the Gentiles, and they came into the fellowship of believers. Thus the crucial question: must those called by Christ to inherit the promises made to Abraham also be circumcised? The gathered elders in Jerusalem consulted the prophets, and they determined that the divine plan for bringing all men and women to unity in Christ's name does not require the circumcision of the Gentiles.

The decision in Jerusalem raises a direct question. If conversion to Christ involves genuine entry into the household of Abraham and full inheritance of the promises, then is it not the case that the "everlasting covenant" sealed in circumcision is suspended or superseded? The question is all the more pressing in Galatians, where St. Paul observes that circumcision is not just unnecessary but spiritually disastrous: "I, Paul, say to you that if you receive circumcision, Christ will be of no advantage to you" (5:2).

However we approach the relationship between the Old and New Testaments, between Sinai and Golgotha, it is crucial that we underline the *everlasting* and *continuous* nature of the covenant first made with Abraham. It is not an easy thing to do. Within the Old Testament itself, the logic of the first five books of the Bible treats the covenant with Abraham as anticipatory, receiving decisive communal form in the law given to Moses. The New Testament describes this law as fulfilled and transformed in Christ. Ever since Christian readers of the Bible have set about to show how this fulfillment and transformation in Christ reveals the true nature and purpose of the Mosaic law.

Both Torah-centered and Christ-centered readings of Abraham presume significant changes. The Mosaic law involves far more than circumcision, and the circumcision of the heart that St. Paul speaks of involves a dramatic revision of what it means to be marked in the flesh. But for all traditional readers, Jewish or Christian, it is a fundamental tenet of belief that the covenant remains the same throughout. The covenant is as reliable and long-lasting as the movements of the planets (Jer. 33:23–26). Speaking of the covenant with David, but expressing the larger theology of covenant that dominates the Old Testament, Ps. 89:33–34 portrays God declaring, "I will not remove from him my steadfast love, or be false to my faithfulness. I will not violate my covenant, or alter the word that went forth from my lips." The coming of Christ underlines rather than rejects this claim of permanence. What is revealed in Christ follows a continuous line of divine purpose. His coming does not deviate but rather continues "as he spoke to our fathers, to Abraham and to his posterity for ever" (Luke 1:55). The innovation (and intellectual excitement) of theology, both Jewish and Christian, comes from showing how all the differences add up to continuity.

St. Paul is typical. He rejects the ritual necessity of circumcision, but he does not dismiss its significance. On the contrary, Paul uses the logic of circumcision as a way to explain the saving work of Christ. "In him," he writes to the Colossians, "you were circumcised with a circumcision made without hands, by putting off the body of flesh in the circumcision of Christ; and you were buried with him in baptism, in which you were also raised with him through faith in the working of God, who raised him from the dead" (Col. 2:11–12). The burdensome threat of judgment against past sins—"this he set aside, nailing it to the cross" (2:14)—and "the promise of the life which is in Christ" (2 Tim. 1:1) is sealed in baptism when "you died to the elemental spirits of the universe" (Col. 2:20). So, by Paul's reasoning, just as Abraham's death to the future of sin is sealed in circumcision, so also baptism "put[s] to death . . . what is earthly" (3:5) and cuts away "the old nature" (3:9). Dying in Christ, we are raised with him to new life, directed to "seek the things that are above" (3:1) and empowered to "put on the new nature" (3:10) so as to enter into what "is hid with Christ in God" (3:3).

St. Paul returns to the question of circumcision and its role in the life of faith again and again, and he consistently argues that in Christ "there cannot be Greek and Jew, circumcised and uncircumcised" (3:11). There is more to say about how to read Paul's views of circumcision below (→17:11a). Yet, however we end up interpreting Paul and however we parse his understanding of circumcision of the flesh and heart, we need to keep the divine affirmation of the everlasting covenant firmly in view: "It is not as though the word of God has failed" (Rom. 9:6). Christ does not come in the power of the Holy Spirit in order to establish a new plan or new path for us to walk. He draws us more fully into the *very same* covenant that was made with Abraham for the sake of the *very same* promises.

17:11a You shall be circumcised in the flesh of your foreskins.

Why circumcision? Why mark the flesh of the penis? In the context of stories of Abraham's reproductive misadventures, there is an obvious fittingness. From Gen. 12 onward, a great deal of the narrative tension flows from the complications of fertility, sexual desire, childbirth, and the succession of generations necessary to sustain the inheritance of Abraham. The sign of circumcision intervenes into and marks one element of the bodily reality that plays a role in the complex psychological and social realities that preoccupy the narrative. Yet, the narrative fittingness of circumcision is not the same as an explanation. Circumcision is certainly not necessary for reproduction. None of the episodes that follow in Genesis would change if Gen. 17 were omitted.

The mark retains an arbitrary, unnecessary character, and this tells us something important about its purpose. Circumcision is a supernatural commandment rather than a natural one. Unlike the commandments given to Noah, circumcision is ordered toward achieving the consummating goal of the divine plan rather than sustaining the created order. It is a sanctifying commandment, and because the divine goal of perfecting us so that we can join God in his Sabbath rest surpasses the powers and expectations of life lived according to the created order, we cannot reason out and explain the divinely ordained means for achieving this goal. For this reason, circumcision prefigures the entire law given to Moses, as well as the fulfillment of the law in Jesus Christ. It is God's gift of holiness, something other than our created natures, something only God can give and we can receive only by way of our created capacity for something greater: obedience.

The sheer ambition of the divine plan—to perfect the entire created order for the sake of rest in God—can too easily tempt Christians to a functional gnosticism. The goal of sanctifying humanity entails dramatic change. Not only must the sinful past give way to a future of righteousness, but also the created order itself must be drawn forward to completion in Christ. This pattern of change is necessarily dualistic: what once was the case must give way to something new. The gnostic view interprets these changes in ontological or metaphysical terms. For example, since we currently live as embodied beings with physical desires and needs, for the gnostic, the dramatic change of redemption seems obvious. It involves being translated from space and time to an altogether different and higher spiritual existence, one free from the limitations of the body. Jesus saves, according to the gnostic view, because he provides the transformative injection of new spiritual substance that motors our lives upward and away from the physical and toward the purely spiritual.

According to this gnostic view, the commandment of circumcision cannot be taken seriously. Marking human flesh moves in exactly the wrong direction. Circumcision takes human will, the rational power of the soul, and directs it downward toward our embodied condition—and the sexual organ no less. The obedience of Abraham fixes his attention on his own flesh, when it seems obvious that we should direct the power of our wills, the highest part of our souls, toward the spiritual. If our destiny is fellowship with God, the gnostic reasons, then surely we need to train ourselves to attend to godlike things: changeless and eternal truths, high ideals, and fine principles of moral behavior that have universal scope. At best, circumcision serves as a cryptic allegory for a moral principle. Perhaps the cutting of the male foreskin teaches a timeless truth about the necessity of sexual restraint. At worst, circumcision reminds the gnostic of the false path of Jewish particularity, and once reminded theology turns on a sharp distinction between the true God of salvation and the tribal deity of Israel.[16]

Few Christians are gnostics in the classical sense of the term. After all, the Old Testament is part of Christian scripture, and the embodied, ritual life of the church claims to embody the spiritual power of salvation. Nonetheless, modern Christianity has tended toward a functional gnosticism in which the divine plan is understood as a progressive universalizing and spiritualizing of religion. What began as the calling of one man that was sealed in his circumcision gives way to a true, inward, and spiritual form of piety. Christianity may have rituals, but it is a religion of love rather than a preoccupation with bodily marks and signs. Fine sentiments and good intentions, so this line of thought reasons, supersede what are taken to be the empty rituals of the Old Testament. After all, we are to live by the spirit of the law, and not by the letter. And why stop with the Old Testament? Surely the priority of the spirit tells us that the rituals of the church and its dogmatic principles are residual forms of Jewish legalism. Didn't Jesus come to bring freedom, not slavery? Thus, not only should circumcision be rejected, but also we should jettison all that it represents: the "marking" of Christians by obligatory confessions of faith, by required rituals such as baptism, by claims that divine authority is located in particular persons or particular texts. So the modern man or woman influenced by the functional gnosticism of our age concludes that it makes as much sense to draw our spiritual aspirations down into the limitations of an old man in Rome or the writings of first-century followers of Jesus as to invest our spiritual futures in circumcision of the penis. Both are hopelessly worldly, enfleshed foci for what should be a universal and spiritual faith.

This crypto-gnostic interpretation of the divine plan takes a great deal of its inspiration and rhetoric from St. Paul's own arguments about the true nature of God's economy. Paul often draws upon contrastive pairings of flesh and spirit, law and promise, bondage and freedom, in order to explain the stages in the divine

---

16. It is a sad truth that many of the founding fathers of modern historical-critical study of the Old Testament trafficked in this juxtaposition.

plan. If we assume the gnostic presumption that all true religion tends toward the universal, the ideal, and the inward, these contrastive pairings easily take on a hard, metaphysical meaning. All matters of the body, all legal forms, all binding commitments become part of the superseded world of immature, body-focused religion from which Christ has set us free. Indeed, taken to its conclusion, Christ's spiritual message has set us free from the dogmas about Christ and even from the literal meaning of the New Testament witness to Christ.[17]

Although widespread in modern theology, the problem with this assumption is that it is antithetical to the biblical witness, and it deracinates Christian faith. Abraham lived in the land of his ancestors, and he was called out and promised a different land. What was once the case for Abraham must become something different in order for the promises to be fulfilled. But this difference occurs within the embodied, particularized world of real human affairs. It does not transport us out of our bodies or out of history. The difference is not one of spiritualization, if by that word we mean a trajectory out of space and time, out of our created condition. The promised future does not move from particular to universal, or from ritual to moral, or from credulous to critical, or from mythological to rational. The dichotomies of modern theology are many, and all of them distort. The move or change is spiritual in a very precise sense. Moving from the house of his father to his wandering condition, and from uncircumcised to circumcised, brings Abraham closer to the final end envisioned by God. In this sense, far from being superseded by anything taught in the New Testament, circumcision sets the pattern. To move forward into the future promised by the covenant always involves a heightened particularity, a more sharply outlined, more well defined, more visible identity as one chosen by God. That Christianity makes the crucifix into the paradigmatic symbol of God's love testifies to this pattern.

In the larger scope of scripture, the commandment of circumcision reinforces the metaphysical heresy revealed in Gen. 12. God chooses a particular household, and then he shapes it. He invades our lives and bodies with commandments that transform our flesh: "This God—his way is perfect" (Ps. 18:30). Sinai extends the perfecting commandment of circumcision to other aspects of bodily existence, as well as into the social and ritual life of Israel. Jewish theologian Michael Wyschogrod is quite aware that Christians read the covenant differently than Jews do. Nonetheless, he observes with irenic intent, "Whatever truth arises out of the covenant between God and Israel, it is never a disembodied truth."[18] Indeed, St. Paul's contrastive terms of spirit and flesh, freedom and slavery, are designed to serve the truth of Christ crucified. According to Paul, the role of circumcision does not get transcended by a leap from flesh to spirit, from time to eternity, from

17. For a classic statement, see Gerhard Ebeling's seminal essay "The Significance of the Critical Historical Method for Church and Theology in Protestantism," in his *Word and Faith*, trans. James W. Leitch (London: SCM, 1963), 17–61.

18. Michael Wyschogrod, *The Body of Faith: God in the People of Israel* (New York: Seabury, 1983), 28.

particular to universal. The circumcised find their place with the uncircumcised where "Christ is all, and in all" (Col. 3:11). This claim about our future in Christ affirms rather than contradicts Wyschogrod's assessment of the basic form of the divine plan. When Christ is all and in all, circumcision is radicalized rather than rejected. All are marked as Christ' own. The cosmos is supersaturated with the particularity of the crucified and risen Jesus.

Thus, in direct opposition to the gnostic view of the divine plan, the future of the covenant in Christ is a future in the body. For all his difficult arguments and sharp contrasts, St. Paul follows the trajectory of the Old Testament, which is a trajectory of intensification. The turn from sin to new life in Christ is not simply a matter of will and intention: "For just as you once yielded your members to impurity and to greater and greater iniquity, so now yield your members to righteousness for sanctification" (Rom. 6:19). Our lives must bear the imprint of the covenant. We must be marked in our flesh, just as the body of the church must be stamped with the image of Christ. We have a future promised in Christ, and it is the same future promised to Abraham. By my reading of the Pauline arguments, circumcision is unnecessary *not* because it is too physical, too focused on the body, too fleshly. Circumcision is set aside by Paul because it is not fleshly enough. As a sign of covenant membership, he argues, circumcision divides the followers of Christ into two camps. In contrast, he envisions a single household of God, one marked by a love that brings unity *in the flesh*, the undivided fellowship of the church.

It is important for us to see that, while St. Paul clearly rejects the necessity of circumcision for Gentile followers of Christ, he affirms the divine project of perfecting his covenant partners in their bodies. He sees the Christian life as akin to a total or comprehensive circumcision. The faithful are called to enter more fully into perfective suffering that brings them into ever fuller participation in Christ. This reflects a commitment to hypercircumcision, not uncircumcision: "We are afflicted in every way, but not crushed; perplexed, but not driven to despair; persecuted, but not forsaken; struck down, but not destroyed; always carrying in the body the death of Jesus, so that the life of Jesus may also be manifested in our bodies. For while we live we are always being given up to death for Jesus' sake, so that the life of Jesus may be manifested in our mortal flesh" (2 Cor. 4:8–11). The same holds for his own person: "I bear on my body the marks of Jesus" (Gal. 6:17). The Pauline economy of salvation is clear. The circumcision of Abraham begins a divine invasion of our flesh, an invasion that is completed in Christ and in which we participate when we follow Jesus in our flesh. Nothing could be further from the gnostic dream.

This argument is carried forward by the church fathers. Circumcision of the heart is more visible in human flesh, not less so. As Ambrose observes, the Lord Jesus "did not circumcise a small part of the body as a sign, but the whole man in truth." To reject circumcision of the foreskin does not leave the body free from obedience to God's commandments; it allows for the full invasion of the flesh by the Holy Spirit. "Circumcision of the part ceases," Ambrose continues, "when circumcision of the whole shines forth. So now a man is saved, not in part, but in his whole body."[19] Origen follows the same line of thinking. The goal of the Christian life is to mark every organ or power of the body: "Each of our members must be said to be circumcised if they are devoted to the service of God's commands" (*Homilies in Genesis* 3.6 in FC 71.99). The requirement of circumcision ends—for the sake of its expansion.

This sounds like an evasion, but church fathers had a very simple question in mind. What would you rather give up, a small piece of flesh or the many sinful desires of your flesh? They knew the answer. We would much rather have our penises circumcised than have our hearts circumcised, for a circumcised heart must submit to the countless disciplines that are necessary in order to root out sin and guide us toward holy lives. Indeed, the most powerful desire of the flesh is to avoid death. Thus, for the early Christian tradition as a whole, the "perfection of circumcision is martyrdom, when the body is perfectly figured in the service of Christ."[20] In martyrdom, the commandment to confess Christ crucified drives all the living flesh of the believer into the service of the covenant. It is the final triumph of the invading will of God, the perfect work of faith.

17:11b It shall be a sign of the covenant.

Adam and Eve's sin involved a fantasy about the future. They turned to creation to find their fulfillment. They chose to live according to the law of the flesh—the circulation of desire and satisfaction that finite goods can provide. The sign of the covenant with Abraham reveals the genius of the divine plan. Circumcision is a *sign in the flesh* that supersedes the *law of the flesh*.

The scope of God's commandment reinforces the way in which circumcision functions in the flesh, but not according to the flesh. Blood links the generations. Yet, in the commandment given to Abraham, the linkage of blood does not govern the law of circumcision. One need not be of the blood of Abraham in order to receive the sign of the covenant. Circumcision is for "every male throughout your generations, whether born in your house, or bought with your money from any foreigner who is not of your offspring" (17:12). Thus, as a sign in the flesh, circumcision is a spiritual sign. It is a sign of covenant membership, not family lineage. The circumcised foreigner is a member, but the uncircumcised descendant is not: "Any uncircumcised male who is not circumcised in the flesh of his foreskin shall be cut off from his people" (17:14).

A juxtaposition of spiritual to carnal needs to find its orientation at this point. What could be more fundamental than the psychological and cultural bonds

19. Ambrose, *On Abraham*, trans. Theodosia Tomkinson (Etna, CA: Center for Traditional Orthodox Studies, 2000), 17.
    20. Ibid., 17.

of blood? We naturally presume that such bonds define our futures. The commandment of circumcision ignores the future made by the bonds of blood. But God does not free us from the law of the flesh by encouraging us to look up or look elsewhere for our futures. Instead, God breaks the power of flesh over our futures by placing the power of his commandments in the same place, in the very member so important for the transmission of life according to the principles of the body. God does not do an end run around a world dominated by the covenant of the lie, the hope that bodily life will provide for us the rest we seek. He comes to defeat it where it dwells: in the flesh. This strategy reaches its culmination in the death of Christ. God puts himself in the place where the law of the flesh seems even more omnipotent than the bonds of blood—the seeming inevitability of death.

17:13 So shall my covenant be in your flesh.

In Gen. 15 Abraham complained that he had no future in the covenant, because he had no son. Abraham cannot see how the covenant can have a future in his flesh, because his body has produced no offspring. This concern finds expression in the classical concern about the need for good works. In order for us to participate in the future promised by God, faith must be made real in the flesh of our lives (→15:1). Now, in circumcision, we learn how God enables us to do the works that will bring us to participate in his promises: he gives commandments that we can in fact perform.

In order to avoid the gnostic temptation, we need once again to return to St. Paul and clarify his account of how the coming of Christ fulfills rather than changes the divine plan of providing us with commandments that we can fulfill. Paul observes that the power of sin prevents him from performing the works of the law, and this can create the impression that God's plan cannot move forward by way of commandments. However, Paul does not set aside the basic Old Testament understanding of the perfection of humanity by way of commandment. Instead, he wants to be clear about the role of Christ in fulfilling the law. One man's disobedience has created for us the fateful future of sin and death, but this is overturned by another man's obedience (Rom. 5:18). In the power of Christ, therefore, Paul can urge us to become "slaves of righteousness" (6:18). Obedience to God's commandment remains the enduring form of discipleship: "Yield yourselves to God as men who have been brought from death to life, and your members to God as instruments of righteousness" (6:13). Law is juxtaposed to grace as paths to obedience, the former unable to attain full obedience and the latter participating in the power of God to accomplish his purposes. Law and grace are, however, one and the same in form and goal, which is why Paul can so easily and naturally speak of "the law of Christ" (1 Cor. 9:21).

17:15 Sarah shall be her name.

The covenant future is not singular. It is corporate, just as the original partnership of Adam and Eve is corporate. Thus, Sarah is given a new name, and for the first time God specifies that Abraham's heir will come from her womb. The new name and the new possibility of a child clearly highlights Sarah's role in the covenant future. Hebrews reads her role in terms of faith, a new economy of hope and conviction that creates a new history for humanity: "Through faith also Sara herself received strength to conceive seed, and was delivered of a child when she was past age" (11:11 AV). A typological link between Eve, Sarah, and the Virgin Mary sheds light on the economy of the new history.

Eve is fruitful, but she gives birth to life-toward-death. The only way for Sarah to avoid participating in the doomed future of the generations from Eve is to not give birth at all. The alternative to sin-infected life is to opt out of the stream of the generations, or in Sarah's case, to be unable to participate because her womb was closed. But God intervenes and gives Sarah a child. It is standard to read Sarah's pregnancy, and the pregnancy of the many barren women in the Old Testament, as an illustration of a theological principle: we depend upon the grace of God. That's quite true, but something more precise is at work here. The point of the divine intervention into the natural process of childbirth is not generic—as if God chose this among any number of other human needs to demonstrate his power. Instead, Sarah's miraculous pregnancy in her old age is one of the crucial concentrations of divine purpose *into* the human condition. Sarah's barrenness took her out of the doomed history of Eve, but the gain is purely negative, an absence of complicity with the power of sin rather than a contribution to a defeat of its hold on humanity. Now, Sarah's unexpected pregnancy brings a child and the beginning of an alternative genealogy oriented toward life rather than death. Her child begins a history that, of its nature, infiltrates the affairs of the children of Eve, as the history of Israel's foreign relations shows.

In this way, Sarah foreshadows the Virgin Mary. Both give birth by virtue of divine intervention, and both for the sake of the plan of salvation. But there is an important difference. Sarah is the anti-Eve by virtue of her barrenness. Her womb is closed to the forward march of the generations after the fall, only returned to fertility by God's intervention and for the sake of another, very different future. But Mary is like Eve in her fruitfulness, quite capable of entering into the ongoing human project of bearing children. As a young virgin she stands on the threshold of the primal commandment: "be fruitful and multiply." So we see a different reaction to the reality of pregnancy. Sarah laughs to herself at the thought of childbirth (→18:12), because she is beyond the age of fertility. Mary's exclamation, "How shall this be?" (Luke 1:34), has a very different motive. She has every reason to think herself fertile, but she has had no sexual intercourse with a man. The barren Sarah wonders, "How can life come to one who *cannot* participate in the way of life-toward-death that began with Eve?" The Virgin Mary asks, "How can life come to one who *has not* participated in the way of life-toward-death that began with Eve?" Sarah's question is answered by appeal to divine power: "With God all things are possible" (Matt. 19:26). What seems unable to give life may by the power of God become a source of life. This teaches us that the children of the first Eve can, by the grace of God, be conscripted into the divine project. Mary's question is very different, and it is answered in a different way. Her pregnancy comes because the source of life, the one who was in the beginning, enters her womb. Mary is the fertile but new Eve. The way of life-toward-death is not redirected but instead superseded by the actuality of life-toward-life. "The first-born of all creation" is the source of life in the Virgin Mary's womb, and the child will live as "the first-born from the dead" (Col. 1:15, 18).

18:1 The LORD appeared to him.

The account of Abraham is organized around six divine appearances, each paired with a declaration (in part or whole) of the promise of land and descendants. In the first appearance, God calls Abraham and gives him the promises (→12:1a). In the second, God commands Abraham to see and walk the promised land (→13:14). In the third appearance, signs and a vision of God's acts of deliverance guarantee the fulfillment of the promises (→15:8). The fourth provides the commandment of circumcision that begins the divine invasion that perfects human creation (→17:2). Now, in this fifth appearance, we come to a dramatized anticipation of the fulfillment of the promise that Abraham shall be a blessing to all the nations of the earth. He pleads the case of Sodom and Gomorrah. He is not chosen for his own sake. Instead, he is favored by the LORD for the sake of all.

18:2 Behold, three men stood in front of him.

The three men by the oaks of Mamre often appear in Christian art as an image of the Holy Trinity. The association of the Father, Son, and Holy Spirit with these verses of Genesis is encouraged by the odd way in which the narrative shifts back and forth between singular and plural. The LORD appears to Abraham. He sees three men, but as befits the double perspective of one LORD as three men, Abraham ends up speaking to him/them in both singular and plural. The narrator participates in the same double pattern: "They said to him. . . . The LORD said" (18:9–10). So, within the strange, shifting literal ambiance of the text, there seems to be one LORD and, at the same time, three persons.

18:4 Rest yourselves.

Abraham sees the three visitors by his tent door, and to his eyes they seem tired and in need of refreshment. He urges them to rest, while he rushes around his household, calling to Sarah for fresh bread and commanding his servant to select a choice calf for slaughter. The image is perplexing. The LORD God who brings all things into existence seems run down, while Abraham, a creature, takes the initiative. The image is also ironic. God is the author of rest, and we are to "rest in the LORD" (Ps. 37:7 AV). And yet here is Abraham offering rest.

Does God tire? A psalm declares: "God my King is from of old, working salvation in the midst of the earth" (Ps. 74:12). Is the work too difficult? Does God need us to step up and fill the gap when he needs a break? Does Jesus need the support of his disciples in Gethsemane? Is he incapable of clothing his own nakedness on the cross? Is Christ vulnerable, requiring our comfort? And if not, then why the scene of the strangers in front of Abraham's tent? Why the extensive Christian tradition of prayer and devotion that focuses on increasing our empathy for the suffering Christ?

Perhaps an answer is found in Jesus's parable of Lazarus and the rich man (Luke 16:19–31). Lazarus lay at the gate of the rich man. He needed the rest of hospitality, but he was ignored. When Lazarus dies, he is carried by angels to rest in the bosom of Abraham. The rich man also dies. From the torment of Hades, he sees Lazarus and appeals to Abraham to warn his brothers to provide hospitality and comfort to those who need rest. Abraham refuses: "They have Moses and the prophets; let them hear them" (19:29). The parable is clearly meant as a commentary on the law and the prophets, but it also conveys an important image of heaven. In the parable, Abraham plays God's role as the provider of rest. Therefore, if we return to the scene by the oaks of Mamre, we can see that Abraham's act of hospitality to the divine strangers need not meet a divine need. Instead, his hospitality brings him into fellowship with—and conformity with—the divine. God provides an opportunity for hospitality, and Abraham is made godlike by comforting the divine visitor. Just as Abraham plays a heavenly role in Jesus's parable, in Genesis Abraham participates in the fulfillment of his covenant future as he plays the role of the one who gives comfort and rest.

Therefore, the proper thing to say about the exhausted divine visitors whom Abraham welcomes—and the dying Jesus over whom we are to rightly weep—is not that God needs rest or sympathy. Rather, God gives us the opportunity to welcome him and to offer ourselves in his service. It is an opportunity to do for the author of rest what he does for us and, in so doing, to draw nearer to God. As Jesus teaches his disciples: "He who receives you receives me, and he who receives me receives him who sent me" (Matt. 10:40). Or elsewhere in the New Testament: "Behold, I stand at the door and knock; if any one hears my voice and opens the door, I will come in to him and eat with him, and he with me" (Rev. 3:20).

18:8 He stood by them under the tree while they ate.

"I tell you," teaches Jesus of the final judgment, "many will come from east and west and sit at table with Abraham" (Matt. 8:11). The movement from a table *for* the LORD by the oaks of Mamre to the table *of* the LORD at the consummation of the age characterizes the history of the covenant. At first, the covenant partner can only observe the meal of divine refreshment. Abraham serves, but he does so at a distance. As the covenant is deepened, commandments regulate who and how human beings may come to join the LORD at the table. The Levitical priests approach the table and minister to the LORD on behalf of all the people of Israel. To complete the covenant, Jesus provides instructions for joining with him at the same LORD's table, now prepared by him in the fellowship of bread and wine. Christ commissions Paul to preach to Gentiles from east and west, baptizing them and bringing them to the table of rest. Thus what begins as a table for the LORD alone, prepared by a man who remains at a distance, ends as the Son's table prepared by his sacrifice, to which all are invited to come near.

18:12 Sarah laughed.

Sarah's laughter is doubt turned to prophecy. Later we read, "God hath made me to laugh, so that all that hear will laugh with me" (21:6 AV). What begins as an impossible dream ends in joy. What is barren and desolate is made pregnant and fruitful, and the dry laughter of unbelief foretells, however unwittingly, the full laughter of celebration. This is why the three-way conversation between the LORD, Abraham, and Sarah focuses on whether and why she laughed. God ends with an emphatic affirmation, not only of his power to raise up children of Abraham, but also of Sarah's laughter: "He said, 'No, but you did laugh'" (18:15). The tone is not one of rebuke. "Indeed," God seems to be saying, "you did laugh, and rightly so. The way forward in the covenant consistently passes through poverty, abandonment, and desolation. I'm sure that the memory of the promises in the midst of this vacancy and emptiness can seem cruelly funny. But 'do not despise the LORD's discipline or be weary of his reproof' (Prov. 3:11). Remember, 'the LORD reproves him whom he loves' (3:12). I have prepared the barren womb for fulfillment. As David will sing, 'The LORD restored the fortunes of Zion, we were like those who dream. Then our mouth was filled with laughter, and our tongue with shouts of joy' (Ps. 126:1–2)."

18:17–19 Shall I hide. . . . No, for I have chosen him.

"Surely the Lord GOD does nothing," we read elsewhere in scripture, "without revealing his secret to his servants the prophets" (Amos 3:7). There are two senses in which God is visible. The whole world testifies to his wisdom as creator, and in this sense, God can no more be hidden than the sun or the moon. We can blind ourselves, but as the source of reality, God never hides himself. In contrast, God's will for our redemption is hidden. Abraham cannot see the future unless he is given a vision. In other words, the God of the philosophers, the Supreme Being, the Highest Good, the Unmoved Mover, can be seen if we will but move ourselves to think clearly. However, the God of Israel, the one who calls Abraham and gives the law on Mount Sinai, who then exiles and restores Jerusalem, and who finally raises Jesus of Nazareth from the dead, can be seen only by the eyes of faith. What is hidden to our natural sight and revealed to the eyes of faith is the identity of God as the one who is the author of the covenant.

The LORD God shows Abraham *who he is* by telling him *what he will do*, and this happens when he calls Abraham and gives him the promises in Gen. 12. The signs and vision of Gen. 15 provide assurance of God's covenant loyalty. But this vision does not entail knowing *how* the LORD's plan will unfold. There remain "great and hidden things which you have not known" (Jer. 33:3). The full scope and import of the divine plan is "kept secret for long ages" (Rom. 16:25), only to be revealed in Christ. And even in Christ, the full form of the covenant initiated with Abraham remains a mystery. Even when the "treasure hidden in the field" is found and bought with the currency of faith, we cannot take the full measure of God's love in the dying and rising of Christ. In faith, we know more and more about God's plan for deliverance. God does not hide himself. To see what God has and will do for the sake of our salvation brings us closer and closer to the inexplicable and sheer existence of God as love. Yet there is always more to know, and we can always draw nearer still.

18:23 Abraham drew near.

"It is good for me to draw near to God" (Ps. 73:28 AV), and the divine plan is to provide for us the means to do so. The covenant of circumcision gives Abraham a way to walk before the LORD in righteousness, and this allows him to enter into intimacy with God. As the divine plan advances, "Moses alone shall come near to the LORD" on Mount Sinai (Exod. 24:2), and he does so in order that God might provide the further steps forward in the covenant. God gives commandments that set aside and sanctify a priesthood that can "come near the altar to minister" (30:20). Through the mediation of the priests, the whole people of Israel can assemble and draw near to the LORD.

The sanctification of a priestly caste is one dimension of the divine plan for bringing Israel near. A second dimension involves the trials of exile and dispersion. As metal purified by fire, the chosen people who are "survivors of the nations" are to "come, draw near together" and return to the LORD (Isa. 45:20). Inheriting the promise that Abraham will be a blessing to all nations, the restored people of Israel function as a magnetic center around which all the nations respond, hearkening to a universal divine call: "Draw near, O nations" (34:1). The gravitational pull of Israel is fulfilled in Christ's exile and dispersion in the crucifixion. Those who were scattered across the globe in the confusion of tongues at Babel are "brought near in the blood of Christ" (Eph. 2:13). In baptism the members of the nations are made both priests and kings of Israel (1 Pet. 2:9). The baptized enter into the sanctuaries of the LORD and they fulfill the pattern of Job, the paradigmatic faithful Gentile: "Like a prince I would approach him" (Job 31:37).

18:32 I will speak again but this once.

As partner in covenant with God, Abraham can provide hospitality and rest for the LORD, and he can draw near to the LORD. As he presses God on behalf of the possible righteous residents of Sodom and Gomorrah, we see that those called to fellowship with God intercede as well. In this way Abraham foreshadows Moses, who intercedes on behalf of the sinful Israelites, as well as the Levitical priesthood that sacrifices on behalf of the people. Abraham even more clearly prefigures Christ. Abraham urges God to accept the righteousness of a few as sufficient for the salvation of the sinful many. Abraham stops at ten, but as the history of the covenant moves forward the righteousness of Christ alone is sufficient for the deliverance of all. Christ Jesus sits "at the right hand of God . . . [and] intercedes for us" (Rom. 8:34). Christ is like Abraham, petitioning his Father on our behalf: "Suppose there was *one* man found righteous, wilt thou not spare the city of man for his sake?"

19:2 My lords, turn aside, I pray you, to your servant's house.

Throughout Genesis, Lot is not so much the antithesis of Abraham as a pale and failed imitation. Here he offers hospitality, as did Abraham. Soon he will offer to "sacrifice" his daughters to placate a dangerous lust, just as Abraham twice "sacrifices" Sarah to satisfy real or imagined lustful desires, first of Pharaoh, then of Abimelech (→12:13). Later Lot will produce sons according to the plan of his daughters, just as Abraham produced Ishmael according to Sarah's scheme. Yet Lot is dissimilar. Like the blind man to whom Jesus applied the first of two doses of cure, Lot can see men, "but they look like trees, walking" (Mark 8:24). Lot perceives the way of righteousness, and yet he misperceives and consistently misjudges. Earlier, he wrongly imagined the Jordan valley to be a new Eden, and he departed from Abraham (→13:10). Now, in Sodom, he resists the blind violence of unrestrained lust, protecting the visiting angels, and yet he is easily lured into incest by his daughters (→19:36). Where Abraham can convince God to consider the possibility of saving Sodom and Gomorrah for the sake of a few righteous men, Lot is unable to persuade even his sons-in-law to save themselves (19:14). Later, after leaving Sodom, Lot misjudges the true nature of safety and rest, first wishing to flee to a nearby city and then changing his mind and retreating to an isolated cave (→19:31).

Throughout the narrative, therefore, Lot should be read as a man inclined toward what is right and good, but as one who fails and falters, because he relies on human discernment and natural powers rather than on the promises of God. He may have been "greatly distressed by the licentiousness of the wicked" (2 Pet. 2:7), but he dithers and lingers (→19:16). He rightly seeks a restoration of Edenic innocence, but he settles in Sodom, unable to distinguish between the luxuries of the city and the abundance of the original garden. Unlike his wife, Lot does not look back with nostalgic loyalty to sinful habits, but he cannot see a way forward. He desires rest, but he wrongly chooses the deathlike isolation of a cave. Such is the fate of life led by the natural light of reason and conscience. Evil may be shunned and the good sought, but weakness of the will tends to neutralize good intentions, and false or finite goods are too easily prized as the highest good. Without the promises that God makes to Abraham, there is no new future for the children of Adam.

19:16 He lingered; so the men seized him.

The episode begins with Lot offering rest to the visiting angels. Seeking to protect them from the lustful violence of the city, Lot even offers his daughters to placate the mob and secure the safety of the visitors, only to have them rejected by the mob (19:8). Lot's actions on behalf of the visitors nearly culminates in disaster, as the disordered desires of the city press against him with deadly force (19:9). Doing evil that good might come eventually produces bad consequences. As Lot's actions reach their well-meaning but futile end, the divine visitors exercise their power. First they pull Lot into the house, saving him from immediate danger. Then they strike the crowd blind. Most importantly, however, the angels save Lot from his own diffidence and hesitation. The mercy of the LORD seizes Lot and brings him out of the city of sin that he was unable to motivate himself to leave.

The narrative emphasizes the reason for the angelic rescue. "God remembered Abraham" and for this reason "sent Lot out of the midst of the overthrow" (19:29). Lot's capacities as an agent and actor do not shape his future. On the contrary, left to his own devices, he would have remained in Sodom to be destroyed. We are not in a different position. Left to our own devices, we would remain in our sinful habits. Fortunately, however, God does not leave us alone, and he does not choose to remember only our merits. For this reason, we rightly appeal to the intercession of the saints. God remembers the saints when he looks upon us in our weakness of will and our continued bondage to sin.

19:24 The Lord rained on Sodom and Gomorrah brimstone and fire.

Modern sentimentality revolts against any linkage between salvation and judgment. It seems impossible to us that God would reveal his love by way of scrutinizing the sin of Sodom and Gomorrah and then punishing accordingly. Isn't love a matter of forgiveness and acceptance?

The Bible speaks against this sentiment. The prophet Malachi reports God's intention: "I will draw near to you for judgment" (3:5). God will do for us what he did for Sodom and Gomorrah. This is good news, not bad, for he did not give them any punishment other than intimacy with himself. "God is a consuming fire" (Heb. 12:29). His love flashes like fire. It is "a most vehement flame" (Song 8:6) that not even our watery indifference and tepid apathy can quench. He will destroy in judgment all that is captive to sin. The flaming coal of his love purifies our hearts and lips (Isa. 6:6). Like the residents of Sodom and Gomorrah, in Christ we die. In judgment we are joined to the Son of Man, who is revealed on the cross (Luke 17:29). For this we should rejoice in thanksgiving rather than recoil in therapeutic horror. "The Lord scourges those who draw near to him" (Judith 8:27), because he desires fellowship with us in his holiness.

19:26 She became a pillar of salt.

"Be very steadfast to keep and do all that is written in the book of the law of Moses," Joshua teaches, "turning aside from it neither to the right hand nor to the left" (Josh. 23:6). The people of God are to do as Ruth did, not "turning back" but instead clinging to the Lord with the pledge: "Where you go I will go, and where you lodge I will lodge" (Ruth 1:16). Faith "run[s] with perseverance the race that is set before us" (Heb. 12:1). We are not to turn back or aside in diffidence, uncertainty, or misguided loyalty to habit, but instead we should be ever "straining forward to what lies ahead" (Phil. 3:13).

It is in the spirit of perseverance that Jesus urges his disciples to "remember Lot's wife" (Luke 17:32). The day on which the Son of Man is revealed will be like the day when Noah entered the ark and when Lot went out from Sodom. Only those who hearken to the call of God will survive the coming judgment, and the response to the call of God must be immediate. We cannot negotiate terms for discipleship. We cannot choose the time and place when the Lord's judgment transforms our lives: "Let him who is in the field not turn back to take his mantle" (Matt. 24:18). To those called to follow him but who wish to return to families and friends to settle their affairs and say their goodbyes, Jesus says, "No one who puts his hand to the plow and looks back is fit for the kingdom of God" (Luke 9:62).

19:31 He dwelt in a cave with his two daughters.

The account of Lot's self-imposed isolation in the cave is complex. Having pleaded with the destroying angels for permission to flee to a city rather than into the hills, Lot suddenly changes his mind. He is afraid to dwell in the nearby town and therefore retreats to an isolated cave. The cave seems to anticipate the cave of Machpelah where Sarah (23:19) and Abraham (25:9) will be buried. True to form, Lot makes a bad choice, seeing as good that which is bad. Earlier, he had imagined the land of Sodom and Gomorrah as an Edenic garden, and he left Abraham in an imaginary "turning back" to original innocence (→13:10). Now he chooses another illusory peace: death. Of course, Lot's choice is not for a literal death, just as the land he chose earlier was not a literal Eden. Nonetheless, isolation from humanity and the hurly-burly of human history is a quite lively and perennial fantasy of rest and respite. The cave represents any number of retreating strategies: losing ourselves in work, numbing our senses with alcohol, making home an isolated sanctuary, building walls of psychological protection. These strategies have no lasting success. Lot's real source of safety and his actual pathway toward rest can be only in Abraham and the covenant with the LORD (→19:16).

19:36 Both the daughters of Lot were with children by their father.

Unlike Lot's choice of a living death, his two daughters continue to share a concern for the future. They want to participate in the forward movement of the generations. However, like Lot, they misperceive and misjudge. They imagine themselves the sole remnant after a worldwide destruction, and they think of the cave as something like Noah's ark. This leads to a plan. The daughters, deceived about their situation, scheme to deceive their father, who is in his own way deceived about the true nature of safety and rest. The upshot is a scene of drunkenness and incest that succeeds in the same way that Sarah's scheme to use Hagar as a means to achieve an heir also succeeds: children are forthcoming. The children follow "the manner of all the earth" (19:31). The sons of Lot are fathers of the Moabite and Ammonite nations. Like the progeny of Ishmael, these nations are not lost in the oblivion of humanity. They figure later in the history of Israel (Num. 23–25; 2 Kgs. 3), and they contribute to the divine plan by way of a chosen remnant (Ruth 4:18–22). Each has a providential role in the divine plan. Even the dead ends have roles to play in the final end (→16:11).

20:2 Abraham said of Sarah his wife, "She is my sister."

This episode repeats the same basic plot of 12:10–20 (→12:13). At this point, however, a son has been promised to Sarah, and this new fact raises the stakes. In the first version, it was not altogether clear whether Pharaoh had sexual intercourse with Sarah before he discovered her true identity. In this version, the narrative is quite clear. God says, "I did not let you touch her" (20:6). Just as the child of the covenant must come through Sarah and not Hagar, so also must the child of the promise be the seed of Abraham and not that of a foreign king. The episode ends with Abraham's prayer of intercession on behalf of Abimelech's wife and his female slaves. He asks that their closed wombs might be opened (20:18). In the very next verse, the LORD does for Abraham and Sarah that which Abraham prayed might happen to Abimelech and his household. Sarah's closed womb is opened.

21:2 Sarah conceived, and bore Abraham a son.

The larger pattern of covenant fulfillment is given in Sarah: "He gives the barren woman a home, making her the joyous mother of children" (Ps. 113:9). Strength does not build upon strength, profit does not follow profit, and success does not lead to success. The way forward in the covenant consistently passes through narrow gates and inauspicious openings. Dry bones and whited sepulchers seem vacant, incapable of a spiritual future, but no more so than an aged and barren woman. The sometimes faithless and always fickle people of Israel in the wilderness, the idolatrous nation driven into exile, the restored temple overrun by moneychangers, the dead man Jesus on the cross, the fearful disciples, and Peter who denies Christ—their unexpected spiritual fertility is prefigured in Sarah's pregnancy.

St. Paul makes use of Sarah's pattern of unexpected fulfillment in his own complex account of the calling of the Gentiles into the inheritance of Abraham. Her barrenness suddenly made fruitful serves as an encouragement to the Gentiles. Do not accept your spiritual desolation and bondage to idolatry as an inevitable future, Paul suggests. True, he implies, you were not married to the LORD in the covenant, and you had no patrimony in the LORD. But it is not his way to favor those already rich in blessings. For it has been written, "Rejoice, O barren one who does not bear; break forth and shout, you who are not in travail; for the children of the desolate one are many more than the children of her that is married" (Gal. 4:27, quoting Isa. 54:1). God gives life where only death seems to reign: first in the womb of Sarah, later in the history of the people of Israel, and most fully and literally in the death and resurrection of Christ. So now, Paul reasons, the Gentiles, long dead in idolatry and sin, are given life in the household of Abraham.

And not the Gentiles alone. The appeal to the barren one who rejoices in her miraculous fertility pertains to Paul's Jewish readers as well. In Romans, Paul quotes a number of scriptural texts that highlight the faithlessness of Israel. "Their eyes [will] be darkened" (Rom. 11:10, quoting Ps. 69:23), just as Sarah's womb was shut up and made empty. "Lord, they have killed thy prophets, they have demolished thy altars" (Rom. 11:3, quoting a description of faithless Israel in 1 Kgs. 19:10). Paul offers a deeply complex account of the role of the law of Moses in relation to the cross of Christ and the Gentiles. However, it is clear that the pattern of blessings in desolation applies as much to the hardened hearts of Israel in his own time as it does to the Gentiles he wishes to encourage. "Their rejection," he writes, "means the reconciliation of the world" (Rom. 11:15). Their desolation in unbelief is the narrow gate through which the Gentiles enter. Thus, it seems clear that Paul envisions the barrenness of Israel as participating in Sarah's joy, not only in the way in which they have given birth to Gentile faith, but also in their own place in the divine plan, living on the threshold of renewal. For "if their failure means riches for the Gentiles, how much more will their full inclusion mean" (11:12).

The history of the Jewish people after the time of St. Paul is multifaceted, and its relationship to Christianity is difficult to parse. Nonetheless, Paul's optimistic evocation of Sarah's pattern of fruitfulness in the wake of barren hopelessness turns out to have an unexpected, prophetic accuracy. The temple in Jerusalem was destroyed shortly after Paul wrote his many letters to the Christian communities. The question he posed became all the more pressing: "Have they stumbled so as to fall?" (Rom. 11:11). The answer that history gives corresponds to Paul's own exclamation: "By no means!" (11:1). The natural branch of the children of Abraham did not join the wild branch of Gentile Christianity that had been grafted on to the olive tree of the covenant (as Paul envisioned would happen). Nonetheless, the new form of Judaism that emerged from the trials of the first century drew nourishment from the shared roots of the covenant.

We do not know "the mind of the Lord," nor are we privy to his inner counsels (Rom. 11:34, quoting Isa. 40:13), so we cannot say what role the renewal of Judaism by talmudic rabbis over and against early Christianity might have played and continues to play in the divine plan. It is difficult to see how the tangled history of interaction, conflict, and debate between Jews and Christians over two millennia has advanced God's purposes—though Genesis certainly seems to anticipate a divinely ordained fraternal enmity. Yet, I think contemporary Jews should be able to rejoice in the fruitfulness of the diverse Judaism of the time of Jesus. It gave birth to rabbinic Judaism and provided the basis for Christianity. Through the missionary work of the church, the Christian interpretation of the fulfillment of the promises to Abraham has converted a great deal of the world, giving birth to a widespread worship of the God of Abraham.

21:10 Cast out this slave woman.

Once again Sarah regrets her plan to create a future for Abraham by way of the slave girl Hagar. For a second time she drives her from the household (→16:2a). The story, however, does not simply double the earlier account. Hagar's child has been born, and we are told that Sarah's desire to see Hagar and Ishmael expelled "was very displeasing to Abraham on account of his son" (21:11). In this instance, therefore, the expulsion of Hagar anticipates Abraham's more famous trial in Gen.

22. Is he willing to sacrifice Ishmael? As an assurance, God provides a double promise: Isaac will inherit the covenant, but Ishmael will found a nation as well. His life will not be for naught. Abraham trusts in the promises and sacrifices Ishmael, not by offering him on an altar, but by sending Hagar and her son out of his household and into the mortal danger of the wilderness.

21:14 She departed, and wandered in the wilderness.

Important parallels between Gen. 21 and Gen. 22 provide good reasons to resist the notion that this second account of Hagar's expulsion is simply a repetition of the first. Just as God's command sends Abraham on his way to Mount Moriah, Hagar is sent out into the unknown at the request of Sarah, which is backed up by the commandment of God (21:12). Like Abraham, who sets out "early in the morning" (22:3), Hagar is sent out "early in the morning" with provisions from Abraham (21:14). Both children come to the point of death, Ishmael from lack of water (21:15), and Isaac bound and ready for sacrifice (22:10). To avert death—and to avert the falsification of the promises made about the futures of both sons—a divine messenger comes with words of deliverance, repeating the promise of a future blessing (compare 21:17–18 with 22:12–18).

The parallels, however, also draw attention to contrasts. Hagar's trial concerns the son whom Abraham received "after the manner of all the earth" (19:31). Ishmael is the worldly son, produced according to a human plan that accepted what seemed to be the realistic constraints of the situation. For this reason, Ishmael inherits a worldly promise. He will be the father of a nation that, like all nations, will live and die by its abilities to protect and advance its own interests under the leadership of someone who is "an expert with the bow" (21:18–20). The subsequent trial of Abraham concerns a son born by the power of God's promises to create a real future. Isaac is the heavenly son and through him will come the nation that lives by the power of God to fulfill his promises, rather than by worldly skill in gaining the upper hand.[21]

21:27 The two men made a covenant.

Earlier, Abimelech appeared as a dark figure, a second pharaoh who takes Sarah into his household (→20:2). In this role, he was poised to usurp Abraham as father, and therefore he was a threat to the future of the promise. But his antagonism to the divine plan was unwitting, and once he realized the true

21. For helpful comparisons between the testing of Hagar/Ishmael and Abraham/Isaac, see Bruce Waltke and Cathi J. Fredricks, *Genesis: A Commentary* (Grand Rapids: Zondervan, 2001), 292, 297.

nature of the situation, he repented and restored Sarah with a great abundance of penitential gifts. Now Abimelech plays the role of an anti-pharaoh, a secular king who wishes to become a continuing ally. He recognizes that Abraham is divinely favored (21:22), and he seeks to secure a proper, lasting relationship to Abraham, whom he sees as the mediator of God's blessings. He pledges peace between his offspring and those of Abraham (21:23), and in the wake of conflict, he does not recapitulate Lot's decision to separate from Abraham (→13:10). Instead, he reunites with Abraham by swearing an oath that Abraham and his flocks may use the well of Beersheba (21:25–31).

The relationship between the elect of God—Abraham, Israel, the church—and the kingdoms of the world is perpetually unsettled. Sometimes the relationship is one of antagonism, even to the point of deadly confrontation. At other times, worldly powers seek alliance with the children of the covenant, sensing that they hold the key to true prosperity. For this reason we cannot reduce the relationship between the people of God and worldly governments, organizations, and institutions to a simple formula. Those called in Christ are to live according to the promise of new life in him. Whether this leads to antagonism to or cooperation with worldly kingdoms depends upon whether the secular world recognizes and seeks the blessings of the covenant. We cannot know ahead of time whether secular governments will be animated by the spirit of enmity or friendship toward the company of the elect.

As a consequence we should be careful when denouncing Constantinianism as a corruption of Christian witness. The social and political movement of late antiquity associated with the Emperor Constantine sought something like Abimelech's covenant with Abraham. According to legend, Constantine put the sign of the cross on his battle standards before a decisive engagement. After winning, he deduced that God is with the church in all that she does, and he set about to provide buildings and endowments for Christian worship and instruction, both to glorify God and to secure divine blessings on the temporal affairs of his people. He thought that if true worship flourished then his reign over all the nations of the earth would prosper. In this sense, Constantine believed in the promise that all the nations will be blessed by the obedience of the children of Abraham.

The account of Abimelech's pact with Abraham highlights the possible legitimacy of the approach represented by Constantine. It is, of course, unstable. The anti-pharaoh can easily again become just plain pharaoh. Moreover, secular government often misconceives the blessing it seeks, imagining that God prospers a nation or a people solely by strengthening its power. But the most threatening danger concerns the church itself. The warm embrace of alliance can place the church in a perilous situation. It is very tempting to accept the "thousand pieces of silver" (20:16) that the secular world offers, the rights and privileges and other forms of social reward that worldly powers provide, and then over time to imagine the silver to be a birthright more decisive and crucial for the church then God's promises. Preserving the favor of secular powers can become more important than "preaching [the] gospel . . . in season and out of season" (2 Tim. 4:2). The powerful are often not rebuked because the leadership of the church wishes to maintain its privileges. The archbishop's palace can seem more precious than the office of teacher and chief pastor. The temptation is great, because the church can mask her tacit submission to worldly powers with rationalizations about the need to maintain a central role in society or to avoid unnecessary and debilitating conflicts that might harm the church.

22:1 God tested Abraham.

For many modern readers, the idea that God tries and tests the faithful offends. We tend to think of loving parents as those who protect rather than try. A good teacher seeks to empower rather than test. We worry about the perils of competition. Encouraging self-esteem becomes the great preoccupation. Everybody is a winner, and prizes and ribbons are on hand for all the participants. True love nurtures, we imagine; it does not challenge and demand, try and judge.

However the scriptures testify otherwise. The trials of Israel in the wilderness are described as the LORD's test, designed to humble the proud independence of Israel and renew covenant faithfulness (Deut. 8:11–20). These trials are ongoing in the biblical history of Israel, always against the background of the threatening perversions of idolatry. After the conquest of the land, the LORD does not permit full and complete dominion. Alien peoples and their strange gods remain, but not as the stubborn residue of the past. Instead they are divinely ordained temptations: "That by them," says the LORD, "I may test Israel, whether they will take care to walk in the way of the LORD as their fathers did, or not" (Judg. 2:22). Later, after their descent into idolatry and division under the ill-fated kings of Israel and Judah, the LORD tries his faithless people with the afflictions of exile (Jer. 9:7). The tribulations of captivity foreshadow an eschatological trial. At the end of the age, the LORD will set aside a remnant, and he will "refine them as one refines silver, and test them as gold is tested" (Zech. 13:9).

God tests the individual as well as the community. When dedicating the temple, the focal point of Israel's cultic life, King David proclaims, "I know, my God, that thou triest the heart" (1 Chr. 29:17). The psalms are full of lamentations uttered by those under divinely ordained duress. However, Job provides the most extensive account of trial, an account that parallels and illuminates the trial of Abraham. Anxious to protect the divine from a direct role as the source of affliction, the opening scene of Job depicts God as authorizing Satan to test Job's faithfulness. Soon Job is stripped of all that he loves. Sword, fire, and crushing stones deprive Job of his flocks, servants, and children. But amid all these afflictions Job is shown to be faithful, and at the end of the book all that was taken away is restored in double portions. What seemed an unbearable loss becomes, through an enduring faith, an unaccountable gain.

Abraham's trial has a similar purifying and redoubling function. Isaac, the beloved son, the child of the promise, the gift of a future with God, plays the same role for Abraham as Job's worldly possessions and familial happiness. And just as the good things of life are taken from Job, Isaac is taken from Abraham by divine commandment: "Take your son, your only son Isaac, whom you love, and go to the land of Moriah, and offer him there as a burnt offering" (Gen. 22:2). The challenge to Abraham's hope is as direct as the challenge to Job's confidence in the goodness of God, perhaps more direct. How can Abraham continue to trust in the covenant if he sacrifices the promised son? As we know, of course, the son is not destroyed by the trial. The angel of the LORD intervenes and directs Abraham's sight to "a ram, caught in a thicket" (22:13). The animal is sacrificed in the place of the son of the promise. Just as Job's possessions and family are restored to him, Isaac is returned to Abraham.

We correctly sense that restoration does not cancel the effects of the trials of Job or Abraham. Job teaches the single most important lesson for anyone afflicted by evil. The speech of God out of the whirlwind gives a spiritual answer to the theological problem of suffering. God says, in effect, "It's not about you." In a similar way, the trial on Mount Moriah has a lasting pedagogical effect. Isaac represents the potency of human fertility. In our bodies, we possess the ability to reproduce and perpetuate our family identities and thus make the future. This kind of future is a central element of the covenant that God makes with Abraham: he is to be blessed by descendants. The trial, however, requires Abraham to deny the role of his natural fertility in the future that God promises. Isaac represents all our worldly efforts to make the future: our plans and projects, our accumulation of goods and savings put aside as a bulwark against unforeseen difficulties, our traditions and habits, and much more. Abraham cannot lift the knife unless he renounces all hope in worldly powers of any sort. The renunciation remains, even as the beloved son is restored.

The dynamic of renunciation and restoration echoes throughout the New Testament. The trial of Abraham enacts the promise of Christ: he who loses his life for my sake shall gain it. The command to offer Isaac is therefore a spiritual gift given by God. It is as a losing of life for Abraham. He can no longer invest his hopes in the natural power of fertility, the power that allows him to live on through his son. And yet, even as he binds his son to prepare to lose him, Abraham gains. Isaac is returned to him as a natural son made spiritual by the power of God's promise. Abraham no longer depends on Isaac's physical survival in order to have a future in the covenant, because he has received him as a gift rather than held on to him as the issue from his loins.

This giving up that prepares one to receive is clearly evident in the passion, death, and resurrection of Christ. The Good Friday events enact what God commands but at the last minute forestalls in Gen. 22, and Easter Sunday completes the restoration of Isaac to Abraham. St. Paul applies this paschal dynamic to all of us. We die with Christ so that we can rise with him. God takes away from us our futile dependence upon earthly powers. In baptism, our captivity to sin is itself taken captive. Our bondage to worldly hopes is bound, as it were, in Christ, just as Isaac is bound for sacrifice on Mount Moriah. And thus sacrificed in Christ, we are not delivered to a spectral, otherworldly place; we are not made into smoke that only God can enjoy. Just as Isaac is restored in the flesh, we rise in Christ in our bodies. We are not unclothed, but further clothed and "swallowed up by life" (2 Cor. 5:4).

With this in mind, I think we can return to our tendency to reject the idea that God tries and tests. Perhaps we like comfortable images of God as a cosmic therapist whose love amounts to a universal scheme to promote self-esteem, because we want to hold on to our lives rather than lose them. The sheer material success of Western culture can heighten our fantasy that worldly realities and powers are able to carry us to a fundamentally new and transformed future. Medical science will stamp out sickness. New farming techniques will feed the world. Democratic institutions will deliver us from political oppression and conflict. Reproductive technologies will perfect the human species. In these and other ways, we pledge loyalty to worldly powers, an investment that St. Paul calls the works of the law. It is a way of living that trusts only in the kind of future that we can imagine building for ourselves.

Yet, if we rely on earthly powers and finite goods—even the seemingly irresistible impulse toward reproduction, even the intrinsic good of parental love—then all is lost. As the author of Ecclesiastes observes with chilling clarity, earthly powers and finite goods decay and cannot protect us from the nothingness of death. The truth is plain to see. The wealthy, child-poor societies of the West suggest that we can no longer trust in the power of sexual desire to produce a future. Nor, as St. Paul points out again and again, can anything other than the power of God deliver us from our self-incurred slavery to sin, which is at root an idolatrous return to inner-worldly powers as the source of our hope. I shudder to think what technological barbarisms will emerge to provide for what women's wombs no longer produce. Thus, if we are realistic about our situation, then we can see that trials and tests are consistent with divine love. They work against our hopeless hope that our finite powers can see us through. To be tested is to be brought back to reality. It is a spank that awakens us.

Trials and tests not only purify us of delusions, but also prepare us for a proper loyalty to the world and its finite goods. A clear New Testament analogue to Abraham's test illustrates: Jesus's temptation in the wilderness (Luke 4:1–13). Satan would have Jesus put his trust in bread and worldly dominion, both of which he rejects. Finally, Satan attempts to bring Jesus to a reversal of roles. Instead of allowing God to try and transform us according to his purposes, Satan urges Jesus to throw himself down from the heights of the temple in Jerusalem and thus put God to the test.

Jesus puts bread and worldly dominion in their proper place, and that's precisely the point of the test. It's not the case that being forced to face reality destroys the world. Just as Isaac is returned to Abraham, so also do the bread and political dominion that Jesus rejects return to play a proper role in the Christian life. Feeding the hungry is a work of mercy, and the just exercise of authority is a social duty. To be tried is to be shorn of worldly hopes, not worldly realities, and this leaves the bread to be exactly what it is, and nothing more: the finite power of nutrition and a focal point for the natural fellowship of a shared meal. The same holds for politics. We need not worship and serve political power as the imagined source of human deliverance, as if we could legislate our way to the kingdom of God. Instead, we can support and participate in the power of the state for the sake of the finite goods it can achieve (Rom. 13:1–7). When we are tried and when our false hopes are dashed, we can render to Caesar the things that are Caesar's—but no more. This is part of the freedom for which Christ has set us free. With a purified hope, we can love the world and remain loyal to it according to its true nature and purpose, rather than the unrealistic images that our idolatrous hope would make of it.

Of course, it is difficult to join with the author of James and say, "Count it all joy, my brethren, when you meet various trials" (1:2). We rarely see the trials in scripture or in our lives as good news. We naturally shy away from any test that probes the inner perversity of our hearts and separates us from our overinflated earthly loves. In the *Divine Comedy*, Dante portrays himself as the seventh and final ledge of the Mountain of Purgatory (*Pugatorio* 27). It is lined by a wall of purifying flames that bar the way forward to the singing fields of paradise and his beloved Beatrice. Virgil, Dante's guide, urges him forward, reassuring him that while there may be torment in the flames, there will be no death. Dante hesitates before the wall of purifying flames—as we all do. We do not want to renounce our worldly loves, which are often dearer to us than life itself. After all, these worldly loves can so easily seem to be the very point and purpose of human existence. But Dante goes through the flames, and he is reunited with Beatrice. We need to be separated from our earthly loves so that we can receive them back, not as sources of our happiness and hope, but as the finite goods of creation that God established in the beginning—not as ends in themselves but as things prepared for perfection on the seventh day of divine rest.

The dynamic of renunciation and restoration that defines Abraham's trial—and all spiritual trials in the Bible—encourages the paradoxical worldliness of faith. We need to be freed from our impulse to live as children "of the world," not in order to escape from finite reality, but so that we can become more fully capable of living "in the world." If we no longer invest our worldly powers and capacities with the vain hope that they can be the point and purpose of human life, then we can actually live as finite creatures with bodies, families, and social institutions, and do so without making them into idols. A purified hope may require a lifetime of trials, many self-imposed as spiritual disciplines that require us to sacrifice the Isaacs of our worldly loves. But the end point remains the same. No longer compulsively trying to make sex or food or children or the triumph of our political judgments into the sources of our hope, we can assess the world realistically. For this reason, trials do not secure divine blessing as extrinsic rewards for iron-willed obedience. They are constituent elements of the gospel itself, as the New Testament reminds us again and again. They purify our loves. They are forms of grace that prepare us to love God and others in God.

22:2 Take now thy son, thy only son Isaac, whom thou lovest, and get thee
into the land of Moriah. (AV)

The imperative "get thee" repeats the formula that opens the story of Abraham. When Abraham is in the country of his father, the LORD commands him, "Get thee out of thy country, and from thy kindred, and from thy father's house" (12:1 AV). Then he renounced his quite natural and healthy loyalty to his parents and his clan. Now he must go with his son, his only son, whom he loves, and "get thee into the land of Moriah" in order to make a deeper sacrifice. In this way, Gen. 22 reiterates the main theme of the entire cycle of stories about Abraham. He has a future only insofar as he trusts in the promises of God. All other means toward a new future circle back to the dead end of sin and death.

22:8 God himself will provide. (NRSV)

Abraham's utterance is an example of unwitting prophecy, just as Sarah's mocking laugh is an unwitting expression of her eventual joy (→18:12). Abraham speaks as does Caiaphas, when he counsels the court of the high priest that it is expedient to sacrifice one man to save the whole people of Israel (John 11:50). Pilate is also an unwitting speaker of the truth when he presents Jesus to the crowd in Jerusalem: "Will you have me release for you the King of the Jews?" (18:39). Moreover, Abraham's unwitting prophecy extends beyond the immediate context of Isaac's sacrifice. He foretells the Passover substitution of the lamb for the firstborn of Israel—and of the paschal substitution of the Lamb of God for the children of Adam: "He who did not spare his own Son but gave him up for us all" (Rom. 8:32).

22:9–10 Built an altar . . . laid the wood . . . bound Isaac his son, and laid him
on the altar . . . took the knife.

In contrast to the earlier episode at Sodom and Gomorrah when Abraham was quite capable of a calculating and extended dialogue with the LORD (18:22–33), we now read of the cold, unquestioning efficiency of Abraham. He is willing, without hesitation or delay, to follow through with the command to kill his son. The chilling effect is heightened by the intimate detail of concrete human actions: the wood on Isaac's back, the fire and knife in Abraham's hand. These realistic features of Abraham's trial and the binding of Isaac are part of what makes this one of the most indigestible scenes in scripture. The text offers no easy exit into symbolism or allegory.

The narrative realism also shifts attention away from generic problems of theodicy. The forward thrust of the action leads us to ask, "Where does such a hard commandment lead?" In this sense, Abraham's trial evokes our anxieties about all the hard sayings of scripture, all the testing demands that seem to call us to sacrifice what it seems natural and good to love. What kind of life really emerges out of the Sermon on the Mount? Where does the cross lead the followers of Christ? Are we to take Abraham's cold, sharp knife of ascetic discipline into our own hands and cut into our own all-too-human and limited selves? Can we be confident that such determined and harsh action will lead to fuller life? Or do we harbor the fear that all is for naught and that we have sacrificed to no good end?

In this way, the theodicy evoked by Abraham's ascent of Mount Moriah is personal, not metaphysical. The binding of Isaac evokes the fear that sacrifice simply ends in renunciation and loss. With his son on the altar and his hand ready to wield the knife, we confront the painful possibility that death is the ultimate end for human life. The train of thought is not difficult to imagine. Perhaps Pharaoh really does have the final word: "I will draw my sword, my hand shall destroy them" (Exod. 15:9). And if so, then the most we can do in life is to negotiate with naked power in order to secure temporary survival and gain some small margin of happiness. There is no God to enjoy, and even if there is one, he does not care for human life or, worse, cares only for the bitter odor of sacrifice. We should therefore renounce pious hopes and take the small pleasures of life where we can find them. Perhaps, this train of thought continues, we should face the facts. The world is governed by religious or secular Molochs, and "the dead who are already dead are more fortunate than the living who are still alive; but better than both is he who has not yet been, and has not seen the evil deeds that are done under the sun" (Eccl. 4:2–3). In a world running relentlessly toward death, this way of thinking concludes, sacrifice wastes what little, passing happiness we might wrestle from an otherwise cruel, indifferent cosmos. We cannot justify hope; therefore, we need to hunker down for the grim task of survival.

This sense of spiritual oppression and despair is not limited to our contemplation of the grim details of Abraham's determined obedience. It is also evoked by the more extended, but equally concrete and quotidian depiction of the passion and death of Christ on the cross. Like the servants of Abraham who seem to evaporate on the day of the commanded sacrifice, the disciples have scattered, and a dark hopelessness dominates Golgotha. Peter denies Christ and weeps bitter tears. Judas Iscariot hangs himself. Pilate washes his hands as the crowd in Jerusalem chants for death. The soldiers spit, mock, and beat. Jesus is prepared for death with the same painstaking care, nailed to the cross with the same grim determination that Abraham used to bind Isaac for sacrifice. Jesus's cry of dereliction, "My God, my God, why hast thou forsaken me?" (Matt. 27:46), seems to express what Abraham might have felt and thought had his hand moved swiftly to draw the knife across Isaac's neck. And in this malignant atmosphere, in the darkness of abandonment, hatred, and cruel disdain for life, the Father really does sacrifice the Son.

There can be no doubt that the central proclamation of Christian hope reaches into the darkest corners of human despair. In Christ, we are asked to dwell upon the stupidity, banality, and sheer ugliness of human wickedness—and unlike Abraham's trial, we are forced to look upon the frightful face of death. The cold, dead bodies of our loved ones stand as painful witnesses. On Good Friday, as the darkness of the day closes in on us, the expressionless faces of death gather in our memories, neither smiling nor frowning. The grave mocks our hope, and as Christ's body is taken down from the cross, there is ample opportunity to wonder whether God is powerful enough or loving enough to provide an alternative. Plunged into the horrible impotence of death, Good Friday gives us a moment of contemplative horror that sounds the depths of faith far more thoroughly than any philosophical formulation of the problem of evil.

22:12 I know that you fear God.

Where modern men and women often see trials as inconsistent with God's love, they also tend to think that the emotion of fear is incompatible with their love of God. It is not an obvious mistake. Fear seems a negative emotion. Aristotle defines fear as pain arising from the anticipation of evil (*Rhetoric* 2). It causes us to recoil and draw away from danger. Love seems quite different. It has moments of jealous turmoil and trembling expectation, but in the main we think of love as unifying. Love unites where fear drives apart. Not surprisingly, Aristotle also says that we cannot love those whom we fear. Why, then, is Abraham commended for his fear? Isn't Abraham a "friend of God" (Jas. 2:23)? How can fear have a role in friendship? In what sense can fear draw us toward God in fellowship, when it seems to keep us in a remote state of trembling obedience?

The puzzle has a literal form in scripture as well. On the one hand, we read that "there is no fear in love, but perfect love casts out fear" (1 John 4:18). On the other hand, the Old Testament consistently endorses "fear of the LORD" as a positive form of covenant faithfulness. The psalmist proclaims, "The fear of the LORD is clean, enduring for ever" (Ps. 19:9). In Deut. 10:12 Moses joins fear, love, and service of God into a single, unified rhetorical question: "And now, Israel, what does the LORD your God require of you, but to fear the LORD your God, to walk in all his ways, to love him, to serve the LORD your God with all your heart and with all your soul?" Isaiah prophesies of a coming day of divine glory that will redeem Israel: "Then thou shalt see, and flow together, and thine heart shall fear, and be enlarged" (60:5 AV). Fear, at least in some aspects of its scriptural sense, seems to operate after the fashion of love.

We need not read the Bible's multifaceted account of fear as a hopeless set of contradictory texts, nor need we adopt the theologically disastrous strategy of reading fear of the LORD as a bad, Old Testament sentiment at odds with the good, New Testament vision of love. If we follow the scriptural account, we can make some distinctions that will help us understand how the covenant begun with Abraham and fulfilled in Christ both overcomes and encourages fear. A debilitating worldly fear is the fear of Cain, who has sown the blood of Abel and shrinks from the consequences of reaping the harvest of his sin. Love casts out this sort of fear. But a spiritual form of fear endorsed by scripture has two moments. The first is a fear of judgment that guides us toward obedience, and the other, the final and everlasting form of fear, involves reverence for and awe of the divine. It is a fear of God's holiness. These distinctions can help us understand why Abraham is commended for his fear at the very moment of his most perfect obedience.

The Bible as a whole consistently teaches that the promises of God free the faithful from worldly fear. Faced with Sarah's infertility, the LORD appears to Abraham and reassures him, "Fear not, Abram, I am your shield" (Gen. 15:1). A situation of troublesome pregnancy that seems the opposite of Abraham's worries opens the gospel stories. Joseph confronts his pregnant spouse and tries to find the most just and humane way to extract himself from the shameful circumstances of her apparent infidelity. An angel of the LORD appears to him in a dream, counseling: "Do not fear to take Mary your wife, for that which is conceived in her is of the Holy Spirit" (Matt. 1:20). Abraham fears the fickle nature of human reproduction, while Joseph fears the way in which sexual desire can draw us into the destroying power of sin. In both cases, the two men fear the finite powers of the world that are indifferent toward the flourishing of human beings.

Worldly fear has a legitimate role in worldly affairs. We should not imprudently fling ourselves into danger. Wisdom urges prudence and discretion (Prov. 8:12). In a certain sense, this worldly fear gives force to the counsel that we should do unto others as we would have them do unto us. After all, they most likely will. Yet, the scriptures consistently recognize that giving priority to a fear of worldly powers is debilitating, paralyzing, and ultimately idolatrous. The Israelites calculate the might of Pharaoh's chariots in comparison to their defenseless columns, and then they cry out to Moses that it is better to serve in Egypt than to die in the wilderness. Their judgment is just in the eyes of the world, but Moses reprimands them. They have falsely assumed that worldly powers rule the world. Against this slavery to worldly fear, Moses urges, "Fear not, stand firm, and see the salvation of the LORD" (Exod. 14:13). The same holds for Abraham's fear of infertility and Joseph's fear of the shame of sin. The LORD rules the world, and to believe in the power of his outstretched arm frees one from worldly fear. As the psalmist sings, "Though a host encamp against me, my heart shall not fear" (Ps. 27:3).

In his reflections on the social destiny of humanity, St. Augustine parses the emotion of fear in a similar way (*City of God* 14.9; see Bettenson 1972: 561–66). Augustine observes, following St. Paul (Rom. 13:1–7), that the fear-inspiring power of the earthly sword has a worldly purpose. Human sinfulness can be restrained by worldly fear, and the wise ruler of the earthly city should acknowledge and try to manage our fears of want, slavery, and death. Yet, however prudent and necessary, social life ordered by worldly fear is as much a spiritual dead end as an individual life organized around worldly loyalties and loves. The earthly city, Augustine writes, is forever "shaken by these emotions as by diseases and upheavals" (*City of God* 14.9, quoted from Bettenson 1972: 566). A fear of suffering and death can too easily be conscripted into the plans of demagogues and tyrants. And even if wisely manipulated, the kind of justice that emerges out of trembling anxiety is outward and unstable. For this reason, Augustine concludes that, although necessary for maintaining order and fending off injustices, worldly fear has no role to play in the heavenly city of peace. The heavenly city lives by the unifying power of a common love of God.

Given that worldly fear has no lasting role, is there a proper form of spiritual anxiety that characterizes the Christian life? In the main, the Bible commends forms of fear that stem from a realistic assessment of God's righteousness. "Do not fear," Moses tells the Israelites at Sinai, "for God has come to prove you, and that the fear of him may be before your eyes, that you may not sin" (Exod. 20:20). The exhortation seems paradoxical—do not fear so that you might fear. But the paradox is apparent, not real. The first fear is worldly. The Israelites want to anxiously retreat from the holiness of God and go back to the less demanding idols of this world. They would rather fear famine and the sword than the judgments of God. But Moses wants the Israelites to reckon with reality. There is no place of refuge. God will put all hearts to the test. If we keep our eyes on this fact, then we will not find ourselves so easily falling into sin. Fear the LORD's power of judgment, Moses implies, and then you won't fear the world and do its bidding.

Modern theologians often worry that fear of eternal punishment somehow corrupts true faith, as if the mere thought of divine judgment casts doubt on God's mercy. Others suggest that a faith motivated by fear of punishment simply reflects a cowering, anxious hedonism that organizes commitments according to long-term calculations about pleasure and pain. But these simpleminded views confuse worldly with spiritual fear. Consider an analogy from the intellectual life. Fear of ignorance or error can be colored by shame and anxiety, but this emotion does not work at cross-purposes to an animating love of truth. The same holds for fear of divine punishment. As sinners, we should recoil from the thought of a righteous judge capable of knowing and punishing all transgressions, and this fear is no more inconsistent with a love of God than fear of error contradicts a love of truth.

We need to be awakened to this spiritual fear of God's judgment. The Bible as a whole and the New Testament in particular encourage us to grieve and weep over our sins (Matt. 26:75). If we tremble with the thought of final judgment, we can better avoid transgression. In this way, a fear of divine punishment is pedagogical. It directs us away from sin and toward righteousness. It guides us, says Augustine, "to lead the right kind of life, the life that is, according to God's will" (*City of God* 14.9, quoted from Bettenson 1972: 565). This guiding fear, however, must come to an end after the faithful enter their reward. Thus the scriptural puzzle remains. Fear of the LORD, we read, is everlasting. This raises an obvious question: What kind of fear characterizes the perfection of the elect? What role can fear play in the gift of fellowship with God?

St. Augustine recognizes that a lasting, heavenly fear of God is something of a paradox. To find a way forward he calls it a "serene fear," because it shares in the "tranquility based on love" that, as St. Paul teaches in 1 Cor. 13:8, "never ends" (*City of God* 14.9, quoted from Bettenson 1972: 565). Whether Augustine is right to think of the everlasting fear as serene, the Bible as a whole supports the apparently odd conjunction of eschatological fulfillment with a shrinking, reverential fear. As Shalom Carmy points out, Isa. 2 contains the eschatological promise of peace ("swords into plowshares" and "spears into pruning hooks" in 2:4), but it ends with the terrifying presence of the LORD.[22] The pedagogical dimension of fear is clearly present. Facing judgment, the people cast away their idols. But even after sin is set aside, the eternal "terror of the LORD" drives them "to enter the caverns of the rocks and the clefts of the cliff" (2:21).

Is should not be difficult to see why the promise of fellowship with God instills an existential horror. How can we draw near to God, even to the point of partaking in the divine nature, without dying to our sinful selves? Here the fear is less concerned with punishment and more concerned with purification. In his modest divine comedy, *The Great Divorce*, C. S. Lewis portrays this fear with his usual insight. The spectral souls who are met by the Solid People at the entrance to heaven can journey toward God only if they give up their doubts, vices, and shame. In Lewis's account, few have the courage to endure their spiritual fears of purification. The reason is simple. As sinners, they cannot imagine being themselves without the deforming qualities that alienate them from God. Sin must be destroyed in order for us to enter the heavenly kingdom. This should be good news, but we are so fully invested in our sinful habits that we see ourselves—our plans, our projects, our personalities—consumed as well. In a particularly vivid scene, Lewis portrays a hissing lizard of lust warning a frightened soul. "Without me," asks the lizard, "how can you live?" The frightened soul turns to his guardian angel for reassurance. God promises new life, he is told, but there is no promise that the transition from sin to holiness will be painless.[23]

22. Shalom Carmy, "'Yet My Soul Drew Back': Fear of God as Experience and Commandment in an Age of Anxiety," *Tradition* 41.3 (Fall 2008): 1–30.

23. C. S. Lewis, *The Great Divorce* (New York: Macmillan, 1946), 99.

At this point, a spiritual fear of purity brings us back to Abraham's trial and puts his situation into an especially clear light. What must be given up can seem so dear to us—and its promised restoration can seem so remote and illusory—that we tremble on the edges of the evangelical counsels, often paradoxically fearing the courage to obey even as we seek divine assistance. Augustine vividly portrays this fear. After he had read the Platonists, he reports that his intellectual objections had fallen away. He was disposed to believe in Christ, but he could not, because he feared the narrowness of the way. He wanted to be rid of the binding chains of his sin, but as he tells us, his desire for new life in Christ was accompanied by a paralyzing anxiety that he could not endure a moral change of such magnitude. The closer Augustine gets to his goal, the more he fears attaining it. He sees the gulf between his sin and God's invitation to holiness, and he fears falling into the abyss.

This fear is everlasting because the gulf between our lives and the life of the Holy Trinity is not just moral; it is ontological. He is creator and we are creatures. The created nature of the human remains forever distinct from the divine nature of the Holy Trinity. This chasm is bridged by grace, but never eliminated. God becomes incarnate, not created, and salvation is a deification of our humanity, not our absorption into the divine nature.

The eternal and unfathomable difference between God and creature explains the everlasting fear that is consistent with a love that draws us ever nearer. An analogy might help. When we walk across a bridge, we may enjoy every confidence that the engineers have done a good job and the span will not collapse. And yet, who does not feel hints of terror when looking over the edge into the depths of the chasm below. This is all the truer of our salvation in Christ. He is our trustworthy mediator, our bridge to eternal life in God, and our confidence in his saving death is entirely consistent with a fearful sense of the depths into which he went on our behalf, depths from which we turn away in shuddering, instinctive horror. Hans Urs von Balthasar observes, "Fear is not abolished, nor is distance eliminated, when grace is given to nature, but it shows up now in its authentic form in Gethsemane and on the Cross and is transfigured as a 'holy fear of the Lord' lasting into eternity."[24] The nothingness of death endured by Christ can never be fathomed—and we rightly fear to look into its gaping, hungry void. As the old spiritual says of the cross, "It causes me to tremble, tremble."

Both the pedagogical fear of divine judgment and eschatological fear and awe evoked by what God has endured for our sakes operate in Abraham's trial. Abraham does not rely on cheap grace. He does not presume upon the riches of God's kindness and forbearance and patience, as if he could evade God's commandments and then throw himself on the mercy of God. Instead, Abraham has a proper awareness that none shall escape the judgment of God, and he acts accordingly,

---

24. Hans Urs von Balthasar, *The Theology of Karl Barth*, trans. Edward T. Oakes (San Francisco: Ignatius, 1992), 287.

wishing not to store up wrath for himself (Rom. 2:1–11). Abraham fears the LORD in the way that Moses urges upon the Israelites, and because he fears, he can be trusted to obey. But there is also the further, reverential sense of fear revealed in the trial of Abraham. If we look to Deuteronomy we can see how. There, Moses shifts the relationship between fear and obedience. One does not so much fear in order to obey as obey in order to fear: "Do all the words of this law which are written in this book," we read, "that you may fear this glorious and awful name, the LORD your God" (28:58). Abraham's obedience brings him closer to God, and this intimacy with the divine produces a reverential, awe-filled fear.

Thus, we can say that Abraham's fear crowns as well as motivates his obedience. When the angel of the LORD says to Abraham, "Now I know that you fear God, seeing you have not withheld your son, your only son, from me" (Gen. 22:13), it is as if the LORD is sizing up Abraham. "I remember your contentious personality when we stood overlooking Sodom and Gomorrah," we might imagine God saying, "and I see how your humble fear of my majesty has kept you silent and you did not dispute my commandment." We can imagine God continuing, "And I remember how you pleaded on behalf of Ishmael, yet now, in your reverence for my purposes, you have not petitioned on behalf of Isaac." And still further, keeping in mind God's foreknowledge of all that will come to pass, it is not difficult to imagine the LORD saying to Abraham, "I see that fear of God has so overtaken your soul that you no longer think of yourself, and unlike Jephthah who will sacrifice his child (Judg. 11:29–40), you do not give yourself over to self-involved grief and lamentation." Thus does the LORD admire Abraham, whom he had chosen and tried. With satisfaction God says to Abraham, "You are now a man who knows how to walk humbly with his God" and you have seen that "the fear of the LORD leads to life" (Prov. 19:23).

22:14 So Abraham called the name of the place The LORD will provide.

God's provision follows an economy that we can see developing in Genesis and throughout scripture. It begins after Cain's murder of Abel. Adam enters into his wife. She bears a son, Seth, and Eve explains his name: "'For God,' said she, 'hath appointed me another seed in stead of Abel, whom Cain slew'" (4:25 AV). The son is not restored, but instead replaced.

When Abraham lifts his eyes and sees the ram caught in the nearby thicket, he offers the animal "instead of his son" (22:13). Although we can see in the background a general commandment to offer the firstborn son to God (Exod. 22:29), in the immediate context, the specific commandment to sacrifice Isaac has no explicit purpose other than to try Abraham. The import of the sacrifice of substituted ram remains obscure. Isaac's life is at stake, but the countercommand, "Do not lay your hand on the lad or do anything to him" (Gen. 22:12), comes before and not after the sacrifice of the substitute. No clear link is established between sacrifice, substitution, and the covenant promise of life. The son is simply restored by an act of God, and then the substitute appears, and the sacrifice is offered.

Although the use of goat's blood by Joseph's brothers to deceive Jacob foreshadows a unity of sacrifice and substitution in the divine gift of new life, it is only in the Passover lamb that this unity becomes the crucial instrument for forward movement into the future promised to Abraham. The punitive death of the firstborn passes over the households that sacrifice the substituted lamb. The Israelite sons live because the lamb dies, and this differs from the scene on Mount Moriah. Isaac is saved by divine decree, and then a substitute is offered; the Israelite sons are saved from death *by* the substitute.

What is important about the subsequent history of Israel and the New Testament is the way in which the beloved son and the ram/lamb merge together. In Isaiah's vision, the descendants of Abraham become sacrificial victims. Personified in the Suffering Servant depicted in Isaiah, Israel "was despised and rejected by men" (Isa. 53:3). She "has borne our griefs and carried our sorrows" (53:4) as she went forward into exile "like a lamb that is led to the slaughter" (53:7). But Israel does not suffer in vain. She shall be raised from her political death to become a light to all the nations; in new life Israel shall be the redemptive center for the divine plan for all humanity (60:3). In the New Testament, Jesus stands in the place of Israel. He is both the substituted lamb of sacrifice and the beloved son of the promise. His death provides "the new and living way" into the inner sanctuary of the house of God (Heb. 10:20). The son dies as the substitute so that all might be saved from death.

22:17 I will multiply your descendants.

The promise on Mount Moriah echoes the promise the LORD makes to Hagar in the wilderness. From Ishmael shall come a multitude beyond measure (16:10), and this serves to vindicate Hagar's affliction. But this great nation will bring the rivalries and conflicts that characterize unredeemed nations: "his hand against every man and every man's hand against him" (16:12). Hagar's son has a future, but not a future capable of reversing the effects of sin and changing the trajectory of history. In contrast, the descendents of Abraham shall be favored by the LORD, and "by [his] descendants shall all the nations of the earth bless themselves" (22:18).

23:2 Abraham went in to mourn for Sarah and to weep for her.

The absence of lament over the dead is a remarkable feature of Gen. 1–12. Abel's blood cries out from the ground, but Genesis makes no mention of Adam or Eve mourning the loss of his life. The generations are recounted. Seth begat

Enosh, Enosh begat Kenan, and so on to Noah. Each receives his full allotment of years, but we read no descriptions of weeping or wailing over the dead. All but those in the ark are destroyed in the great flood, but God alone seems to notice and regret their deaths. It seems that men and women can feel jealousy, lust, and shame, but not the bitterness of loss. It is as if death were simply a nonnegotiable fact of life for the children of Adam and Eve, no more to be mourned than the setting of the sun.

But with Abraham come the promises: land, prosperity, and the immortality of countless descendants. A new future suddenly comes into view, one hallowed on Mount Sinai and fulfilled in Christ. Abraham trusts in the promised future. In signs and visions he sees the mighty acts of God that will guarantee its triumph. And in this future, death has no role; it is swallowed up and destroyed by the divine invasion of human history. What once seemed so normal, natural, and inevitable becomes alien and unnecessary. The fundamental thrust of Abraham's trial on Mount Moriah tells the tale: obedience to God's commandments brings us into a future in which we receive life as a gift.

Then Sarah dies—just as Noah and his sons died before; just as her own son, Isaac, and his sons and the sons of his sons will die in their own time; just as those we love will die; just as you and I will die. And for the very first time in the Bible, we find a scene of mourning. Abraham enters Sarah's tent and weeps over her dead body.

Abraham's tears mark the beginning of what Hans Urs von Balthasar calls "the dramatic rhythm" of the divine economy of salvation.[25] By Balthasar's reading, the progressively deeper divine involvement in covenant history produces a "continual raising of the stakes." Heaven and hell, Mother of God and the Great Harlot, Christ and antichrist, everlasting joy and the eternal lake of fire—these and other images from Revelation mark the end point of an ever intensifying rhythm that begins with Abraham's call out of his father's household. The promises of God create a new future, and the ever increasing light of this future throws the legacy of the past, the trajectory of fallen flesh toward death and dissolution, into an ever darker shadow.

Abraham's mourning over Sarah provides a witness to the psychological effect of this dramatic rhythm. The covenant promise cannot help but sharpen the contrast between the legacy of the past and the promised future, and this throws death into a new light. We are created for fellowship with God, not for the grave. The covenant has opened up a future in which death can be seen only as an anguishing defeat, an unnecessary blow, a cruel counterstrike by an enemy in final retreat. Thus the paradox of faith: belief in God's promises heightens rather than softens the existential pain of death. The victory of Christ on the cross intensifies our sense of death's wrongful hold on life, and faith in the resurrection of the dead

25. Hans Urs von Balthasar, *Theo-Drama*, vol. 4: *The Action* (San Francisco: Ignatius, 1994), 56–58.

sharpens rather than blunts the loss. The scroll swallowed by John of Patmos is sweet to the mouth and bitter to the stomach (Rev. 10:9–10).

The ancient Greeks and Romans understood the paradoxical relationship between hope and grief. "Cease to hope," writes Stoic philosopher Seneca, "and you will cease to fear" (*Letters* 5). Expect little, he suggests, and you will not be disappointed. "Make your peace with destiny," he urges, because if we accept the deliverances of fate, then death will not disturb (*Letters* 91).[26] In our increasingly post-Christian culture, a hard-nosed realism preaches a similar wisdom. We are to recognize that we are part of the cycles of life and death that characterize all things. We need to accept that our world is a mere speck and that the short career of humanity is an insignificant moment on the timeline of the universe. The death of a loved one is thus inevitable (natural!), and, viewed biologically and cosmologically, the death of an individual is of no consequence. Why, then, should we mourn at all, other than to manage our psychological pain toward the rational goal of equanimity and acceptance of the facts of life?

The sentiment was not unknown to biblical authors. "Who knows whether the spirit of man goes upward and the spirit of the beast goes down to the earth?" asks the author of Ecclesiastes (3:21). If we can believe that "man has no advantage over the beasts" (3:19), then the way is open to the dark consolation of life without hope. Death no longer threatens; it can even attract and reward those impressed by the futility of life: "I thought the dead who are already dead more fortunate than the living who are still alive" (4:2). Perhaps a vivid sense of the emotional risk of faith in the covenant led those who collected and passed down the scriptural tradition to include Ecclesiastes. The temptation to escape from the pain of life vivified by promise is powerful. Acquiescence to death can seem a wise concession to the inevitable.

Yet the scriptures as a whole are clear. Death has no role in the future that God promises, and faith in God's promises blocks the therapy of hopelessness that allows us to accept death. God promises life, and the stakes are raised. Affliction, anguish, and tribulation become more real and more intense as victory seems more certain. The final stages of a long, arduous journey are characterized by a heightened agony as the end comes into view. To see the finish line, to know the race is won—the expectation of rest makes the last effort all the more agonizing. We are rightly driven to near madness by the thought of those killed in Hitler's concentration camps in the final weeks of the war. The end was so near. Their deaths were so unnecessary. For the same reason we are not wrong to mourn at any graveside. The promise of life makes death less emotionally manageable, not more. The triumph of the divine plan increases sorrow even as it leads to joy, just as childbirth anguishes the mother even as it brings life (John 16:21).

26. *Seneca: Letters from a Stoic*, trans. Robin Campbell (New York: Penguin, 1969), 38, 182.

23:3 Abraham rose up from before his dead.

Hope may heighten grief, but Abraham does not weep forever. Stricken by the power of death—what could be more powerful, we often wonder?—he straightens himself and prepares for action. God gives life, not death, and Abraham, the recipient of the promises, cannot remain bowed down before Sarah's corpse forever. Abraham will not serve death. It can afflict. It can bring deep and lasting pain. But death will not dictate the course of his life. Abraham goes to the local chieftains. He wants a burial place for Sarah. He want to put her "out of my sight" (23:4).

Out of my sight! It is a shocking thing to say about the body of a loved one, but it is a sentiment repeated in the Bible. Jesus chastises one who would follow him, but who wishes to delay in order to bury his father. "Let the dead bury their dead," he says (Matt. 8:22 AV). The principle is not general, as if Christ came to abolish the law (both natural and revealed) that compels children to mourn for, bury, and remember their dead parents. Rather, like Abraham who rises from his distress, those who follow Christ must recognize that even as death continues to crush life, it cannot control the future. "O death, where is thy victory?" asks St. Paul with haughty confidence in the power of life. "O death, where is thy sting?" (1 Cor. 15:55).

Resistance to the emotional control that death tries to exercise over our lives is woven deeply into Jewish and Christian practices of burial. The Jewish prayer for the dead is stunningly indifferent to the deceased. Like Abraham who puts Sarah out of his sight, the Mourner's *Kaddish* gives no space for remembering the dead and excludes any mention of loss. It brazenly ignores the grave, calling simply for the triumph of the covenant and glorifying in the power of God. The Mourner's *Kaddish* begins, "May His great Name grow exalted and sanctified in the world that He created as He willed." In the middle is a petition for the triumph of the LORD's kingship in our lifetime. It ends, "Blessed, praised, glorified, exalted, extolled, mighty, upraised, and lauded be the Name of the Holy One." This central, fundamental prayer of Jewish life is a verbal punch, an affirmation of life that is plunged like a spear as deeply as possible into the nothingness of death that seeks to haunt our lives. The covenant of life and not the shadow world of death "shall be as frontlets between your eyes" (Deut. 6:8).[27]

A funeral mass has the same basic logic. We've all known the anguish of loss and have wept tears of impotence as we have sat in the pews. At one time or another, everyone rages against death: why, why, why? And when we don't rebel, we broker compromises in our minds to soften the pain. Nobody lives forever. He had a good life. She's in a better place. We turn to the bittersweet presence of the dead in the caverns of our memory, and we feel the numbing vacuum of their absence in our

---

27. For profound meditations on the role of mourning and the Jewish affirmation of life, see Joseph Soloveitchik, *Out of the Whirlwind: Essays on Mourning, Suffering and the Human Condition*, ed. David Shatz, Joel B. Wolowelsky, and Reuven Ziegler (New York: Ktav, 2003).

lives. Death brings many emotions that cannot be mastered, which is why it can so bewitch and control our lives. And yet, when the eulogies are over, the priest prepares and consecrates the bread and wine. The faithful line up to receive, and next to the casket at the front of the church, the bread of life hits the tongue. In the eucharistic celebration of the funeral mass, it is as if the church turns from the legitimate work of mourning in order to put a stick in the eye of death.

I have little doubt that the restless humanism of Western culture takes a great deal of its energy from the ways in which Jews and Christians mourn and bury. We are not trained to reconcile ourselves to death. We do not make peace with the dark destiny of the grave. We put the dead Sarah out of our sight, not with a therapy of forgetfulness that denies her memory, but in order to turn toward what we take to be our true inheritance: life.

23:6 A mighty prince among us.

The Hittite description of Abraham seems hyperbolic. Although we have read of Abraham's miraculous defeat of foreign kings with 318 men (→14:14b), Genesis also describes Abraham's fear and submission in his encounters with Pharaoh and King Abimelech of Gerar. Perhaps, then, at this point the text elevates Abraham in order to dramatize a juxtaposition. Unlike the pharaohs of Egypt, Abraham does not want to heap up stones into a huge monument visible for miles around in order to memorialize his dead wife. He envisions nothing like the tombs of Lenin and Stalin in Red Square. Nor does Abraham wish for an ancient version of the Lincoln Memorial or Washington Monument. Mighty princes have the power to marshal resources toward grandiose public monuments to the dead, but Abraham formulates no such plan. Abraham is mighty in a promised future, not mighty in a desperate effort to forestall the power of time to erode memory and erase the past.

23:9 Let him give it to me in your presence as a possession for a burying place.

The extended negotiation between Abraham and the Hittites who control the land is more than an illustration of ancient bartering methods. Abraham is faced with Sarah's dead body, a reality that not only conveys the cessation of time and possibility, but also decays. The dissolution of the human body after death testifies to the power of chaos, the *nihil* of disorder and decomposition. Abraham does not just want to hide Sarah's dead body underground, as if the power of death should be managed and minimized by pressing its reality to the margins. Abraham does not express a desire for the dark, empty reaches of forgetfulness. For this reason, the Hittite offer of burial privileges is not sufficient. Abraham needs to possess a piece of the land so that Sarah can be buried in a small, symbolic fulfillment of the promise. Owning a small plot of the promised land allows Abraham to ritually relocate the dead Sarah into the geography of the future, which is a place of life. In this way, her death is neither counteracted by human efforts to defeat decay by a grand gesture of memory nor evaded by a strategy of forgetfulness. Instead, the dead body finds a real place in God's promised future.

Ancient Romans buried their dead outside the walls of their cities. The decaying reality of death was not allowed to pollute the urban economy of life. Early Christians followed this pattern at first, limited by financial resources and local customs. But when Christianity gained a margin of political power, the bodies of buried martyrs were exhumed and transported into the cities for reburial within the confines of the churches, setting the precedent for the subsequent tradition of crypts and church graveyards. The effect is to recapitulate Abraham's purchase of a piece of the land. Instead of following a ritual pattern that expels the polluting power of death from the city of the living, the common Christian practice of burying the dead in church crypts and graveyards places their bodies in a place consecrated to the power of life.

Both Abraham's desire to buy a burial place in the promised land and conventional Christian practices of burial serve as literal figures for St. Paul's teaching on baptism. Like Sarah's burial in the land of the promise, baptism incorporates the believer into Christ Jesus, and this buries us "into his death" (Rom. 6:3). It is a ritual burial that ensures our participation in his risen life. "As Christ was raised from the dead by the glory of the Father," St. Paul continues, so too we now "walk in newness of life" (6:4). Thus, to be buried with Christ places us firmly in his future of risen life, just as Sarah's burial in the promised land plants her in the future of the covenant.

24:1 The Lord had blessed Abraham in all things.

Coming immediately after the extended negotiations for a burying place, this verse effectively restates the promises of the covenant and their fulfillment. The death of Sarah does not prevent Abraham from being blessed *in all things*. The atmosphere of blessing is reinforced by our learning nothing of Sarah's actual burial, another subtle reminder of the scriptural rejection of death as a focal point for life in the covenant.

24:2 Abraham said to his servant.

In general, the literary character of Genesis moves from the archetypical toward the particular. From Adam through Noah, the narrative reads like a legend. Events take place on a worldwide stage, and the characters seem more like types than individuals. With the calling of Abraham, the narrative comes into focus. From episode to episode, however, readers can feel disoriented. The Abraham account lacks the tight skein of storytelling found in the later chapters on Joseph. Nonetheless, readers begin to see ordinary men and women acting on a recognizably human scale. There is narrative realism even if a single narrative thread cannot be easily followed.

Now the human texture of the narrative intensifies. Abraham commissions his servant to find Isaac a wife from among his kin. The servant makes subtle and effective efforts to find just the right woman for Isaac. Rebekah's family deliberates on the merits of the match. In these and other ways the narrative becomes more intimate and more detailed. What began from an impossibly eternal perspective— "in the beginning"—now seems entirely realistic and accessible. The trajectory is certainly unexpected. Who would imagine Abraham and his servant emerging from the cosmic frame of reference in Gen. 1? High theological abstraction seems more natural. Yet now we have a long story of very human interactions, and we can easily picture Rebekah with her brothers and parents as they weigh the offer of marriage presented by the forthright servant who seems to possess an impressive store of gifts. The topic is fit treatment for a Henry James novel.

We can explain this trend in general anthropological terms. Cultural imagination treats the distant past in grand, heroic, and mythic terms, but as the past draws near, we begin to cut historical actors down to our own size. Fair enough, but we should not remain insensitive to the ways in which the literary character of scripture also conveys distinctive theological judgments. The more God becomes involved in the world, the closer the covenant comes to its universal fulfillment— and yet, at the same time, the more distinctively human the world itself becomes. Grace not only perfects nature, it humanizes nature by sharpening its particularity and vindicating the integrity of individual lives.

We can see this combined movement toward both universal fulfillment and intensified human particularity recapitulated in the Gospels. Jesus begins more as a type than as a man. At the outset, he seems an oracle, miracle worker, sage, and figure of prophecy fulfilled. However, by the end of the Gospels he has become all too human: vulnerable to the powerful, overcome by suffering, and capable of death. When the LORD fulfills his covenant with Abraham in the suffering, death, and resurrection of Jesus, the promised future of new life arrives, not by delivering us from our humanity, but by ordering the particularity of the world—even its insane drive toward death ("crucify him")—toward the consummation of the divine plan.

This trajectory toward a quotidian realism is very important, because our religious imaginations often make us think otherwise. Joseph Soloveitchik, one of the great Jewish thinkers of the twentieth century, observes that the urge to transcend the particular is perennial. *Homo religiosus*, Soloveitchik's personification of the impulse toward transcendence, seeks "divine secrets and eternal mysteries."[28] Such a person is not satisfied with the here and now. He cannot rest

---

28. Joseph Soloveitchik, *Halakhic Man*, trans. Lawrence Kaplan (Philadelphia: Jewish Publication Society, 1983), 7.

in the limitations of the finite. Driven by a desire to "discover the source of the plenitude of being and the fullness of the cosmos in supernal ontic realms that are pristine and pure," *homo religiosus* sets about to climb up the great chain of being to attain "an existence that is above empirical reality."[29] Piety is ascetic and ecstatic for *homo religiosus*. The bonds of the body must be broken; the limits of finite knowledge must be overcome in a single, piercing thrust of the religious imagination. The shimmering ideal of the Eternal and the Absolute entices us "beyond the bounds of concrete reality."[30]

While we may not use terms such as *homo religiosus* and never speak of "supernal ontic realms," the religious impulse that Soloveitchik describes is surely familiar. We see its basic profile in the contemporary commonplace: "God is too big for any one religion." We find *homo religiosus* in the seeker-personality that restlessly experiments with meditation and sifts through sacred books, looking always for the spark of the divine that can be detached from the earthbound demands of traditional religions that operate within the limitations of their rules, institutions, and histories. The desire for life purified of the finite fuels a spiritual protest against the church and her all-too-worldly reality, to say nothing of priests and pastors forever limited by our common, imperfect, and fallen humanity.

Yet the biblical trajectory is otherwise. A world consummated by its entrance into the seventh day of Sabbath rest is more real and not less so, more particularized, more determined and ordered in its details. God invades by the agency of commandment, and the life of faith sharpens the outlines of finitude. The knife of circumcision marks finite human flesh with divine purpose. The laws for the Day of Atonement invest the natural, timeless beauty of sunsets and sunrises with images of the high priest and sacrifices in a temple built according to an exceedingly detailed plan. Yom Kippur is saturated with specific actions rather than freed from the coils of contingent events, just as the eucharistic sacrifice at the center of Christian worship recalls and reenacts specific events in Jerusalem rather than delivering us from the particularity of our lives. This testifies to a theological truth. Human life divinized by fellowship with God is more embodied and more human. It is not shadowy and spectral, drained of the concrete realities of created life.

Soloveitchik calls the religious personality that participates in the divine invasion of reality "halakhic man," because such a person orders the world according to the detailed, this-worldly requirements of Jewish life. Unlike *homo religiosus*, who "attempts to extricate himself from the narrow straits of empirical existence and emerge into the wide spaces of a pure and pristine existence," halakhic man "longs to bring transcendence down into this valley of the shadow of death—i.e., into our world—and transform it into a land of the living."[31] Evoking the deep priority that scripture as a whole gives to divine initiative over human striving,

29. Ibid., 13.
30. Ibid., 16.
31. Ibid., 40.

Soloveitchik summarizes the basic difference as follows: "*Homo religiosus* ascends to God; God, however, descends to halakhic man."[32] "Holiness, according to the outlook of Halakhah," he continues, "denotes the appearance of a mysterious transcendence in the midst of our concrete world, the 'descent' of God, whom no thought could grasp, onto Mount Sinai, the bending down of a hidden and concealed world and lowering it onto the face of reality."[33]

There can be no evading the basic dispute between Christianity and Judaism about the way in which God descends to humanity. But the trajectory of God's holiness downward and into the concrete—a spiritual arc quite different from upward striving toward a distant God untainted by contact with finitude—marks a fundamental agreement. The very idea of incarnation intensifies the divine project of invading a sin-deformed world. St. Paul has many difficult and complicated things to say about the role of the law of Moses in the path of Christian discipleship. But it is clear that he had no commerce with the transcendent hopes of *homo religiosus*. This is why Paul's letters can toggle back and forth between proclamations of the gospel and detailed concerns about particular communal practices. The good news of Christ penetrates and transforms real human affairs. The gospel follows the literary trajectory of Genesis: forward into the concrete details of humanity rather than up and away from the lives we actually lead.

24:6 See to it that you do not take my son back there.

Commissioned to find a wife among Abraham's kin, the faithful servant worries about his prospects: "Perhaps the woman may not be willing to follow me back to this land" (24:5). The implication is clear. Wouldn't the whole expedition be more successful if Isaac went along? After all, it is the young man whom the woman shall marry, not the dutiful servant. Abraham's response is emphatic: by no means should Isaac return to the land and family that Abraham left behind.

Abraham's sharp response conveys an important truth about covenant history. The promises tear Abraham and his descendent out of the blind forward movement of time made possible by the ordinary cycles of birth, death, and inheritance. The servant must go back in order to find Isaac a wife, but Isaac himself, the bearer of the seed of the future, must not allow himself to be reabsorbed into the logic of time, hope, and expectation that characterizes the fallen world.

Abraham's worries about the danger of sending Isaac back are well founded. Faced with a fearful future, the Israelites in the wilderness pine for the real but familiar liabilities of life in Egypt. In a certain sense, the countless returns of Israel to idolatry involve spiritual returns to the land and kin of Abraham. They are backward-turning efforts to make life endurable by the propitiation of inner-

32. Ibid., 45.
33. Ibid.

worldly and created powers. But this return cannot work, because the world was created for the sake of the seventh day. As Abraham commands his servant, we may also need to constantly return to the world in order to provide for the future. Children must be conceived and raised. Crops must be cultivated and harvested. We need to make treaties with neighbors and prudently defend against the vagaries of nature and our fallen humanity. But in so doing, we should no more return our faith and hope to the powers of the world than the servant should take the child of the promise back to the land of his ancestors.

24:58 I will go.

It is not Isaac but Rebekah who recapitulates the pattern of Abraham. She, like Abraham, is from the house of Terah: "Born to Bethuel the son of Milcah, the wife of Nahor, Abraham's brother" (24:15). There are differences. Living in the household of her birth, she does not receive a direct call from God. Instead, Rebekah is called by Abraham's servant to leave her homeland. Moreover, where we can speculate about the bonds of affection and familial security that might have prompted Abraham to stay in his father's house, Rebekah's story includes an explicit scene of temptation. After promising Rebekah to Abraham's servant ("take her and go"; 24:51), Rebekah's brother Laban and her mother wish to delay Rebekah's departure: "Let the maiden remain with us a while, at least ten days" (24:55). This call for delay offers a brief foreshadowing of Laban's long delay of Jacob's return, and it reflects a basic fact about human life: the gravitational force of our past is powerful. We are not only bound by guilt and transgression. The rightful claims of familial love and duty encircle us. However, like Abraham, Rebekah hearkens to her call. When consulted about her future, she simply says, "I will go."

24:67 So Isaac was comforted after his mother's death.

Although Abraham commands otherwise, in a spiritual sense Isaac returns "back there." He dwells upon death, and he is locked in the past. He will not heed, he cannot heed, the call of the LORD to "go forth." In fact, the overall characterization of Isaac in Genesis suggests that Isaac never follows Abraham's pattern. He is a passive and largely silent figure. When Rebekah arrives, she finds Isaac at Beer-lahai-roi, Hagar's well (16:7–14), and he is wandering disconsolate (24:63), not unlike the despairing Hagar who wept over what she imagines to be the impending death of her son (21:15–21). Rebekah, not Isaac, is the one who embodies the pattern of Abraham. She leaves her father's house and goes forth, and she does so solely on the promise of marriage. Isaac, the one who carries the physical seed of the promise, needs Rebekah. She comforts him. Her life is directed toward the promised future. He inherits the body of Abraham, as it were, and she his soul.

Read in this way, the extended story of the servant's journey "back there" serves as an allegory for redemption in Christ. Jesus is both servant of the Father and his beloved Son. As servant, Jesus is sent "back there" into the land defined by the nothingness of sin. There, he finds Rebekah, the human spouse that the Father longs to bring into fellowship with his beloved Son. Jesus the servant offers Rebekah, a daughter of Eve, betrothal to Jesus the beloved Son. Rebekah accepts, and the journey of the servant ends as the elected spouse is delivered from the land of her fathers (sin) and brought into the land of the promise (new life in Christ). This allegorical reading is spelled out in some detail in Ambrose's sermon "Isaac, or the Soul," which turns out to be much more a mediation on Rebekah, the soul who desires union with God, than a treatise on Isaac, the passive body of the promise. Rebekah serves as a lasting figure for the church in Ambrose's exegesis, while Isaac is superseded by Christ as the spouse of the promise (FC 65.9–68).

25:1 Abraham took another wife.

Many commentators have noticed the relative anonymity of Isaac. He has little to say, and his own story is absorbed back into Abraham's and forward into Jacob's. The way in which the narrative follows up the story of Isaac's marriage with a report that Abraham married a second wife prevents the son from shining on his own. Moreover, Abraham has more children by his second wife, Keturah, and this continued fertility contrasts strongly with Isaac's inability to produce children with Rebekah. The continuing fruitfulness of Abraham contributes to the overall sense that Isaac is more a placeholder than a personality, more a link in the chain of ancestry than a character with his own projects and purposes. Where Abraham starts anew, Isaac seems simply to continue on.

There are doubtless many ways to read the somewhat indistinct role of Isaac in Genesis. Yet, coming as it does so soon after the call of Abraham, the ways in which Isaac blurs into the lives of his father and sons suggest something important about salvation history: the call of Abraham initiates a single divine project that will press forward to its successful conclusion. There will be many developments and apparent diversions, but there will be no more new beginnings, no stark changes in direction. This important feature of covenant history, one signaled by the literary interweaving of the generations that flow from Abraham forward, should influence our reading of the Old and New Testaments. Between them there is no break, no hiatus, no disjunction. They bear witness to the same, single divine project.

25:9 Isaac and Ishmael his sons buried him.

The sons are separated by both the worldly enmity of familial conflict and the larger divine plan of election. But now the gravitational force of filial piety draws the two brothers together in order to bury Abraham. In this scene, fulfillment of the covenant promise is momentarily foreshadowed. God sets apart his chosen people, not for their own sakes, but for the sake of bringing the blessings of the Sabbath to all of humanity. For a period of mourning, the two brothers work shoulder to shoulder to carry their father to his place of rest.

Yet, finite loves by themselves, even the fundamental and potent ties that bind family members together, cannot bring a lasting peace. God comes to us in and through his election of finite flesh, but the divine fruitfulness of what God has chosen does not translate into a plenary potency for created reality. Modern notions such as an incarnational spirituality or a sacramental worldview are fundamentally misguided. The powers naturally resident in creation cannot bootstrap their way to the seventh day of creation. God does not wave a magic wand over everything. He chooses a particular people, place, and person, and from a single point in creation he works toward the consummation of all things. The narrative implicitly emphasizes the particularity of the divine plan when it follows up the scene of fraternal unity in burial with a renewed emphasis on the covenant privilege that flows through Isaac. "After the death of Abraham God blessed Isaac his son" (25:11). The blessing gives heavenly sanction to Abraham's decision to give "gifts" to the children of his concubines while reserving "all he had" for Isaac (25:6).

25:22 If it is thus, why do I live?

Rebekah speaks in the voice of the created order itself. Nature regenerates itself with the natural blessing of new life. But "what gain has the worker from his toil?" asks the preacher (Eccl. 3:9). What possible purpose does the gift of life serve if it is so immediately and inevitably conscripted by human sinfulness into a fraternal struggle that can lead only to death? Election is the answer to this question. God's decision to wrench a single life from the deadly struggle creates a new possibility. God's promise to Abraham answers Rebekah's question. Conflict and suffering define the present, but they will not define the future.

25:23 Two nations.

The divine plan begins with the call of Abraham. The call cuts him off from those to whom he was bound by family loyalty. He is sent from his father's household. We have already asked: Why must the divine plan set son against father? Why does redemption cut against the grain of our worldly loves? (→12:1b). But we have not fully confronted the question of particularity: Why Abraham? Why does the narrow path toward divine blessing run through the children of Abraham rather than through another man, another tribe, another nation? Why Isaac instead of Ishmael? Why Jacob instead of Esau?

To a certain extent, the narrative gives its answers. Ishmael is the son of a servant, while Isaac is the son of the wife; the one was the son of human efforts to overcome impediments, the other was the son purely of the promise. The circumstances that distinguish the two sons from each other thus made the choice of Isaac fitting. St. Paul makes much of the difference, linking the works of the law to slavery and the grace of the promise to freedom (Gal. 4:21–31). Whether we follow Paul's reading, the divine plan worked out through the children of Abraham seems to have a coherent shape and logic.

Now, however, the element of arbitrariness in the divine project comes fully into view, one that pushes us back to Gen. 12 and redoubles the scandal of God's unexpected investment in the sheer particularity of a single clan as the instrument for fulfilling his plan. The circumstances of Jacob and Esau in the womb allow us to see that questions of character and personality have no purchase. Both children are from the same mother and same father, coequal in so many ways. The question necessarily arises: why Jacob instead of Esau? The question points toward a deep theological puzzle: What explains the seemingly arbitrary will of God? What can justify the apparent injustice of the divine decision to call Abraham in the first place, to confer his favor upon Jacob instead of Esau, to choose Israel instead of any other nation, to save the baptized instead of the unbaptized? These questions haunt both Christian and Jewish doctrines of election.

One strategy is to read forward in the narrative in order to find reasons that explain the fittingness of God's choice. This involves identifying key qualities—negative for Esau and positive for Jacob—that explain the divine preference. Ancient interpreters were quick to exploit suggestions within the text. Esau's preference for hunting and his hairy skin indicate a brutal, animal nature. The scene of ravenous hunger when he gives his inheritance away for a bowl of soup seems a clear indication of Esau's preference for transient material satisfactions over the lasting benefits of spiritual goods. Jacob, in contrast, has his eye on what matters most. Thus, God foresees the bad character of Esau and the righteousness of Jacob, and he wisely chooses the one who merits his favor.

The biblical narrative gives both Jacob and Esau personalities, but the problem is that the evidence is extremely mixed. While Esau may be impetuous and shortsighted in his hunger, Jacob is hardly the paragon of virtue. He appears to entrap his brother. Moreover, as the plot thickens, he participates in Rebekah's strategy of deception and lies to his father. When all the evidence is in, a neutral judge would be hard put to declare Jacob innocent and Esau guilty. Both brothers seem less-than-ideal children of the promise. Subject to the sin of Adam and Eve, they both participate in the dead end of inner-worldly human conflict. Wicked Esau does not afflict innocent Jacob. Rather, after their conception, "the children struggled together" within Rebekah's womb. As St. Paul teaches, "none is righteous, no, not one" (Rom. 3:10).

There is a further reason why the problem of election cannot be solved by recourse to merit. St. Paul explicitly addresses the question of God's justice in election in Rom. 9–11. The larger context is a long reflection on the shift in divine favor from the Jews (descendants of Abraham "according to the flesh"; 9:5) to the followers of Christ. Paul wants to be clear: the call of God operates according to no earthly measure, no human standard, no calculation of merit. He draws upon the story of Jacob and Esau to illustrate. Though they were sons of one man, Isaac, and though morally equal in Rebekah's womb, one was chosen and the other not. Why? Paul's answer is direct: "In order that God's purpose of election might continue, not because of works but because of his call" (9:11). If we protest against the apparent injustice of simply choosing one and not the other, Paul's reply is again uncompromising. He quotes Exod. 33:19, which concerns Moses's intercession on behalf of the Israelites, whose faithlessness makes them entirely undeserving of their chosen role: "I will have mercy on whom I have mercy, and I will have compassion on whom I have compassion" (Rom. 9:15). Paul immediately provides his interpretation of the divine declaration. "So it depends," Paul writes of the entire trajectory of divine election from Abraham through Jacob to Sinai and into his own time, "not upon man's will or exertion, but upon God's mercy" (9:16). God elects for the sake of bringing his plan to fulfillment; he does not elect in order to recognize or champion our efforts and projects.

In the Augustinian theology that has dominated the religious imagination of the Christian West, St. Paul's reasoning is summarized with the observation that sinners are saved in Christ by grace alone, *sola gratia*. This principle takes its most rigorous form in Calvin's doctrine of election: the circumstances of those brought into fellowship with God in Christ are no more relevant than the qualities or character of Jacob in comparison to Esau. Our destinies turn solely on the divine decision, not on our works or merit. Unlike Calvin and the Reformed tradition, Luther and his followers put less emphasis on the doctrine of election and more on salvation by faith alone, *sola fide*. Although faith has warmer connotations than predestination and the remote world of God's eternal decrees of salvation and damnation, the effect is the same: God calls those whom he saves, and for no other reason than whom he calls he saves. The Catholic response to the Reformation at the Council of Trent differs not at all on this point: "Faith is the beginning of human salvation, the foundation and root of all justification, without which it is impossible to please God and to come to the fellowship of His sons." Faith itself is a disposition given by grace. "We are therefore said to be justified gratuitously, because none of those things that precede justification, whether faith or works, merit the grace of justification" (session 6.8).

In view of this universal affirmation of the priority of grace, it is very tempting to fixate on the sheer contingency of God's saving will and reject it as arbitrary. We imagine that if there is nothing about Abraham or Isaac or any member of the covenant that explains his election, then God chooses on the basis of a whim or in an offhanded, thoughtless manner. Unless there is a clear "because," we worry that the whole biblical account of salvation reduces to a divine game of "eanie, meanie, mynie, mo."

At work in this worry are assumptions based on our experience of human choices. In nearly all cases, we choose for a reason, but when we don't care about the outcome, we simply let go of reasons and allow the choice to go where it will. "Coke or Pepsi?" someone asks. We reply, "I don't really care." We make our choice without really thinking about it. In other instances, the choice is not so much unthinking as endlessly changing. Our flittering, fickle will goes first this way and then that. On the spur of the moment we decide to drive to see a friend, only to change our minds halfway when we realize that we no longer want to see him. Not surprisingly, therefore, we think of arbitrary choices as unstable and unreliable, as without purpose or close attention. The arbitrary choice is indifferent. Thus the typical image of predestination: a remote deity moving lifeless pawns on a heavenly chessboard.

But is the typical image of predestination sound? Are we right to assume that all choices that cannot give reasons are indifferent, unreliable, remote, and thoughtless? Consider our desperate situation. It is good news that God does not choose for the sake of the justice or righteousness or goodness or piety of those he elects. For if he did so, then none would be found worthy. Only God's wanton disregard for our moral and spiritual worthiness makes fellowship with him possible. That God tosses reasons aside does not signal that he does not care, but instead indicates a love that tosses aside the fact that the beloved does not deserve to be loved. Here our complaint against the inexplicable nature of election ends up in litigation against divine mercy, as St. Paul notes in Rom. 9 and as Augustine points out in his defense of the doctrine of predestination.

The universal stain of sin is not the only reason why God's love invariably seems arbitrary to us. God could love us generically, according to general principles. He might identify a standard of judgment and allocate his blessings. But he does not want us in measured lots or carefully weighed loads. Instead, God's love seeks to meet us face to face in our irreducible particularity, and this desire is necessarily made real by a spontaneous and not calculating will. It must be so. To love because of the quality of the person makes love conditional and therefore vulnerable. If it is beauty, then the beloved worries about the inevitable diminishments of age. Even if it is virtue, uncertainty remains. If I love my wife for her high moral character, then I might rightfully transfer my love when I meet someone more righteous still. In fact, my reason for loving compels me to do so. Thus, it is no accident that as love predominates it discards reasons and reaches toward the purest particularity of the person. The highest romance is to say, "It is you alone that I love, and I love you just because you are who you are." Love becomes fuller as it appears more and more inscrutable. Such a love is neither indifferent nor fickle. Quite the contrary, love without motive or reason invests everything in the particularity of the beloved, and this makes love invincible. Nothing can speak against a love that has no reasons.

Of course, no human love is free of reasons. I can look into the eyes of another and embrace her in the sheer particularity of her individuality, but not for long. Soon enough, the embrace ends, and I see and judge her appearance, her intelligence, and her character. But God's love is omnipotent, and he can do what you and I cannot: love us forever in our pure particularity, and in so doing draw us to himself. St. Paul suggests this intimacy of espousal when he points to Deut. 30:14, which emphasizes the kiss of divine election: "The word is near you, on your lips and in your heart" (Rom. 10:8). With the covenant begun in Abraham, God plunges into human affairs with a terrible determination. Only a sudden, reasonless love can strike so quickly, so deeply, so permanently. And we cannot enter God's embrace without abandoning our objection to his lack of reasons.

To a great extent, the standard spiritual mistrust of the doctrine of predestination stems from a latent spiritual pride that encourages us to survey the divine plan from above and coolly judge its merits. In our minds, we observe God's heedless love from the perspective of eternity. When we object that choosing Jacob over Esau is unjust, we are putting ourselves next to God, watching him move his pawns on the chessboard, challenging his strategy, questioning his rationale. And if we are beside God rather than before him, then how can we not be dismayed? For God can no more share with us his reasons than a close friend can explain a sudden, precipitous fall into love. Experience tells the tale. A man's friends are those most offended by the arbitrariness of love. "What do you mean you can't go out for a beer? What do you mean you're skipping baseball practice? What are you thinking? Come to your senses! Don't mess up our plans."

The same offended sense of desertion holds for the common spiritual objection that predestination violates the principles of justice. We have our ideas about how the world should be run, and we've made our plans accordingly. We have made all sorts of commitments to live according to certain standards, and we have settled expectations. Thus, what seems like a solicitous horror that God might leave somebody out of the plan of salvation masks a personal affront. The fierce purity of God's love eclipses reasons, motives, and judgments we can share. We partake in God's nature only insofar as we know *that* God reaches out to grab us—Christ crucified and risen—and not because we know *why*.

We need to press the analogy of human love one final step forward. Those who stand beside rather than before us often worry about the strangely inscrutable character of our loves. Parents worry, "Are you sure she's the right one?" Long-time friends who have consoled us when past loves have gone wrong offer wise counsel: "Be careful and think things through this time." But amid all the sensible concern and good advice that surrounds our fallible, fragile adventures of love, the beloved himself or herself does not fear the blinding force of the love, at least not in the first heat of its flashing fire. The beloved is strangely reassured that the question "why me?" has no answer. The sheer *fact* of love sways the heart. Love's reasonless abandonment to another is what gives love its burning necessity. This is why God's name is good news. The name is not Perfect Justice or Everlasting

Goodness or Sober Reason. The name is YHWH, the God of Abraham, Isaac, and Jacob, the one who will choose whom he will choose. Far from pointing toward a fickle or indifferent deity, the name directs us toward the deepest mystery, the mystery pronounced in the name of the Father and the Son and the Holy Spirit: "God is love" (1 John 4:8).

25:34 Esau despised his birthright.

This episode is rich with irony. The elder brother has been chosen to serve the younger, and yet, with his bowl of soup, the younger brother is poised to serve the hungry elder. And precisely because ready to serve, Jacob finds himself at an advantage: the mighty elder brother is about to be put down from his throne (Luke 1:52). Yet, more than a pattern of reversal is at work. God's prophecies are not mechanically fulfilled. Human reality corresponds to what God ordains. In this case, Esau seems culpably negligent. Perhaps he has failed to make provisions for an unsuccessful hunt, or perhaps his account of his hunger is hyperbolic. In any event, Jacob's bargain should strike him as ridiculous: a bowl of soup for Abraham's birthright! But Esau's hunger makes him feel as though he is on the brink of death, so he readily takes an oath to hand over his rights as the firstborn son. Esau seems a man so controlled by his bodily desires that the precious things of God are of no moment to him.

Other passages in scripture seem to support this reading. In Obad. 10 and Amos 1:11, the children of Esau are depicted as rightly punished by God because of the sins of their forefather. Hebrews 12:16 portrays Esau as an immoral and irreligious man and uses his example to warn against the perils of a lax, undisciplined faith. Yet it is important to recognize that Esau's wickedness flows from the choice of election rather than motivating or triggering it. God's intervention into history forces the issue of sin. Esau is drawn into the ever intensifying drama of antagonism between good and evil, between truth and the lie. God invades space and time through the particularity of his chosen people, and this action brings forth the spirit of resistance (→4:7). Elected to serve the younger, Esau no more willingly plays his role in God's purposes than Adam and Eve wished obediently to play their roles. The powers of the world coil around him and draw him into their purposes. Unable to participate in the divine plan on his own terms, he falls more deeply into the counterplan of the devil. There is no third way (→3:1a).

Human sinfulness has a role in the divine plan. Esau is wrong to bargain away the blessings of God, but because of his sinful fixation on his bodily hunger the way is clear for the promise to flow toward Jacob. This is one of many moments throughout Genesis when human sins are quite real but nonetheless providential. It is a *felix culpa*, a happy fault. Foreshadowing the story of Joseph and his brothers, Esau does evil, but God puts it to good use.

26:5 Because Abraham obeyed my voice and kept my charge,
  my commandments, my statutes, and my laws.

Comparison with Deut. 11:1 ("his charge, his statutes, his ordinances, and his commandments") gives the impression that Abraham did more than obey the occasional commandments of God. Rather, it seems he followed the way of life laid out in detail on Mount Sinai. The conclusion, motivated by the pleonasm in this verse (charge, commandments, statutes, and laws), is fitting. The full scope of the Torah is latent in the commandment of circumcision. To live according to the sanctifying will of God involves the whole of human life and not occasional obligations and duties. Indeed, the entire divine economy of salvation fulfilled in Christ is latent in the initial call of Abraham from his father's house. The elect are torn out of the flow of worldly affairs and given a new future, one directed toward the triumph of holiness. Through signs and visions of the fulfillment of the covenant promises (→15:18), Abraham participates in the shaping power of God's redemptive plan. There is a deeper, fuller shaping of character and identity in the law given to Moses and fulfilled in Christ. The trigger is not the detonation. Nonetheless, the divine intention is the same from fuse to explosion (→17:7).

26:18 Isaac dug again wells of water which had been dug in the days
  of Abraham his father.

The LORD appears to Isaac in a time of famine and repeats the covenant promise. Isaac stays in Gerar, and he repeats the wife-as-sister ruse that Abraham employed in order to protect himself against the perceived danger of hostile, lustful, and more powerful strangers. As was the case in both of Abraham's deceptions, Isaac's prevarication is both discovered and turns out for the best. Abimelech commands his subjects to respect Isaac's conjugal rights, and Isaac flourishes, just as Abraham was strangely enriched rather than harmed by Pharaoh (12:16) and Abimelech (20:15–16). But economic success brings conflict rather than peace, repeating a pattern already established when Abraham's and Lot's servants quarrel over cattle and grazing rights (13:7). Resolution comes when Abimelech visits Isaac, a scene reminiscent of the earlier blessing of Melchizedek and the gifts offered by the king of Sodom (14:19–21). Now, at the center of Gen. 26, these implicit narrative repetitions are given explicit form in the threefold redigging of Abraham's wells.

The literary effect is direct. It is as if Isaac's role is being spelled out in bold letters for readers. He is a patriarch because he outwardly recapitulates the figure of Abraham. This recapitulation is reinforced in the repetition of the covenant promises. What was sworn to Abraham will be fulfilled in Isaac, and by implication just as Abraham obeyed the voice of God, so also must Isaac obey. To enter into the covenant involves walking in the ways of the LORD.

However, the outward recapitulation of Abraham's pattern is not matched in these chapters by inward development. Many traditional readers impute virtues to Isaac in order to buttress his role as patriarch, often emphasizing his Christlike role as the willing sacrifice to be offered by Abraham on Mount Moriah. However, the Genesis narrative portrays Isaac much less sympathetically. From birth to death, the bulk of the life of Isaac either reaches back into the more fundamental life of Abraham or moves forward into the more detailed life of Jacob. Unlike Abraham and Jacob, Isaac never faces his own trials and tests, and he never leaves the land of the promise. When he is the focus of narrative attention, Isaac hardly seems a man of virtue. He lacks discretion (e.g., in the sexual play with Rebekah that gives away his deception; 26:8). His judgment is questionable. Not only does he prefer Esau, but even in this preference he fails to secure for Esau a good marriage (26:34–35), something Abraham went out of his way to secure for him. Rebekah, his wife, seems the more fully developed character. She embodies the pattern of Abraham when she departs from her father's house, and she is the one who ensures that Abraham's promise is properly transmitted though Isaac to Jacob (→24:58).[34]

On the whole, then, readers seem encouraged by Genesis to draw the conclusion that Isaac matters only as a placeholder, the sometimes unwilling and often unwitting link in the chain of inheritance. He is not careful to do all that God has commanded, and he seems an almost accidental rather than intentional patriarch. Yet Isaac cannot be dismissed as an unimportant, transitional figure. After all, the tradition insists on his role. The LORD is the God of Abraham, Isaac, and Jacob. Thus the puzzle: why, exactly, is the largely passive, derivative, and unaccomplished Isaac a patriarch?

Perhaps the warning to the Israelites in Deut. 4:2 provides the clue: "You shall not add to the word which I have commanded you, nor take from it." This warning is repeated at the end of Revelation (22:18–19). With this standard of transmission in mind, we can return to Isaac and better understand his place as a patriarch. After all, in spite of his passivity and his flaws Isaac successfully (if unintentionally) passes on his inheritance to Jacob. In the most basic sense, we can say that Isaac adds nothing to the pattern of Abraham, and because of his wife's schemes he takes nothing away. Isaac does nothing more—nor less—than transmit the promise from his father to his son. This giving of what has been received is the sole form of his righteousness, and it defines his role as a patriarch. Flaws and weaknesses aside, Isaac passes on the promise, and that is enough.

Isaac's seemingly unconscious success in his role raises an important question about human intentions. Are inner experiences, sentiments, and commitments necessary for us to participate in the divine plan of sanctifying the world through the covenant with Abraham? The question is not only important, but it is also

34. For a detailed and helpful discussion of Isaac's recapitulation of Abraham, his failures of character, and Rebekah's indispensable role, see Kass 2003: 376–403.

fraught. Many readings of St. Paul's distinction between law and gospel explain the difference in terms of the relationship between inner sentiments and ritual performance. Works-righteousness, by this way of thinking, involves outward conformity to religious duties, doing something apparently righteous, but for the self-regarding sake of spiritual rewards. This legalistic piety, so this way of thinking assumes, has no inner purchase on the soul. In contrast, faith in Christ transforms the heart of the believer, providing a real, enduring, inner basis for worship and moral transformation. With this distinction in hand, it is then tempting to interpret the historical conflicts between Judaism (law) and Christianity (gospel), as well as between Catholicism (legalism, works-righteousness) and Protestantism (faith, Christian liberty), as a matter of superficial, outward, legalistic conformity over and against genuine inner commitment and transformation of the heart.

This temptation needs to be resisted, because it turns out to be very difficult to sustain either side of the standard dualism between outer and inner identity. Consider the case of the supposed empty legalism of ritual conformity to Jewish law. In most cases, rabbinic opinion teaches that religious duties performed without a specific intention remain efficacious. It is not necessary to be thinking of the theological purpose of the dietary laws in order to properly obey them. Continuous practice is sufficient. This seems precisely the picture of Isaac. He lacks the inner faith and virtue of Abraham, but nonetheless he remains a patriarch by retaining the outward forms of Abraham's life.

However, the picture is not so simple. According to Joseph Soloveitchik, the relative unimportance of intention in the performance of the law is not universal. Some commandments necessarily involve the inner life of the faithful. The commandment to pray, for example, cannot be outwardly fulfilled. It must have an inner component. Thus, Maimonides observes, "Prayer without *kavannah* [intention] is duty bound to recite his prayer over again."[35]

The Christian tradition may or may not put more emphasis on inwardness than traditional Judaism does, but without a doubt it shares in the complexities observed by Soloveitchik. The picture is not simple. The example of law that St. Paul gives as working death in him is not an outward, ritual commandment. It is the tenth commandment, "You shall not covet," a commandment entirely concerned with intention (Rom. 7:7). The crisis of obedience does not come about because of a ritualized neglect of the inner life. It occurs because our inner lives are under the spell of sin, which is why Paul argues for a deeper, fuller circumcision in Christ, a circumcision of the heart that flows from an intensified and fulfilled application of the holiness of the law (→17:11a).

Yet inwardness is not the whole story, and the drama of salvation is not solely a battle for purity of heart. Like Judaism, Christianity has its own affirmation of the efficacy of outward actions performed without regard to inner intentions. The

---

35. *Hilkhot Tefillah* 4.15, quoted from Joseph Soloveitchik, *Worship of the Heart: Essays on Jewish Prayer*, ed. Shalom Carmy (New York: Ktav, 2003), 20.

Donatist controversy in fourth-century North Africa concerned the legitimacy of bishops and priests who had compromised themselves in various ways during periods of persecution. St. Augustine's solution was to formulate a view of sacramental action that emphasized the office rather than the person. So, by his reckoning, the sanctity of the church and the grace of God in sacraments such as baptism, ordination, absolution, and the Eucharist flow to the believer without regard to the inner state of the priest or bishop performing the act. The action itself is sufficient to convey the promise of new life in Christ. This view we find in Isaac. He plays his role in spite of himself. The blessings he gives to Jacob are efficacious, and they secure the future of the covenant—even though he gives the blessings in spite of rather than because of his own goals and intentions.

27:5 Now Rebekah was listening.

Eavesdropping, a family conflict over favorite sons, a plot to deceive, a bald-faced lie—Jacob's inheritance seems to emerge out of less-then-noble circumstances. Ancient interpreters did their best to mitigate the apparent immorality of the story. The two sons are first described in 25:27: "When the boys grew up, Esau was a skilful hunter, a man of the field, while Jacob was a quiet man, dwelling in tents." On this basis, Esau's identity as a hunter could then be read as pointing to a bloodthirsty, violent nature, while Jacob's toward a bright, young scholar, or so ancient readers concluded. Thus, Jewish literature in the centuries just before Christ contains a sharply drawn and moralizing contrast. Jubilees 19:14 retells the stories of the patriarchs, and in doing so, adds its own commentary to Gen. 25:27: "And the youths grew, and Jacob learned to write; but Esau did not learn, for he was a man of the field, and a hunter, and he learned war, and all his deeds were fierce." The same holds for *Targum Onqelos*, which modified the verse to dramatize the difference between the two sons: "And the two boys grew up, and Esau was a skilled hunter, a man who went out to the fields, but Jacob was a perfect man who frequented the schoolhouse."[36] In other words, Jacob studied Torah and therefore deserved divine favor.

The interpolated moral juxtaposition of the virtuous Jacob to the vicious Esau is not surprising. If we align Jacob with righteousness and Esau with wickedness, then the story is not about an intrafamily squabble between a father's favorite and a mother's favorite. Rather, the real story, so this reading suggests, is the triumph of a good son over an evil one. And given the importance of the covenant itself, this way of juxtaposing the two brothers leads directly to thoughts about the larger and hoped-for triumph of good over evil. Everything fits into a convenient formula: the righteous prosper, but the wicked fall like grass (Ps. 1:3–4). The

36. Both sources quoted from Kugel 1998: 357, 354, who also discusses ancient attempts to adduce moral justifications for Jacob's emergence as heir to the promise.

troublesome lies and deceptions recede from view. God is not intervening into the hopeless, universal disaster of sin by way of a heedless love. Instead, he remains at a comfortable distance, patiently separating the sheep from the goats according to principles of justice that we can understand (→25:23).

However, the plain sense stands in the way. Rebekah's scheming and Jacob's lying are difficult to domesticate with general pictures of good and bad characters. Scripture itself speaks against Rebekah and Jacob. As the mother's scheme unfolds, a deception is counseled and performed against a background that biblical readers cannot help but bring to bear on their interpretations. On Sinai God commands, "Thou shalt not bear false witness" (Exod. 20:16 AV; Deut. 5:20), and St. Paul warns against "do[ing] evil that good may come" (Rom. 3:8). The difficulty is compounded by the explicit solicitude that God expresses for the blind, a solicitude conjoined with harsh condemnation of those who exploit them: "Cursed be he who misleads a blind man on the road" (Deut. 27:18). Thus a worrisome question worms its way into our minds. How can the future patriarch inherit his role on the basis of an outright lie? Jacob obtains Abraham's inheritance in a way that seems to compromise the sanctity of the covenant and make a mockery of God's law.

Some ancient Jewish readers pursued a subtle strategy of interpretation (Kugel 1998: 359–60). After Rebekah overhears and formulates her plan of deception, Jacob appears in his furry disguise to deliver the savory meal to Isaac. Isaac asks a simple question: "Who are you, my son?" At this crucial point, instead of reading Jacob's response as a simple lie ("I am Esau your first-born"), a whole tradition of interpretation breaks the sentence into two parts. The first sentence responds (truthfully!) to one possible sense of Isaac's question. When asked, "Are you my son?" Jacob answers with a simple "I am." In the second sentence Jacob then tells Isaac a further (and not a terribly germane) truth: "Esau is your first-born." As the encounter unfolds, the old, enfeebled patriarch finds himself puzzled by the contradiction of hairy hands that feel like Esau's, but a voice that sounds like Jacob's. This leads Isaac to ask a direct question: "Are you really my son Esau?" (27:24). But instead of reading Jacob's response ("I am") as a lie, this same line of reading treats it as a technical truth: after all, Jacob exists, does he not?

In their concern for the moral character of the patriarchs, the church fathers differed very little from ancient Jewish readers. They were also anxious to minimize the apparent immorality of Rebekah's and Jacob's deceptions. St. John Chrysostom worries that Jacob's duplicitous response to Isaac's question will provide Christians with excuses for their own convenient and self-serving lies. But instead of a strategy focused on parsing the sentences in the text, Chrysostom turns to casuistry. He urges readers not to "idly pry into what happened," for fear that some might draw the conclusion that lying is permissible. "Rather," he observes, "grasp its purpose in not being done for the reason of earthly greed but because he was anxious to win his father's blessing" (*Homily* 53.9 in FC 87.83). Jacob's motive was filial piety, an honorable desire to gain the approval of his father.

Of course, this strategy of exculpation is not more persuasive than a reading that somehow manipulates Jacob's duplicitous answers into technical truths. It runs aground on St. Paul's warning not to do evil that good might come. For this reason, Chrysostom shifts to a providential reading that focuses on God's will rather than on Rebekah's or Jacob's actions. "Don't take the view in this case that the words spoken by Jacob were deceitful," although, as Chrysostom implies, they were; "rather, consider that God wanted his prediction to take effect and so arranged everything to happen this way" (*Homily* 53.10 in FC 87.84). After all, as Chrysostom persuasively argues, the entire narrative of deception seems far-fetched. Rebekah overhearing the conversation, her rapidly implemented scheme, the quickly cooked meal, the improbable success of Jacob's hairy disguise, and most of all Isaac's credulity—how could Jacob have succeeded were it not for God's faithful loyalty to his plan that the elder shall serve the younger? Finally, Jacob receives the blessing, and as soon as he leaves, Esau returns from his hunt (27:30). Here, the sensitive reader feels something deeper at work. What could possibly explain the narrow, miraculous timing that allows Jacob to secure the blessing, asks Chrysostom? Nothing, he answers, other than the rather obvious fact that "the hand of God was active to preserve the young man" (*Homily* 53.14 in FC 87.87).

The appeal to divine providence does not solve the problem of deception that has long troubled readers who rightly worry about the way in which the story can be read as a justification for lying. It merely transfers the problem of evil, as it were, from Rebekah and Jacob to God. Nonetheless, if we follow Chrysostom and allow ourselves to think of Rebekah and Jacob and of Isaac and Esau as actors in a larger drama, then we are encouraged to read this passage for insight into the divine plan rather than ethical guidance. In this way, Chrysostom points to an approach that follows St. Paul's assessment of the relation of our mortal flesh to our divine vocation: "We have this treasure in earthen vessels, to show that the transcendent power belongs to God and not to us" (2 Cor. 4:7). We should look to see what God is doing with Jacob (the treasure) rather than sizing him up as a moral exemplar (the earthen vessel). "He hath not beheld iniquity in Jacob, neither hath he seen perverseness in Israel" (Num. 23:21 AV). Why not? Because the LORD has something he plans to do with those whom he has chosen: "There shall come a Star out of Jacob, and a Sceptre shall rise out of Israel" (24:17 AV). Election looks to the future.

With this interpretive approach, we do not need to build up Jacob as the morally superior son and run down Esau as an immoral man with base appetites. Election makes the man rather than the man meriting election (→25:23). Esau struggles against his role. When the time comes, he will not serve his younger brother, and this response rather than any innate character flaw makes him wicked. And how is Jacob "made"? Kass offers a perceptive assessment of the story of Jacob's efforts to supplant his brother. "In his striving with his brother, Esau" he writes, "Jacob must avoid becoming either Cain or Abel. In relation to his father from whom he steals his brother's blessing, he must avoid being Ham, a man who sees his father's nakedness and refuses to cover it up" (2003: 406). The comparisons enrich our reading of Jacob's deception, because they frame the story in the larger context. The malice of sibling rivalry is muted by a deception that avoids open conflict. The insensitivity and blindness of a father is covered over by a scheming wife who gives good advice to her son. Sin is not yet defeated, but it is tamed, softened, and constrained. The wheels of salvation history are beginning to turn. The promised future begins to make a difference. The knife of circumcision begins to make its way toward the human heart.

27:27 So he came near and kissed him.

The larger Christian tradition has read the success of Jacob in gaining Isaac's blessing as a prophecy of the emergence of the Christian church as the heir to the promises fulfilled in Christ. The pattern of younger supplanting elder is clearly present in St. Paul's allegory of the children of Hagar (those who inherit the fleshly, earthbound Jerusalem) and the children of Sarah (those who inherit the promised, heavenly Jerusalem) in Gal. 4:21–33. In Rom. 9:12 Paul applies Gen. 25:23 ("the elder shall serve the younger") to the relation of Jews to the followers of Christ. Thus, when considering the relation of Jacob to Esau, St. Augustine observes, "Hardly anyone of our people has taken it as meaning anything else but that the older people of the Jews was destined to serve the younger people, the Christians" (*City of God* 16.35, quoted from Bettenson 1972: 698).

How are *we* to read this pattern of the younger taking the place of the elder? One approach is usually termed "supersessionism." By this reading, the church supersedes or replaces the synagogue as the carrier of the divine promise. In its most radical form, the replacement is complete. The covenant made on Mount Sinai has a specific but limited purpose: to provide the old covenant—the law and prophets—that prepares for the coming Messiah. Jesus's suffering, death, and resurrection fulfills this covenant, and therefore it has no further purpose or validity. Paul seems to argue for a complete replacement. The Sinai covenant that structures Jewish life had a custodial purpose that, once Christ comes in fulfillment, is no longer necessary (Gal. 4:1–2). Now the synagogue has no role, and indeed, to continue in the Mosaic law becomes a cardinal sign of sin and rebellion. "I do not nullify the grace of God," Paul proclaims, "for if justification were through the law, then Christ died to no purpose" (2:21). With these citations from Paul, therefore, it is easy to conclude that Judaism after Christ is nothing more than a willful loyalty to an outdated mode of faith, a denial and rejection of Christ's saving death, and a refusal to accept the saving truth that Christ and the church have superseded Moses and the synagogue.

A commentary on Genesis is no place to provide a comprehensive interpretation of St. Paul. It is sufficient to note that he says very different things elsewhere.

229

In his reflection on the mystery of election in Rom. 9–11, Paul insists that God's promises are irrevocable and that God has not rejected his chosen people: "As regards election they are beloved for the sake of their forefathers. For the gifts and the call of God are irrevocable" (11:28–29). Those who continue to follow the law on Mount Sinai are not irrelevant to the future of the covenant fulfilled in Christ; on the contrary, they have a continuing, providential role. So what shall it be? Does the continued existence of Judaism after the death and resurrection of Christ signify only rebellion and unbelief, or do Jews have a positive role to play in the triumph of the gospel?

Paul is utterly unequivocal about the identity of Christ as the promised Messiah, and he treats Jewish resistance to the gospel as a debilitating blindness. There is no double covenant operating in Romans—or for that matter anywhere in the New Testament. The divine plan moves in a single, torturous, but unbroken line from Abraham through Moses to the life, destruction, and finally restoration of Jerusalem, and from there to the life, death, and resurrection of Jesus, and onward to the gift of his spirit to the church. This commitment to just one salvation history that begins with the calling of Abraham places severe pressure on Paul's line of reasoning. On the one hand, Jesus is God incarnate in whom all are saved. He completes the divine plan. On the other hand, "God has not rejected his people whom he foreknew" (Rom. 11:2). These two theological truths force speculation about the strange drama of salvation that incorporates rather than sets aside Jewish rejection of Jesus as the Messiah. The single, unbroken history of the covenant is not a simple, streamlined sequence of events.

Paul's approach does not involve backing off from a claim about the universal saving role of Christ. Instead, Paul affirms that Jewish unbelief after the coming of Christ has a providential role. "A hardening has come upon part of Israel," he writes, "until the full number of Gentiles come in" (Rom. 11:25). Rather than the church replacing the synagogue without remainder, Paul sees the elder brother's service of the younger as an ongoing component of salvation history, one that continues after the death and resurrection of Christ. Life in obedience to Sinai and without faith in Christ plays a part of the divine plan, not just to prepare for his coming, but also contributing in a mysterious way to the missionary work of converting the Gentile nations.

In his mediations on Jacob and Esau, St. Augustine comes to a similar conclusion. Because Isaac is deceived, his blessing of Jacob is unwitting, as his subsequent horror of sudden self-awareness when Esau returns testifies. Yet the blessing remains efficacious. Augustine works with this combination of blind and unintentional but nonetheless real and effective blessing as he plots the Genesis story of Esau the elder and Jacob the younger onto Judaism and its relation to Christianity in his own day. "Isaac is the Law and the Prophets," he writes, making Isaac into a personification of the Old Testament as a whole, "and Christ is blessed by the Law and the Prophets, even by the lips of Jews, as by someone who does not know what he is doing, because the Law and the Prophets are themselves not understood."

The figural exegesis is compact. Isaac not only represents the Old Testament, but he (merged together with Esau in this reading) also represents its "unwitting" use by Jews, who think their prayers await the Messiah, when, in fact, they bless the Messiah who has already come. "Our Christ," Augustine continues, "is blessed, that is, he is truly spoken of, even by the lips of Jews who, although in error, still chant the Law and the Prophets: and they suppose that another is being blessed, the Messiah who is still awaited by them, in their error" (*City of God* 16.37, quoted from Bettenson 1972: 700–701). In this way, the prayers of the synagogue give aid to the prayers of the church.

Our present cult of tolerance cannot tolerate Augustine's straightforward observation (which simply repeats Paul's judgment) that Jews are in error. In view of the dreadful history of Christian anti-Judaism—expulsions, pogroms, and the Holocaust—it is tempting for Christians to favor a more inclusive view. After all, who are Christians to assign Jews roles in the economy of salvation?

Yet as St. Paul and St. Augustine knew, we do not have the freedom to rearrange God's plan in order to try to compensate for our moral and spiritual failures. We are not the ones assigning roles in the divine economy of salvation. The direction of the divine plan is in the hands of God, and faith in Christ commits one to a view that, to be quite frank, assigns roles to everyone in the end, as Revelation makes clear. Judaism has its own vision of the unfolding of the divine plan, and Torah observance necessarily assigns roles to the Jew and Gentile alike. The only way to avoid ordering the world into a hierarchy of elder and younger—or their reversal—is to give up on the particularity of the divine plan. One is either circumcised or not, baptized or not. Because God invades the world and redeems it from the inside, we can participate only insofar as we take sides according to the lines that God draws. To want salvation without distinctions amounts to telling God to keep his distance.

Our present, perverted sensibilities about truth, sensibilities that recoil from anything sharp, determinate, and consequential, should not blind us to an obvious fact. It cannot be true that both Christians and Jews are right about Jesus of Nazareth: either he is—or is not—the promised Messiah. This St. Augustine and the Christian tradition as a whole have recognized, as did the ancient rabbis and the Jewish tradition through the centuries. But as St. Paul in Rom. 9–11 and St. Augustine in his reading of Gen. 27 make clear, one can both affirm the lordship of Christ and acknowledge the ongoing contribution of Jewish prayer and practice to the glorification of his name. Instead of fantasies of some sort of grand religious convergence, the legacy of Christian anti-Semitism should cause us to sober up and see that there is a crucial difference between a view in which the church replaces the synagogue without remainder and a view of the elder who continues to serve the younger in the economy of salvation. The former makes the continuing existence of Jews an offense to Christianity. The latter welcomes Jewish prayer and obedience, even as it interprets this prayer as bearing witness to the Messiah whom Jews reject.

27:38 Esau lifted up his voice and wept.

In his reflections on the relation of church to synagogue, St. Paul quotes Deut. 32:21 (Rom. 10:19: "I will make you jealous of those who are not a nation; with a foolish nation I will make you angry"), a passage in which Moses foretells God's decision to use the Gentile nations to provoke Israel with jealousy, just as their idolatry has made God jealous. The theme of jealousy takes us directly back to the story of Jacob and Esau. News of Jacob's successful deception sparks bitterness in Esau, and in his jealousy he hates Jacob for the favor his brother has found in the eyes of God. Rebekah warns Jacob that his older brother wants to kill him: "Behold, your brother Esau comforts himself by planning to kill you" (Gen. 27:42). The divine plan forces the issue: Esau will either move forward into his role as elder in service of the younger—or backward to recapitulate Cain's destiny.

Perhaps Paul was attracted to the figures of Jacob and Esau as sources for understanding the relations of church and synagogue, because the early pattern of their relations followed the story of the brothers so closely. As the Acts of the Apostles depicts, like Esau, the Jewish leaders in Jerusalem sought to destroy the new cult of Jesus. But Paul is hopeful. Esau's jealousy and anger do not send him backward to recapitulate Cain's homicide. In spite of himself, Esau moves forward. Jacob is blessed and sent away to find a wife from his mother's people, and this leads Esau to reconsider his preference for purely foreign, Hittite wives. He turns to the tribe of Ishmael for a mate (28:6–9). The elder may be destined to serve the younger, but the vocation of the younger also serves to advance the elder in relation to God, even if by way of the dangerous, conflict-laden emotions of jealousy, bitterness, and anger. Moreover, after many years away, when Jacob returns, he is reconciled to his brother. It is a scene pregnant with a typological relevance for the relations of Jews and Christians, but one that remains an as-yet-unfulfilled figure (→33:4).

28:2 Arise, go to Paddan-aram.

Isaac sends Jacob where Abraham would not send him. Abraham sensed Isaac's spiritual passivity—he would go and perhaps never return. Jacob, however, is like Rebekah. In spite of trials and difficulties that threaten to prevent his return, Jacob comes back. He can live in an enforced exile—and still remain faithful to his inheritance. He has Abraham's personality to match Abraham's vocation.

28:12 He dreamed that there was a ladder.

In recent decades, theologians have criticized the otherworldliness of traditional Christian piety. Moral theologians have recovered a more positive assessment of bodily life, especially in the area of human sexuality. Liberation theologians have emphasized the worldly reality of God's promises. Freedom and flourishing are not purely spiritual. They have a concrete, political dimension as well. The promises of God fulfilled in Christ make a difference in the world.

Without a doubt the stories of the patriarchs support a recovery of human embodiment and history as the site of divine transformation. The covenant with Abraham initiates the divine invasion of space and time (→17:11a). The divine project is to redeem and transform the fallen world rather than facilitate our escape by way of mystical transports (→24:2). The covenant moves forward in time (Abraham's descendents will be blessed) and outward to the far reaches of the earth (by Abraham all the nations will be blessed). This horizontal movement may be punctuated by divine visitations and the upward look of worship, but in the main the adventures of Abraham, Isaac, and Jacob are inner-worldly. The very mundane reality of fallible human actors, the realistic drama of generational succession, and the promise of the land emphasize the tangible reality of fellowship with God. Faith is not a pie-in-the-sky hope for a disembodied rest in a far away heavenly realm.

Yet, it is as false to limit faith to this life as it is to think of it as entirely otherworldly. Both errors stem from a false separation of the immanent and transcendent, the temporal and eternal, the carnal and spiritual. The journey to God is woven together with the journey into the future of the blessing promised to Abraham. Faith reaches upward even as it reaches forward and outward. This is dramatized in Jacob's own journey from his father's house. On his way to find a wife and take his role in producing children that will ensure a future for the covenant, Jacob dreams of a ladder to heaven. In the history of theology, Jacob's ladder has served as an image of the movement of the human spirit upward to God. The traditional reading is fitting, and it does not pull us away from the forward, this-worldly thrust of the narrative. The two movements—forward toward a wife and upward toward God who transcends space and time—operate together in the life of Jacob. After all, although the ladder reaches upward, he is not called to ascend the ladder in order to leave his worldly life behind. He does not stop and remain in his place of vision. He offers worship, makes a vow, and then continues on his way.

Because the bodily, historical dimension of the covenant cannot be separated from the transcendent and spiritual aspect, we need to avoid separating the realities of life from a love of God. Jacob's desires are distorted by sin, but the basic direction of his worldly aspirations is essentially compatible with his divine inheritance. Jacob is not called up and out of life. Grace perfects rather than destroys nature. Moreover, it is telling that the angels first ascend and then descend the ladder. They take Jacob's vision upward into a vertical economy of divine transcendence, only to return his vision to the horizontal economy of this world. And after the vision, Jacob enacts the movement of the angels. He offers the upward movement of worship: "Jacob rose early in the morning, and he took the stone which

he had put under his head and set it up for a pillar and poured oil on top of it"
(28:18). Then he makes a vow and dedicates the place as the future site of God's
house (28:20–22). He does not linger, but instead resumes his forward journey
(29:1).

Of course, it is very tempting to fix all attention on the upward-reaching ladder
and in this way to treat Jacob's dreamlike vision as the moment of transcendence
that completes and fulfills God's promise of rest. We can plainly see that the lives
of finite, embodied creatures are characterized by suffering and death, and so we
think of deliverance in metaphysical terms. Lasting happiness comes from release
from finitude and embodiment and deliverance into a realm of limitless, spiritual
existence. Thus the normal dichotomies of ancient gnosticism arise: finite versus
infinite, time versus eternity, and body versus spirit.

These days we do not so much regret our embodiment as despair over our
historical and cultural particularity. We can see that there is a deep contingency
to our religious faith. We could have been born in India as Hindus or in China
as Confucians. This contingency seems a threat to the universal, eternal truth
of Christ, and so we begin to separate the historical teachings of Christianity
from its purportedly timeless core. Or we read the latest book on postcolonial
interpretation of scripture, and it fills us with dread. The particularity of tradition seems a pointed, aggressive weapon for cultural imperialism. With these
thoughts in mind, we wish to soften and weaken the concrete and highly focused
invasion of God's purpose into the world. Instead of moving forward with Jacob
into the history of the covenant, we turn Christianity into a symbolic medium
for our everlasting, upward movement to the God who is above all cultural and
historical distinctions.

The effect is similar to ancient gnosticism. In order to overcome the finite constraints of historical teachings, we do our best to deracinate the gospel. Schleiermacher and Hegel disagreed intensely, because they offered two very different
paths toward a dehistoricized account of the truth of Christ. Schleiermacher
interpreted the historical forms of Christian teaching as expressions of an inner
religious feeling of absolute dependence. In contrast, Hegel saw Christianity
as a system of teaching and practice that brought Western culture to a point of
transparent self-understanding. In spite of this difference, they both thought that
Christianity was the most perfect *instance of* or *vehicle for* religious truth. Like
the covenant of circumcision and any other particular element of salvation history, Christ crucified and risen represents, mediates, or instantiates some deeper,
more universal religious truth that remains at a distance from history, untainted
by time, unsullied by embodiment.

The witness of scripture consistently speaks against this impulse to turn the
particularity of salvation history into the medium for or symbol of a transhis-
torical, supratemporal truth that transcends time and place. Jacob's vision of the
ladder clearly underlies John 1:51. Philip brings Nathaniel to Jesus, who already
knows him. Nathaniel marvels that Jesus is a seer. Nathaniel's religious imagination

is natural. He sees Jesus as a man infused with remarkable powers from above, someone who transcends the limitations of ordinary human sight and perception. Jesus appears to agree, simply upping the ante and magnifying his sublime status: "Truly, truly, I say to you, you will see heaven opened, and the angels of God ascending and descending upon the Son of man." Yet what seems to be an appeal beyond space and time unfolds in John's Gospel (and the Synoptic Gospels) in an unexpectedly inner-worldly fashion. Christ's crucifixion and bodily resurrection turn out to be infinitely greater and more sublime than any revelation of Jesus's ability to transcend the limitations of space and time. This commitment to particularity is reinforced by John 1:51. Christ is the very ladder upon which the angels ascend and descend. He is not a window onto a greater reality; he is the living medium of commerce between heaven and earth.[37]

The Scholastic tradition has a convenient distinction that helps us distinguish between the occasional irruptions of the vertical dimension into ordinary affairs and the saving presence of God that brings us into the lasting fellowship of his Sabbath rest. The power of a seer to transcend space and see at a distance is preternatural, something outside or beyond the normal or natural. In contrast, our saving participation in the life, death, and resurrection of Christ is supernatural, a fulfillment and transformation of our created human nature. The preternatural is discontinuous with the ongoing flow of history. In contrast, the supernatural transforms history. When we participate in the liturgies of Good Friday and Easter Sunday, we place ourselves within Jesus's passion, death, and resurrection. The events may be freighted with universal significance, but they are very this-worldly: sweaty, bloody, and very much a local event. The experience may include intense emotional moments, visions, and revelations of God, but none are otherworldly in a preternatural sense. On the contrary, the liturgical recapitulation of Jesus's passion, death, and resurrection plunges us into the history of the supernatural, which is nothing more or less than the sequence of events that God undertakes to fulfill his promise to Abraham. The central saving mystery of Christian faith does not rise up and out of space and time, but rather both ascends and descends upon the crucified body of Christ. The particularity of human life is not transcended. In worship and prayer, our lives are saturated with the fulfillment of God's promises.

29:1 Jacob went on his journey.

Like Abraham, Jacob leaves his father's house. But in an important sense, Jacob's life moves in the opposite direction. Abraham comes into the land of the

---

37. For an interesting discussion of the links between John 1:51 and the midrashic tradition's use of Jacob's ladder, see James L. Kugel, *In Potiphar's House* (New York: HarperCollins, 1990), 114–15.

promise, while Jacob leaves it. We can overplay the difference. Abraham walks the land, not as one who possesses it but rather as the firstborn of a noble family who anticipates his inherited estate. He sees the future of the promises. He receives the sign of circumcision. He buys a small plot in the promised land as a place for burial. But he does not enter into full possession of the promise. Abraham remains a pilgrim (→12:7). But the pilgrim life is even clearer in the case of Jacob. His first step forward toward full possession of the future of the promises requires him to find a wife and secure progeny—and this first step necessitates a period of exile in the household of Laban. And although he eventually returns, Jacob never settles into the blessings promised to Abraham. His presumptuous sons keep him on the move (→34:1). Finally, at the lowest point of homeless despair, when his sons claim that Joseph has been killed by a wild beast, Jacob's grief becomes so great that he wants to depart to Sheol (37:35), the place of permanent exile, the very antithesis of the promised land.

The wandering of the patriarchs—tellingly, Isaac is most stable and least favorably portrayed—indicates something important about life in the covenant. The covenant promises worldly fulfillment: progeny, place, and prosperity. These promises seem to encourage a stable, this-worldly attitude. Family surrounds the patriarch. The places of burial pull with gravitational force, and, of course, with prosperity comes heavy luggage. But in Genesis the promises impel the elect forward. The promises are about the future, which draws all things forward to their fulfillment. Therefore, the journey, nearly always reluctant because of our attachment to the false promise of life lived according to the rules and principles of present life, is a primary motif, and it continues to be so throughout the Old Testament. In the Christian tradition, the idea of faith as a journey remains primary. Both the church and the individual believer are often described as pilgrims: strangers in a strange land, seeking to return to their homes. The future that God promises may be a place and time, a real future for us to inherit in our finite, created bodies, but it is the present transfigured, not extended. Everything God has created has a role, but nothing about this time and place feels right in comparison to the promised future.

29:11 Jacob kissed Rachel, and wept aloud.

Passions blind, but they also push us forward, because they excite and energize the will. Jacob begins his journey with a general idea in mind: to avoid the murderous anger of his brother and find a suitable wife among his mother's people. Wandering eastward, he encounters shepherds who tell him that he has arrived in Laban's neighborhood. The story reports a leisurely conversation among those who have gathered their flocks around a closed-up well, waiting for its daily opening. Then, with the arrival of Rachel, Jacob is galvanized. He leaps up and in a superhuman feat of strength rolls away the stone covering the mouth of the well. Love may not conquer all, but it certainly gets young men to do remarkable things.

There is a dualistic view, both ancient and modern, that sees cool reason as the seat of human dignity and hot passions as subversive powers. Plato wished to ban the poets from the ideal republic, because he saw the way in which beautiful words can sway the passions, move opinions, and motivate actions. The same holds for families and the affections between parents and children. Plato wanted universal wisdom to reign, not the loyalties born of particular loves. Of course, his own beautiful dialogues show a more realistic view; passions cannot be eliminated, and the wise should engage them and direct them toward a proper service of reason's ends. Aristotle makes this view explicit. The doctrine of the mean outlines a role for moderated and constrained passions, a balanced approach that stabilizes and guides the life of a virtuous person. The courageous person is not cowardly and driven by fear, but is also not rash and insensitive to danger. The temperate soul recognizes a rightful desire for pleasure, but moderates and limits its power by prudence.

The church fathers certainly adopted this classical view of the well-ordered soul, but they were also influenced by the larger biblical view of the human condition. We are creatures animated by a desire for something greater than ourselves, and for this reason, the agitations of the soul caused by the passions cannot be viewed simply as bodily turmoil to be ordered and disciplined by reason. Dynamism is built into the human condition. We are not satisfied with simply knowing that which is greatest. We want to love and serve it. This is why, for the Old Testament as a whole, idolatry and not ignorance threatens us; false loves rather than immoderate loves stand as the deepest and most dangerous temptation.

Because his thought was guided by the Bible, St. Augustine saw that love gives direction to life. "A material body is borne along by its weight in a particular direction," he writes, "as a soul is by its love" (*City of God* 9.28, quoted from Bettenson 1972: 463). Because our love is our weight, the heart must be directed toward God. In him we find a rest that is not the same as the equilibrium or moderation prized by so much of ancient culture. Instead, our true rest is born of intense and unequivocal devotion, the peace that comes from knowing that one's future is utterly committed to the beloved. Faith does not dampen passion. On the contrary, it enflames us with passion, now properly directed toward what we truly desire. As Gregory of Nyssa observes, "Through desire above all we are brought nearer God, drawn up, by its chain as it were, from earth toward him" (*On the Soul* in NPNF[2] 5:449). Thus the central exhortation in both Judaism and Christianity: "You shall love the LORD your God with all your heart, and with all your soul, and with all your might" (Deut. 6:4).

A great deal is at stake here, and the issue remains very contemporary. It is not coincidental that an ancient ideal of the passions and their management works within a view of history that tends toward decay. One staves off the dispersing forces of desire, which in each moment seem to fixate on passing satisfactions.

The same holds for history and the grinding wheel of time. One seeks to escape by loyalty to timeless truths or with more modest efforts to carve out a temporary zone of stable happiness. The Roman poet Lucretius combines both. To know that all reality can be reduced to atoms and their interactions frees us from illusions about life. Once freed, we can get on with what really matters: avoiding pain and seeking pleasure as best we can.

Our contemporary intellectual culture differs dramatically from pagan antiquity, but it shares a similar view of the way in which a life of reason frees us from the dead end of passing passions. The ideal of critical reason is simple: tear off the masks of ideology that disguise the self-interest and desire for power that are, in fact, the driving forces of history. For most of the modern era, this unmasking was seen as a preparation for receiving a higher truth. Critical reason exposes idols and empty dogmas and frees us to receive the true, trustworthy dictates of reason. The defining feature of postmodern intellectual culture has been a loss of confidence that any higher truth exists. Our job, therefore, is to see ourselves as the human animals we truly are—bundles of primitive passions given diverse cultural forms. There is no lasting truth, and neither you nor I nor human history have an end that fulfills and perfects us. The best we can do is to manage ourselves and the cultural process that surrounds us so as to prevent unnecessary suffering. In this way, a deflationary, skeptical humanism ends up echoing Lucretius.

In contrast, as the forthright and entirely uncritical report of Jacob's hot passion illustrates, the biblical view treats passion as the engine of destiny, for good or ill. Our desire for truth and our striking tendency to fall in love with a vision of human destiny is not an unfortunate fact to be domesticated by critical reason. After all, our loyalty to the future of sin cannot be broken by cool reflection. Syllogisms may have irresistible logical force, but they easily shatter on the chains that bind the will. Nor is postmodern irony effective. It may insulate against error, but it cannot move toward truth. Only a counterloyalty, a counterlove, can set us free from our bondage to false loves. Love enflamed burns away hesitations, delays, and our self-imposed impediments.

Furthermore, the end that God desires for us is supernatural. It is not something we can reason our way toward and then settle upon as proper goal for human life. Only the madness of love and its arrogant disdain for human limitations can motivate us to seek fellowship with God. Thus, the sheer ambition of the promise of salvation encourages a view of the human in which the urgency of desire plays a more fundamental role than deliberations of reason. Love—understood to include all the intersecting influences of bodily passions that give this too-often-idealized word its heated connotations—makes the man.

Christianity and Judaism prize the gift of reason. But neither misconceives its role and overestimates its power. As John Henry Newman recognized, to misconstrue reason in relation to passion brings us to a dryness of mind that makes our knowledge of truth empty and ineffectual. The intellect needs to be informed, but it also must be energized, and to do so the passions must be engaged. General ideas, universal principles, formulas and theorems—these and other powerful tools of reason help orient us in the world. Yet to know where you are is not the same as knowing which way to go. We must decide what in this world we shall love and in which direction we will travel. This decision involves an act of the will that reason itself seems rarely able to motivate. Thus, not surprisingly, Newman describes our situation in a way that calls to mind Jacob's encounter with Rachel. "The heart is commonly reached, not through the reason, but through the imagination, by means of direct impressions, by the testimony of facts and events, by history, description," he writes. "Persons influence us, voices melt us, looks subdue us, deeds inflame us. Many a man will live and die upon a dogma: no man will be a martyr for a conclusion."[38]

29:26 Why then have you deceived me?

Laban ensures the revenge of the firstborn. Jacob does not see the irony. Instead, he protests that he has been deceived. For the most part, the interpretive tradition sides with Jacob. Laban is portrayed as a wicked man who lies and cheats. Yet traditional readers are not univocal. One ancient Jewish midrash brings out the way in which the deception of Jacob seems fitting retribution for his deception of Isaac: "All that night he kept calling her 'Rachel' and she kept answering him 'Yes?' 'But the next morning, behold, it was Leah.' . . . He said to her, 'Liar and daughter-of-a-liar!' She answered: 'Can there be a schoolmaster without any pupils? Was it not just this way when your father called out to you 'Esau' and you answered him?'" (*Genesis Rabbah* 70.19, quoted from Kugel 1998: 380).

30:1 She envied her sister.

Jacob's household is the original community of Israel, as the twelve tribes descended from the twelve sons make explicit. The dysfunction and dissension within the family foreshadow later events, both in Israel and in the life of the church. The naked account of the failures of Jacob's household, the proto-Israel, reminds us that election comes by grace alone and not as a result of some sort of inner purity or righteousness that merits the covenant. "We have this treasure in earthen vessels," writes St. Paul of the glory of God made visible in the face of Christ, "to show that the transcendent power belongs to God and not to us" (2 Cor. 4:7). The elect are promised a future of blessedness—not a present state without blemish.

38. John Henry Newman, *Discussions and Arguments* (London: Longmans, Green, 1899), 293.

30:14 Give me, I pray, some of your son's mandrakes.

This scene of Rachel's seemingly unquenchable desire for worldly goods recapitulates Esau's ravenous hunger. But there are important reversals. In the first episode of bartering, Esau the firstborn gives up his birthright. Here, Rachel the second-married gives up the favor she has attained in Jacob's eyes. Rachel buys the mandrakes from Leah at the price of Jacob's fertility. This substitution of first wife for the second serves, perhaps, as a warning. True enough, God has chosen the elder to serve the younger. But we should beware: "For if you have been cut from what is by nature a wild olive tree, and grafted, contrary to nature, into a cultivated olive tree, how much more will these natural branches be grafted into their own olive tree" (Rom. 11:24). Rachel was "wise in [her] own conceits" (11:25), and this worldly wisdom ensures that neither she nor her sons rise to the kind of supereminence that ensures that the covenant future flows through her progeny alone. No one son will replace Jacob as the sole recipient of the promises. All the brothers are grafted onto the tree of the covenant.

30:25 When Rachel had borne Joseph, Jacob said to Laban, "Send me away, that I may go to my own home and country."

Jacob has many children in Paddan-aram, and although the growing family is portrayed in scenes of jealousy and bitterness, the place seems to be fruitful. But there is something about Joseph. With Joseph's birth, Jacob wants to return to the land of his inheritance. Jacob's sudden desire to return foreshadows Joseph's divinely appointed role. From his birth, Joseph is the motor of Jacob's future and therefore motor of the future of the covenant.

This subtle narrative marker of Joseph's special role contrasts with the very explicit divine designations of Abraham, Isaac, and Jacob as the sole recipients of the promise. Abraham is called out of his father's house. Isaac is the chosen son instead of Ishmael, Jacob instead of Esau. In each case, the divine voice divides and separates for the sake of the future of the covenant. Not so Joseph. He will be separated from his brothers, but only by their evil intentions, and it will be a separation that God uses toward the end of their eventual reunion and collective survival. This different role marks a decisive development in the divine plan: no longer will an individual patriarch carry the covenant forward. Now all the children constitute a corporate partner. The clan receives the promises, and individuals are chosen to serve the covenant by serving the people of God. In this way the focus and preoccupation of the Genesis narrative shifts. Instead of the drama of establishing the *boundaries* of the chosen people—Abraham as distinct from his father's household, Isaac as opposed to Ishmael, Jacob and not Esau—Genesis turns to identifying the *saving center* that gives life to the chosen people.[39]

This reading of Joseph as the archetype for a new role in the future of the covenant can be found in early traditions. Psalm 81:5 treats Joseph as a synecdoche for all of Israel. One ancient Aramaic translation directly identifies Joseph with Joshua, the leader of the community (Maher 1992: 106). In both instances, Joseph is being read as the animating, indispensable center of the divine plan. Taken in this sense, Joseph's role foreshadows the Torah and temple—and, for Christian readers, Jesus Christ (→37:2). However, in the later chapters of Genesis, this role is often equivocal. Joseph serves as a warning about the dangers of blurring the boundaries of the covenant. His brother Judah makes the crucial offer of himself as a substitute to bear the punishment of another (→44:33), and Judah—not Joseph—inherits the royal and messianic roles (→49:8).

30:32 Every speckled and spotted sheep.

Jacob wants to leave, and Laban is willing to negotiate with him over the conditions of his departure. But Jacob has learned his lesson. Laban is not a man to be bargained with, for he is a shifty character who is likely to get the best of any deal. So Jacob comes up with a plan. He will take only the occasional speckled and spotted sheep from Laban's flock and raise them. For a period of time, Jacob will care for this motley flock, and Laban will receive all the pure white and black sheep produced under Jacob's care. Laban sees this as a very good deal, for in the ordinary course of things, the vast majority of sheep born are either entirely white or black. "Good!" he says to Jacob, "Let it be as you have said" (30:34).

Jacob differs from both Abraham and Isaac. They find wealthy patrons—or, more accurately, by the providence of God wealthy patrons find them. In contrast, Jacob's worldly prosperity must be won by effort and craft. In this way, Jacob draws the covenant closer to the form of life commanded in the garden of Eden. He does not just let nature or events go their course. He gives his sheep water in runnels specially constructed to induce the birth of spotted lambs. He exercises dominion, breeding/tilling and keeping the sheepfold/garden given to him by Laban. But the result is not self-sufficiency. Jacob's flock grows in a way favorable to his well-being, but God will have to intervene and restrain Laban (31:24) in order for Jacob's work to serve the future of the covenant.

39. One clear sign of this shift is that the portions of Genesis that Paul uses in his letters concern Abraham, Isaac, and Jacob before the birth of Joseph. The problems of Torah observance and circumcision are, for Paul, problems of boundaries and entry into covenant membership. These issues now move into the background as the narrative shifts from the career of Jacob to the collective destiny of his sons.

31:13 Return.

The voice of the angel of God in Jacob's dream is clear: go back to the land of your birth. But the subsequent narrative is far less clear. After the vision of the ladder, God promises to keep Jacob safe from harm and to return him to the land of the promise. But in what sense is this promise fulfilled? Does Jacob really "go home"? True enough, he leaves, but the family seems to move from place to place rather than resting in a state of divine favor. Jacob delays a return to his father's dwelling place until the patriarch is on his deathbed (35:27–29), and although he stays for a while (37:1), famine eventually drives him to Egypt, and it is there and not in the land of the promise that he dies. Moreover, Jacob's life seems as unsettled as his migratory patterns. Instead of peace and rest, he goes from conflict to conflict: with Esau, with Laban, with his sons, with his beloved Joseph at the end of his life when he blesses Ephraim first and then Manasseh, and most importantly with the divine stranger at Jabbok. Even when he is not an antagonist, Jacob finds his life agitated by conflict: between Leah and Rachel, between his sons and foreigners, between Joseph and his brothers. Jacob is ever striving, ever contesting, ever pushed forward by the struggles and conflicts of his large family.

The divine commandment to return is nothing more than an imperative form of the divine promise to fulfill the vow that can be traced back to Abraham. "Return!" means "Enter the blessings I have prepared for you for the sake of your forefathers." Certainly, Jacob's unsettled life encourages us to read the imperative as initiating an eschatological movement forward to the final end of all creation, rather than a worldly journey back to images of childhood security and stability. Even when he returns to his father's house, Jacob's journeys are not over. Even when Joshua leads the people of Israel back into the land, or when the remnant of exiles returns from Babylon to rebuild Jerusalem, the history of the covenant is not consummated.

Even though Jesus is the pioneer and perfecter of faith, the one who has persevered to the end and is seated at the right hand of God, those who are baptized into his death find themselves in Jacob's position. We are called to inhabit the blessings promised, but in this life we are always arduously en route, afflicted and made lame by the weight of sin that only the ministrations of Christ can heal. Rather than comfortable and at rest, belief in the promise subjects one to hard struggles, often accompanied by suffering (Heb. 10:32). The fight must be fought, and the race must be run (2 Tim. 4:7), "for here we have no lasting city, but we seek the city which is to come" (Heb. 13:14).

31:19 Rachel stole her father's household gods.

Laban gets a taste of his own medicine. He "stole" Rachel from Jacob by substituting Leah. Now, Rachel spirits away the small statues of the gods of Laban's

household. It may be poetic justice, but Rachel's act breaks the divine commandment against theft. Unlike the deception of Isaac, this transgression is not directly
related to the transmission of the covenant, so the act does not put immediate
pressure on our presumption that the path toward fellowship with God should
be pure and free of sin. Nonetheless, Rachel is a source of the twelve tribes of
Israel, and her transgression would seem to stain the inheritance. Once again, the
covenant household appears to be a source of sin, not sanctity.

As in the case of Jacob's deception (→27:5), ancient readers developed a
strategy of exculpation. Rachel stole in order to free her father from the temptations of idolatry. "Her purpose in this was on God's behalf; for she said: 'Now
we are going our way. Can we leave this old man in the midst of his idolatry?'"
(*Genesis Rabbah* 74.5, quoted from Kugel 1998: 384). Some church fathers offer
a similar reading of Rachel's intention. If the household gods were unavailable,
then Laban will remain loyal to God alone—or so this line of interpretation
suggests. Of course, this reasoning runs aground on the Pauline principle not
to do evil that good might come (Rom. 3:8). And in any event, if we take the
patriarchs and matriarchs as prototypes for corporate Israel, then the entire impulse toward exculpation is wrongheaded. The body of the faithful carries the
divine project forward, and this project seeks to redeem creation from within.
Until the divine project is brought to completion, that chosen people is always
being made holy. As the instrument of God's will for all humanity, *being made*
holy rather than simply *being* holy invariably means that the sinful worldliness
of our fallen humanity is present along with the righteousness that God uses to
sanctify creation.

32:7 Jacob was greatly afraid.

Jacob has good reasons to fear reunion with Esau. He has usurped his older
brother, and he expects retribution. If we follow through with the figural interpretation of Jacob and Esau as types for the church and synagogue that St. Paul
develops (→27:27), then we can see a contemporary relevance.

Today, Christians are justifiably anxious when encountering Jews. They fear
that they will receive a just retribution for their long history of anti-Judaism, not
in the form of physical attack, but rather as moral censure. Furthermore, just as
Jacob continues with his clever schemes, setting aside presents to buy off Esau and
instructing his servant in the proper manner of supplication, so also do we see a
great deal of moral posturing on the part of the contemporary churches as they
fall over themselves to apologize for a past history of anti-Judaism—even as they
intensify their investment in theological antinomianism. The unctuous phrase
that Jacob uses for Esau, "my lord," is insincere. He has no intention of submitting
to his brother, or if so, then only out of necessity and only as long as it will take
to regain the upper hand. The same holds for the general postmodern cult of the

victim, which drives so much Gentile guilt about the treatment of Jews in Western history. It is a stylized guilt, a reassuring stance of moral self-denunciation.

Jacob, however, realizes that he has reached the limits of his capacity to manipulate events. If Esau wishes to play the role of Cain and destroy the one who has been chosen, then no gifts or concessions or ritual acts of submission will satisfy him. Nothing short of Jacob renouncing his claim to God's promises will do. But Jacob cannot renounce the future that God has assigned him. The way forward seems blocked. The logic of the matter divides them: either the elder shall serve the younger or he shall not. Jacob fittingly offers a prayer of petition that places his future in the hands of God. "Please, LORD," his prayer asks, "be faithful to your promised future, because I do not have the power to bring it to pass." God alone has the power to deliver Jacob from the seeming dead end of fraternal rivalry. God alone can prevent Esau from sliding back into the role of Cain—and Jacob into the role of Abel.

Jacob's problem and his turn toward a prayer of petition shed light on the difficult relations of church and synagogue. From the outset, the conflict arose from Christian claims about Jesus of Nazareth, which, like Jacob's usurpation of Esau, concern the future of the covenant. This source of antagonism has remained alive, and the Jewish refusal to affirm Jesus as the promised Messiah has offended and inflamed Christians over the centuries. Doubtless there are many other causes for the persecutions and pogroms that have stained the history of Christian Europe, to say nothing of the role of nineteenth-century racial "science" in the modern anti-Semitism that culminated in the horrors of the Nazi campaign of extermination. But the fact remains: Christians and Jews are divided over the nature of God's fulfillment of his promise to Abraham, and this division has to be weighted with the religious passions that properly accompany fundamental beliefs. The church can no more overcome the long history of anti-Judaism by renouncing her claims about Jesus than Jacob can be reconciled to his brother by giving up the blessing he has received from Isaac. It is absurd to imagine that we can overcome the legacy of our moral and spiritual failures by denying Christ. On the contrary, as Jacob expresses in his prayer, the way forward requires a redoubled trust in the power of God's promises, for God alone can deliver us from the hands of our elder brothers. "When I am afraid" of the complicated burden of Christian history, "I put my trust in thee" (Ps. 56:3).

32:20 I may appease him.

It seems as though Jacob backslides into a strategy of placation. He offers generous gifts and engages in carefully orchestrated acts of ritual submission. Perhaps the placation suggests only halfhearted trust in the power of God to protect those whom he has chosen. The promise moves forward in earthen vessels, and Jacob demonstrates on many occasions that those chosen by God are simultaneously righteous and sinful. But we can also read Jacob's plans for appeasing Esau as entirely in keeping with his trust in God. After all, it is a false faithfulness that justifies inaction by recourse to grand claims about the unworthiness of human action and the supervening power of God. The future of the covenant rests in God's hands, but this does not excuse us from undertaking our own efforts. Reconciliation depends upon God's providence, but the divine plan calls for us to play an active role, rather than to sit on the sidelines of the divine project as passive spectators.

32:24 A man wrestled with him.

The struggle and its inconclusive outcome are highly ambiguous. Jacob's opponent, at first an unknown man, seems to recapitulate Esau, against whom Jacob struggled in Rebekah's womb. The opponent also echoes Isaac, against whom Jacob struggled by way of subterfuge in order to secure the patriarchal blessing. The strange man may even evoke Laban, with whom Jacob strove to marry Rachel and gain worldly wealth. Yet, in the end the opponent blesses Jacob—as did Isaac unwittingly.

Jacob's description of the contest uses a biblical image that is a standard trope for salvation: "I have seen God face to face, and yet my life is preserved" (32:30). This evocation of danger and blessing, life-threatening peril and divine encounter, seems to sum up the trajectory of Jacob's life. Does the wrestling match set Jacob against an enemy, or does it bring Jacob into intimate contact with a friend? Is the life of the chosen a curse, or is it a blessing and gift? Does the covenant bring heavy burdens and deep suffering, or will it bring peace and prosperity?

The interpretation of Jacob's struggle in Hos. 12:4–6 suggests a view of God as both enemy and friend. The context is a prophetic pronouncement of divine lament over the faithlessness of Israel. In the prophecy, Jacob's wrestling match becomes an image of Israel's disastrous sinful struggle against God's promised future: "He strove with the angel and prevailed" (12:4). This is not good news, for it means that faithless, prostitute Israel succeeds in shaking off her divine vocation. She will not be a willing covenant partner with the LORD. Yet, the prophetic use of Jacob's wrestling match does not end there. Hosea continues, portraying Jacob/Israel as weeping with regret over his unnecessary struggle with God—one that he has unfortunately won! Jacob/Israel petitions God for favor. The sanctity and power of God's name is invoked, and then the prophecy turns to speak to the reader, conveying the moral of the story of Jacob's wrestling match with God: "So you, by the help of your God, return, hold fast to love and justice, and wait continually for your God" (12:6).

This intracanonical use of Jacob's struggle implies an interpretation of the exchange that ends the wrestling match. The mysterious man says, "Let me go, for the day is breaking" (Gen. 32:26a). In the context of Hosea, the breaking day is the day of judgment, the coming of God in wrath, the day that the decay and destruction of Israel suggests is near. Israel has struggled against the will of God, but time is running out. With this in mind, the prophecy in Hosea reads Jacob's response as a decisive change of heart: "I will not let you go, unless you bless me" (32:26b). Jacob/Israel turns from fighting against the LORD to clinging to God. God is an enemy to the wicked and friend to the righteous, and therefore whether the covenant is a curse or a blessing depends upon the human partner. A repentant heart that clings to God as the source of righteousness can turn wrath into comfort, judgment into forgiveness.

At first glance, the plain sense of Genesis gives no strong support to a reading that turns the aggressive Jacob into a repentant supplicant. But the figural interpretation suggested by Hosea's use of the elements of Jacob's struggle has persuasive logic. Jacob seems to both struggle against and tenaciously cling to his adversary. Moreover, 32:26 and Jacob's tenacious grip function as the pivot of the episode. Before this verse, the adversary is a nameless man who can easily be read as representing the enemies of Israel, the human forces that God will allow to prevail in judgment against a sinful Israel. Yet, as the wrestling ends, the former adversary is revealed to be God himself. The providential power behind the afflictions now blesses Jacob. In Hosea, the same is promised to Israel as she endures the travails of exile. The one who authorizes affliction does so in order to bless those who cling to the LORD as the only source of salvation. The wisdom of God "is a tree of life to those who lay hold of her; those who hold her fast are called happy" (Prov. 3:18).

There are further reasons for the interpretation found in Hosea, ones that have to do with the place of the mysterious wrestling match in the larger story of Jacob. This scene of reentry into the promised land is clearly related to the dream of the ladder that precedes Jacob's departure (→28:12). After the vision of the ladder, Jacob anoints the stone that served as his pillow. He then takes a vow that involves a strange reversal of responsibility for the covenant with Abraham. Normally, the covenant has a *because-therefore* structure. God says something that can be glossed, "Because I have chosen you, therefore you are my people." After the vision of the ladder, Jacob turns this around and makes the covenant dependent upon his assessment of God's faithfulness. The covenant seems to be a bargain in which Jacob claims the upper hand: "If you reliably show that you have chosen me, then I will make you my God." In a crucial sense, then, Jacob sets himself up as over and against God as an equal partner: "You may judge me, but beware, I'll judge you as well."

Now, as Jacob prepares to reenter the land of the promise, the context has changed. Jacob has served Laban for a long time, and as he returns to his homeland, he worries about the danger of his forthcoming encounter with Esau. In Gen. 28 Jacob had planned to wait and see whether God will give him what has been promised. Now, after his difficult life of exile, it is hard to see how God has given Jacob what he demanded: clear evidence that he has been blessed. Perhaps, therefore, we are to read the beginning of the wrestling match as an echo of his previous challenge to God: "If God will be with me" Jacob seems to be saying in his aggressive, grappling efforts to pin God down, "then the LORD shall be my God" (28:20–21). By this reading, the nightlong duration of the wrestling is meant to suggest the futility of a spiritual disposition that seeks to lash God to terms we devise, a futility that leads only to a maimed life: "Jacob's thigh was put out of joint" (32:25). Yet, as the wrestling match moves to its end, Jacob does exactly the opposite of what he pledged after his vision in Gen. 28. He holds on to God—he makes the LORD his God—and this in spite of long servitude to Laban, in spite of conflict in his household, in spite of worries about the murderous resentments that his brother very likely harbors against him. Like Israel in exile, in spite of his trials, Jacob holds God close, and therein is he blessed.

Read in this way, we can harmonize the plain sense of antagonism found at the beginning of this episode with the concluding atmosphere of blessing and piety. Prideful self-sufficiency fuels the fantasy of equality with the divine. God will be my God, but only on my terms. This form of sinfulness brings the human creature into conflict with God. In this sense, like Jacob, insofar as we sin, we fight against God, and he is our enemy. And yet this very tendency toward self-sufficiency is defeated over the course of Jacob's life. In this sense, God is *for* Jacob as the one who is *against* him as the providential power that orchestrates events that seem harmful at first glance but serve to chasten and educate the patriarch. God does the same with the people of Israel over the course of the centuries. They undergo trials that prepare them for deeper fellowship. The dynamic plays out in our lives. God fights back against our sinfulness, and in so doing, the LORD takes our side by standing against us, just as a parent in resisting the self-destructive rebelliousness of a child works against the will of the child in order to work for the well-being of the child (→22:1).

Ezekiel's prophecy makes explicit the double role of God as both aggressor and defender. The scene is the siege of Jerusalem, which the LORD himself leads as a fitting punishment for the sins of the city. Yet, Ezekiel says that at the very same time as God attacks, he is also within the city, looking for an agent whom he might put forward to defend his beloved dwelling place: "I sought for anyone among them who would repair the wall and stand in the breach before me on behalf of the land, so that I would not destroy it" (22:30 NRSV). It seems paradoxical: God both assaults and defends, both condemns in judgment and contends for mercy. But the scene actually makes sense. Of necessity, God's holiness overwhelms and undoes fallen humanity, but at the same time, God allies himself with his elect in order to secure safe passage through the purifying fires of judgment. Of course, this comes to a dramatic climax in Jesus's passion and death. God becomes the one whom he sought, the one who will stand in the breach.[40]

40. See Robert W. Jenson's comments on Ezek. 22:23–31 in *Ezekiel*, Brazos Theological Commentary on the Bible (Grand Rapids: Brazos, 2009).

32:28 Your name shall no more be called Jacob, but Israel.

Name changes signal new identities (→17:5). The blessing that accompanies the new name adds to the atmosphere of benediction. The name closes the wrestling match that tests Jacob's perseverance, and the name sets the stage for Jacob's career in his homeland. In this sense, the new name is the final ordination of Jacob as patriarch: go forth to receive your inheritance. That the new name denotes the nation that will claim Abraham's inheritance—and will have a history marked by many occasions of conflict with God—only reinforces this interpretation.

Yet the details of the text raise interesting difficulties. What is the meaning of the new name? The answer is not obvious. Jacob shall be called Israel, because "you have striven with God and with men, and have prevailed." This translation follows the Masoretic Text, the standard Hebrew version, which certainly fits nicely with wrestling in the larger context. But it does not fit perfectly. Kugel clarifies the perplexing diversity of translations and points out that, whatever role we assign to God (either as Jacob's ally or adversary), during the night at the Jabbok ford, Jacob wrestled with only *one man* (1998: 394–95). Who, then, are the "men" against whom Jacob struggled? Furthermore, in what sense could any person strive with God and prevail?

In the Septuagint and Vulgate, the difficulty is relaxed by the decision to read a slightly different sense into the Hebrew. Instead of "to struggle," the word can be related to a root that means "to rule" or "to be strong." This shifts the emphasis somewhat. Instead of the name pointing back to the wrestling match, it signals an overall evaluation. Jacob has shown himself a man of powerful strength in his match with God, and this allows for the obvious inference that his descendants will be princes among men. Thus the Septuagint reads: "Your name shall no more be called Jacob, but Israel shall be your name. For you have been strong with God, and you will be powerful with men." The Vulgate is even clearer: "For if you have been strong against God, how much more shall you be powerful against men?" By this reading, Jacob's status in relation to God—whether by way of cooperation (the Septuagint preserves the ambiguity) or contest (which Jerome's Vulgate translation specifies)—gives him priority with respect to the rest of humanity.[41]

One reading of Jacob's role in Genesis supports the Septuagint interpretation of the new name. In Rachel's womb Jacob struggled, and as a young man he continues to struggle, first for Isaac's blessing and then for Rachel. Now, the name "Israel" comes in response to a struggle, once again framed as an effort to secure a blessing: "I will not let you go, unless you bless me" (32:26). Overall, then, we can say that Jacob struggled with God for the future of the covenant. In this way, God and Jacob are allied toward a common purpose, even if God throws up roadblocks and creates difficulties. This alliance is palpable in the complex scene

---

41. See Jerome's explicit development of the point in *Saint Jerome's Hebrew Questions on Genesis*, trans. C. T. R. Hayward (Oxford: Clarendon; 1995), 70 §32.28–29.

of Isaac's deception. Rachel and Jacob's conniving takes place in a sequence of events that has all the markings of divine providence (→27:5). Thus, if we expand the covenantal logic of Jacob's success to evoke the *sola gratia* structure of God's election of his people, then "Israel" means something along these lines: "For you have been chosen by God as the instrument of his invasion of human history for the sake of the struggle toward its redemption and consummation, and therefore you shall be blessed among the nations."

This tilt in the direction of the Septuagint, with "strong with" meaning "in alliance with God," does not rule out Jerome's reading in the Vulgate, which endorses "against God" as the proper sense. Both senses are regularly included in the biblical vision of God in relation to his beloved (→32:24). The LORD can be both for and against, or more precisely, God can be for us by being against us, always for the sake of the fulfillment of the divine plan. Moreover, there is a spiritual sense in which the faithful can struggle with and afflict God. This possibility guides the influential Jesuit commentator Cornelius Lapide, who follows the Vulgate reading of the new name and places Jacob "against God." By his reading, this teaches us that Jacob masters God by way of ardent and unceasing prayer. The spiritual sense is then obvious: we should follow Jacob's example and live up to the new name. With tireless petition we should "assault" God to win his favor, as did the Canaanite woman with her determined efforts to win the favor of Jesus (Matt. 15:21–28) and as the widow did with her persistent demand for justice (Luke 18:1–8).[42]

The whole question of the meaning of Jacob's new name is complicated by the church fathers, who by and large accepted a popular etymology that allows for an interpretation of the name "Israel" as "he who has seen God."[43] With this reading, Gen. 32:30 becomes the focal point for a proper, spiritual interpretation of the entire episode: "So Jacob called the name of the place Peniel, saying, 'For I have seen God face to face, and yet my life is preserved.'"

To shift from "struggled" to "seen" as the fundamental root in Jacob's new name can seem wildly divergent, but a closer look shows otherwise. It is a biblical truism that one cannot see God and live, so much so that Job views his encounter with God in the whirlwind as an overwhelming, unaccountable honor (Job 42:1–6). A lasting vision of God is not a worldly possibility; it is reserved for the age to come, when the creature is purified of all defect and can enter into fellowship with God in all his holiness. St. Paul's famous dictum depends upon this eschatological

42. Cornelius Lapide, *Commentarii in sacrum scripturam* (Paris: Berche & Tralin, 1875), 1.264.

43. Origen gives this interpretation of the name in *On First Principles* 4.3.12 (in *Origen: On First Principles*, trans. G. W. Butterworth [repr., Gloucester, MA: Peter Smith, 1973], 307), as does Augustine in *City of God* 16.39 (Bettenson 1972: 704). This is not a strictly Christian tradition; see Kugel 1998: 387 for ancient Jewish sources. However, the Christian belief in Jesus as God incarnate certainly supports an emphasis on the vision that the Jewish tradition after the destruction of the Jerusalem temple does not.

limit: "For now we see through a glass, darkly: but then face to face" (1 Cor. 13:12 AV). Thus, the church fathers read the name "Israel" as "he who has seen God," because they took the name to give precision to the blessing already promised to Abraham. The full form of the covenant promise is that we will become partakers in the divine nature, a future that the late antique world often thought best expressed in terms of vision. It is a destiny that the Bible portrays in the same way: "Blessed are the pure in heart, for they shall see God" (Matt. 5:8).

Guided by the patristic interpretation of the divine name, therefore, we can read the Jabbok episode as a recapitulation of Abraham's lament over the lack of a son and his subsequent vision of the future of the covenant in the signs and dream of Gen. 15 (→15:8). Jacob struggles with God in the same sense that Abraham laments. He grasps God, seeking reassurance. "I've spent years in exile," we can imagine him saying. "I've been deceived and harshly treated by my father-in-law. My wives quarrel. My brother very likely wants to kill me when I return. Tell me, O LORD, how are my father's blessings a gift and not a curse? How is being chosen a source of joy rather than grief, rest rather than travail?" In his brief moment of vision—"I have seen God"—Jacob sees the end. He has a glimpse of the face of God, the fullness toward which the history of the covenant strains: "Thy face, LORD, do I seek" (Ps. 27:8).

32:32 Therefore to this day the Israelites do not eat the sinew of the hip.

When God says to Abram, "No longer shall your name be Abram, but your name shall be Abraham," Genesis and the rest of the Bible and subsequent tradition obeys (→17:5). Thereafter the patriarch is always called Abraham. This is not true for Jacob. We read, "Your name shall no more be called Jacob, but Israel" (32:28; 35:10), but Genesis, the rest of the Bible, and the subsequent tradition seems to disobey. Jacob remains Jacob. Jesus speaks of the God of "Abraham, Isaac, and Jacob," not of "Abraham, Isaac, and Israel."

The way in which the story of Jacob's solitary struggle with the man/angel/God concludes with an aside about the dietary laws of the people of Israel suggests an explanation. Jacob has two roles. The first role is that of a patriarch, successor to Abraham and Isaac. God chooses one man as the vehicle for advancing his plan, and Jacob is that man in his generation. But with Jacob this approach to advancing the divine plan is suspended. Thus Jacob's second role comes to predominate. He is the father of a clan that will carry the covenant forward collectively, rather than transferring it from single chosen son to single chosen son. And the nation will do so by way of their obedience to distinctive communal practices, of which dietary laws are visible and daily, as this concluding verse reminds readers. We should say, then, that Jacob is to Israel as Christ is to the church. As an individual actor, he remains Jacob, but his seed, his power of life, moves forward in his sons, their families, and the families of their families. They provide the body that bears the promise forward. All twelve sons constitute Israel. The man is Jacob; his future is Israel.

33:4 Esau ran to meet him, and embraced him.

Jacob's anxiety about Esau seems to have been misplaced. His brother does not merely refrain from attacking; Esau calls Jacob "brother" and embraces him. In the larger context of Genesis, this unexpected outcome seems unnecessary, even inappropriate. After all, hasn't Jacob outfoxed all his adversaries up to this point, and hasn't he struggled with God in a wrestling match? Abraham managed to defeat the armies of foreign kings with only 318 men, so why can't Jacob also miraculously triumph over Esau and his 400 men? Moreover, this tender scene of brotherly reconciliation seems false to the way in which both Genesis and the rest of the Bible depict the subsequent history of the two clans. Jacob ends up separating himself from Esau rather than living in brotherly harmony, and in Exod. 17 and Num. 20 the descendents of Esau are depicted as enemies of the people of Israel.

The way in which this scene of embrace cuts against the grain of the larger story strongly suggests an eschatological reading. God's plan of invading human reality by way of a chosen people will bring conflict, as the biblical history of Israel and the gospel stories of Jesus testify. The world no more wants its privileges and prerogatives usurped than Esau wanted his birthright taken by Jacob. But God does not choose the few in order to destroy the many. On the contrary, Abraham is called so that all the nations of the earth might be blessed through him. Esau's embrace of Jacob foreshadows the reconciliation of all by the thin, narrow line of the elect.

The typological potential of this scene of reconciliation also has specific relevance for the relations of Jews and Christians. If we follow the Pauline reading of Jacob and Esau as figures for the church and the synagogue, then we can find hope in this passage. Two brothers are reconciled, foreshadowing the reconciliation of church and synagogue. Perhaps this hoped-for reconciliation will follow the pattern of Jacob and Esau, with the synagogue taking the initiative, and the church playing the role of servant, bowing before the elder brother. It is a telling reversal of Isaac's blessing—"let thy mother's sons bow down to thee" (27:29 AV)—and it is a chastisement to the church's historic role as powerful lord over the lives of Jews in the Christian West. Moreover, the servant role is so deeply woven into the fabric of the New Testament, so closely associated with the person of Jesus, that the view of the church in relation to the synagogue suggested by a typological reading of Jacob and Esau brings to mind the promise of discipleship: those who follow Christ and serve the servant shall see the face of the Lamb (Rev. 22:4). As the bowing Jacob says to Esau, whom God has ordained to serve his younger brother, "Truly to see your face is like seeing the face of God" (Gen. 33:10). But one cannot know the specific shape of the future. Figures never come clear until they are fulfilled.

251

5

NEED FOR ATONEMENT

"Now there comes a reckoning for his blood" (42:22)

34:1 Dinah the daughter of Leah.

This extended episode of rape and revenge seems to turn on a series of inversions that throw key elements of the covenant into a dark shadow. Fertility, marriage, circumcision, the promise that Abraham's progeny will be a blessing to the nations—these key elements of the divine plan are distorted and abused.

The central role of fertility is clear at the outset of the career of Abraham and his descendents. Twice Abraham says that Sarah is his sister, seeming to offer her up to the desires of more powerful men in order to save his skin (→12:13). It is a pattern repeated by Isaac with Rebekah (→26:18). In each case, the integrity of marriage and the roles of Sarah's and Rebekah's wombs in the service of the covenant are threatened. Their fertility could have been easily coopted by foreign powers, but God forestalls the danger. In the case of Dinah, however, the outcome is reversed. She "went out to visit the women of the land," and right away Shechem, the powerful son of the local ruler, "saw her, he took her, and lay with her, and defiled her" (34:2 AV).

The scene is not unlike when Jacob first saw Rachel. Shechem is smitten. But unlike the young Jacob, Shechem thinks he has the resources to take immediate and permanent possession of what he wants. He goes to Hamor, his father. Shechem demands that Hamor use all his powers to secure Dinah as his wife. Shechem does not just want to use Dinah for his pleasure. He wants to conscript her into the larger communal project of reproduction. He wants her womb for the sake of building a future for the house of Shechem.

This emphasis on the communal nature of Dinah's rape tends to be overlooked by modern readers, because we so often think of rape in terms of violence and coercion.[1] By our thinking, rape is a crime against the woman as an individual. But Genesis does not give us the personal perspective. We do not learn anything about Dinah's condition after her rape, nor do we learn if she has any interest in Shechem's burning desire to make her his wife. Instead, the text draws out the communal consequences. Hamor and Shechem go to Jacob to negotiate for Dinah. Like a corporate titan used to getting what he wants, Shechem is willing to pay any price: "Whatever you say to me I will give" (34:11), while Hamor clarifies the goal of melding the clans, an alliance that will follow in the train of the marriage. "Make marriages with us; give your daughters to us, and take our daughters for yourselves," Hamor offers. "You shall dwell with us; and the land shall be open to you; dwell and trade in it, and get property in it" (34:9–10).

Here we see a narrative form of the rhetorical move made in countless places throughout the Old Testament: sexual defilement symbolizes wayward idolatry; religious harlotry threatens to return the chosen people back into the mass of fallen humanity. With this in mind, we can see how the defilement of Dinah threatens to spread like an infection. It begins with Shechem simply grabbing a young woman and using her for pleasure. He wants her without any regard to her role as part of the communal project of procreation. But human desire is never purely personal. It always expands toward a communal form, which is why vice invariably corrupts cities as well as souls. Shechem plans to conscript Dinah's fertility—and the future of Jacob's entire clan—into the Shechemite project, the normal, worldly project of producing enough children and accumulating enough property to ensure survival. For this reason, we need to read the defilement of Dinah against the background of any number of biblical prohibitions against intermarriage, idolatry, and communal disloyalty to the covenant. As is the case for all the women in Genesis, her fertility represents the future. Where her womb goes, there goes the future of Israel.

It is no coincidence that Jacob says nothing and does nothing. His new name, Israel, has been given, and this signals a shift from individual to collective identity (→32:32). Thus, "the sons of Jacob" rather than the singular patriarch respond to Shechem and Hamor. True sons of their father, they deceive, and they do so in a dramatic fashion. They pretend not to care about the defilement of Dinah's rape and the larger defilement of intermarriage. Instead, the brothers express a half-truth. They protest that it "would be a disgrace to us" for Dinah, and for the rest of the clan, to marry into a community not marked by circumcision. But the unspoken falsehood is plain to see. Those not called cannot make themselves

1. For a helpful discussion of this point and a reading of the episode that has shaped my interpretation, see Kass 2003: 477–92.

chosen by adopting the sign of circumcision as their own. Circumcision may be necessary, but it certainly is not sufficient. In any event, the sons of Jacob have no intention of treating the sons of Hamor as members of their clan. Instead, Simeon and Levi wait until all the males of the city of Shechem are recovering from their circumcisions. Then they attack, kill all the males, plunder the city, and do to all the women what Shechem did to Dinah: "Their wives, all that was in the houses, they captured and made their prey" (34:29).

Simeon and Levi's actions hardly seem noble. The narrative itself reports Jacob upbraiding them—"you have brought trouble on me" (34:30)—although perhaps we should discount Jacob's response, since he worries about the consequence only for himself. Notice the "me, me, me" refrain throughout 34:30–31. But there are other narrative clues. God makes no appearance in the story to encourage, command, or commend the action. More importantly, the thematic content provides a strong reason for interpretive dismay. God promised Abraham that his progeny will be a blessing to all the nations, and God gave Abraham circumcision in order to perfect the flesh of his chosen people. Yet the sons of Jacob have turned circumcision into a sign of death. Therefore, it is very difficult to read the overall story as anything other than a perversion of the covenant.

At this point we need to be careful to avoid a moralistic critique of Simeon and Levi, as if they should have set aside their anger and accepted union with the Shechemites. After being chastised by Jacob, Simeon and Levi respond, "Should he treat our sister as a harlot?" (34:31). Jacob gives no response, because the answer is clear enough. Dinah and her fate matter for the future of the people of Israel. Something *must* be done about her defilement. The wombs of Israel represent her future, and they cannot be conscripted to serve another people, another project, another future. To let Shechem have his way threatens to bring about the triumph of "harlotry," which means the assimilation of nascent Israel back into the spiritual condition of fallen humanity. So, in this sense, Simeon and Levi have the right motive: they want to make clean that which has been defiled. They want to protect the future of the covenant. But their methods are hopeless. What they do to the Shechemites parallels the flood. They try to remove defilement by destroying all that is unclean.

If we allow that the sons of Jacob have good motives, then we can step back and see the larger role of this bleak episode in the transition from the stories of the individual patriarchs to the concluding account of Joseph and his brothers. God appears immediately after Simeon and Levi ask Jacob their rhetorical question. He commands Jacob to build an altar (35:1). This foreshadows an important truth about defilement and its remedy, a truth that is given full expression on Mount Sinai. Humans cannot use moral and political agency to overcome the infection of sin. When we try to do so, we risk a catastrophic misanthropy. We war against sin, and because it is woven into the fabric of our humanity, the death and destruction of humanity become the solution. In contrast, the altar that God commands points us in a different direction. We can use the power of the sword to restrain sin, but the solution to its defiling, infecting power is to be found in ritual rather than political action. The future of the covenant must be protected by a code of holiness rather than a strategy of worldly action. Defilement must be brought before God for atonement, for only God's sanctity is powerful enough to cleanse without destroying.

The modern moral imagination no longer trusts in the power of atonement. Not surprisingly, therefore, recent centuries have seen a return to Simon and Levi's strategy. Beginning with the French Revolution, modern radical politics has sought to destroy the power of evil by eliminating those who carry its infecting power. If inequality oppresses humanity, then the sure route to justice is to execute the aristocrats or destroy capitalism or root out the oppressive conventions of bourgeois morality. We often think of these goals as progressive, and we excuse their excesses. It was once common to say that communists were just liberals in a hurry. But the Nazis diagnosed the disease of the human condition in the same way, differing from Russian revolutionaries only in substituting Jew for capitalist as the infecting source of defilement. In both cases, prisons were filled and mass graves dug—an outcome always looming when modern men and women pursue political cures to spiritual diseases.

35:2 Put away the foreign gods that are among you.

Jacob chastises his family for idolatry. Perhaps Rachel was transfixed by her father's household gods and kept them (→31:19). No explanation is given. But coming in the aftermath of the extended episode of revenge for the rape of Dinah, the accusation is significant. Simeon and Levi felt that something must be done to remedy the defilement of their sister, a defilement that threatened to overwhelm the entire clan. Yet all the while the household has been embroiled in spiritual harlotry! The brothers succeed in their plan, but the defilement remains. The earthly sword cannot reach to the roots of sin.

In the wake of Jacob's chastisement, the clan puts away their foreign gods, but only outwardly and not in the broad sense of purifying themselves of the corrupting defilement of worldly loves. The family spirals downward. Beloved Rachel dies in childbirth (35:17–18). The curse of Eve is doubly fulfilled as her labor pains are joined to death. Then, the theme of sexual defilement that triggered the story of Dinah's rape returns, this time within the clan itself: "Reuben went and lay with Bilhah his father's concubine" (35:22). This transgression does not lead to a richly developed episode, as did the rape of Dinah, yet the parallel is reinforced: just as Jacob kept silent when faced with news of Dinah's defilement, he does nothing when told of this transgression.

Thus, Genesis seems to be raising questions about patriarchal authority and the succession of the covenant. Ever since his wrestling match at the Jabbok ford, Jacob has become passive. He does not respond to the rape of Dinah. He tolerates idolatry. He does nothing about the defilement of his own bed. Against this background of passivity, and with the death of Isaac in view (35:29), the question of inheritance that dominated the narratives of Abraham, Isaac, and the young Jacob comes to the fore. Who will succeed Jacob? Who will receive the inheritance? Is it to be Simeon or Levi—who demonstrated their decisiveness in protecting the covenant from destruction by assimilation into the city of Shechem? Or shall it be Rueben—who seems to have signaled his decision to usurp Jacob's role as progenitor by sleeping with Billah, his father's concubine?

None of the obvious sons seem auspicious. Simeon and Levi have used the sacred sign of circumcision as a tool for political deceit, and they stand as symbols of destruction, not blessing. Reuben seems to have taken Jacob's own deceit of Isaac to the next stage, and not for the sake of the promise, but instead for worldly pleasure. More importantly, neither Abraham nor Isaac nor Jacob came to their inheritance by way of their natural powers. They were not chosen because they were stronger or more decisive or possessed the crucial power to reproduce. They received the promises because they were chosen by God. Thus, as Jacob joins Esau to bury his father, the question rings all the more loudly. Who will God chose as Jacob's successor?

The rest of Genesis provides the answer. No son will inherit the covenant in the way that Isaac inherited it from Abraham, and then Jacob from Isaac. The overall impression we receive from the many episodes in Jacob's life suggests why. Unlike Abraham and Isaac, Jacob has been supremely successful in expanding his clan. He has twelve sons, not two. Jacob has been fruitful in the flesh. But he has not guided his clan toward holiness of life. Jacob has not been fruitful in the spirit, a fact made evident by the bitterness and rivalry between his wives, the ill-conceived political strategy of Simeon and Levi, the persistent presence of foreign gods, and Reuben's usurpation of his concubine. Perhaps the problem is not with Jacob, but instead rests in the path of covenant inheritance. Perhaps the divine choice of one man needs to expand to the election of a nation. The stage is set for a shift in the divine plan. All the brothers will inherit the covenant. Instead of asking, "Who will inherit the covenant?" Genesis begins to ask a new question: "Who will find a way to overcome the debilitating, defiling effects of human sinfulness that threaten to destroy Israel and derail the future promised to Abraham?"

36:1 These are the descendants of Esau.

Like the genealogy of Ishmael, the verses devoted to the descendents of Esau foreshadow the fulfillment of the promise to Abraham: through him all the nations shall be blessed. To have children is to have a future, and the generations of Esau are a natural sign of the supernatural reality of deathless life with God. Neither Ishmael nor Esau is chosen. Both are progenitors of nations that will afflict the people of Israel. This is especially true for Esau, whose descendants include Israel's archenemies, the Amalekites, which certainly encourages an eschatological reading of the blessing promised to Abraham (→33:4). Nonetheless, neither Ishmael nor Esau disappears into the anonymity of the nations. They have genealogies in Genesis. They have futures that revolve around the chosen people.

37:1 Jacob settled. (NRSV)

The departure of Esau makes room for Jacob to settle into the land of the promise. His journey seems over. And yet it is not to be so. Jacob and his clan will have to pull up stakes and flee to Egypt in order to survive a seven-year famine. In this way, Jacob is truly a figure for the people of Israel. Their settlement is never permanent, their dynasties never enduring, their temples in Jerusalem never eternal.

Like the land to which Jacob returns and into which he settles, the church has received a promise that is real and enduring. Yet, at the same time, and like Jacob and the people of Israel, the church remains on the move—*semper reformanda*, always in need of reform, always to be refined by further travails. The church cherishes what she has been given, but she knows that God calls her forward to a perfection that will involve countless leave-takings, penances, and renunciations. The movement of the church into the future is not at odds with the permanence of her inheritance. Jacob settled. In his old age he "took his journey with all that he had" (46:1). In death he returned. Even in departure, the land of the promise retains a specific gravity.

37:2 These are the generations of Jacob. (AV)

Other than a side story about Judah and his daughter-in-law Tamar, the history of the family of Jacob is largely the story of Joseph. Yet he is not the next patriarch. The LORD is the God of Abraham, Isaac, and Jacob, not the original three plus Joseph. Instead of successor to Jacob, Joseph is one brother among twelve; nonetheless, the narrative focuses on him. He is the unwitting legatee for Israel, the representative, the one on whom the fate of the many depends (→30:25). Joseph is paradoxically the object of envy, the favored son whom the brothers wish to destroy—and whom they (unwittingly) seek out as their savior. They wish him dead, and yet he is the source of life for them. They hate Joseph and in so doing work against the divine plan for forming a holy people ("you shall not hate your brother"; Lev. 19:17), but their hating triggers a course of events that ensures their survival. Rejected by his brothers, Joseph carries the future of Jacob's clan as the shepherd carries the lamb on his shoulders.

The role of Joseph in the larger context of Genesis is signaled by the strange way in which his story is introduced. "These are the generations of Jacob," we read in the AV, but no long sequence of "begats" follows. Instead of the usual genealogical list, the text immediately launches into the story of Joseph. The RSV tries to mitigate the way in which the plain sense leaves us hanging by offering a translation that seems to better fit what follows: "This is the history of the family of Jacob." But this reading obscures the rather obvious textual signal. Genealogical lists regularly function as expressions of the forward thrust of time. A good, long list of descendants evokes the gift of time that stretches forward to the fulfillment of the promises. Here, however, the textual signal for a genealogy ends up pointing toward Joseph alone. It seems he will carry the future for Israel. As the story unfolds, what seems an odd textual anomaly turns out to make sense. What some modern critics think of as a poorly handled insertion by simpleminded editors—generations without a genealogy?—is actually an artful device for signaling an enlarged sense of what is necessary in order to secure the future of the covenant. Joseph does not serve this future by assuming the role of patriarch and taking a privileged place as the next person in a narrow line of succession. He begets a future for Israel by saving his clan from famine.

The shift from biological succession to an elaboration of roles within the community is decisive, and it reaches its most explicit form in the differentiated roles assigned by Jacob in his final blessings of his sons (→49:2). The shift indicates precisely what it means to say that the covenant calls us to walk according to the spirit rather than the flesh. Joseph serves the future of the covenant by virtue of his role as provider for others. This role is in no way at odds with the physical needs of his brothers. On the contrary, in order to play his role Joseph must have the grain of Egypt at his disposal. But the role differs dramatically from the way in which Jacob served the future of the covenant as progenitor, as the physical seed of the future. From Jacob's loins comes life. Not so Joseph. He has children, but they have no singular role for the future of the clan. Instead, Joseph is the one who can and does serve the needs of his brothers, and this role matters decisively for the future of the covenant. Jacob does what God commands in the garden: "be fruitful and multiply." Joseph does something new, something more. As the beloved son, he rescues the very brothers who wished him harm.

For Christian readers, Joseph's role as the source of life for his brothers begs for a christological interpretation. The basic features of the narrative suggest the theological structure of the story of Jesus's life. Just as Joseph is the beloved son of Jacob, hated by his own kin, so also does the beloved Son of God come "to his own home, and his people received him not" (John 1:11). Yet, just as the effort to destroy Joseph leads to the salvation of his family, so also does the suffering and death of Jesus end up securing salvation for the human family. But a christological reading does not depend simply on the broad outlines of the story. The cogency of a sustained christological reading depends upon the accumulation of details that establish typological parallels. Typological readings are more like webs woven from multiple lines of connection than single, heavy cables of direct inference.

To consider the details of a christological reading of Joseph all at once rather than piecemeal does more justice to the traditional impulse. Moreover, it is useful to give the typological reading in a single push. This allows for other, different sorts of comments to be developed in the course of the ensuing chapters that are otherwise obscured by the christological figure. A christological interpretation does not supersede or silence these other interpretations. There is a great deal to say about Joseph and his brothers that should not be mapped onto the life, death, and resurrection of Christ. But this diversity does not speak against a christological interpretation. Instead, it reminds us that the scriptures convey a plenitude of sense. The sacred text resists a single line of interpretation.

Joseph has problems with his brothers. He seems to be a youthful tattler, running to his father to report on the perhaps less-than-ideal behavior of his brothers as shepherds of their father's flocks (37:2). He is impolitic, telling his brothers about dreams that put him into a position of superiority (37:5–11). But the narrative is fairly clear. The main problem is that Israel (a telling use of the collective, honorific title that is weighted with the future) loves Joseph more than he loves the others (37:4). He is the beloved son, and this favored status produces envy in his brothers, an envy that reaches murderous intensity. It is in this general atmosphere of menace that the Joseph story of affliction begins. The brothers are out with the flocks, but Joseph remains behind with his father. Jacob then says, fatefully, "Come, I will send you to them" (37:13). Joseph obediently goes and, in going, enters fully and defenselessly into his brothers' world of deadly scheming and plotting.

It does not take sophisticated theological training or an overactive imagination to see the incarnation of the Son of God in the opening of Joseph's story. The Father sends his beloved Son into the world, and the Son takes on the vulnerability of human flesh precisely in order to seek us out as brothers.[2] Like the good shepherd of the gospel, Joseph is not set above his brothers in order to be exalted, but in order to serve them. "I am the good shepherd," teaches Jesus, "I know my own [sheep] and my own know me" (John 10:14). Sent to save the lost, the good shepherd will search and find them (Luke 15:4). Once found, he will not lord over them, but instead will call them brothers (Matt. 12:48–50). So, were someone to meet Jesus on the road from Galilee to Jerusalem and ask him, "Whom do you seek?" his answer would be the same as Joseph's urgent reply to the stranger he meets in the fields after being sent by his father: "I am seeking my brothers" (37:16).

Joseph finds his brothers. They receive him with malice rather than love. Although the eternal Son through whom all things were made "came to his own home," because of the sin that reigns among the children of Adam, "his own people

---

2. Thus Ambrose: "Joseph was sent by his father to his brothers, rather by that Father 'who has not spared his own Son but has delivered him to us all' (Rom. 8:32)" (*De Ioseph* 3.9 in FC 65.193).

received him not" (John 1:11). "They saw him afar off, and before he came near to them they conspired against him to kill him" (Gen. 37:18). The atmosphere of conspiracy facing Jesus in Jerusalem differs very little: "The chief priests and the elders of the people gathered in the palace of the high priest, who was Caiaphas, and took counsel together in order to arrest Jesus by stealth and kill him" (Matt. 26:3–4). But Reuben intervenes and forestalls immediate action, not unlike the voices in the high priest's palace who warn, "Not during the feast, lest there be a tumult among the people" (26:5). Reuben's reasoning also echoes in the account of Jesus's passion. "Shed no blood," he says (Gen. 37:22), echoing the prohibition given to Noah (9:6). The reasoning is recapitulated when the chief priests rebuff Pilate's attempt to return Jesus to them for judgment: "It is not lawful for us to put any man to death" (John 18:31).

Of course, unlike the incarnate Son who suffers death, Joseph does not die, and this seems an important break in the figure. But the break is not as great as it seems. In the first place, the empty, waterless pit into which Joseph is thrown evokes the larger biblical theme of "the pit," an image of death's imprisonment. In the canon as a whole, to go down into the pit serves as a metaphor for death, and to be saved by a merciful God delivers us from the pit. The image is repeated many times in the psalms and the prophets: "O LORD, thou hast brought up my soul from Sheol, restored me to life from among those gone down to the Pit" (Ps. 30:3). In Proverbs, the pit serves as a catchall image for the dead end of sin, which is death itself. The image is taken up in Revelation. Out of the bottomless pit emerge the woes (Rev. 9) and the beast (11:7) that afflict the earth. Into the bottomless pit go those who are not written in the book of life (17:8). Clearly, then, Joseph's temporary imprisonment in the pit evokes countless biblical echoes that lead us to think of death and the imprisonment of the soul in hell.

In addition to the prominent role of the pit as an image of death, Joseph's survival in his temporary imprisonment suggests a robustly trinitarian reading of Jesus's crucifixion. The incarnate Son suffers death: "He was cut off out of the land of the living" (Isa. 53:8). Yet, as the source of life itself, the second person of the Trinity is too powerful to be held by death: "He was not abandoned to Hades, nor did his flesh see corruption" (Acts 2:31). The crucified Son breaks the strong doors of death's dark prison: "I died, and behold I am alive for evermore, and I have the keys of Death and Hades" (Rev. 1:18). So, in an important sense, what seems like a break in the figure is in fact a confirmation. Joseph's temporary imprisonment parallels the Son of God's temporary imprisonment in the tomb of death. The eternal Son really does go down into the depths of death's dispersing power and annihilating nothingness—yet even there, like Joseph, he has a future in the love of his Father.

Here we see one of the ways in which typological reading does not ignore or efface the distinctive texture of Old Testament types. The figures are not proof-texts that serve as inert evidence for Christian claims. The clarity of the Joseph story on its own terms shines light on the mystery of Jesus's saving death. Consider the difficulty of understanding a basic creedal affirmation: the incarnate Son of God dies on the cross. If we turn to Joseph, then a line of reflection opens up. Even in the pit Joseph lives, and soon he is sold into slavery to passing Ishmaelites (Gen. 37:27–28). With this in mind, we can turn to the truth that, for our sakes, the incarnate Son sells himself into the thrall of the devil, so that, as the deathless power of life, he might taste death and drink to the final dregs the most bitter consequence of our common slavery to sin. Or to use the literal sense of Joseph's fate as a slave, we can say that, in death, the incarnate Son allows himself to be taken prisoner by the power of death, so that he can destroy its stronghold.

In these figures, the literal sense of Genesis drives the christological reading, not the other way around. Some interesting details give further illustration. In Joseph's initially ill-starred career in Egypt, he is accused of betraying his master's confidence, and he is thrown into the pit or prison once again. There, he interprets the dreams of two fellow prisoners, who, like the two prisoners crucified beside Jesus, have very different destinies: one for life and the other for death (Luke 23:39–43). Pharaoh's cupbearer is restored to his station in life, but he does not remember Joseph. Two years pass, and Pharaoh has anxious dreams that cannot be interpreted by his wise men. In this atmosphere of dread, the cupbearer recalls Joseph and commends him to Pharaoh. Restored to freedom, Joseph shaves and receives new clothes.

The movement is sudden and dramatic: from the depths of prison to a transformed face and new clothes. With this concrete image of Joseph refreshed and renewed, the reader can turn to St. Paul's eschatological vision of humanity disrobed and then reclothed in garments fit for the heavenly kingdom (2 Cor. 5:1–5). The accounts of the risen Christ have a similar structure. Like Joseph, Jesus comes out of prison, and like Joseph shaven and given new clothes, the risen Christ comes out of the prison of death not as a disembodied spirit but instead in a body purified and clothed in incorruption. Christ triumphs over death in the body of his flesh, which is renewed and reclothed rather than transcended and left behind. Thus the figure of Joseph raised by Pharaoh from the depths of prison clarifies a fundamental truth about God's promise of new life in Christ: eternal life will renew rather than cancel or leave behind our created nature.

A typological reading of Joseph as prefiguring Christ can yield still more fruit. Years pass between Joseph's release from prison and his saving engagement with his brothers. Here again, the literal sense of Genesis gives depth to a theological truth provided by the New Testament. Revelation commends patient endurance for those who believe in the risen Lord. The time of the final fulfillment of the promise has yet to come. Compare this announcement of eschatological delay with the strikingly elongated and complicated account of Joseph's reconciliation with his brothers. Joseph has the power of life. He controls the storehouses of Egypt. Yet he seems to create complications and delays and trips back and forth, all of which heighten the anguish of history. In the end, the delays seem to have no obvious purpose, bringing only grief to Joseph himself (→43:30). The reader easily falls into a sentiment that yearns for the concluding reconciliation. "Please," we urge Joseph, "reveal your true identity to your brothers. Save yourself and your kin from the anguish of delay!" This yearning evokes the ending of Revelation: "Come, Lord Jesus!"

37:9 I have dreamed another dream; and behold, the sun, the moon, and eleven stars were bowing down to me.

Joseph's first dream portrays his preeminence over his brothers, but with an image that strikes an odd note. Although Jacob and his clan tend sheep, Joseph dreams of wheat fields. The second dream, however, is odder still. Joseph pictures the heavenly bodies bowing down before him. Jacob and his dead mother, Rachel, have been added to the eleven brothers as his supplicants. Not only does this reverse the commandment to honor father and mother, but the entire image cuts against the larger biblical vision of the role of the heavens. The sun and the stars do not pay homage to any mortal; rather, they "declare [the] righteousness" of God (Ps. 50:6) and "praise [his] wonders" (89:5). "The heavens are telling the glory of God; and the firmament proclaims his handiwork" (19:1). They do not trumpet Joseph's glory or his accomplishments. In another psalm we read, "Praise him, sun and moon, praise him, all you shining stars!" (148:3). The referent is clear. The heavens are to praise the LORD, not Joseph.

On its face, the dream cannot be true. Joseph is a man, and it is vainglorious for him to imagine that he can play the divine role. Perhaps, then, the dream should be read as signaling a deep flaw in Joseph. The young lad is not a perfect child. He is full of himself and needs to be brought down a notch. If we adopt this reading, then Joseph's immediate rebuke by Jacob makes good sense (37:10). Moreover, if we assume that Joseph has a flawed personality, then the next scene is more easily understood. Jacob calls Joseph and sends him to find his brothers at Shechem (37:12–14). It hardly seems a wise mission for a loving father to give to his favorite son. Jacob must know that Joseph is resented by his brothers. Moreover, the place he sends him, Shechem, is hardly auspicious. It not only evokes memories of the deadly ire of Simeon and Levi, but it will also be the place where the kingdom of David will be divided (1 Kgs. 12:1). Perhaps the patriarch feels that Joseph needs to be humbled by his brothers. The subsequent events unfold accordingly. Joseph is enslaved and imprisoned. God himself gives Joseph trials by which to purify his character.

Of course, a christological reading of Joseph takes the dreams at face value. The seemingly idolatrous image of the heavens bowing down before Joseph becomes evidence that the entire sweep of the Joseph story is about something more than the events narrated. Furthermore, it is not clear that the dreams are fulfilled in the subsequent encounters with his brothers (→42:8). The dreams are certainly not fulfilled when Jacob is reunited with Joseph. He never bows down before his son. This lack of fulfillment encourages us to say that the dreams are not about Joseph son of Jacob, but instead about Joseph, the figure of Christ. The dreams are not fulfilled until the Messiah comes. "Who is He," asks Ambrose, "before whom parents and brothers bowed to the ground but Jesus Christ?" (*De Ioseph* 3.8 in FC 65.192). The Son of God incarnate is exalted above all things, and the heavens rightly bend their knee and proclaim his glory (Phil. 2:9–11).

37:23 Coat of many colours. (AV)

The obscure Hebrew is translated by the Septuagint as *poikilos* ("spotted, varied"), which the tradition in the West has assumed refers to a multicolored fabric. Recent translations opt for alternatives based on speculative philology ("long robe with sleeves" in the RSV). This decision to substitute uncertain alternatives for traditional translations is a wonderful example of the all-too-common modern penchant for adopting readings that have little to recommend them other than the opportunity to break with the past. After all, a new translation cannot claim to be a new translation unless it offers new translations.

37:27 Come, let us sell him to the Ishmaelites.

There is nothing straightforward about Joseph's fate. At first his brothers coalesce into a unified reprise of the Cain and Abel episode: they conspire to kill their brother (37:18). But very quickly they fall into debate about what to do. Reuben evokes the covenant with Noah ("shed no blood") and tries to delay the murderous plan. After putting Joseph into the pit, the brothers then dillydally, taking time to eat. Ishmaelites approach, and Judah formulates an alternative plan. Seeing, perhaps, the senselessness of murder, he asks, "What profit is it if we slay our brother and conceal his blood?" (37:26). His reasoning is sensible. Wouldn't it be better to be rid of Joseph by selling him into slavery rather than for the brothers to pollute themselves with the blood of their own brother? But suddenly Midianites traders appear, and they, not Joseph's brothers, end up selling Joseph to the Ishmaelites. The brothers seem unaware. Only after they finish their meal and go back to the pit do they discover that Joseph is gone.

Some readers iron out the confusing action by imagining a cooperative and elaborate sequence of exchanges, but without much success. Historical critics handle this confusing, almost comic scene of plans made, unmade, remade, and then foiled by recourse to distinctions between underlying textual traditions. "According to one (J)," writes von Rad, "Joseph was sold by his brothers to the Ishmaelites; according to the other (E), Joseph was sold from the cistern in an unguarded moment by the Midianites" (1972: 353). But this observation about different textual traditions deepens rather than explains the puzzle. Are we to imagine that the scribes and temple elites responsible for the final form of Genesis lived in an incense-induced stupor, mindlessly stitching together different traditions? It seems an implausible assumption, and instead we should consider the possibility that this episode deliberately conveys something about the self-defeating nature of human sin. The brothers cannot sustain their murderous consensus. Delays brought by both indecision and the allure of a good meal gives time for complications to emerge. The greed of others (the Midianites) ends up thwarting both Reuben's and Judah's plans. In the end, the brothers, who at first seemed so clearminded in their wicked plan to kill Joseph, are entirely confused about what has happened to him. They are bumbling participants in an evil sequence of events.

Evil is the privation of the good, which in its metaphysical form is a diminishment of reality. Therefore, evil cannot achieve lasting form in a coherent, workable plan. This is why there is always something darkly, pathetically comic about wickedness: the Unabomber in his Montana cabin penning long diatribes, Hitler dreaming of the glory of the Reich in his Berlin bunker in the final weeks of the war, the propaganda machine of the old Soviet empire churning out slogans for the workers. Given the pointless death and suffering caused, the images rightly horrify—but they also amuse in their surreal absurdity. Thus, a deep fact about evil—its bumbling, comical, and self-defeating character—is evoked by the ragged edges found in the final form of the story of Joseph's fate at Shechem.

38:6 Her name was Tamar.

As Joseph goes into slavery, his older brother Judah also leaves Jacob's household. He finds a wife, Shua, from among the Canaanites, and he has three sons. Solicitous for the future of his line, Judah arranges for his eldest son to be married to Tamar. But the LORD does not look with favor on Judah's sons, perhaps because Judah has separated from the clan and is seeking his own future without his brothers.[3] Tamar's husband, Judah's eldest son, dies. Custom requires that the next oldest son fulfill the conjugal duties of his dead brother. Therefore, Judah gives Onan to Tamar, but he is struck dead by the LORD as well. This leaves Judah with only one son, Shelah, the youngest. He anxiously withholds Shelah from Tamar on the pretext that he is too young. The same anxiety leads him to encourage Tamar to return to her father's house, where she is to wait for the younger son to come of age. This woman seems to have put a curse on his house, and Judah worries that his line will come to an end. Better to give up on future grandchildren than to risk the only child he has left.

Tamar's removal from Judah's household and then the death of Judah's wife trigger a course of events that lead the father to impregnate his daughter-in-law.

---

3. For an excellent discussion of Gen. 38 that focuses on Judah's ill-fated departure from the clan and his call to repentance by way of Tamar's scheme, see Kass 2003: 526–38.

In a scene true to the spirit of Jacob, Tamar uses a disguise in order to trick Judah into unwittingly blessing her with pregnancy, a state of fruitfulness that vindicates her role as his eldest son's wife. She cleverly convinces Judah to leave his signet, chord, and staff as signs of his identity in order to protect her against charges of immorality when her pregnancy becomes obvious. The contrast is striking. Joseph's brothers present a false sign of Joseph's death to Jacob, the multicolored cloak that they have deliberately stained with animal blood. By contrast, when called to account, Tamar is able to present the true signs of life to Judah. "My pregnancy," these signs tell Judah, "is from your seed." Instead of death falsely signified, Tamar's sign saves herself and her child. When she gives birth to twins, she secures the future of life for Judah's household.

The significance of this side story as an interruption of the dominant story of Joseph is not obvious at first glance, and modern critics too easily use the device of source criticism to simply dismiss the need for any accounting of its role in the larger narrative. Once one establishes that it is from such-and-such source, then one can say that the later editors had to find a place for it, and they plopped it down willy-nilly in Gen. 38. Von Rad provides a classic example. "Every attentive reader," he writes with serene confidence, "can see that the story of Judah and Tamar has no connection at all with the strictly organized Joseph story at whose beginning it is now inserted. This compact narrative requires for its interpretation none of the other Patriarchal narratives" (1972: 356–57). This quick and confident rejection of interpretive responsibility is one of the ways in which modern biblical study manifests a disturbing exegetical negligence.

In fact, attentive readers can see a connection. The singular focus of the story of Tamar in Gen. 38 is childbearing, and this emphasis on fruitfulness foreshadows the role of Joseph in relation to his brothers. The side story begins well enough. Judah sires three sons. It seems, in other words, that Judah and his brothers were right. They do not need Joseph. Children represent the future, and Judah's initial success seems to secure a future. Yet what seems is not so. Judah's two older sons are struck dead, the first for no stated reason other than being "wicked in the sight of the LORD." Onan, the second, is struck dead because he is tellingly reluctant to contribute to a future that he cannot possess on his own terms. "But Onan knew that the offspring would not be his," we read, "so when he went in to his brother's wife he spilled the semen on the ground, lest he should give offspring to his brother" (38:9). Onan is too much a son in the image of his father. Onan is not willing to give over his seed of the future to Tamar and his dead brother, just as Judah and his brothers were not willing to give over the future of Jacob's inheritance to the care of Joseph.

The father recapitulates the sin of the son. Onan's death causes Judah to withhold his youngest son, which is simply a paternal form of Onan's withholding of his sperm from Tamar. If we anticipate a future episode in the story of Joseph and his brothers, we can say that Judah prefigures Jacob, who withholds Benjamin and is willing to endure famine rather than risking the death of his youngest son

(→42:28). Judah would rather endure a famine of childbearing than risk the complete death of his line. However, in a way that prefigures Jacob once again, the death of Judah's wife forces the issue. Without a mate, Judah has no vehicle for reproduction. The future is blocked. The famine of childbearing threatens to kill the family name. The sheer necessity of sexual desire drives Judah into the arms of Tamar, just as the specter of death by famine finally overwhelms Jacob and forces him to allow his sons to take Benjamin to Egypt (→43:1).

Still further parallels suggest a close connection between Gen. 38 and the larger story of Joseph and his brothers. Like Joseph, who disguises his identity when his brothers come seeking some relief from the threat of famine, Tamar disguises herself when Judah seeks relief from his sexual famine. By virtue of the disguise, what seems the simple satisfaction of sexual hunger for Judah is, in fact, the redemption of his future. Tamar's cleverness and intrinsic fertility, like Joseph's talent as dream interpreter and agricultural czar in Egypt, delivers Judah from the famine of children in his house. Judah recognizes this fact when he proclaims, "She is more righteous than I, inasmuch as I did not give her my son Shelah" (38:26). The reason for Tamar's superior righteousness points directly to the central issue in the story: the question of who shall carry forward the future of Jacob's clan. Against Judah's (and Onan's) intentions, Tamar takes responsibility for the future, just as Joseph will.

39:2 He became a successful man.

Abraham succeeds in finding beneficent (and unlikely) patrons. Pharaoh and Abimelech load him up with riches, and Melchizedek appears out of nowhere to offer a blessing. Clever Jacob gains a large flock from Laban by way of creative, magical husbandry. But of all the characters in Genesis, Joseph is the one who seems born for success. Not even the schemes of his brothers can keep him down. He rises to prominence as chief slave in the household of Potiphar, captain of Pharaoh's guard. But this success seems a false start, for it comes to naught in the lust-inspired scheming and deceit by Potiphar's wife. What seems like success ends with Joseph in the pit once again.

Although this story of failed seduction and vindictive betrayal concerns the fate of Joseph, like the story of Tamar, a reader can be forgiven for being puzzled. The digression is detailed and dramatic, but how does it fit with the larger story of Joseph's betrayal by his brothers, followed by his reconciliation with them and his exercise of power to save them? Of course, the story might not fit in any direct way. We should not discount the possibility that the Bible likes a good story for its own sake. However, a good story can be a good story—and something more.

In the broadest outlines, handsome, successful Joseph attracts the desires of Potiphar's wife. She wants a handsome man with a good portfolio. She is the adulteress who loves the goods of this world rather than righteousness. Because of the christological role that Christian readers give Joseph, there is a strong impulse to see him as the perfectly virtuous, Christlike man.[4] The episode with Potiphar's wife would seem an obvious support. It establishes that Joseph is like Jesus: a righteous man who must endure unjust persecutions. This impulse is not unique to Christian readers. In 1 Maccabees 2:51–53, for example, Joseph's trial of temptation is one of the great deeds of old, one equated with Abraham's trial on Mount Moriah. But Joseph is not so obviously virtuous in other episodes. With his ambitious dreams, he seems a vain young man rather than the paragon of virtue. Later, Joseph dresses like an Egyptian and marries an Egyptian, more the model of faithless assimilation than holy virtue. For this reason, rabbinic readers looked for clues in the story of his temptation, hints that Joseph was less than perfect. In commenting on Gen. 39:6, Rashi supposes that Joseph is now handsome because he vainly curls his hair. The image seems fanciful, but that Genesis highlights Joseph's beauty is not a good sign. David was a good-looker, and he ends up in bed with another man's wife. In contrast, Jesus is described as many good things, but never handsome. Rashi also reports (in comments on 39:11) the older opinion that Joseph actually entered the empty house with the intention of sleeping with Potiphar's wife and is saved from the sin of adultery only by the sudden, miraculous appearance of his father's image.

Joseph's role is unequivocal. He becomes the indispensable savior of Jacob's clan. But whether or not we adopt Rashi's suggestions, we should see that Joseph's character is much less clear in the narrative than his role. For this reason, we should avoid projecting moral and spiritual perfection onto Joseph. We should read his seduction, refusal, and subsequent bad fortune as telling us something about the worldly fate of those chosen by God, instead of as a handbook for virtue. "In the world you will have tribulation," Jesus warns his disciples (John 16:33). As Joseph's story shows, however, the tribulation will end, and "your sorrow will turn to joy" (16:20). Joseph's seduction sends him on the downward path into the pit once again, and this sets the stage for his even more dramatic restoration to favor as Pharaoh's right-hand man.

40:8 Tell them to me, I pray you.

Joseph is handsome, and he is good with accounts, as his success in running Potiphar's house suggests. Moreover, he is a born leader. The captain of the prison guard puts him in charge. Yet his otherworldly powers as an interpreter of dreams rather than his worldly talents spring him from prison and catapult him to his

4. Ambrose sees him as "a mirror of purity" who can teach us virtue of chastity (*De Ioseph* 1.2 in FC 65.189), and when he gets to the episode of seduction, Ambrose emphatically rejects any suggestions of complicity on the part of Joseph: "He is absolved by the testimony of scripture" (*De Ioseph* 5.24 in FC 65.205).

role as de facto ruler over all Egypt. But the path forward is narrow and circuitous. Joseph's success as a seer leads to no immediate benefit. Two prisoners have dreams that need interpretation, and Joseph offers to do so with a bold claim to interpret on behalf of God—another instance where Joseph seems dangerously vain, even to the point of proclaiming himself godlike (→45:13). He interprets his prisoners' dreams, with sorrowful accuracy for the one and joyful accuracy for the other. Pharaoh's former baker will be executed in three days, and in three days the former butler will be restored to his position of honor at Pharaoh's side. Yet, once restored, the butler forgets about Joseph, and his tribulations as an unjustly imprisoned man continue.

The dream interpretations in prison interact with the equally long and seemingly unnecessary digression into Joseph's experiences in Potiphar's household. With Potiphar, Joseph demonstrates his capacity to run a large, complex household. In the prison, he demonstrates his favored status as a vehicle for divinely inspired (and therefore accurate) interpretations of dreams. Both qualities play a role in his ultimate success and the assumption of the power in Egypt, a role that will be necessary to save his brothers. As the chosen instrument of redemption, Joseph has the capacity to rightfully and justly command human affairs. But when all is said and done, Joseph remains in prison, a forgotten man. The digressions into the details of Joseph's effectiveness as Potiphar's servant and his role in prison as an astute interpreter of dreams seem to tell us that what is wanted is not simply a man with ample worldly talents, nor a seer with unique insights into the ways of God's providence. He must be raised from prison. He cannot spring himself. Like Abraham, Isaac, and Jacob, he must be chosen for his role. He is not a self-made man.

41:14 Pharaoh sent and called Joseph.

A crisis of dreams and interpretation in Pharaoh's household triggers the butler's memory, and suddenly Joseph is taken from prison and restored to life (on the significance of shaving and new clothes, →37:2). Unlike the butler, Pharaoh does not wait for events to prove the accuracy of Joseph's interpretation of his dreams. Instead, in what can seem only precipitous and divinely foreordained, Pharaoh immediately assents to Joseph's interpretation. And just as quickly, Pharaoh draws the unexpected link between his two talents. Pharaoh's dream foretells a dire famine that will require first-rate leadership. And who better to lead them than Joseph, the man who can interpret dreams? After all, in him the Spirit of God seems to reside (41:38–39). Events prove Joseph right about Pharaoh's dreams—and prove Pharaoh perceptive in his choice of Joseph as his all-powerful grand vizier. Famine comes, and Joseph succeeds in laying up enough stores for survival, so much so that Egypt becomes the storehouse for the whole world. Pharaoh is greatly enriched as a result of Joseph's talent as both dream interpreter and national agricultural administrator (→47:21).

41:45 Pharaoh called Joseph's name Zaphenath-paneah; and he gave him
in marriage Asenath, the daughter of Potiphera priest of On.

Joseph is raised out of prison and put in charge of all Egypt. But at what price?
He receives the linen clothes of Pharaoh's court, a new name, and a wife from
the priestly caste of Egypt.[5] God makes Joseph fruitful, as the name he gives to
one newborn son indicates (Ephraim: "to be fruitful"). Yet the cost of Joseph's
success seems to be renunciation of the ways of his father, as his other son's name
suggests (Manasseh: "making to forget"). Clearly, readers are meant to confront
the ambiguity of Joseph's success. Unlike the incarnate Son of God who can be
completely loyal to his divinity while completely loyal to his humanity, Joseph
is an ordinary man. He cannot be both son of Jacob and what amounts to being
the adopted son of Pharaoh. One of the identities must give way to the other. It
seems that the Egyptian side becomes supreme.[6]

41:57 All the earth came to Egypt to Joseph to buy grain.

Joseph's ascent from the solitary depths of prison to the role of Egyptian potentate in charge of the food supply during a famine places him at the center of
human life. With his great storehouse of grain, Joseph seems ready to fulfill the
promise to Abraham that his children shall be a blessing to all the nations. Yet the
Bible does not end here! And the way it continues is telling. The worldwide stage
is set: everybody needs food. But 42:1 dramatically reduces the narrative focus to
Jacob and his sons. From this point forward, aside from a brief return to the global
significance of Joseph's overflowing storehouses (→47:21), the Genesis narrative
stays focused on the narrow particularity of Jacob's clan. The accordion of the biblical scope of divine concern has opened to its maximum breadth for a moment,
only to compress immediately to the concentrated point of divine invasion begun
in Abraham. Joseph is poised to feed the whole world, but it is more important
for the future of God's plan for creation that Jacob's clan be fed bread so that it
can survive to receive the commandments of God. This is the political form of
the metaphysical concentration of the divine plan: the sanctification of the elect
few matters more than feeding the worldwide many. Famine relief allows for the

---

5. *Targum Pseudo-Jonathan* is so worried about Joseph's apparent fall into Egyptian assimilation
that it interpolates a circuitous life story for his new wife, making her into a child born to Dinah and
Shechem and then reared by the wife of an Egyptian priest (Maher 1992: 138). The same targum
finds a way to restore a beard to clean-shaven Joseph. His brothers fail to recognize him not because
he has been so thoroughly Egyptianized (which would include a clean-shaven face), but because
the now-mature Joseph has a beard (1992: 139). This interpolation draws Joseph back into the
Israelite orbit, while the canonical text has him moving in the other direction.

6. I am indebted to Kass's astute observations (2003: 550–72) about the ways in which Joseph
adopts an Egyptian identity.

continuation of life, an unequivocal but finite good. However, the consummation of the divine plan in and through the chosen particularity of Israel transforms life and gives it the supernatural possibility of fellowship with God.

42:3 Ten of Joseph's brothers went down to buy grain in Egypt.

From the call of Abraham forward, the main thrust of Genesis has been the problem of how the covenant will secure a reliable future. Abraham and Isaac confront the problem of infertility. Jacob is engaged in a potentially deadly rivalry with Esau and then endures an exile in Laban's household before returning home. Yet, as Jacob's life story evolves, the focus shifts. Unlike Abraham and Isaac, Jacob does not need to struggle with infertility. Instead, the problem he faces takes shape as the difficulty of achieving an enduring communal form of life. As the episode of Dinah's rape suggests (→34:1), as well as the much briefer references to family idolatry and Rueben's usurpation of Jacob's concubine (→35:2), the primary issue is clan survival rather than inheritance. The narrative turns toward the problem of communal continuity rather than reproduction. In Joseph's story, this problem is dramatized by the threat of famine and the need for grain. The clan needs bread in order to survive. But as the story unfolds, it is clear that the problems of communal survival are much more complex. A well-fed clan is not necessarily a unified clan, one capable of avoiding deadly, fragmenting fraternal violence.

The brothers are sent by Jacob because of the threat posed by the famine. Just as the future of the covenant requires new life in children, so also must it sustain life with grain. But it is telling that "ten of Joseph's brothers" go down to Egypt rather than "ten of Jacob's sons." The image of the childless Abraham lamenting his lack of an heir recedes into the background. We no longer face the problem of a blind old father groping to discern whether he can trust the son whose hairy skin feels like Esau but who sounds like Jacob. The patriarchal father-to-son problem of the future that dominates Gen. 12–27 is behind us. Now the Israelite brother-to-brother problem comes to the fore: How can the pollution of sin be overcome without the destruction of the clan? How can Joseph avoid using his power to take revenge? How can the shamed brothers stand with Joseph rather than remain perpetually prostrated in their guilt?

These questions can be expressed in the vocabulary of the Pentateuch taken as a whole. Viewed retrospectively and negatively, the story of Joseph and his brothers is under the shadow of Cain. Will fraternal enmity end in death, or will the band of brothers affirm the vocation of the covenant? Will they reverse the direction of Cain's choice and become their brother's keeper? Viewed prospectively and positively, the story looks toward the code of communal holiness outlined in Leviticus: "You shall not hate your brother in your heart, but you shall reason with your neighbor, lest you bear sin because of him. You shall not take vengeance or bear any grudge against the sons of your own people, but you shall love your neighbor as yourself" (19:17–18). To use the language of the altar, Joseph and his brothers present readers with the problem of atonement, which is one reason why the Christian reader finds christological parallels in the Joseph story so irresistible.

The need to overcome the taint of sin by way of a love that seeks reconciliation and creates unity is the obvious theme of the story of Joseph and his brothers. But there is a subtle, secondary theme as well, one that also has to do with communal flourishing. Joseph's new role as Pharaoh's right-hand man suggests the problem of assimilation, a problem that was also prominent in the rape of Dinah. Shechem represented the threat of absorption into the cultures of powerful neighbors. Now the threat has migrated into the clan. Joseph is crucial for the future of Israel, but he consistently appears aloof and superior in his chariot. He seems a clean-shaven Egyptian figure with an Egyptian wife. His success will save Jacob's clan, but the power to sustain their lives seems to have been bought at the price of covenant forgetfulness. Here again Leviticus provides the intracanonical agenda: "Every one of you shall revere his mother and his father, and you shall keep my sabbaths: I am the LORD your God. Do not turn to idols or make for yourselves molten gods" (19:3–4). Does Joseph leave the ways of his father in order to become Pharaoh's adopted son? Unlike Daniel, a later dream interpreter whom the Bible champions for his courageous loyalty to the ways of his forefathers, Joseph seems to slide easily into the pagan culture of Egypt. As the drama unfolds, it is telling that Judah, not Joseph, will make the decisive offer to stand as a substitute to bear the punishment of another.

Viewed in this way, the entire story of Joseph suggests the problem that gives pathos to Esther. What is necessary for communal survival: a life of strict faithfulness, or a flexibility that enables the leaders of Israel to attain worldly power? This problem is not made explicit in Genesis. But it is not far from the surface, especially since faithful readers of Genesis know that the good things that Joseph provides for Jacob and his clan in Egypt will turn into slavery and the threat of genocide in future generations. Furthermore, unlike the explicit problem of intracommunal conflict, the Joseph story provides no clear answers to the latent, unspoken problem of how to properly use foreign, worldly powers for the sake of the future of the covenant. But of this ambiguity and reticence one can hardly complain. No obvious formula is forthcoming from the rest of the Old Testament. Esther and Daniel coexist in the canon. Nor does the New Testament speak in one voice. The book of Revelation depicts a final separation of worldly and heavenly loyalties, but the impulse to read this as a warrant for separating from the world is counteracted by Rom. 13:1–7 ("let every person be subject to the governing authorities") and 1 Pet. 2:13–14 ("be subject for the Lord's sake to every human institution").

42:8 Joseph knew his brothers, but they did not know him.

Our commonsense observations about the way in which weakness, vulnerability, and power influence our self-presentation give the story of Joseph and his brothers part of its pathos. Joseph has all the cards, and his brothers have every reason to fear him. Not only is he a powerful overlord, but also he is the brother whom they have wronged. If they were to discover his true identity, then surely they would fear revenge. It is easy to imagine that this fear motivates Joseph's efforts to disguise his true identity. If they knew, they might beg for mercy out of desperation. They might be motivated to make shameless appeals to whatever feelings they imagine Joseph having for their father. Therefore, if Joseph (and the readers) are to have any confidence that the actions of his brothers are sincere, then his brothers must remain ignorant of Joseph's true identity, which is precisely the way the story unfolds. If they don't know, then he can observe them rather than be subjected to their efforts to renew and recover their fraternal roles.

It has long been a platitude that ancient men and women had a different sense of self than modern men and women. The ancient sense of self, we are often told in the broad strokes of our freshman Western civilization classes, is much more external and communal, while the modern is more introspective and individual. The literary device of hidden identity in the story of Joseph and his brothers suggests that such easy dichotomies are, at best, only half true. The clear narrative purpose of Joseph's hidden identity is to create a situation in which he can observe his brothers and their actions with confidence that they are not disguising what they would otherwise say and do. There is something about his brothers that Joseph wants to flush out. He wants to know their deepest attitudes toward brotherhood.

Yet, as we shall see, Joseph himself is an unsteady character in the drama. So perhaps it is best to put the point in terms of literary structure and editorial contrivance. Genesis wants to expose what the brothers are really thinking and what they really care about. For this reason, Joseph hides in order to expose. The brothers broke the bonds of the clan when they threw Joseph into the pit. They envied and hated him, even to the point of sacrificing him. Reconciliation with Joseph will turn on his recognition that they now have a new attitude toward the clan, one based on the love of the brother, even to the point of self-sacrifice. In other words, this ancient text gives an account of an extended trial, an elaborate, multistage back-and-forth designed to strip away opportunities for insincere manipulation and expose the true sentiments of the protagonists. Genesis wants to get to the bottom of fraternal conflict.

But the distinction between sincere and insincere is too crude. The brothers are, of course, sincerely obsequious to the man they see as an Egyptian overlord. They bow before him as they ask for grain, seeming to fulfill his dream of the bowing sheaves of wheat: We read that "Joseph remembered the dreams which he had dreamed of them" (42:9), but we do not know what Joseph thought while he was remembering. Readers should not assume fulfillment. The brothers think that they are bowing to a powerful man, and doubtless they are doing so out of a calculated conformity to convention, rather than out of any heartfelt acceptance of his superiority as a powerful Egyptian. But more importantly, they are certainly not bowing down to Joseph *as* Joseph. They never do so, which must force us to look back on the original dreams as highly equivocal rather than as straightforward prophecy (→37:9).

42:9 You are spies.

Joseph takes the first step toward developing a complicated and multistage test of his brothers. With all the menace of powerful rulers who can dictate life and death, he accuses them of being spies. This is the crucial narrative turn, and it raises an obvious question. Why doesn't Joseph just reveal himself to his brothers? Why does he accuse them and set in motion a sequence of events that seems to make everyone suffer? Jacob will anguish over Benjamin. The brothers will be afflicted by fear and anxiety. Even Joseph himself ends up weeping. The answers turn on the problem of reconciliation.

Joseph cannot simply embrace his brothers, because he has gone a long way toward losing his identity as Joseph son of Jacob (→41:45). In the dialogue that follows, for example, Joseph swears a number of times "by the life of Pharaoh." Perhaps the phrase is meant only to reinforce our sense that Joseph is disingenuously playing the role of an Egyptian, all in order to keep his brothers in the dark. But we can also wonder if the expressions are not sincere. After all, the brothers have failed to recognize him, and perhaps for good reason. Has Joseph become so assimilated, so comfortable in his new role, that even his brothers don't know him? Has the new name that Pharaoh bestowed on him taken over his psyche? If so, then the sudden appearance of his brothers may have shocked the complaisant, forgetful Joseph. Read this way, the claim that they are spies is not a calculated ruse. Instead, he blurts out what seems a very improbable accusation: "You are spies, you have come to see the weakness of the land" (42:9). It is a self-protective reaction. Joseph needs to buy time for himself, so that he can recover from the initial shock and decide what he wants to do about the sudden appearance of his brothers.

The narrative (like life itself) does not dictate a single interpretation of motive. The rash accusation may stem from Joseph seeing his bowing brothers and recognizing that they offer an unsatisfying, merely outward fulfillment of his dream of fraternal obeisance. Joseph has been an Egyptian potentate for long enough to know how people react to those who have the power of life and death. "They're bowing, it's true," we might imagine Joseph saying to himself, "but they're doing so simply because I'm powerful and they want grain. Their words and actions tell me nothing about their real attitude toward me. Would they bow to me if they knew I was Joseph, the brother they were ready to kill?" With these thoughts in mind we can easily imagine Joseph hatching a plan. "I'll put them in a difficult situation," he might be thinking, "and then I can expose their true sentiments."[7]

This line of interpretation is reinforced by Joseph immediately conjuring up an ordeal to try his brothers. "By this you shall be tested" (42:15), he says to the ten brothers who have come to him. "Send one of you and let him bring your brother, while you [plural] remain in prison" (42:16). Yet, a reading that emphasizes Joseph's shock and inner uncertainty is also reinforced at this point. The initial form of the test seems poorly conceived, more an act of retribution than an effective test. To keep nine and send back one tests only a single individual rather than the brothers as a family. Joseph needs to be reconciled with all his brothers, not a single brother who happens to be selfless.

After further reflection, Joseph revises the test. He keeps just one brother, Simeon, in prison, while sending the others home to bring back Benjamin. We can imagine him saying to himself, "I know what they did to me to satisfy their own desires when I was vulnerable. Now let's see what they'll do to Simeon, whom I now hold hostage. Do they care for him so little that they will sacrifice him to save themselves? Their behavior will tell me what their true attitude would be toward me, if they had somehow discovered me when I was a slave and in prison rather than as powerful prince!"

Finally, the test that Joseph designs begins to wind its way to success. The brothers seem to come to a new awareness of their situation. When the fate of the vulnerable single brother in prison becomes clear, the rest of the brothers draw a link between the trial they now face and what they did to Joseph years ago in Shechem. They see clearly. When Joseph was in the pit, they sacrificed him to satisfy themselves. Now, with Simeon imprisoned by a haughty, dangerous, and seemingly fickle Egyptian potentate, they find themselves in a similar situation. The easiest thing to do would be to depart and never return. The obvious parallels provoke a painful moment of self-knowledge. "Then they said to each other," the narrative tells us, "in truth we are guilty concerning our brother, in that we saw the distress of his soul, when he besought us, and we would not listen; therefore is this distress come upon us" (42:21).

This moment, however, is an inadequate basis for reconciliation. Rueben immediately follows with a rebuke that evokes once again a spirit of division among the brothers: "Did I not tell you not to sin against the lad? But you would not listen. So now there comes a reckoning for his blood" (42:22). Joseph is portrayed as turning away and weeping after overhearing this exchange. But why? Perhaps he fears that he sees his brothers as they truly are. They are expressing regret, true enough, but they only fear the consequences for themselves. Not surprisingly they seem ready to set upon each other in bitter recrimination. Does Joseph cry,

---

7. This is the way in which Jubilees 42:25 reads Joseph's actions: "Joseph devised a plan whereby he might learn their thoughts as to whether thoughts of peace prevailed among them" (quoted from Kugel 1998: 462).

therefore, because he fears that his brothers enduring selfishness will cause them to fail the test? Surely this is a plausible reading, but we need to look again and see another thread intertwined. When his brothers came before Joseph to ask for grain, what did he see if not the distress of their souls, a fear about the future that was in his own soul when he lay in the pit? So we can imagine Joseph asking himself, "When they came to me, did I listen with sympathy and a desire to restore the brotherhood? Was my accusation that they are spies really any different than Reuben's accusing words to the other brothers?" Perhaps, then, Joseph cries because his brothers serve as a mirror. They reflect back to Joseph his own bitter feelings of recrimination, feelings that hover on the edge of doing to his brothers as they once did to him. After all, his first plan was to throw all but one into prison, a reenactment of their decision to throw him into the pit ($\rightarrow$37:27).

42:28 Their hearts failed them.

Joseph commands his servants to secretly put the money the brothers have paid for the grain back into their grain sacks. The narrative gives no explanation of Joseph's motive. Does he want to atone for the harsh trial he is putting them through, or does he want to demoralize his brothers still further? Whatever the intent, the effect is clear. The presence of the returned money heightens anxiety: "What is this that God has done to us?" the brothers ask (42:28). Perhaps they are worried that their father, himself a man of deception, will think that they have stolen the grain, a conclusion that will hardly make him confident when they explain why Simeon is not with them. "And why should he trust us?" they might ask themselves. "We have already deceived him about the fate of Joseph."

The brothers are correct: "Those who plow iniquity and sow trouble reap the same" (Job 4:8). An atmosphere of distrust characterizes their return. Jacob does not dispute the truth of their story, but he withholds Benjamin, and therefore the brothers cannot return to save Simeon. The trial of Joseph and his brothers seems doomed to fail. Jacob the father ends up playing the role of Judah the father ($\rightarrow$38:6). Just as Judah withheld his youngest son from Tamar, now Jacob is withholding Benjamin. Judah gave up hope in children. Faced with the death of his two older sons, he was unwilling to risk the few joys of life that he had left. Jacob has the same reaction. He has no hope that Simeon can be restored to him. God's promises mean nothing now. "You have bereaved me of my children," laments Jacob in a moment of sad acquiescence to a vision of the clan destroyed by fraternal enmity. "Joseph is no more, and Simeon is no more, and now you would take Benjamin; all this has come upon me" (42:36).

Jacob's thoughts follow a bitter, downward path: "All hope is lost," he seems to say to himself. "It is better to cling to the small sparks of life that somehow survive in a cruel world." To Reuben who pleads for permission to take Benjamin back to Egypt in order to secure Simeon's freedom, Jacob replies firmly, "My son shall not go down with you" (42:38). Jacob sees only the specter of death, even to the point of entertaining a destiny of empty nothingness for himself: "His brother is dead, and he only is left. If harm should befall him on the journey that you are to make, you would bring down my gray hairs with sorrow to Sheol." The promises of God seem powerless and empty. The covenant seems to have come to a dead end.

43:1 Now famine was severe in the land.

In *On First Principles*, Origen observes that the suffering necessarily entailed in bodily existence plays a providential role. Our vulnerability to pain, hunger, desire, and fear influences us and guides us toward salvation. God is like a homeopathic physician, using the suffering of the body in order to cure the soul.[8] The despairing figure of Jacob provides a clear example. He seems closed in upon himself in a pessimistic assessment of the future. Left to himself, perhaps he would have become accustomed to his hopelessness, and the clan would have fractured permanently as the surviving sons sought their individual survival in the face of their father's refusal to allow them to take collective action. But Jacob's belly makes him vulnerable. Pangs of hunger and fear of death induce him to reopen the issue of return to Egypt.

Jacob proposes an impossible plan: "Go again, buy us a little food" (43:2). Judah reminds him that the grand vizier of Egypt has told them not to return without Benjamin. There can be no food without the youngest son. The narrative drives home the pressure that hunger exerts upon Jacob. It guides the hopeless patriarch unwillingly but fortunately down the path of hope. Judah pleads: "Send the lad with me, and we will arise and go, that we may live and not die" (43:8). They can get no hearing with Joseph without Benjamin. Jacob's clan cannot survive as a clan without Benjamin's journey to Egypt. But Judah speaks a greater truth than he knows. Not only does the clan need grain; it also needs to be restored to unity. The fate of Jacob's flesh and the future of the covenant are tied together. They cannot have grain without Benjamin. Jacob and the remaining brothers know this quite well. What they do not know is that the twelve brothers cannot be reconciled without Benjamin. Both are necessary for the realization of Judah's hope: that we may live and not die.

43:14 If I am bereaved of my children, I am bereaved.

The threat of famine and the words of Judah succeed in persuading Jacob. As a result, Jacob repeats Abraham's binding of Isaac. He sacrifices his youngest son, whom he holds dear. As Judah departs with Benjamin and the rest of the

8. *On First Principles* 3.1.13 in *Origen: On First Principles*, trans. G. W. Butterworth (repr., Gloucester, MA: Peter Smith, 1973), 181–83.

brothers, and the caravan disappears over the horizon, Jacob has lost all his sons. He is bereft of progeny. In the solitude of his tent, the promise to Abraham seems to have reached a bitter, empty end.

43:18 The men were afraid because they were brought to Joseph's house.

They are not afraid of Joseph, of course, because the returning brothers do not know that he is Joseph. Instead, they are anxious when Joseph's servants quickly usher them into Joseph's house. "It is because of the money, which was replaced in our sacks the first time," they speculate, worried that the powerful Egyptian has engaged in a deliberate ruse to enslave them. This sense of vulnerability and powerlessness once again impairs genuine communication. The colloquy between Joseph and his brothers about the money has precisely the falsity of a ritualized encounter between the weak and the powerful. The brothers plead their innocence and sincerity, pointing to their having brought the money back, along with more to buy a second load of grain. Joseph reassures them, "Rest assured, do not be afraid; your God and the God of your father must have put treasure in your sacks for you; I received your money" (43:23). The distancing language of "your God" and Joseph's reassuring lie hardly moves the colloquy toward any real reconciliation. Ritual bows follow, along with hints of a stilted conversation about Jacob's health. The artificiality of the entire sequence is reinforced by the elaborate eating arrangements. Joseph, although powerful, is a foreigner, and he cannot eat with the Egyptians, but he must maintain his hidden identity, so he does not eat with his brothers. The brothers seem as divided as ever. Perhaps Jacob was right to despair.

43:30 He sought a place to weep.

If Joseph wept previously out of a bitter fear that his brothers had not changed—or out of the realization that he was not really different from them—in this scene the emotional atmosphere is quite different. "His heart yearned for his brother" (43:30). The possibility of reunion is near, and the tears reflect the pain of postponement. Joseph is Pharaoh's grand vizier, and the whole world comes to him for grain. He is in full control of the situation, and yet he cannot avoid suffering. He seeks (perhaps only half-knowingly) a reconciliation that must be real rather than simply declared. It must occur across what Greek philosophers recognized as the agony of time, for to endure time is to suffer change. The agony of time, however, is good news for Joseph and his brothers, because they must change in order to be reconciled.

God created the world in six days, and on the seventh he rested. From the very beginning, the divine intention was to bring all things into the rest of the seventh day, so that they might not only participate in the goodness of created reality, but also in the glory of God, the uncreated source of all reality. But the man and the woman sinned, and they ruptured the relation of created reality to God. Thus began the agonizing delay of the world's consummation, the delay that is the history of the world. From Cain to Terah, the father of Abraham, this delay was futile, and the agony of time pointless. The generations tumbled forward, but toward no end other than the self-chosen futility of seeking to rest in finite things. With the calling of Abraham, however, history finds a center, and the forward thrust of time in the Bible is concentrated toward the single end of fulfillment.

The paradox of time, from a human perspective, is that we suffer it more as we see its fulfillment more clearly. To know that Benjamin is near and will be restored as a brother—and not be able to reach out and enjoy his embrace—this is deeper and more painful anguish than the simple loss that death and the eroding passage of time imposes. Joseph sees the end, but he must endure the time that separates him from the end (→23:2). He must suffer delay, because he must change; he must be transformed from the brother cast out, the brother partially absorbed into an alien culture, the brother who continues to distrust his clan, into a brother among brothers, united to them in love.

Joseph's role as supreme Egyptian master, however, suggests something more than the human perspective. In a certain sense, and in this scene most pointedly, Joseph is the sovereign of the time he spends with his brothers. His deceptions and subterfuges dictate the sequence of events. He has the power to stop the whole affair. If he wished, he could embrace Benjamin and cast his brothers into jail. But he does not, because the future of the covenant requires the reconciliation of the brothers, not Joseph's personal happiness, and certainly not release from the agonies of time. As a result, Joseph's own anguished weeping provides an occasion to contemplate the mystery of God's sovereign participation in time. God himself endures the delay necessary for the fulfillment of the plan initiated in Abraham, an anguishing delay fraught with enmity and unbelief, a delay so unaccountably capacious that St. Paul exclaims, "O the depth of the riches and wisdom and knowledge of God!" (Rom. 11:33).

It is a theological mistake to ascribe suffering to God, if by suffering we mean the literal sense of pathos as change. God is impassible. He is the eternal and unchanging source of changeable reality. God never wavers in his decision to bring all of creation into the seventh day of rest. It is a purpose undeterred and unaltered by sin and transgression. We have time precisely because God's impassible goodness says to the nothingness of evil, "It will not be so!" But it is permissible, as an aide to contemplation, to consider the cost of this unsurpassable divine determination. We can imagine the tears of the Godhead. We can consider the agony of one who sees the triumph of love with utter clarity and without the slightest doubt—but who also endures the insane, impossible reality of sin and the terrible necessity of delay.

A beautiful, compelling diptych from the sixteenth century encourages us to contemplate this properly qualified by a real sense of divine suffering. Painted by an unknown Netherlands artist called the Master of the Lille Adoration, one panel portrays the Holy Trinity. The conventional elements of traditional images of the Trinity are the crucified Son, the regal Father, and a dove representing the Holy Spirit. Yet in this diptych, the crucified Son, eyes closed and face ashen in what a viewer can only imagine as death, rests limply against the side of the Father. The Father, whose right arm draws the Son to him, looks out at the viewer with eyes of infinite sadness. The atmosphere of surpassing sorrow is intensified by the garments and headgear worn by the Father. Influenced perhaps by Jews then immigrating from Spain, the Father looks more like the high priest of the temple than a late medieval king. He is the one who slew the victim. He has done at the heavenly altar what Father Abraham did not have to do on Mount Moriah, sacrificing his beloved Son by sending him into the deepest depths of sin's ill fruit, the source of our need for the transforming agonies of time.

Joseph changes his mind, and he changes his identity. God has no need for such changes. But insofar as Joseph desires something not yet present—the truth about his brothers, a truth in which he needs to find a place—he is implicated in the agonies of time. God's desire for us, unlike Joseph's, is clear and unwavering. But in a similar way, it implicates him in our history. God is forever the one who creates for the sake of the seventh day. His resulting implacable, unchanging "no" to sin's desire for another future draws God into the agonies of the time. In this sense, then, the impassible God suffers his impassibility. He sorrows in the anguish of what will be but is not yet, not in spite of, but because of his unchanging identity as the one who will be who he will be.

44:2 Put my cup, the silver cup, in the mouth of the sack of the youngest.

Joseph sets up the denouement. He commands his servants to place a silver cup in Benjamin's sack. This allows him to level an accusation of theft against Benjamin alone. The accusation divides the brothers once again. Just as Simeon was cast into prison, tempting the brothers to forsake him and save their own skins, now Benjamin is at risk. Will the brothers rally to save him, or will they care only for themselves?

44:33 Let your servant, I pray you, remain instead of the lad as a slave
to my lord; and let the lad go back with his brothers.

Judah's speech is a complex rhetorical appeal. Deferential but forceful, it tells of Jacob's plight and pulls at Joseph's heartstrings, evoking the doleful consequences of Jacob's despair over the loss of Benjamin: "When he sees that the lad is not with us, he will die; and your servants will bring down the gray hairs of your servant our father with sorrow to Sheol" (44:31). But the crux of the speech is Judah's offer to stand as a substitute for Benjamin. In this crucial moment, Judah reaches backward to the first rupture between brothers in Genesis, and he reverses the direction of events. Unlike Cain, Judah is willing to be his brother Benjamin's keeper. Unlike Cain, he is willing to suffer on behalf of his brother rather than inflict suffering on his brother. This dramatic reversal bears directly upon Joseph's situation. Years ago Joseph lay in the pit, put there by the Cain-like hearts of his brothers. In that moment, hovering on the edge of death, Judah gave merely prudential reasons to spare Joseph's life—"What profit is it if we slay our brother and conceal his blood?" (37:26)—advising instead the profit (and avoidance of bloodguilt) that would come from selling Joseph into a life of slavery. Now, in marked contrast, Judah offers to become a slave, not just to save Benjamin, but to save his father and what remains of the clan: "I fear to see the evil that would come upon my father" (44:34).

Jacob has already received the communal name "Israel." He has fathered many sons. The clan is very much in the forefront of the action from Gen. 32 onward as the narrative focus shifts from the succession of the patriarchs toward communal survival. In this verse the shift is complete. The old pattern of brotherly rivalry that reaches all the way back to Cain and Abel and that haunts the covenant as it is passed from Abraham to Isaac and dominates the transmission from Isaac to Esau is now reversed. Instead of grasping for the good inheritance, Judah chooses the bad one. And he does so for the sake of his brother. In choosing the least portion, however, Judah receives the greatest of Jacob's blessings (→49:8). Here, Judah, not Joseph, prefigures Christ.

45:2 He wept aloud, so that the Egyptians heard it, and the household
of Pharaoh heard it.

The test suggests more than strong emotions. A larger frame of reference for the reconciliation of Joseph with his brothers is being evoked. The whole city hears Joseph's cries as they might hear the ringing of the tocsin. What happens to the clan of Jacob is not a personal, private matter. Joseph may have all the grain that the world needs, but the future of Israel matters more deeply and permanently. The human future as a whole depends upon the ability of the clan to overcome the power of human sin to define human destiny. Only the reconciled elect can serve as an instrument of the divine plan of sanctifying the whole world. Thus Jesus prays on behalf of his followers "that they may all be one; even as thou, Father, art in me, and I in thee, that they also may be in us, so that the world may believe that thou hast sent me" (John 17:21).

For all the drama of the scene, and in Judah's offer of himself as the rich anticipation of Christ's suffering for our sakes on the cross, it is important to realize that the reconciliation is not perfect. Joseph's brothers never entirely accept his warm embrace (→50:15). The story brings a crucial reconciliation, one necessary for the future of the covenant. To have returned without Benjamin would have sent Israel to a bitter death. But Genesis does not tell of the final reconciliation, the one that need not be renewed daily (Heb. 7:27), the reconciliation made possible in Christ's atoning sacrifice, which makes all humanity "one body through the cross" (Eph. 2:16).

45:7 God sent me before you to preserve life.

To those who protest that the Old Testament has a narrow, parochial view of God as a tribal deity, Joseph's words provide the response. The LORD calls Abraham and sends him as a forerunner who carries forward the promise of life. What seems like an inauspicious course of events is, in fact, the narrow path of the divine plan. In the pit, Joseph teeters on the edge of death as his brothers contemplate his future (→37:27). He narrowly escapes into slavery, only to fall again into the pit of prison after an ill-fated encounter with Potiphar's wife (→39:2). The same held for Abraham. He was an obscure man with a barren wife who narrowly escaped childlessness, a condition that epitomizes the overall obscurity of the people of Israel in the great history of ancient empires, as well as their struggle for survival over the course of many centuries.

The small scale of the divine plan—the one man who goes before the many for the sake of life—is reinforced when Joseph repeats his interpretation of his travails and gives a more specific picture of how God has used him to preserve life. "God has sent me before you," he tells his brothers, "to preserve for you a remnant on earth" (45:7). In the biblical history of Israel, the conquest of the promised land and the subsequent political history of the judges and kings of Israel suggest an expansion of the chosen people as the divine instrument of redemption. But with the fall of Jerusalem and the exile, the scope begins to contract, and the restoration recorded in Ezra and Nehemiah emphasizes the role of a saving remnant. The future of the covenant comes to rest on the fates of smaller and smaller groups, returning to the atmosphere of Genesis. It is not surprising, then, that followers of Jesus came to see him as the Messiah, the single man in whom the divine plan is fulfilled, a contraction even more extreme than the initial call of Abraham to leave his father's house with his childless wife.

The obscure man with the barren wife, the brother sold as a slave, the remnant of Judeans who cling to their ways even in exile, the Galilean preacher crucified with two thieves in a Roman province—the narrow focus of the biblical narrative cannot help but seem odd. It seems ridiculous to believe that the creator of the universe invests himself and his purposes in such small, feeble realities. Our rebellion against smallness emerges again and again as a perennial objection to the metaphysical inversion, the priority of particularity found in the biblical vision of redemption. The mean words of scripture seem hopelessly fragile. What if Abraham never existed? What are we to make of the authority of scripture, which is, after all, a text formed out of previously existing narrative traditions? The same holds for institutions of church authority. What could possibly lead us to think that some three hundred men could gather at the Council of Nicea and reliably describe God as a Trinity of persons? How can anyone believe that an old man in Rome is able to infallibly define doctrine?

There is no refutation of the rebellion against smallness. It is motivated by a natural religious impulse, and it is well supported by the philosophical intuitions of natural reason. Who doesn't find it implausible that the eternal and changeless deity should use time-bound and fragile means to achieve his purposes. Far more fitting would be methods akin to mathematical formulas or logical truths, things invulnerable to time and irresistibly powerful in their truth. Or so we imagine. But God reveals himself otherwise. What is most godlike will not serve the divine purpose, which is to transform rather than destroy a sin-infected world. The divine plan is for God to counter sin with the real presence of his holiness in human life, and this requires the small, thin needle of a syringe rather than the baseball bat of necessary truths or global proclamations. The divine plan fights the infection of sin with a counterinfection of holiness.

45:13 You must tell my father of all my splendor in Egypt.

Joseph remains an equivocal figure. He exclaims to his brothers, "I am Joseph" (45:3), but readers cannot be entirely sure. Is he still bewitched by his role as a god-like Egyptian potentate? When faced with the temptation to sleep with Potiphar's wife, he is able to resist. But does Joseph avoid the harlotry of embracing life as an Egyptian? His emphasis on his Egyptian splendor suggests the view of Israelite participation in foreign cultures found in Esther—survival requires working within the system. But it can also serve as a warning, and perhaps Joseph is deliberately portrayed in Genesis as a troublesome figure. He not only views himself as an Egyptian, but he gives his brothers fine Egyptian clothes as well (45:22). Is Joseph a subtle seducer? Until the giving of the law on Mount Sinai, the children of Israel have no way to give a durable permanence to their identities. Without the law and its invasion of every detail of human life, Joseph can commit himself to his brothers at one moment and then very quickly fall back into the Egyptian mentality. Doubtless Joseph is the heroic rescuer, but his ambivalent character seems to positively beg for the law. Sinai will end dual loyalties. The comprehensiveness of the law leaves no neutral ground, no place for us to toggle back and forth between obedience to God and obedience to the ways of the world. With the law, the life of obedience becomes comprehensive and continuous rather than selective and occasional.

46:4 I will go down with you to Egypt, and I will also bring you up again.

Readers know the fate of Jacob's clan in Egypt—slavery and oppression for many generations—and this throws a shadow over the final chapters of Genesis. The wonderful family reunion and great good fortune for Jacob and his sons are actually the beginning of the archetypical period of Israelite affliction. The pharaoh who invites Jacob's clan to Egypt will give way to a pharaoh who forgets Joseph and enslaves Jacob's descendents.

Reading this episode with the eventual bad outcome in mind is appropriate, not only because we have no evidence that any community of ancient readers ever did otherwise, but also because the narrative atmosphere of the Joseph story participates in the later history of Israel. God comes to Abraham in a vision, and the canonical reader of Genesis knows that the future of the divine promise is fraught with the suffering of future generations (→15:18). Joseph's rescue of his brothers requires trial and suffering something that comes to Israel later in her history. In this way, the entire complex of stories associated with Joseph evokes the anguish of the divine plan, and it feeds the impulse to find christological parallels. The disciples are like Jacob. They take the divine promises at face value, but Jesus knows that there will be a long way to go before the LORD will bring up those who go down: "The Son of man must suffer many things, and be rejected by the elders and chief priests and scribes, and be killed" (Luke 9:22).

46:8 These are the names of the descendants of Israel.

In 37:2, the promised generations of Jacob are not forthcoming, and the Joseph story begins. Now readers get the full family list, and the genealogy serves as the closing bracket to the story of Joseph and his brothers. From a literary perspective, however, that the brackets were opened in the first place needs explaining. As we have seen, the patriarchal problem of succession recedes with Jacob, and the communal problems of survival come to the fore. The brackets are opened, so to speak, because the question is open. In the face of fraternal sin, can the clan of Jacob survive as a clan rather than as twelve separate patriarchates? This question needs to be answered—however tentatively and ambivalently—before the narrative can give its readers the genealogical sign that the covenant has a future. The reconciliation of Joseph with his brothers gives the answer. The offer of atoning self-sacrifice by Judah has the power to overcome the defilement of sin that threatens to permanently rupture the clan (→44:33). Now the text can close the brackets opened in 37:2 and give readers the genealogical signal of a continuing future.

46:34 For every shepherd is an abomination to the Egyptians.

Once again the figure of Joseph toggles back and forth, shifting roles between adopted son of Pharaoh and son of Jacob, solicitous about the identity of the people of the covenant. He prepares his family for an audience with Pharaoh, and he emphasizes the importance of their roles as shepherds. Because Egyptians regard shepherds as taboo, Pharaoh will want to keep the tribe in Goshen, on the margins of the nation. Readers are not told why Joseph thinks this is such a good plan, but in view of the question of identity that swirls around Joseph throughout the narrative, the obvious reason is that relative separation will provide less chance for assimilation.

Joseph preps his brothers, as would any good courtier who knows how to manipulate a more powerful boss. But the larger canonical context gives his advice a dark meaning. Perhaps a margin of advantage can be gained by anticipating an Egyptian disdain for the nomadic way of life that characterizes Jacob's clan, but it can hardly be auspicious for Joseph's brothers to settle in a place where their defining work is "an abomination." Therefore, Joseph's role seems uncertain. Is he really the rescuer of Israel, or has he set up the chosen people for more suffering? Is he truly gaining advantage for his brothers, or is he only drawing attention to the ways in which they will grate against the mores of the majority culture? In an important sense, the answer is yes to both sides of these questions. The way of redemption involves suffering, and the true advantage of Israel is her inability to simply blend into the nations.

47:21 As for the people, he made slaves of them from one end of Egypt
　　　 to the other.

In a sudden and unexpected shift, Genesis reintroduces the larger geopolitical consequences of the famine that provides the background for the entire drama of Joseph and his brothers. The people come to Joseph, pleading for the bread of life: "Give us food; why should we die before your eyes?" (47:15). First the people give Joseph all their money in exchange for grain, and then their cattle. Finally, when their wealth is exhausted, the multitudes come to Joseph and offer themselves and their land: "We with our land will be slaves to Pharaoh" (47:19). Joseph accepts the offer on Pharaoh's behalf, enslaving the population while they offer wholehearted, worshipful thanks: "You have saved our lives; may it please my lord, we will be slaves of Pharaoh" (47:25).

At first glance, it is difficult to know quite what to make of this digression, especially since it concludes with a report of the subsequent law concerning the land of Egypt, which speaks of the one-fifth portion to be possessed by Pharaoh rather than the enslavement of the entire nation. Von Rad resorts to the strange claim that "the narrator lived in an enlightened, awakened period, which was very interested in life in foreign lands. There is therefore nothing more behind this narrative than the intention of telling how such strange economic conditions arose in a foreign land" (1972: 410–11). One can only marvel at the way in which the otherwise quite sound modern interpretive assumption that some passages serve to explain the origins of nations and practices can be deployed willy-nilly to explain away difficult passages.

We need to do better. This episode recapitulates the earlier description of the whole world flowing to Egypt for salvation from famine (→41:57). That earlier evocation of a grand fulfillment of the promise that Abraham's children shall be a blessing to the nations stood in dramatic juxtaposition to the subsequent collapse of the narrative down to a narrow focus on the fate of Jacob's clan. This microscopic focus can seem a diversion from the real issue: the redemption of the world. But as we have seen since Gen. 12, God's plan involves contraction for the sake of penetration to the core of our humanity. Now, in this episode, readers get a hint of the danger of a vision of salvation carried out on a grand scale. If we seek the renewal of life from a powerful, world-historical figure such as Joseph, the global agricultural commissar, then we are on the road to slavery. Our reliance on bread is very real. Famine can kill and destroy physical life. But the original deception in the garden was precisely the lie that our physical lives matter supremely (→3:4). We should by all means seek the sustaining goods of creation, but we must not imagine that they provide the bread of life, for if we do, then we will become their slaves.

48:5 And now your two sons.

Genesis 48 depicts Jacob's special blessing of Joseph and settles the fate of his two sons. The text gives us two different traditions. The first and shorter tradition portrays Jacob adopting Joseph's sons: "Ephraim and Manasseh shall be mine, as Reuben and Simeon are. And the offspring born to you after them shall be yours; they shall be called by the name of their brothers in their inheritance" (48:5–6). The implication is clear. Because Jacob adopts Ephraim and Manasseh, Joseph receives a double portion of Jacob's inheritance. He is the father of two tribes. But the gift has a cost. The tribes will bear Joseph's sons' names, not his own. Motivated by an enigmatic remorse over the burial of Rachel, the gift has the effect of erasing Joseph's name from the later political history of Israel.

The second and longer passage depicts Jacob blessing Joseph's sons. Ironically, Joseph, who dreamt of his older brothers bowing down before him, now insists on primogeniture. In a sense, Joseph is like Isaac, who also prefers the elder son. And like Isaac, Joseph is outfoxed by Jacob, who crosses his hands to ensure that the younger son receives the greater blessing. The outcome is in any event the same as the earlier scene of adoption. Jacob's name and those of Abraham and Isaac will be carried forward by Ephraim and Manasseh—and not by Joseph.

Genesis 48 is not entirely clear. At the very end, Jacob promises Joseph a special portion of land that Jacob "took from the hand of the Amorites with my sword and with my bow" (48:22), as if Joseph's descendants would continue under his own name. Nonetheless, the chapter as a whole epitomizes the eccentric status of Joseph in the clan. From the outset, his dreams, his vainglorious temperament, and his Egyptian ways keep him from fitting in with his brothers. His very success in Egypt, which was absolutely crucial for the survival of his brothers, seems to compromise his identity and block a role for his name in the future of Israel. He is undoubtedly the crucial brother, the rescuer. We read of no brother harboring objections to Joseph's double portion. He seems to deserve a special status in the clan. Yet that special status puts Joseph's name outside the normal history of Israel. It is as if Joseph's success has made him too dangerous for the future of the clan, and he must be suppressed even as he is honored. And as Joseph is suppressed, the place of rescuer to be glorified remains open. Joseph's name is put aside, and the Old Testament as a whole continues to await the savior whose name every tongue shall confess.

49:2 Assemble and hear, O sons of Jacob.

More reprimand and prophecy than blessing, Jacob's final benediction to the clan does at least three obvious and important things.[9] First, Jacob passes along the patriarchal inheritance, and he does so to the many brothers rather than to only one. In this way, the scene serves as an explicit affirmation of the general trend of Genesis away from individual agency in Abraham, Isaac, and Jacob toward communal agency in Israel. Second, Jacob repeats the standard rejection of primogeniture found throughout Genesis. He explicitly elevates Judah over his older brothers: Reuben, Simeon, and Levi. Finally, by assigning different roles to the generations that flow from each son, Jacob emphasizes a spiritualizing trend in Israelite identity. Roles are inherited within the tribes, and in that sense the biological reality of reproduction continues to be crucial. But the function of each tribe within the collective Israelite project gives blood inheritance its distinctive forms. The tribes not only have a future by virtue of successive generations. They are ordained to a particular vocation in the larger life of Israel. The natural forward thrust of reproduction is supernaturalized.

49:8 Judah, your bothers shall praise you.

Jacob's blessing of Judah is the longest and the most important for the history of both Judaism and Christianity. The turn of events in Genesis is ironic. Joseph has the dreams of supremacy, and nearly all the action from Gen. 37 to this point turns on his actions and personality. However, in the end, it is Judah and not Joseph who inherits the royal role.

---

9. *Targum Pseudo-Jonathan* treats Jacob's final words as pure prophesy. Jacob calls his sons to tell them "the concealed secrets, the hidden times, the giving of the reward of the righteous, the punishment of the wicked, and what the happiness of Eden will be." Indeed, but for divine intervention to ensure discretion, Jacob would have revealed the time of the promised "King Messiah" (49:1) (Maher 1992: 157).

The promise that "the scepter shall not depart from Judah" (49:10) is treated by nearly all subsequent strands of the biblical tradition as a synecdoche for the role of kingship that emerges from the tribe of Judah. David, of course, provides the paradigmatic fulfillment of this prophetic promise. But the Davidic monarchy comes to an end, and this forces a rereading of the promise that the scepter shall not depart. Both Jewish and Christian readings shift the sense away from actual kings of Israel toward the future rule of the anointed king, the messianic king. This general shift has a role to play in the way the New Testament presents Jesus of Nazareth.

The messianic potential of Jacob's blessing of Judah becomes explicit in the prophecies of Zechariah. Jacob's blessing describes the king who will rule all the nations as one who is "binding his foal to the vine and his ass's colt to the choice vine" (Gen. 49:11a). Zechariah's vision of the messianic king incorporates this verse in the following way: "Lo, your king comes to you; triumphant and victorious is he, humble and riding on an ass, on a colt the foal of an ass" (9:9). Matthew's Gospel echoes this passage from Zechariah and tells us that Jesus commanded his disciples to go and bring to him an ass and a colt. The gospel writer quotes Zech. 9:9 in order to drive home the fulfillment of the messianic promise in Jesus, a promise that reaches back through Zechariah all the way to Genesis. In this way, the gospel writer has tightened the links between Jacob's latent messianic blessing in Genesis, Zechariah's explicitly messianic prophecy, and the actions depicted in the life of Jesus.

The subtle ways in which the New Testament weaves strands of prophecy both backward into Genesis and forward into Christ is evident elsewhere. Jacob's blessing of Judah continues: "He washes his garments in wine and his vesture in the blood of grapes" (Gen. 49:11b). The image echoes in a number of messianic passages. Isaiah 63:1–3 famously depicts the coming of the LORD in wine-colored garments made red by the blood of those whom he has trampled in his wrath, just as a winemaker tramples his grapes. As we turn to the New Testament, we see once again a reinforcing move, one that takes the Isaiah passage and sharpens its connection to Genesis. Revelation 19:12–15 evokes the prophecy from Isaiah, but in so doing adds an additional description—the Messiah's "eyes are like a flame of fire"—in an image that echoes the final verse of Jacob's blessing of Judah: "His eyes shall be red with wine" (Gen. 49:12). This evocation of Isaiah with supplementation has an important canonical effect. It redoubles the connection between Genesis, Isaiah, and the apostolic witness to Jesus Christ.

The way in which Matthew's Gospel and Revelation clarify the prophetic uses of Gen. 49 is nearly invisible compared to the protological project of John's Gospel and the rethinking of salvation history by Paul. Yet the subtle strategy of drawing the great messianic prophecies *both* forward toward Jesus *and* backward to Jacob's blessings at the end of Genesis testifies to the larger project of early Christian biblical exegesis. The goal was not to read creation and fall in Gen. 1–3 and then to vault over the history of Israel to the solution provided by the incarnate *logos*. Systematic theology can give this impression. The creation-fall-redemption sequence provides the basic structure for the opening sections of Athanasius's *On the Incarnation*. But Athanasius also works to show the fulfillment of messianic prophecies, including 49:10! His goal—and the goal of the larger Christian tradition—was to provide an account of God's economy or plan of salvation that builds up a complex and tightly woven web extending from creation through covenant to fulfillment in Christ. The universality of the opening chapters of Genesis was carefully knit into a full-scale interpretation of every possible aspect of the Old Testament. This profound intellectual investment in discerning the role of the minute and manifold details of the entire sweep of the Old Testament was the exegetical way in which the Christian tradition expressed the surprising divine decision to redeem the world from within, by way of the particularity of the elect rather than from above and by way of universal concepts and principles.

Immanuel Kant and Friedrich Schleiermacher had very different views about the nature and role of Christian faith in the modern world, but on one point they agreed. They rejected the role of the Old Testament as the indispensable context for the truth of Christ, the promised savior of the world. By their reckoning, Old Testament prophecy and the history of covenant have no value for the exposition of Christ's saving work. After all, the limited, tribal focus of Abraham and his progeny was immersed in merely local religious regulations, a religious sensibility that both Kant and Schleiermacher found antagonistic, because it cut against what they took to be the universal moral and spiritual power of the Christian message. The cogency of Christian claims about the saving significance of Christ needs to be rethought in general, universal terms. What matters, they argued, is how Jesus speaks to some feature of our universal humanity.[10]

The problem is that almost the entire Old Testament concerns the particular history, teaching, and revelations accorded to the descendents of Jacob. Schleiermacher was clearminded. In his great systematic theology, the Old Testament dies a death of many qualifications. He allows some value as a "husk or wrapping" for universal truths made clear in the New Testament, but "whatever is most definitely Jewish" in the Old Testament "has least value."[11] Of course, the "Jewish part" turns out to be most of the Old Testament after Gen. 12. Thus it is not surprising that Schleiermacher set aside the Old Testament as "simply a superfluous authority" for Christian theology.[12]

Most modern theologians have been more muddy-headed than Schleiermacher. They have not thought through the exegetical significance of a view of Jesus as metaphor for being fully human, as a symbol of divine love, or as an archetype of moral purity. The authority of the Bible may be affirmed, but other than the crucial

---

10. For an excellent account of the theological rationale for the turn away from the Old Testament in Kant and Schleiermacher, see Kendall Soulen, *The God of Israel and Christian Theology* (Minneapolis: Augsburg Fortress, 1996), 57–80.

11. Friedrich Schleiermacher, *The Christian Faith*, ed./trans. H. R. Mackintosh and J. S. Stewart (Edinburgh: Clark, 1899), 62 §12.3.

12. Ibid., 115 §27.3.

stage-setting account in Gen. 1–3, most of the Old Testament turns out to be irrelevant. This neglect is a natural consequence of any view of God's redemptive plan that fails to accept the divine contraction of his purposes into the particularity of those whom he chooses. As long as God redeems from above rather than from within the fleshly particularity of human history, the Old Testament after Gen. 12 will be felt as a spiritual burden to be explained away—or politely ignored.

This turn away from the Old Testament has not been without consequence. During World War II, Henri de Lubac gave a series of lectures addressing the great moral and spiritual crisis of the Nazi triumph and French capitulation. His diagnoses were diverse, but in one instance he observed that a prevailing spiritual impotence and lack of will stemmed from "the renunciation of knowing and using the Bible."[13] Theologians and pastors had their favorite gospel parables and Pauline phrases, but the overall sweep of the biblical vision of human destiny had no purchase, because the Old Testament had become remote, unknown territory. "Many theologians," he bemoaned, "themselves forego acquiring a deeper knowledge of it, considering it an obscure domain, reserved for exploration by a few, rare specialists."[14] The effect of this failure to engage the Old Testament, according to de Lubac, is a loss of the sense of the sacred. Unable to see Christ in the history of Israel, we have lost the ability to see our own lives, lived now and at this time in history, as deeply penetrated by the call to faith in Christ.

At the same time in Western history, Dietrich Bonhoeffer drew the very same conclusion. In prison for his role in the Hitler assassination plot, Bonhoeffer reflected on the deepest sources of modern spiritual impotence in the face of evil. He observed that faith has migrated to the margins of everyday life and that God seemed too much above and beyond rather than amidst and within a sin-shattered world. What could help us recover God incarnate? Bonhoeffer recognized that the God within the world—the LORD who calls Abraham and commands his circumcision—this God is very much present in the Old Testament. But we are in love with our universal notions and have trained ourselves to ignore the Old Testament. As Bonhoeffer observes, "We still read the New Testament far too little in the light of the Old."[15]

De Lubac wished to recover the "sacred atmosphere" for our lives.[16] He intuitively recognized the need for a historical and narrative mode of theological exposition. The sacred atmosphere becomes real as we undertake the infinitely complex and never-ending project of seeing the vast sweep of the Old Testament and its fulfillment in Christ, as well as the living reality of the Word of God in the history of the church. As de Lubac recognized, the traditional modes of biblical exegesis provide the paradigmatic method for linking the Old Testament with the New, and both to

13. Henri de Lubac, *The Mystery of the Supernatural*, trans. Rosemary Sheed (New York: Herder & Herder, 1998), 226.

14. Ibid.

15. Dietrich Bonhoeffer, *Letters and Papers from Prison*, trans. Reginald H. Fuller, ed. Eberhard Bethge (New York: Collier, 1972), 286.

16. De Lubac, *Mystery of the Supernatural*, 231.

contemporary reality. The plastic, absorptive, and unending strategies of allegorical and figural exegesis illuminate world history, the geography of the soul, the moral life, and Christian doctrine and practice. In this exegetical project, concepts play an important role. For example, *creatio ex nihilo* seems an indispensable conceptual commitment that Christians (and Jews) make at a highly abstract level—and against the grain of the plain sense of the opening verses of Genesis (→1:2). The same holds for a distinction between created nature and our supernatural vocations in fellowship with God (→2:2). Yet these and other theological commitments serve the interpretive project; they do not govern it. They facilitate the deeper and more fundamental theological project: pulling together, as best as we can, an overall reading of the biblical account of God's redemptive plan. This work of stitching together a comprehensive interpretation never ends. It reaches through all the details of scripture rather than floating above the text with broad theological generalizations. The echo of Gen. 49:12 in Revelation is exemplary. It reaches through Isaiah to Gen. 49:12 in order to give us a vision of the return of Christ in glory.

50:15 When Joseph's brothers saw that their father was dead, they said, "It may be that Joseph will hate us."

Joseph's reconciliation with his brothers is real; however, it is neither prefect nor everlasting. Rightly or wrongly, the brothers feel that they continue to have reasons to fear Joseph's vengeance. In keeping with Jacob's deceitful ways, they make up a story to protect themselves. Their father, they report, commanded them to ask Joseph to forgive them. Joseph does forgive them. He reiterates his view that their desire for his death years ago was used by God to bring life to them now.

The anxiety that the brothers continue to feel, and Joseph's reiteration of his reassuring view of God's providence, suggests the fragile state of the covenant future. The brothers' sin against Joseph may have been a *felix culpa*, a blessed fault, as Joseph explains. Yet the brothers have difficulty believing that one wronged can live without retribution. The economy of sacrifice outlined in Leviticus addresses this unbelief, not by denying the moral and spiritual intuition that fuels the fear animating Joseph's brothers, but instead by showing the way in which the rupture of human sin can be overcome and the blood of Abel silenced.

50:25 God will visit you, and you shall carry up my bones.

Joseph dies, but unlike Jacob, he is not carried to the land of his fathers to be buried with his ancestors. Instead, Joseph's body is embalmed, given over to the Egyptian art of suspending rather than completing or redeeming time. And he is put in a coffin. Thus, Genesis ends with a scene that aches for the fulfillment of the promise. A body waits for its final rest.

BIBLIOGRAPHY

Frequently cited works are listed here. Other works are documented in the footnotes.

Bettenson, Henry, trans. *Augustine: Concerning the City of God against the Pagans.* New York: Penguin, 1972.

Kass, Leon R. *The Beginning of Wisdom: Reading Genesis.* New York: Free Press, 2003. Reprint, Chicago: University of Chicago Press, 2006.

Kugel, James L. *Traditions of the Bible: A Guide to the Bible as It Was at the Start of the Common Era.* Cambridge: Harvard University Press, 1998.

Maher, Michael, trans. *Targum Pseudo-Jonathan: Genesis.* Aramaic Bible 1B. Collegeville, MN: Liturgical Press, 1992.

von Rad, Gerhard. *Genesis: A Commentary.* Translated by John H. Marks. Revised edition. Old Testament Library. Philadelphia: Westminster, 1972. Reprint, 1974.

SUBJECT INDEX

SCRIPTURE AND ANCIENT
SOURCES INDEX